CRITICAL INSIGHTS

All Quiet on the Western Front

by Erich Maria Remarque

CRITICAL INSIGHTS

All Quiet on the Western Front

by Erich Maria Remarque

Editor
Brian Murdoch
University of Stirling

Salem Press
Pasadena, California   Hackensack, New Jersey

Cover photo: John Kobal Foundation/Hulton Archive/Getty Images

Published by Salem Press

© 2011 by EBSCO Publishing
Editor's text © 2011 by Brian Murdoch
"The *Paris Review* Perspective" © 2011 by Ruth Franklin for *The Paris Review*

∞ The paper used in these volumes conforms to the American National Standard for Permanence of Paper for Printed Library Materials, Z39.48-1992 (R1997).

Library of Congress Cataloging-in-Publication Data
All quiet on the western front, by Erich Maria Remarque / editor, Brian Murdoch.
    p. cm. — (Critical insights)
Includes bibliographical references and index.
ISBN 978-1-58765-719-1 (alk. paper)
    1. Remarque, Erich Maria, 1898-1970. Im Westen nichts Neues. 2. World War, 1914-1918—Germany--Literature and the war. I. Murdoch, Brian, 1944-
    PT2635.E68I663 2011
    833'.912—dc22

                                                                  2010030208

PRINTED IN CANADA

Contents_____

All Quiet on the Western Front and Other War Novels

All Quiet on the Western Front as a Film

Resources _____

About This Volume_____

Brian Murdoch

It is easy to forget that *All Quiet on the Western Front* was not written in English but in German. Though *Im Westen nichts Neues* (literally, "nothing new in the west") is well established as an international novel and has been translated into an astonishing number of languages, it *is* a German novel, with German soldiers, set in the context of a lost war. Much of the critical analysis of the novel, therefore, has appeared within the context of German studies, and where articles in this collection have quotations in German, translations are provided. However, even within German studies, Erich Maria Remarque's novel was for a long time more fully treated in the English-speaking world than in Germany. This may have something to do with the fact that Remarque spent much of his life in the United States and that the novel's first cinematic adaptation is still an important Hollywood film. More recently, an increase of interest in Germany has produced some excellent studies, and those who read German will find the essays and bibliographies in the *Remarque Jahrbuch/Remarque Yearbook*, which is published in Remarque's hometown of Osnabrück, indispensable. For all that, the theme of *All Quiet on the Western Front*—the experience of the (mostly young) ordinary soldier in World War I—is and likely always will be a universal one.

This selection of new essays and critical reprints has been assembled to accomplish several tasks: to demonstrate the novel's internationalism; to locate it in its double historical context (double, because it is set in World War I but was written during, and can be related to, the precarious years of the Weimar Republic before Adolf Hitler came to power); to give an idea of how the work has been received inside and outside Germany over the years; and to show that it is a major work of German and world literature with a continuing significance.

In the essays specially written for this collection, Ruth Franklin makes clear the importance of the novel, while Thomas F. Schneider locates it within the war literature of the Weimar Republic. Mark Ward assesses responses to the novel both in the years immediately following its publication and in the decades that have followed up to the present day. Peter Hutchinson examines the ways in which the novel is an antiwar statement (hinted at by Remarque himself in the prefatory statement to the work, which is significantly *not* by the first-person narrator of the story as such) and focuses on the different ways in which the novel can be read. Matthew J. Bolton, finally, sets Remarque's novel against an eminently comparable work, Hemingway's *A Farewell to Arms*, a work from "the other side" (which, however, is always a questionable concept for an ordinary soldier in any army).

Of the reprinted essays, the first group, looking at the early impact of the work, begins with some comments from a very important critic indeed—the author himself, Erich Maria Remarque. Here, he is in correspondence with a British general, Sir Ian Hamilton, who had read the first translation of the work by Arthur Wellesley Wheen, and was (after some initial hesitation) greatly impressed with its depiction of the ordinary soldier. In this unusual discussion between an Allied general and a German private, it becomes clear that Remarque designed his work to elicit a response from a specific body of readers, those who (in Remarque's own words) had been destroyed by the war even if they had survived the shelling. The entire aim of the work, then, is to portray the lost generation of ordinary soldiers who were also, in their own way, heroes. Hilton Tims, in an excerpt from his recent book on the life of Remarque, gives a general background to the production of the novel and the immediate effects of its publication, and this background is looked at in rather more depth by Alan F. Bance. Bance uses the word "bestseller" in his title, and, indeed, the work has always been in print somewhere since its publication, even if the Third Reich banned and burned it. Bance's view that the novel could be all things to all readers is worth considering, but it is particularly significant that he places the novel in its written context, that is, in the Weimar Republic. The work is historical, written at a distance of some years from the events it por-

trays, and this presentation can be related in various ways to the intellectually fruitful, but doomed German state that preceded Hitler's
Reich. A final piece in this section is from a book that is of considerable
general importance, Modris Eksteins's *Rites of Spring: The Great War
and the Birth of the Modern Age*. Eksteins looks closely at the novel
and its inception but also places it into a very broad context and raises
all kind of questions about the ways in which the war was remembered
(and also forgotten). His study forms a bridge to the next section.

The second group of reprinted pieces considers the novel as literature. Harley U. Taylor, Jr., and Richard Arthur Firda—two of the earliest American scholars to devote major studies to Remarque—examine
the novel first as a reflection of the generation of young men most affected by the war and then as an echo of aspects of Remarque's own experiences. Both also look at the effect of the book in its time, tying
these studies in with the previous section. The other reprints in this section concentrate more closely on the work as a literary production as
such. Richard Schumaker rightly stresses Remarque's craftsmanship
by looking closely at how he accomplishes shifts in time and perspective, especially with his inclusion of the views of the young soldiers of
a possible future. Like Schumaker, Richard Littlejohns takes issue with
the idea that the work is only about the war, stressing that it is about the
effect of war on people and picking up neatly the universality of the
work voiced already in the Hamilton-Remarque correspondence. Last
in this section is a chapter from my own recent study of Remarque's
novels. I sometimes have to state the obvious about *All Quiet on the
Western Front*: it is not really an autobiography, even though, of
course, some of Remarque's own experiences were used. Rather,
though the novel is almost entirely narrated in the first person, its motto
and ultimate statement both come from outsiders. I include the whole
of my chapter to stress the importance of the novel's sequel, *The Road
Back*, which picks up and clarifies a number of the points left open or
confused in *All Quiet on the Western Front*, not least of which is that
the idea of comradeship, which is often highlighted in discussions of

the first novel, breaks down very quickly after the war is over and certainly does not justify the war.

The third section of reprints contains comparative pieces. The years around 1930 saw the production of a massive number of novels about the war, both in Germany and elsewhere, as writers sought to give some sort of meaning to the war. A chapter from Ann P. Linder's important book on German writing about the war as a whole gives an introduction to several other German works in the genre (most of which were translated), and sets Remarque's work in this context. In the other essay in this section, Kim Allen Scott also looks at Weimar literature in general, but her main comparison is with a now little-known but extremely interesting work by Rudolf Binding, whose memoir *A Fatalist at War* also appeared in translation in 1929. The similarities and the differences between the two works are equally striking, and where Remarque's work was banned by the Nazis, Binding (who died in 1938) actually defended National Socialism.

A final section offers two pieces on the film of the novel made by Lewis Milestone in 1930, which has become a classic of early cinema. John Whiteclay Chambers II presents an overview of the film and its history in what is, in fact, the first chapter of a book concerned with the *Second* World War in film—an indication that Milestone's film has become a yardstick for war films in the same way the novel has become one for antiwar writing. Milestone's film was condemned by the emergent Nazis in Germany, who famously disrupted its showing. Kathleen Norrie and Malcolm Read compare the film and the Nazi response to it with a contemporary German film, G. W. Pabst's *Westfront 1918*, which is also a classic and equally antiwar. It was a source of confusion for the Nazis, who first condemned it and then tried to use it against Milestone's work. *Westfront 1918* closes with the word *Ende* ("The End") on the screen, but with a question mark after it. The idea would have worked as well for *All Quiet on the Western Front*, a novel that raises questions we need to keep asking.

THE BOOK AND AUTHOR

On *All Quiet on the Western Front*_____

Brian Murdoch

It is a myth that Erich Maria Remarque was a one-novel author. Before he won international acclaim with *Im Westen nichts Neues* (*All Quiet on the Western Front*), Remarque, who was born Erich Paul Remark, had written three other novels, the first of which was a thin and rather sentimental artist-novel called *Die Traumbude* (1920; The Dream Room) that Remarque (not without good reason) would later dismiss, even changing his name to distance himself from it. A second novel went unpublished, and a third appeared only in serial form. After the success of *All Quiet on the Western Front*, which was published with considerable hype as a magazine serial in 1928 and then in book form in 1929, Remarque would write ten more novels as well as a handful of short stories. Like *All Quiet on the Western Front,* all of these later novels were highly successful, widely translated, and, in most cases, filmed. Many are of the same high quality as his best-known work, and in them Remarque deals regularly with the serious themes of the twentieth century—two world wars and their aftermath and the problems of the refugee—and always (and the point is an important one) in a readable fashion. *All Quiet on the Western Front* benefits greatly from being read together with these novels, especially its sequel, *Der Weg zurück* (*The Road Back*), which appeared in 1931 and is a real continuation of its precursor. It begins just after, and indeed refers to, the death of Paul Bäumer, the narrator of *All Quiet on the Western Front*; yet, the new narrator, who survives the war and has to cope with the period that follows, is so much like Paul Bäumer that they are almost interchangeable. And both novels benefit from being read alongside six related short stories, since collected as *Der Feind* (1993; The Enemy), that Remarque published in the American magazine *Collier's* during 1930 and 1931.

Despite the success of all his other works, however, *All Quiet on the Western Front* remains Remarque's best known. Published at a time when countless novels about World War I were appearing across Europe and the United States, it almost immediately became a best seller. For a long time, it was the yardstick against which other war novels—whether German, English, or American—were measured, as was Lewis Milestone's 1930 film adaptation in the war film genre. Today, the novel stands as one of the relatively few German novels to achieve the status of an international classic. It has been translated into approximately fifty languages, as Thomas F. Schneider's bibliography of translations attests, and there are numerous English editions, including a comic-book version. The book is now so familiar in the English-speaking world that readers sometimes forget it was originally written in German.

The novel is deceptively simple. It is hardly difficult to summarize: its narrator, the young soldier Paul Bäumer, who, with his classmates, has joined the army straight from high school in 1916, recounts a series of episodes reflecting his experiences of the war. The narrative moves among vivid scenes of actual warfare (on wiring or on sentry duty, under heavy fire, in a dugout, on a patrol), flashbacks to Paul's training, and periods of respite behind the lines, at home on leave, and in a military hospital. Interspersed, however, are a number of passages in which Paul reflects on the nature of the war and the effects it is having on him and will likely have on his, his comrades', and his country's future.

From this brief synopsis, it may well seem that the novel is little more than a kind of documentary journalism. Indeed, when it was first published (and still today even, among some readers), it was often taken as autobiography. Some of Remarque's fellow soldiers even condemned him for failing to render faithfully episodes they thought they recognized from their service, apparently not noticing that Remarque's central character does not, unlike his creator, survive the war.

The novel is, in fact, far more complex than this. It is indeed a first-person narrative, but because the entire novel is filtered through Bäumer's eyes, one must be wary of taking the narrator's understanding of the war for Remarque's. Bäumer, who is a consistently drawn character in his own right, is intelligent, perceptive, literate, and polite but also politically naive and inexperienced in many areas of life. He is young, too young indeed to have had any responsibility for the outbreak of the war, which is at a stalemate when he and his classmates and the young workers from his home join the army. All of these qualities have a bearing on the situation in which Bäumer suddenly finds himself. He and his compatriots are brutalized by the killing and exposed to horrific scenes of carnage, and yet Bäumer, ever genteel, remains self-conscious about using scatological phrases and cannot bring himself to explain to a nurse that he needs to go to the lavatory.

At the same time, Bäumer is typical enough to represent other soldiers. Since he is observant, he can also perceptively describe to us the other young men who have been drawn into the war. Many chapters begin with "we," the first-person plural that, depending on context, can embrace all of the Allied and German soldiers together, the German army alone, a single company, Bäumer's platoon, the group of boys who volunteered with him straight from grammar school, or just the narrator and another soldier. In this war of attrition, however, all of Bäumer's comrades—last of all his mentor, the older man Katczinsky—are killed, and at the end, just before his own death, Bäumer is forced in upon himself, speaking only of "I." Then, of course, he too is killed, and a postscript is added by a different voice, which speaks of him objectively but also speculatively: the narrator tells us that Bäumer had an expression on his face that made him look as if he were content with how things ended. Yet while Bäumer may have *looked as if* he were content, the reader must decide if this is true or not.

It is through omissions such as this—especially those arising from Bäumer's sometimes naive philosophizing—that Remarque obliquely addresses his reader. At the bedside of a mortally wounded comrade, Bäumer comments that the whole world ought to be made to go past this bed and this dying nineteen-year-old, and, of course, this is what Remarque is doing to his reader. Often Bäumer will comment that he cannot pursue an idea further at the moment but that it must be returned to after the war, and these remarks are also directed toward the reader. Ten years after its defeat, the German Weimar Republic was still trying to make sense of the war. Some avowed that it had been a horrific and wasteful undertaking, a thing that should never again be done; others believed that it had been a baptism of fire, terminated only by the shame of a punitive treaty.

All Quiet on the Western Front was only one of the many war novels that sought to adjudicate the meaning of the war during the 1920s and 1930s. In comparable German novels produced during the period, central figures (who are often first-person narrators) were ordinary soldiers, stretcher bearers, women, children, and even a horse (who, without any conceivable responsibility, is very much a victim). Some of these novels were militaristic and portrayed war as a testing, a forging of the personal or national character. Especially prevalent in Germany, they often depicted war graphically and realistically. Others, more trivial versions of the militaristic novel, presented war as an adventure. The idea formed the basis for a whole genre of "books for boys," and Remarque, in an alternative version of his novel's short preface (which appeared in the first English, but not the first German, book edition), was careful to dissociate his novel from these books, explicitly rejecting the idea that war could ever be an adventure. Though some critics would find what seem to be adventurous aspects in Remarque's novel—as when the central group guards a food depot and the soldiers have a feast—they can be explained by the soldiers' need to seize any chance of frivolity while they can; the meal is consumed under fire, and shortly afterward the central character is wounded and hospitalized.

Still others were antiwar novels. *All Quiet on the Western Front* is of this sort in the sense that, while it presents the war and the sufferings of those in it realistically, vividly, and, indeed, deliberately horrifyingly, it does not (whatever the Nazis thought) belittle the courage of the frontline soldiers. Its message is that war is an evil because of how it affects those who play a part in it—not just through death and injury but also through brutalization and deprivation as well as through the material and philosophical problems that confront those who, unlike Bäumer, survive.

Yet it is always worth asking what is *not* in a given work. Early critics of the novel faulted it for lacking a clearer political message and failing to show a positive revolt among the soldiers—even though, in reality, the bulk of the soldiers did not disobey their commanding officers. For all these lacks, however, there *is* a political aspect to the work, chiefly in its criticism of the hypocritical, empty rhetoric and irresponsible nationalism of those who are ostensibly in charge of the welfare of the young. In effect, the novel indicts them for the betrayal of a whole generation; it also condemns war profiteering.

Further, the novel lacks a historical analysis of the beginning of the war, which allows Remarque to present it as something over which the soldiers have no control. Because the point of view is consistently that of the ordinary solider, there is no mention of strategy. Likewise, Germany's defeat, which is also not actually shown because Bäumer falls just before the armistice, is not explained (and certainly not blamed on German politicians' supposed betrayal of the army, as in Nazi propaganda). The defeat is portrayed as simply a matter of overwhelming military force (including the fresh troops provided by the entry of the United States in the later stages) and the Allied blockade. The Nazis burned the novel in 1933 because it was supposed to have insulted the frontline soldier, but Remarque makes it explicit that the German army loses the war *not* because its soldiers are less capable than the Allied troops but simply because they are overwhelmed. The soldiers carry on, they do not revolt, and nobody deserts in the proper sense (only one soldier absents himself, but to return to Germany rather than to escape to, say, the Netherlands).

Although very many aspects of the war are covered, offering within a limited space a broad view of a very large-scale event, the novel also displays some noteworthy absences. Very few officers appear—indeed, almost none above the equivalent of drill-sergeant rank—and these are, in any case, a hated breed. Bäumer shows us an obnoxious major, a decent lieutenant, and also (briefly and from a distance) the kaiser, but that is it. Mention of the unpleasantness of the noncommissioned officers (and although Himmelstoß may be a martinet, his techniques harden the soldiers enough to keep them alive) leads us to consider the main omission: Where is the enemy, at least in formal terms? A comically naive discussion of the impossibility of one country insulting another country breaks down in the novel, but it is designed to provoke thought. To be sure, the opposing (usually French) forces are shown, and one is even named, Duval, whom Bäumer kills in terror. But the real enemies are different. On a personal level, the enemy is military authority; in broader terms, death itself. Bäumer and his comrades are fighting not against an enemy but rather to stay alive, perhaps even fighting against war as such, which is perceived as a kind of external force over which they have no control and of which they are therefore victims. Even when the soldiers are on the attack, they are like automatons, and Bäumer's commentary underlines this. This concept is important. It transformed what could have been a strictly German novel, a novel written by a German for Germans, into an international one, one that would appeal to all ordinary soldiers—whether they fought in the German or the Allied armies—who were determined not to fight again.

In the end, none of the questions Bäumer poses are answered explicitly. *All Quiet on the Western Front* has sometimes been dismissed as trivial, as popular or populist writing, as storytelling without much substance. Recent studies, however, have come increasingly to highlight the skill behind the construction and presentation of the work, its shifting patterns and styles, its movements in time, its development—for Bäumer *does* develop as the war gradually takes away all those around him—its subtleties and its challenges to the reader, all while retaining the reader's interest. This last point is not negligible. In some respects the novel *is* a simple one: its message is that the mechanized warfare of World War I had terrible consequences, especially for the uncomprehending and innocent young soldiers. The application to any war is clear.

All Quiet on the Western Front is, finally, a memorial to an event in human history of a magnitude that is still hard to come to terms with, an event that took or damaged the lives of many young people—both the soldiers and those they left behind. International and universal, and even at an increasing distance from the trenches of nearly a century ago, the novel retains its impact, and the relevance of the questions it poses to readers has not diminished.

Biography of Erich Maria Remarque_____

Diane Andrews Henningfeld

Erich Paul Remark, as he was known before changing his name to Erich Maria Remarque in 1920, was born on June 22, 1898, in Osnabrück, Germany. His father was a bookbinder. The family was poor and moved often; as a result, young Erich attended several different schools.

Remarque was talented in music, art, and literature and even thought of becoming a professional musician. Instead, he chose to enter teacher's training. Yet in 1916, at the height of World War I and before he was able to begin his career as a teacher, he was drafted into the army and sent to Flanders on the Western Front. On July 31, 1917, he was wounded and sent to a hospital to recover. Remarque's mother, who had been ill for some time with cancer, died while her son was in the hospital. This death appears to have profoundly affected Remarque.

During his hospital stay, Remarque began his writing career, completing a novel called *Die Traumbude* (1920; The Dream Room). Published after the war, the novel, for which Remarque had to sell his piano to cover printing costs, was a sentimental and romantic account of his circle of friends and would later become an embarrassment to Remarque, who found the writing poor and immature.

After his release from the hospital, Remarque had some trouble with authorities for wearing a lieutenant's uniform and medals he had not earned. By all accounts a handsome young man, the medal incident demonstrated Remarque's tendency toward flamboyance. During the early 1920's, Remarque had several jobs before becoming an editor of *Sport Im Bild* (*Sport in Pictures*) in 1925. It was at this time that he married Jutta Ilse Zambona, his first wife.

While at *Sport Im Bild*, Remarque began publishing articles and stories. No one could have predicted from these, however, that he would produce a work of such stature as *All Quiet on the Western Front*. In 1927 Remarque reportedly fell into a deep depression, which he attributed to his war experiences, and found that many of his former comrades were also suffering emotional disturbances from the war. Consequently, he began working on *All Quiet on the Western Front* for cathartic purposes. He believed that if he committed his memories to paper, he could overcome the depression they caused. He finished the book at the end of 1927, but initially had difficulty finding a publisher for it. Eventually, *All Quiet on the Western Front* was serialized in the paper *Vossische Zeitung* in November and December of 1928 and excited a great deal of public interest.

Remarque attempted to describe his project in the brief preface to *All Quiet on the Western Front*: "This book is to be neither an accusation nor a confession, and least of all an adventure, for death is not an adventure to those who stand face to face with it. It will try simply to tell of a generation of men who, even though they may have escaped shells, were destroyed by the war." For Remarque, the most important message of his novel was that war destroys more men than it kills.

All Quiet on the Western Front is set during the last two years of World War I, along the German lines in France. During this time, the Germans were losing strength just as the Americans entered the war. The novel tells the story of young Paul Bäumer and his high school classmates, who enlist in the German army at the urging of their teacher, Kantorek. The young recruits soon learn that war is not the glorious, heroic experience their elders taught them it is, but instead a brutal, futile business. Remarque's story is told from the point of view of a German foot soldier; however, his descriptions of the horrors of war transcend national boundaries. When it was published, Allied and German veterans alike recognized their experiences in Remarque's novel.

After its serialization, *All Quiet on the Western Front* was published in book form in January, 1929, and was an immediate best seller. Some attribute the success of the book to the massive publicity campaign undertaken by its publisher prior to the book's release. However, most critics agree that the book touched a nerve not only among the German people but also among veterans all over the world. Yet, although the book was wildly popular, it generated considerable controversy. Remarque soon became the subject of intense media and political scrutiny. Most notably, the Nationalist Socialist German Workers' Party, or the Nazi Party, rabidly criticized the book for its pacifist philosophy and for its supposedly negative depiction of German soldiers. Remarque was accused of being a French Jew whose name was really "Kramer" (Remark spelled backward), a piece of nonsense that has proved surprisingly hard to dislodge. In fascist Italy, the book was banned almost as soon as it was printed. When Carl Laemmle's 1930 film adaptation of the novel reached German cinemas, Nazi protesters disrupted the showings and eventually succeeded in getting it banned. In 1933, the Nazis publicly burned the book. On the other side of the Atlantic, however, the novel and the film were instant critical and commercial successes, with the film garnering several Academy Awards.

Meanwhile, Remarque began working on his next book, a sequel to *All Quiet on the Western Front* called *Der Weg zurück* (1931; *The Road Back*, 1931). In this book, he follows a group of veterans after the war, demonstrating the ways in which their lives have been destroyed. The novel was not the commercial success of *All Quiet on the Western Front* and received a more positive critical response in the United States than it did in Germany. After completing the book, Remarque realized that the growing power of the Nazis endangered him. He moved his money out of Germany and himself to Switzerland, where he remained until 1939. During this time, he and his wife divorced, only to remarry in order to expedite her emigration from Germany. In 1938, Germany took away his citizenship.

While in Switzerland, Remarque continued his writing career, publishing a novel titled *Drei Kameraden* (1938; *Three Comrades*, 1937). The German edition of the book, like many of the novels by German émigré writers at the time, was published in Amsterdam, Holland. In this novel, Remarque details the lives of three Germans between the years of 1923 and 1930, again returning to themes of friendship and displacement that had so marked his earlier work. Film versions of both *The Road Back* (1937) and *Three Comrades* (1938) were made in the United States and enjoyed commercial, if not critical, success.

In 1939, Remarque moved to the United States, living first in Los Angeles, California, and then New York City. During these years he wrote a number of novels and worked as a screenwriter. After divorcing Jutta Ilse Zambona a second time, he married the actress Paulette Goddard in 1958. The couple spent their time in New York, Italy, and Switzerland. In 1970, after a period of failing health, the seventy-two-year-old writer died in a hospital in Locarno, Switzerland.

Erich Maria Remarque was perhaps not the most talented writer of his generation. Nevertheless, nearly all of his dozen or so novels have been filmed, most of them are still in print in Germany, and several are unjustly neglected (especially his novels of World War II), overshadowed by the success of *All Quiet on the Western Front*. Further, while critics may not view *All Quiet on the Western Front* as one of the greatest works of twentieth century literature, none deny that it is an extremely important book. Thus the impact of *All Quiet on the Western Front* on society, politics, film, and literature confers on Remarque a higher status than he might otherwise have achieved. Throughout the novel, Remarque provides a ghastly look at the realities of war. Perhaps more important, his novel has come to define the experience of World War I, not just for Germans but for everyone who fought in the war.

Bibliography

Barker, Christine R., and R. W. Last. *Erich Maria Remarque*. New York: Barnes & Noble, 1979. An excellent introduction to Remarque's career, this study covers all of his major fiction.

Firda, Richard Arthur. *"All Quiet on the Western Front": Literary Analysis and*

Cultural Context. New York: Twayne, 1993. One of Twayne's masterwork studies, this is an excellent tool for students of the novel.

_____. *Erich Maria Remarque: A Thematic Analysis of His Novels*. New York: Peter Lang, 1988. Contains a good deal of helpful biographical material. Useful also for Firda's interpretation of the later novels.

Gilbert, Julie. *Opposite Attraction: The Lives of Erich Maria Remarque and Paulette Goddard*. New York: Pantheon, 1995. Primarily a biography and love story. Gilbert also provides detailed notes and an excellent bibliography.

Kelly, Andrew. *"All Quiet on the Western Front": The Story of a Film*. New York: I. B. Tauris, 1998. Focuses on the film made from Remarque's novel. Describes the film's origins and production, as well as its reception by critics and audiences.

Murdoch, Brian. *The Novels of Erich Maria Remarque: Sparks of Life*. Camden House, Rochester, N.Y.: 2006. Examination of Remarque's life and writing is an excellent resource for anyone interested in his works, but particularly for those who know him only as the author of *All Quiet on the Western Front*. Murdoch portrays Remarque as an artist, shedding light on his personal life and his reputation as a playboy. His entire body of writing, even his lesser-known novels, fall under close scrutiny as Murdoch examines the works individually, paying attention to their recurring themes and motifs.

Owen, C. R. *Erich Maria Remarque: A Critical Bio-Bibliography*. Amsterdam: Rodopi, 1984. An excellent source for finding additional critical commentary on Remarque.

Taylor, Harley U., Jr. *Erich Maria Remarque: A Literary and Film Biography*. New York: Peter Lang, 1989. This detailed study provides excellent background information on Remarque's family origins, his early years, military service, and the filming of *All Quiet on the Western Front*. Includes bibliography, chronology, filmography, and index.

Wagener, Hans. *Understanding Erich Maria Remarque*. Columbia: University of South Carolina Press, 1991. Separate chapters on all of Remarque's major work, interweaving biographical background with literary analysis. Includes a chronology, notes, and an annotated bibliography.

The *Paris Review* Perspective

Ruth Franklin for *The Paris Review*

On December 8, 1930, Joseph Goebbels, accompanied by two hundred Nazi storm troopers, went to see *All Quiet on the Western Front*. The epic film was adapted from Erich Maria Remarque's phenomenally successful novel, published just a year earlier, which had already sold more than a million copies in Germany alone. Translated into a dozen languages, it would eventually be hailed as the greatest war novel of all time by critics in Germany, England, France, and the United States.

Goebbels—then one of only ten Nazis elected to the Reichstag—did not share their high estimation of the novel. He called Remarque a "slicked-over fashion-monkey" and accused him of "treachery toward the German soldiers of the World War." At the cinema, he watched from the balcony as his minions, shouting, "Jews out! Jews out!," released mice, stink bombs, and sneeze powder in the theater, forcing the screening to be cut short. The storm troopers repeated the propaganda stunt night after night until the "film of shame," as Goebbels called it in his diary, was finally banned. "With that action," he wrote, "the National Socialist movement has won its fight against the dirty machinations of the Jews." One of Goebbels's first acts upon his appointment as propaganda minister in 1933 was to stage the infamous burning of "degenerate" books on Berlin's Bebelplatz. Remarque's novel, unsurprisingly, was among the thousands in the flames.

Despite his foreign-sounding name (originally spelled Remark), Remarque counted himself among the very German soldiers whose honor Goebbels had supposedly been defending. Born in Westphalia in 1898, he became a conscript at age eighteen and was transferred to the western front a year later, in June 1917. After the war, he held various odd jobs—cemetery stonecutter, race car driver, and advertising copywriter. He was working at an illustrated sports magazine when he wrote *All Quiet,* completing the manuscript, he later claimed, in just five weeks.

"Beside me a lance-corporal has his head torn off. He runs a few steps more while the blood spouts from his neck like a fountain." Hendrik Hertzberg, writing in *The New Yorker,* recalled reading *All Quiet* as an adolescent boy and being haunted for years afterward by that image. Reflecting on the depiction of violence in recent cinema, Hertzberg worried about the effects on the human psyche of the "desensitization program" effected by decades of exposure to ever more violent imagery: "We are benumbed, so much so that to produce the emotional impact that could once be achieved by a few lines of type in a paperback now requires the services of armies, so to speak, of technicians and skilled craftsmen." But in the eighty years since its publication, *All Quiet* has lost none of its rhetorical power. It still feels fresh, even to a reader well acquainted with the contemporary literature of atrocity—because it was the progenitor of this literature.

The novel's anecdotal, episodic style and clarity of voice have led readers often to mistake it for the author's war diary. But unlike Paul Bäumer, the protagonist ("hero" is not the right word for this deeply antiheroic book), Remarque served on the front for only a month before he was wounded; he spent the remainder of the war in the hospital. As is the case with every work of fiction that appears so minutely to reproduce reality—"It is not the artful construction of fancy, but the sincere record of a man's suffering," wrote T. S. Matthews in his review of the novel for *The New Republic*—the mirroring effect signals the workings of a great talent. Remarque may have dashed off his novel in a month, but he was able to do so, he explained, only because he was already so intimate with its subject matter. "It was really simply a collection of the best stories that I told and my friends told as we sat over drinks and relived the war," he said in an interview.

Veterans reminiscing do not moralize and neither does Remarque's narrator, who is nineteen at the start of the book and so recently out of school that, in one of the novel's droller moments, he and his fellow conscripts sit around laughing over the inutility of their so-called education. The stories he tells do not have a deeper point or a greater meaning, other than to demonstrate the ugliness of war. *All Quiet* is a dramatic novel—with its subject matter, how could it not be?—but it entirely lacks a narrative arc. No one is transformed by the war, no one achieves greater depth of character, no one learns the true meaning of courage or solidarity, no one finds or loses God. "We are forlorn like children, and experienced like old men," says Paul in one of the novel's most famous lines. "We are crude and sorrowful and superficial—I believe we are lost." It is these men, the men of the "Great War," who are the true "lost generation," not the dissolute expatriates who populate the cool prose of Ernest Hemingway or the fantasies of Henry Miller. They are lost because war has become their only reality.

Remarque establishes this from the very first episode of the novel. Paul's tone is honest, matter-of-fact; he speaks with a kind of cynical realism. "Today is wonderfully good," he tells us, certainly in comparison with the day before, when nearly half the company of 150 men were killed in a shelling attack. Yesterday was bad, but today is good— the cook, not realizing the volume of the losses, prepared enough food for the entire company, giving each man in effect a double ration. Afterward, the men pass the "wonderfully carefree hours" of the afternoon sitting together in a common open-air latrine. Once they were embarrassed by such "enforced publicity" for their bodily functions; now they calmly read letters, smoke, or play a game of skat, setting the lid of a margarine tub on their knees as a table.

But the realities of the war cannot be held at bay for long. Later that day, the men go to the hospital to visit their friend Kemmerich, who does not yet know that his leg has been amputated. Müller, another of the company, eyes Kemmerich's boots jealously, but none of the soldiers has the heart to tell the wounded man he won't be needing them anymore. Later Paul reflects on the subtleties of this interaction. There is nothing wrong with Müller's coveting the boots, he explains, "he merely sees things clearly."

Were Kemmerich able to make any use of the boots, then Müller would rather go barefoot over barbed wire than scheme how to get hold of them. But as it is the boots are quite inappropriate to Kemmerich's circumstances, whereas Müller can make good use of them. Kemmerich will die; it is immaterial who gets them. Why, then, should Müller not succeed to them? He has more right than a hospital orderly. When Kemmerich is dead it will be too late. Therefore Müller is already on the watch.

Müller does manage to get the boots; after he dies, Paul inherits them. "They fit me quite well," he remarks. "After me, Tjaden will get them, I have promised them to him." A similar lack of sentimentality characterizes the works of Holocaust writers such as Tadeusz Borowski, who, like Remarque, was later castigated by an unsympathetic government for his unsanitized portrayal of his compatriots' actions during wartime. While Borowski is often credited with pioneering this coolly cynical tone, it may well have originated with Remarque. (Borowski must have read *All Quiet*, which appeared in Polish in 1930.)

All Quiet is known as both a war novel and an antiwar novel—a reputation that might once have seemed paradoxical. But by the twentieth century, it might well have been impossible to write literature celebrating the heroism of war. The *Iliad*'s dramas of honor and revenge sound to us like the pulsings of an alien culture; Horace's old cry "*Dulce et decorum est pro patria mori*" comes now from Owen's bitter mouth. We know that war is terrible beyond our imaginings. The contemporary reader—after Stalingrad, Auschwitz, Hiroshima, Vietnam—may even come to a novel about trench warfare with a certain complacency: Haven't we seen worse, much worse?

"The author has nothing new to say," Matthews wrote in his 1929 review, "but he says it so honestly and so well that it is like news to us." Just as the teenaged Hertzberg was haunted by the image of the decapitated man, I suspect that each new reader of this novel will come away from it with a crystallization of war's horror in a single catastrophic image or scene. It might be the moans of wounded horses after a particularly severe shelling: the sound, Paul realizes, "is not men, they could not cry so terribly." Or the attack that breaks out while the company happens to be in a cemetery, forcing Paul to take shelter in an open grave; afterward he contemplates the mercy killing of a young recruit with a shattered hip: "Every day that he can live will be a howling torture. And to whom does it matter whether he has them or not—." Or the cries of a dying soldier that continue for two days while the company desperately searches for him: "He must be lying on his belly and unable to turn over. . . . The voice is so strangely pitched that it seems to be everywhere. The first night our fellows go out three times to look for him. But when they think they have located him and crawl across, the next time they hear the voice it seems to come from somewhere else altogether."

If there is anything resembling an epiphany in this resolutely down-to-earth novel, it would have to be the episode in which Paul stabs a French soldier who falls into the shell hole where he is hiding. When day breaks, he is horrified to see that the Frenchman is still alive. Paul bandages the man's wound with his own tunic and brings him water, and is consumed with guilt after his death. "'Comrade,' I say to the dead man, but I say it calmly, 'today you, tomorrow me. But if I come out of it, comrade, I will fight against this. . . . I promise you, comrade. It shall never happen again.'" But when he tells the story to his friends, they reassure him that he could not have acted differently. "I listen to them and feel comforted, reassured by their presence. It was mere drivelling nonsense that I talked out there in the shell-hole. . . . 'It was only because I had to lie there with him so long,' I say. 'After all, war is war.'" The epiphany is retracted.

And just as well. The weakest moments of *All Quiet* are the explicitly political ones, particularly the episode in which the kaiser comes to visit the troops, who marvel at his undistinguished looks and later debate the reasons (or lack thereof) for all the bloodshed. One suspects that it was scenes like that one—along with the glamorous lifestyle Remarque enjoyed while living in exile in Switzerland (he had an affair with Marlene Dietrich, whom he called by the same nickname as his beloved sports car), not to mention his enviable ability to turn out best seller after best seller—that bestowed upon the author his middlebrow reputation. But *All Quiet* is one of those rare novels that has earned its popularity. It may not bring news—a fact ironically underscored by the book's original German title, *Im Westen nichts Neues*—but it retells it in indelible ink. As Paul says at one point, "Bombardments, barrage, curtain-fire, mines, gas, tanks, machine-guns, hand-grenades—words, words, but they hold the horror of the world."

CRITICAL
CONTEXTS

The Weimar Republic and
the Literature of the Great War_____

Thomas F. Schneider

"Finally the truth about war," the real truth about the Great War, proclaimed the more than 450 reviews of Erich Maria Remarque's *Im Westen nichts Neues* (*All Quiet on the Western Front*) published from 1928 through 1930. Roughly five thousand to six thousand publications on the war had appeared before *All Quiet on the Western Front*, yet that little word, "finally," suggested that all of them had failed to draw a true picture of the war. It implied, too, that the most important criterion critics used to judge literary representations of the Great War was "truth." Though, of course, critics used the word in different contexts and with different meanings, depending on their political or ideological points of view, this criterion was not new in 1928. The literary, but first of all cultural and political, discussion of real and "truthful" representations of war had started already during the war as a result of the new experiences modern warfare brought to the trenches of the western front. It was in this context, then, that the Ullstein publishing house announced the serialization of Erich Maria Remarque's new novel by calling it a "true picture of war" written not by an author "by profession" (J.E.) but by an authentic war veteran. Now, exactly ten years after the armistice, Ullstein said, the time had come to present and discuss the real war and its meaning in history and contemporary society.

I

The war enthusiasm during August 1914 of several European countries involved in the outbreak of World War I has been widely discussed and analyzed (see Gollbach; Prangel; Linder; Schöning; Marsland). Approximately one million poems and thousands of narratives were written that gave expression to the enthusiasm and (in the German cultural context) the hope for change that war would bring to the entrenched society of the *Kaiserreich*. These poems and narratives represented and extrapolated from an image of war created during the liberation wars at the beginning of the nineteenth century. In this image, a self-determined individual fought for the kaiser and for the fatherland in a war mainly characterized by rapid movements and individual soldiers' "heroic" acts. This image had already begun to crack during the Franco-Prussian War of 1870-1871 as it was defied by the ongoing guerrilla war in the south of France in 1871 and the fact that most of the dead were not killed in action but by diseases. However, as time passed, German authors such as Theodor Fontane reinstated the former image of war, and by 1914, after more than forty years of relative peace, the Franco-Prussian War had been nearly forgotten.

In September 1914, the advance of the German armies stopped on the river Marne, and German soldiers found themselves stuck in trenches, attacking Allied forces burrowed into other trenches and making no obvious progress. The ideological reasons used to justify beginning the war now seemed contradictory to the reality of war. Thus the flood of publications and reports on the war, written especially for those who stayed on the home front, became more necessary than ever. A new interpretation of the war, one that provided "new" reasons yet did not contradict the "old" ones, began appearing at the end of 1914.

The main guidelines for describing and interpreting the war can be found in these writings. They attempt to treat "the whole thing": both the war itself from a historical and ideological point of view and the experiences and deeds of the individual soldiers. They try to evaluate the war's horrors, give sense to the war's apparent senselessness, and provide the individual soldiers—who, in these writings' definition, are not able to judge the war from their "worm's-eye view"—with a reason they should go on fighting and suffering. Although these writings do portray the individual as material in the matériel battle, trench warfare does not lead to his demoralization. Rather, the soldier's awareness of his superior morals and values gives him a new self-assuredness. Though the soldier faces dehumanization, the loss of self-determination, and the constant threat of death, these hazards are interpreted in such a way as to re-create the individual from the faceless masses of soldiers, from the matériel of war. The old image of war, in which the individual is able to change the "whole thing" by being heroic and courageous, is nearly gone. All that remains is his ability to maintain his humanity.

During the war, the German public was bombarded by these reports and publications on the war, and the guidelines these publications created had a strong impact on how contemporary histories, autobiographies, and literature represented the war. Countless numbers of these books on the war were published. Even the *Hinrichs Halbjahrs Katalog*, similar to today's *Books in Print*, stopped its attempt to list the German war literature in a special edition after five editions in 1916. The publications listed under "literature" alone fill thirty small-print pages with dozens of titles.

One of the main factors contributing to the popularity of war literature was the publication, starting with the beginning of the war, of series of books dealing with the war. *The German War, Friend and Foe, War and Victory*, and other series published more than one hundred titles each that focused on nearly every aspect of modern life in connection with the war. Published in print runs of sometimes more than 500,000, these cheap books offered an image of the war in which the new and modern weapons and the new experiences of war were almost seamlessly integrated.

They sublimated the dehumanization of the individual soldier by producing new heroes who could control the new weapons such as airplanes or submarines and use them to accomplish their missions. Mainly officers who emerge from the masses by skillfully handling the machines of which they are part, these heroes are self-determined. These heroes have fears, they have doubts, and they are aware that they may be killed by chance—the part of the war that they cannot control. Yet, by overcoming these psychological obstacles, these heroes strengthen their wills and power as well as their ability to fight for the kaiser and the fatherland (or just their lust for hunting or adventures in foreign countries). Though these books never denied the new structure of war, they did create new myths through metaphorical comparisons between the war in the skies and hunting or the adventurous struggle of the individual to get home to Germany from China or Paraguay in order to fight for the kaiser. Illustrations and the precise identification of locations, times, and events lent the books authenticity. In short, author, text, and illustration were combined into a harmonious unity, giving readers the impression that what they were reading was not an adventure story but the war itself, the "true" war.

II

During the war, censorship prevented pacifist and even critical war literature from being published in the German *Kaiserreich*. This should be emphasized because antiwar literature was published in other countries and is still the main part of the canon of war literature and of scholarly studies of war literature. German antiwar literature only appeared in exile, mostly in Switzerland, where it was published by the Max Rascher publishing house in Zurich. In 1917 the Alsatian René Schickele, himself a pacifist novelist and literary journal editor, began publishing antiwar prose by writers of a variety of nationalities. One such writer, the Austrian Andreas Latzko, had such success with his stories *Menschen im Krieg* (1917; *Men in War*) that Schickele was encouraged to continue his program with Henri Barbusse, Leonid Andrejew, Romain Rolland, and Leo Tolstoy. In contrast to the usual German war literature of the period, these texts showed how modern warfare, particularly trench warfare, results in dehumanization. War inevitably leads to insanity and murder in these texts, and there is no way out of the war and no way to stop the killing.

The most successful and, for German war literature, most influential book to come out of René Schickele's publishing program was the German translation (by L. von Meyenburg) of Henri Barbusse's *Le Feu* (in German *Das Feuer*, and in English *Under Fire*). Written in 1915 and first published in French in 1916, the novel was translated into German and smuggled into the country in 1918. Barbusse's novel fulfills the standards for war literature—it claims to be authentic, its story is chronological, and its narrator/protagonist is identifiable with its author—yet it also changes them. The "hero" of Barbusse's "diary of a platoon" is not a single person but a group of soldiers, the platoon. The novel's topic is not the single, exemplary fate that re-creates the soldiers' individuality but the slow vanishing of the social differences among the French soldiers of various class origins and of the national differences between the French soldiers and their German opponents. Written in 1915, before the main materiel battles of Verdun and Passchendaele, the novel creates stunning images of a modern war. The final chapter, "Dawn" ("Morgengrauen" in German, which can also be read as "morning horror"), shows the trenches filled with water and mud after days of rain, which has stopped the fighting. The mud-covered soldiers cannot identify one another; the soldiers from both sides of the front are equal and completely deindividualized. This leads to the recognition of the other, of the solidarity among all soldiers, which is, in Barbusse's eyes, a socialistic salvation.

Without doubt, Barbusse's popular *Le Feu* influenced German war literature as well as the image of modern war outside literature. But Barbusse did not create new standards for representing the war—he just reworked the standards for pro-war literature and thus stayed in discourse with them. His descriptive methods were not novel and could easily be adopted and used by pro-war authors, as can be seen in the work of Ernst Jünger. The criterion for evaluating war literature—even an antiwar literature—then, remained "truth"—that is, how accurately a work of literature captured the image of modern warfare, not the way in which it described the war.

The armistice and the end of the war generally did not change the standards and conventions of war literature. During the war, fiction and documentary had so intermingled that, even today, it seems impossible to distinguish between the two; likewise, both pro-war and antiwar literature of the early and mid-1920s used fact as well as fiction to pursue their ideological and political purposes. Some critics, such as Modris Eksteins, have assumed that in the 1920s the public got tired of war literature. Yet this verdict is fairly incorrect because the literature produced during the war, especially pro-war literature, continued to fulfill its ideological function. Not war but peace was subjected to criticism. And not the lost war but the Treaty of Versailles—which Germans largely believed was full of unfair, punitive Allied demands—was blamed for the social, economic, and political catastrophes Germany endured throughout the decade. The most popular literature of the period described the German army as unbeaten and heroic and provided the public with guidelines for interpreting the postwar present. The (very) few examples of antiwar literature were censored and sometimes even prosecuted by legal action.

A distinction should be made, however, between "documentary" publications, such as the forty-volume *Schlachten des Weltkrieges* (Battles of the World War, 1921-1930), and expressly fictional texts, such as Arnold Zweig's *Der Streit um den Sergeanten Grischa* (1927; *The Case of Sergeant Grischa*) or Leonhard Frank's *Der Mensch ist gut* (1919; Man Is Good). The standards for postwar fiction about the war demanded that the author should be a veteran; that the events described in the text should have been experienced by the author; and that the events should be verifiable (and, therefore, exact dates and locations had to be given). Further, these standards prevented fiction about the war from formulating interpretations of the war. On a literary level, the war could be used as background for any kind of human subjects and topics, but valid texts about the war should show no obvious tendency or political meaning. Instead, they judged the war itself as meaningless. It had been cruel, and every soldier on the front had suffered from the war in some way, yet the German soldiers had fulfilled their duty. Postwar society and politics were the results not of the war itself but of postwar political events (such as the Versailles treaty) and the responsibility of the governing politicians—the democrats.

III

Erich Paul Remark—who, in 1921, would change his name to Erich Maria Remarque—was drafted into the German army on November 21, 1916. After more than six months of military training in Osnabrück and Celle, he was sent to the western front in Flanders on June 12, 1917. On July 31, the first day of the third Ypres battle, he was wounded in his left leg, right arm, and neck and sent to the Duisburg hospital, where he stayed until October 31, 1918. The end of war prevented him from being sent to the front again. While in the hospital, he questioned other wounded soldiers about their war experiences and, in late 1917, began writing a "novel" about the war. The death of his mentor and fatherly Osnabrück friend Fritz Hörstemeier halted his work in March 1918, and Remarque instead wrote *Die Traumbude* (The Dream Room), a novel about his experiences as an adolescent before the war, which was published in 1920.

In the fall of 1927, for no obvious reason, Erich Maria Remarque, now journalist for *Sport im Bild*, a fashionable Berlin literary periodical published by the national conservative Hugenberg trust, renewed his wartime plans and wrote a novel titled *Im Westen nichts Neues* (*All Quiet on the Western Front*). Remarque worked out at least three versions of the text before he handed the typescript over to the highly respected S. Fischer publishing house in early 1928. The text was rejected because the publisher thought the market for war literature was oversaturated and that any type of war novel would be a flop. Through many hands the typescript finally reached the bourgeois and liberal Ullstein company in the early summer of 1928 and was accepted.

Remarque had written a "novel," his third one after *Die Traumbude* and the serial *Station am Horizont* (1927-1928; Stopping Point on the Horizon). It was meant to be the first part of a trilogy describing the fate of German soldiers during the war, their homecomings, and the difficulties they face as they try to reintegrate themselves into postwar civilian society. Ullstein invited Remarque to a meeting on August 6, 1928, and presumably (no documents are available) forced him to change the whole text of *All Quiet* in order to align it with the period's standards and criteria for war literature.

Remarque changed the novel from one that was, if not antiwar, at least critical of war into a text that, like other war novels of the period, refuses to offer an explicit interpretation of the war. He deleted all the passages that expressly criticized the war, its causes, and its senseless-ness, and added sentences and passages that relativized critical state-ments. For example, the famous staff corporal, Himmelstoß, who in the typescript version was meant to be a representative example of mil-itarism and military thinking, became an exception, a curiosity. The new passage ended, "Es gab auch viele anständige Korporale, die vernünftiger waren; die anständigen waren sogar in der Überzahl" (*Westen* 31) ["There were many other staff corporals, the majority of whom were more decent" (*Quiet* 25)]. The young soldiers' suffering remains in the new version, yet now they suffer not from the military system itself but from a vicious sergeant called Himmelstoß.

Other changes concerned the general critique of war. For example, the sentence "Wir entschuldigen nichts mit Notwendigkeit, mit Ideen, mit Staatsgründen" ["We don't excuse anything due to necessity, to ideas, to reasons of state"] was changed to "Wir sagen nichts gegen Notwendigkeit, Ideen, Staatsgründe" ["We don't say anything against necessity, ideas, reasons of state"]. The sentence appeared in the serial-ized version of the novel but was later completely deleted from the book edition.

In chapter 9, Remarque completely changed the famous discussion among the soldiers about the sense and causes of war after the kaiser's visit. The original typescript showed Paul Bäumer reflecting that the discussion is typical for the ordinary soldier, who observes the war "aus der Froschperspektive"—that is, from "a worm's-eye view"—and judging the discussion as a tragic expression of resignation. In Re-marque's revision, however, Bäumer fails to reflect on the conversa-tion and remains on the level of the soldiers. The discussion finishes with Albert remarking: "Besser ist, über den ganzen Kram nicht zu reden" ["The best thing is not to talk about the rotten business"], to which Kat responds, "Wird ja auch nicht anders dadurch" (*Westen* 206) ["It won't make any difference, that's for sure" (*Quiet* 209)].

In its published version, *All Quiet on the Western Front* meets the standards and criteria of war literature—its narrator expresses opinions of the individual soldiers only and nearly always takes them back. Nothing is expressly antiwar. As in Barbusse's *Le Feu*, the novel's protagonist is a group of soldiers, not the reflecting Paul Bäumer.

But the Ullstein company still was not certain that even the depoliticized version of *All Quiet on the Western Front* would meet with success. Preparing the first World Congress of Advertisement in late 1928, the company embarked on a marketing campaign for the book that was unprecedented in German publishing history. The serialized print in the *Vossische Zeitung* was announced on November 8, 1928, and commenced on November 10, 1928. The ambivalence of the marketing campaign becomes evident when one takes into account that these November days were not only the tenth anniversary of the armistice (and German revolution) but also the fourteenth anniversary of the 1914 Battle of Langemarck, in which, as myth had it, fervently patriotic young German soldiers were massacred as they charged the Allied lines, and which right-wing groups yearly observed. Ullstein announced the text *All Quiet on the Western Front* as a documentary without "tendency"—a nonpolitical novel that nevertheless provided a new perspective on the war: that of the ordinary soldier. Ullstein created in Remarque a "new" author, too, one who could have been identical with the protagonist of *All Quiet on the Western Front*, Paul Bäumer. Ullstein let it be known that Remarque was in his early thirties (he was exactly thirty years old), which readers took to mean that he could have enlisted in 1914; that he enlisted deliberately, which is definitely untrue; and that all the events described in the text were experienced by the author himself (J.E.). This text *and* its author now fulfilled the standards and criteria for war literature.

The serial of the novel was an unexpected success. It boosted the

Vossische Zeitung out of the red, and thousands of letters to the editor reached Ullstein, some of which were at once published in the *Vossische Zeitung* to advertise the novel further. The book's publication was scheduled for late January 1929, after the usual Christmas business, so that it would stand alone as an extraordinary event in the book market. For weeks before its publication, it was announced and advertised in newspapers. Journals that did not belong to the Ullstein company were allowed to print one chapter of the text gratis, and Ullstein offered complete shopwindow displays to booksellers—something that was then unprecedented in German publishing. Parts of the text were also printed on leaflets.

Meanwhile, the text changed again with the book edition. Some passages were deleted and replaced by new ones, increasing the amount of sex and crime in the novel (for example, the chapter 10 hospital scene with Lewandowski was added, though it was unknown to the American reader until 1975 because it was censored in the United States). As no handwritten or typescript documents of these passages exist, however, it is not known whether the new passages were written by Remarque or by someone at Ullstein.

On January 29, 1929, the day the book was published, or in the days that closely followed it, all of the Ullstein newspapers published enthusiastic reviews of the book by well-known authors such as Carl Zuckmayer, Bernhard Kellermann, and Fritz von Unruh, all of whom fought in the Great War and were thus legitimated to write about it. All remarked that *All Quiet on the Western Front* was "finally" telling the "truth" about the war.

At the same time, Remarque was living up to his new biography in interviews and in life. He declared that he had written the novel in six weeks, and without making any corrections, in order to "overcome" his war experiences and depressions. He denied that the novel had any political bias and instead emphasized that he "just" wanted to describe what happened to young men thrown into the war. This was exactly the opposite of what he originally intended—that is, what *happens* (not *happened*) to young people coming home from the war—but what else could he do? The Ullstein marketing campaign was extremely successful, and even after the book was published it continued publishing a steady stream of brochures and leaflets that collected and quoted positive as well as negative reviews. *All Quiet on the Western Front* became the best- and fastest-selling novel in German literary history; moreover, the text was discussed not in a literary context but in a cultural and historical one.

At first, public approval of the novel was nearly complete: left-wing as well as right-wing critics agreed with the Ullstein campaign that *All Quiet on the Western Front* was telling the "truth" about the Great War. But in spring 1929, opinions began to change. Sales figures were still rising, but as public debate turned to issues such as the construction of the country's first pocket battleship, the *Panzerkreuzer A*, and the re-militarization of Weimar Germany, as well as the Young Plan for the German reparations, more and more critics, especially democrat and bourgeois ones, began to regard *All Quiet on the Western Front* as an antiwar novel. At the same time, those in the political center claimed Remarque's former "novel" for their political position.

Ullstein changed its marketing campaign slightly with the book edition, which probably helped attract the controversy. The company had marketed the serial version as a testimony of the war experiences of the generation who fought in the war, yet it proclaimed the book version to be the war testimony of all participating German soldiers and, even more, a virtual memorial to unknown soldiers who had fallen in the war (Germany at that time had no official nationwide memorial for these soldiers). The chairman of the poetry section of the Prussian Academy of Arts, Walter von Molo, was even quoted on the front cover as saying, "Remarque's book is the memorial to our unknown soldier—written by all dead." Thus Ullstein changed the marketing campaign slightly. The serialized version was a testimony of the war experiences of a young generation, the classes of the 1890s. The book version claimed to be the war testimony of all participating German soldiers and, even more, a virtual memorial to the soldiers killed in the war. *All Quiet on the Western Front* now stood in a strict opposition to another virtual memorial of the Great War, Adolf Hitler. In nearly every one of his speeches of that time, Hitler pointed at his own war experiences as a "simple private" who suffered barrage and gas attacks and claimed them to be average, a rhetorical strategy that would give him the legitimation he needed to ascend to power in Germany. The supporters of the democratic Weimar Republic now assembled behind *All Quiet on the Western Front*, while right-wing (and left-wing) critics and enemies of the Republic opposed the text. Left-wing critics opposed the text for not describing the social and economic reasons for the war in a socialist way.

The discussion of the book now became an exact mirror of the political situation of the late Weimar Republic. Though for different reasons, the Left and Right alike became opponents of the book and denied that it contained any truth. The biography Ullstein had fabricated for Remarque began to unravel, and critics, especially those on the Right, tried to undermine the author's legitimacy by unearthing his early, romantic writings and his various name changes as well as concocting stories and rumors that would later become legends. A year after so many critics had written about the truth of *All Quiet on the Western Front*, hardly anyone outside of a small group of young people who fought on the western front saw any truth in it at all.

In the wake of this controversy, *All Quiet on the Western Front* became the touchstone of German war literature. In the years following its publication, hundreds of texts appeared that, from various political viewpoints, would try to prove, ex negative, that it was a false representation of the war and claim to provide the true image of war. Discussions of these texts were mainly restricted to political criticism and rarely touched on the text's literary qualities. Critics did not deny the cruelty of war (in this respect, they considered Remarque truthful) or even the senselessness of dying—but they condemned Remarque for failing to interpret the war (all such interpretations were deleted by

Ullstein) and for asserting (as Ullstein's marketing campaign made him appear) that *All Quiet on the Western Front*'s depiction of the war was representative of all soldiers' experiences of the war.

Yet *All Quiet on the Western Front* did not create a new image of the Great War. Comparing the published version of the text with, say, National Socialist war literature, only a few differences can be seen. The latter tends to have even more confusing scenes (in a sense of innovation), especially among depictions of suicide, fear, horror, or self-mutilation. The National Socialist texts also emphasize how war experience builds camaraderie between the soldiers, resulting in a new social phenomenon: men forged by the storm of steel of the matériel battle to form a new society. And, in contrast to *All Quiet on the Western Front*, these texts depict the "worm's-eye view" as necessary. Rather than refusing to offer an interpretation of the role of the individual soldier in the war, as *All Quiet on the Western Front* does, these texts make it clear that the individual is fully integrated into the group, making him part of a greater community and a greater purpose. Man as material becomes an individual again because he knows that he is a respected and useful part of the entire war effort. *All Quiet on the Western Front* offers no such interpretation; moreover, Remarque's next novels *Der Weg zurück* (1931; *The Road Back*, 1931) and *Drei Kameraden* (1938; *Three Comrades*, 1937) demonstrate that, in Remarque's view, comradeship is not able to withstand the social demands placed on the veterans in the postwar era. That this general social emptiness was an outcome of the war was the most dangerous claim of *All Quiet on the Western Front* for its critics. And this was the reason why Joseph Goebbels, as part of National Socialist cultural policy, mounted an opposition to the film adaptation in 1930, finally succeeding in banning it December 1930.

The Ullstein publishing house's attempt to gain hegemony over the interpretation of the Great War in the Weimar Republic thus failed. The changes the house made to the text of *All Quiet on the Western Front*, along with its attempts to install Remarque as a legitimate author of war literature, were only the first steps of a campaign aimed at bolstering the democratic political system of the Republic. Remarque and his novel were just an inducement for a political controversy that had long been in the making. When the National Socialists succeeded in banning the movie, the discussion of the novel was effectively finished. And with the National Socialists' 1933 government takeover, the political debates that started with the discussion on *All Quiet on the Western Front* in 1929 were at an end.

Yet despite the controversy the novel sparked in Germany, readers from all over the world have taken *All Quiet on the Western Front*—even in its depoliticized version—as a valid description of the front lines of modern war—and as an indictment of war. Thus Remarque's original intentions for the novel have at last been fulfilled.

Works Cited

Bartov, Omer. *Murder in Our Midst: The Holocaust, Industrial Killing, and Representation*. New York: Oxford UP, 1996.

Chambers, John Whiteclay, II. "*All Quiet on the Western Front* (U.S., 1930): The Antiwar Film and the Image of Modern War." *World War II, Film, and History*. Ed. John Whiteclay Chambers II and David Culbert. New York: Oxford UP, 1996. 13-30.

Eksteins, Modris. *Rites of Spring: The Great War and the Birth of the Modern Age*. Boston: Houghton Mifflin, 1989.

Erll, Astrid. *Gedächtnisromane: Literatur über den Ersten Weltkrieg als Medium englischer und deutscher Erinnerungskulturen in den 1920er Jahren*. Trier: WVT, 2003 (ELCH 10).

Gilbert, Julie. *Opposite Attraction: The Lives of Erich Maria Remarque and Paulette Goddard*. New York: Pantheon, 1995.

Gollbach, Michael. *Die Wiederkehr des Weltkrieges in der Literatur: Zu den Frontromanen der späten Zwanziger Jahre*. Kronberg: Scriptor, 1978.

Howind, Angelika. "Ein Antikriegsroman als Bestseller. Die Vermarktung von *Im Westen nichts Neues* 1928 bis 1930. " *Erich Maria Remarque 1898-1970*. Ed. Tilman Westphalen. Bramsche: Rasch, 1988. 55-64.

J.E. Rev. of *Nichts Neues im Westen*, by Erich Maria Remarque. *Vossische Zeitung* (Berlin) 8 Nov. 1928: 1.

Kelly, Andrew. "*All Quiet on the Western Front*": The Story of a Film. 1998. New York: I. B. Tauris, 2002.

Linder, Ann P. *Princes of the Trenches: Narrating the German Experience of the First World War*. Columbia, SC: Camden House, 1996.

Marsland, Elizabeth. *The Nation's Cause: French, English, and German Poetry of the First World War*. New York: Routledge, 1991.

Prangel, Matthias. "Das Geschäft mit der Wahrheit. Zu einer zentralen Kategorie der Rezeption von Kriegsromanen der Weimarer Republik." *Ideologie und Literatur (Wissenschaft)*. Ed. Jos Hoogeveen and Hans Würzner. Amsterdam: Rodopi, 1986. 47-78.

Remarque, Erich Maria. *All Quiet on the Western Front*. Trans. A. W. Wheen. Boston: Little, Brown, 1929.

_____. *Im Westen nichts Neues*. Berlin: Propyläen, 1929.

Schneider, Thomas F. *Erich Maria Remarques Roman "Im Westen nichts Neues": Text, Edition, Entstehung, Distribution und Rezeption (1928-1930)*. Tübingen: Max Niemeyer, 2004.

Schöning, Matthias. *Versprengte Gemeinschaft: Kriegsroman und intellektuelle Mobilmachung in Deutschland 1914-1933*. Göttingen: Vandenhoeck & Ruprecht, 2009.

Stanzel, Franz Karl, and Martin Löschnigg, eds. *Intimate Enemies: English and German Literary Reactions to the Great War, 1914-1918*. Heidelberg: Winter, 1993.

Ziemann, Benjamin. "Die deutsche Nation und ihr zentraler Erinnerungsort. Das 'Nationaldenkmal für die Gefallenen im Weltkriege' und die Idee des 'Unbekannten Soldaten' 1914-1935." *Krieg und Erinnerung: Fallstudien zum 19. und 20. Jahrhundert*. Ed. Helmut Berding, Klaus Heller, and Winfried Speitkamp. Göttingen: Vandenhoeck & Ruprecht, 2000. 67-91.

The Reception of
*All Quiet on the Western Front*_____

Mark Ward

It is commonplace, when considering literature relating to World War I, to say that the conflict had been so devastating for what became known as the lost generation that effectively a decade had to elapse before the war could be confronted in literary form. The years 1927 through 1929 saw the publication not only of Erich Maria Remarque's *Im Westen nichts Neues* (1929; *All Quiet on the Western Front*, 1929) but also of Arnold Zweig's *Der Streit um den Sergeanten Grischa* (1927; *The Case of Sergeant Grischa*, 1927), Ludwig Renn's *Krieg* (1928; *War*, 1929), and Ernst Glaeser's *Jahrgang 1902* (1928; *Class of 1902*, 1929), and subsequent years saw many more treatments, from a variety of perspectives, of the momentous events of 1914-18. Of all these treatments, however, it was, and is, Remarque's novel that has had the most enduring impact, not only within a German or European context but also around the world. It rapidly became a best seller, with 1.2 million copies selling in the first year after it was published, and it has subsequently been translated into approximately fifty languages. The reasons for its success, however, were at the time, and remain, a topic of debate and contest, although the circumstances surrounding the novel's publication do provide some insight into its initial impact.

All Quiet on the Western Front was written in late 1927 and submitted to the prestigious S. Fischer Press. To this day, it is not clear why the imprint turned it down, but the novel eventually did appear on January 29, 1929, with the Ullstein Propyläen Press, thanks to the efforts of Fritz Roß, the son-in-law of Hans Ullstein. But there appear to have been doubts about whether the book would sell. The contract that Ullstein issued to Remarque guaranteed one thousand marks per month over a two-year period but also included a clause stating that Remarque would have to partially repay any deficit. That said, the

Ullstein Press took great pains to try to ensure the success of the novel. In 1928 the work appeared in serialized form in the *Vossische Zeitung* newspaper, which sold out during the weeks in which the serial appeared—from November 10 to December 9—something that was unprecedented. The *Börsenblatt für den deutschen Buchhandel* (Stock Market Journal for the German Book Trade) of June 10, 1930, recorded that the newspaper "had taken the risk of publishing such a realistic war novel in its entertainment section with some hesitation because everybody had in their minds that phrase that had been heard a thousand times: 'We do not want to hear anything more about the war'" (54). The substantial advertising campaign that preceded the publication in novel form included, among other things, posters on advertising pillars that changed weekly:

Week 1: It's coming.
Week 2: The great war novel.
Week 3: All Quiet on the Western Front.
Week 4: By Erich Maria Remarque.

After its publication, the daily sales on occasion reached fifteen thousand copies, and the Ullstein Press, having run out of paper and cloth, began employing up to seven printing works and binderies.

The book was also promoted through the distribution of leaflets containing commentary by a broad range of readers including the parliamentary president, famous writers, politicians, readers of the *Vossische Zeitung*, press reviews, and ordinary women readers. Common to these various voices is the shattering effect that the novel had on them; a feeling that it was true to the experience of those who fought in the Great War; a recognition of the warning it sounded; and an appreciation for the novel's first-person narration, which tells the story clearly and simply and without any attempt to propagandize. There are also frequent comments to the effect that the novel is a fitting monument to the soldiers.

The dramatist Carl Zuckmayer, who had served as an officer in the war, observed, "It will be the same for hundreds of thousands who took part in the war as for me: that they rediscover a part of their own life history in this book"; the novelist Stefan Zweig, who had adopted a pacifist stance toward the war, recorded:

> In order to know what the last generation suffered in the war, every German should read this book that is unprecedentedly true and mercilessly disturbing. It overpowers without being partial, it distresses without exaggerating. Perfect work of art and incontrovertible truth at the same time.

It was the ordinary women readers who stressed the status of the book as a warning. Thus Else von Holten wrote: "This plea for peace should lie in thousands of copies on the Christmas table. The girls of today are the mothers of tomorrow." And taking up the same motif of the Christmas table, Paula Weiß, a teacher from Berlin, wrote:

> May this in book form fall into thousands and thousands upon thousands of hands. Mothers should read it and place it on the Christmas table for their growing sons. Those who work with their brains or with their hands, teachers and educators, doctors and priests, women in nursing and charitable organisations, they should all have knowledge of this work.

Among the politicians whose words are recorded are those of the president of the German Parliament, Paul Löbe:

> Remarque has set up a memorial to the field-grey mass of millions of unknowns, that will be as enduring as ever a monument would be. This book is great by virtue of its simplicity and stirring by virtue of its truthfulness.

The former state president Hermann Hummel said simply: "I am convinced that a huge number of people, those who took part in the war of all countries, will feel their soul deeply affected by this book."

Judging by these remarks, it would seem that the novel and its writer articulated the feelings and experiences of a generation. The frontline soldier who fought and died for reasons and causes he could not comprehend is embodied in the central figure of Paul Bäumer. But such a view is very partial and, indeed, misleading. At the time of its publication and subsequently, *All Quiet on the Western Front* has proved to be a text with an almost unparalleled power to polarize its readers. Criticism, sometimes scandalous and personal, of both man and work has rained down from both the left and the right wings of the political spectrum.

What has often been seen as a strength of the text—namely, its refusal to adopt a political position on the rights, wrongs, and causes of the war, concentrating instead on the simple human experience—was castigated by the Left. While acknowledging the power of Remarque's text, the left wing missed in it any analysis or presentation of the causes of the war, which, for them, were intimately connected with the structure of capitalist and bourgeois society. The silence of the text on these matters constituted for them the novel's failure as well as its guilt. Indeed, the critic Helfland uses a word as strong as "lie" in discussing the novel. Remarque's unwillingness to use the text as a means of provoking protest and resistance, he writes, is "the toxin of passive obedience" (qtd. in Rüter 158).

On the other hand, the Right saw Remarque as trying to elevate the perspective of a private individual into an all-embracing vision of the war that was inconsistent with their understanding of it. Additionally, the Right identified a pacifist dimension in the text that again was inconsistent with their understanding and that was seen as dangerous because of the seeming objectivity of the narrative. In the words of one such critic, "For me the book is not a memorial, rather a desecration of a corpse" (Pflug qtd. in Rüter 160).

In the immediate period after the novel's publication, a number of lengthier anti-Remarque writings were published. Of these the most interesting is the satire by Mynona ("Anonym" spelled backward), the pseudonym used by philosopher and minor expressionist and Dadaist poet Salomo Friedländer. The work is titled *Hat Erich Maria Remarque wirklich gelebt?* (Did Erich Maria Remarque Really Live?) and, in the course of some 250 pages, Friedländer undertakes a scurrilous personal assault on Remarque's character, trawling in detail over his early writings. At the same time Friedländer attacks *All Quiet on the Western Front* for its prevarication and, hence, its capacity to provoke violently conflicting reactions. This attack met with a riposte from Kurt Tucholsky, who saw himself as a liberal democrat and a pacifist and who wrote, among other things, social criticism and satire. The riposte, titled "Hat Mynona wirklich gelebt?" (Did Mynona Really Live?), was published originally under one of Tucholsky's pseudonyms, Ignaz Wrobel, in the journal *Die Weltbühne* (The World Stage), of which he was coeditor, on December 31, 1929. After a brief satirical introduction, in which Tucholsky has Mynona claiming to have sabotaged Remarque, Tucholsky turns his attention briefly to *All Quiet on the Western Front* before attacking the way in which Mynona had himself attacked Remarque. He judges that Remarque's novel is "not a great work of art, but a good book" and continues, "Through the unspeakable stupidity of those in right-wing circles, the book has acquired an aura of pacifism; this tendency was in all probability not intended by Remarque" (283). Tucholsky raises, but does not develop, issues of stylistic quality.

Peter Kropp, in a pamphlet titled *Endlich Klarheit über Remarque und sein Buch "Im Westen nichts Neues"* (Finally Clarity About Remarque and His Book *All Quiet on the Western Front*), adopts a strategy similar to Mynona's in attacking Remarque's character. Arguing that Remarque did not live through many of the episodes he depicted in the novel, Kropp rejects the assertion that the power of the book lies in its transcription of Remarque's personal experience. Instead, he ascribes the novel's success to Remarque's publisher: "It appears to me that the secret power of the book lies in the skilful advertising of a capitalist publisher and in the common dirty jokes" (8). He goes on to lament the absence of heroism from the novel: "Can one write a war book without praising that life-giving high element that we simply call heroism?" Fearful of the book's influence, he issues the cry: "Get this book out of schools. Onwards to the struggle so that a spiritual decline does not follow on the economic decline" (15).

Of other contemporary responses, a few more should be mentioned. In 1929, Wilhelm Müller-Scheld published the booklet *"Im Westen nichts Neues" eine Täuschung (All Quiet on the Western Front*—A Deception). Among other things, Müller-Scheld finds that the soldiers of Remarque's novel lack any sign of pride or confidence; however, his main concern is that the novel lacks focus, which he attributes to the prominence of Paul Bäumer and the dominance of his limited perspective. Also, in 1929, Dr. Gottfried Nickl's *"Im Westen nichts Neues" und sein wahrer Sinn. Betrachtung über den Pazifismus und Antwort auf Remarque ("All Quiet on the Western Front" and Its True Meaning: A Consideration of Pacifism and a Reply to Remarque*) appeared. Since this work was distributed through the National Socialist Party network, it achieved very substantial dissemination. The front cover reads:

The monument of shame that was erected in the book *All Quiet on the Western Front* for our heroes of the World War has now been toppled. Everyone must be aware of these revelations about Remarque and his war novel. The scales will then fall from the eyes of everybody who has been blinded and led astray by Remarque.

The political dimension of Nickl's writing emerges clearly from statements; for instance, pacifism, he writes, "is the same false doctrine in the area of ethics as is Marxism in social matters" (12). He also emphasizes the fact that the novel was published by a press owned by the Jewish Ullstein, and, like Kropp, he fears that the novel may have a negative impact on German youth:

Instead of the heroic spirit that allowed our incomparable army to triumph in the field for four and a half years against half the world, the pernicious ideology which speaks out from Remarque's book will raise and lead German youth land will result in a future Germany lying on the ground, impotent and quiescent. (36)

E. Erbelding, with his *Im Westen doch Neues* (1930; Something New on the Western Front), penned more than four hundred pages of an attack on Remarque targeting what he sees as his pacifist stance, and, in the manner of others writing from a right-wing perspective, praising the German troops and their heroism, which he believed Remarque had denigrated. Franz Arthur Klietmann's *Im Westen wohl was Neues* (1931; Probably Something New on the Western Front) has at the top of its title page the words "Contra Remarque," and, by way of a preface to 174 pages of vitriol, Klietmann writes: "This book is an accusation against a degenerate who is trying to besmirch the German heroic spirit, because his emaciated bone marrow and his wilfully nerve-wracked body, destroyed by his own hand, could not grasp what the great struggle did for the German soldier at the front." Klietmann then proceeds to take scenes from *All Quiet on the Western Front* and rework them in a different light in order to criticize the novel's central character and present him as unrepresentative. Remarkably, Klietmann's hero does not die at the end but becomes a Bolshevik.

One other ordinary voice is also worth noting here. In a review of Thomas Levenson's 2003 book *Einstein in Berlin*, Freeman J. Dyson, having read of the Nazi activities at the time of the Berlin showing of the film of *All Quiet on the Western Front*, concludes on a personal note:

One of my relatives, who is now 94 years old, has lived in Germany all her life. Many years ago I gave her Remarque's book to read and she found it very moving. "This book is wonderful," she said. "Why didn't they let us read it when it was published? That was before the Hitler time, but we were told it was disgusting and shameful, and that respectable people should not read it." So the respectable Germans of her generation, even those who were not Nazis, did not read Remarque. I had always wondered why, and now I know. (812)

A number of common features emerge from these contemporary receptions of Remarque's text, one of which is the frequent use of forms of parody and, indeed, quotation. Using the pen name Emil Marius Requark, Max Joseph Wolff published *Vor Troja nichts Neues* (1930; All Quiet on the Trojan Front), an attack on Remarque that, yet again, questions what are seen as the pacifist dimensions of the novel. Remarque's work also picks up on another charge repeatedly leveled against Remarque, namely, that he wrote *All Quiet on the Western Front* in order to make money. Remarque certainly profited from this novel, but, as critics have repeatedly observed, he continued to lead a modest lifestyle in the years immediately after its publication and certainly did not flaunt his wealth, although he was famously given a six-cylinder Lancia Cabriolet of which he was very fond. Carl Otto's *Im Osten nichts Neues* (1929; All Quiet on the Eastern Front) is a straight imitation of Remarque's novel and aims to simply point out that experiences elsewhere were just as horrific as those depicted by Remarque. In 1930, Evadne Price published (as Helen Zenna Smith) *Not So Quiet . . . : Stepdaughters of War*, a novel that offers a female perspective on the war.

One final factor that led to the very diverse but nevertheless huge reception accorded to Remarque's text was the release by Universal Pictures Corporation on April 29, 1930, of Lewis Milestone's famous film adaptation. George Abbott and Maxwell Anderson wrote the screenplay. The review by Mordaunt Hall that appeared in the *New York Times* the following day has only one negative observation, namely: "Some of the scenes are not a little too long and a few members of the cast are not Teutonic in appearance." Otherwise, the review has only praise for the film's fidelity to Remarque's text, for its "harrowing and pulsating" realism, and for its powerful portrayal of disillusionment. The film premiered in Berlin on December 4, 1930, amid demonstrations orchestrated by the National Socialist Party against its alleged anti-German sentiment. An open letter to Remarque from Curt Emmrich in the *Deutsche Allgemeine Zeitung* on December 10, 1930, drew attention to the fact that there were two versions of the film in circulation, one for the German cinema and one for other countries. The latter, Emmrich claims, contains scenes that put down both the German people and the German army. Given, he argues, that Remarque has arrogated to himself the position of speaker for a generation, he asks Remarque to dissociate himself from this version. But this and other controversies surrounding the film were ultimately of little consequence since Joseph Goebbels succeeded in getting the film banned, and by 1933, under the new National Socialist regime, the book was banned as well and subsequently fell victim to the wave of book burning.

One episode in the 1940s demonstrates just how tenacious was the influence of Remarque's novel. In 1943 Remarque's younger sister, Elfriede, had been denounced in Dresden for publicly asserting that Hitler would lose the war. At her trial the Nazi judge, Dr. Roland Freisler, sentenced her to death by the guillotine and is alleged to have said that this was because the Nazis had been unable to capture her brother.

Popular interest in *All Quiet on the Western Front* then follows a curious path. Following the end of World War II there was, perhaps unsurprisingly, a relatively mild flurry of interest as a later generation struggled to come to terms with the events of 1939-45. However, any direct literary influence on this generation is harder to discern. Alfred Andersch's novel *Winterspelt*, published in 1974 (English translation, 1978) and dealing with the Ardenne offensive of 1944, is clearly indebted to Remarque. Director Douglas Sirk's 1958 film *A Time to Love and a Time to Die* is based on Remarque's novel *Zeit zu leben und Zeit zu sterben* (1954; *A Time to Love and a Time to Die*, 1954); it deals with events of World War II but is indebted to *All Quiet on the Western Front*.

A further visual realization was the 1979 television movie of *All Quiet on the Western Front*, directed by Delbert Mann. It is generally felt that, though good (it won a Golden Globe and an Emmy Award), this adaptation does not have the raw power of Milestone's version. John Pym's May 1980 review in *Monthly Film Bulletin* is something less than flattering: "Made as a theatrical feature but shown on American TV (at the behest of Remarque's widow Paulette Goddard), in three one-hour slots, this ploddingly expensive film is as redundant a remake as one could conceive."

Having failed to find a suitable location in either Britain (the Ministry of Defense refused cooperation) or West Germany (war damage and reconstruction simply meant an absence of locations), the film's producer turned to the town of Most in what was then Czechoslovakia. Alan Road, writing in the *Observer Magazine* on November 11, 1979, finishes his article by anticipating the kind of comparison between the substance and circumstances surrounding the publication of the novel in 1929 and the issues of the later twentieth century:

> When Milestone's "All Quiet on the Western Front" was first released there were violent demonstrations outside cinemas by members of the nascent Nazi Party. Even while the new film was being made, descendants of those Nazis were demonstrating against the persecution of suspected war criminals in West Germany. Perhaps it is time for another warning against the dangers of rampant nationalism.

Perhaps more remarkable was the premiere on April 2, 2003, in Osnabrück of the opera of the novel with music by Nancy van de Vate.

In 1988, the ninetieth anniversary of Remarque's birth, the Remarque Society in Osnabrück announced the "Remarque Year 88." Among the events taking place that year were exhibitions, film showings, and an academic conference, all of which achieved significant international representation. The year's academic purpose was to consider the totality of Remarque's oeuvre, and the year saw the publication of a two-volume bibliography that collected together copious material relating to Remarque's literary works and their filmic realizations. However, *All Quiet on the Western Front* dominated the press coverage of the event—Remarque's second novel was, and remains, the central point of orientation for readers and scholars. Indeed, the view of Remarque as a one-book author remains very tenacious. Little known and not widely read is the sequel to *All Quiet on the Western Front*, *Der Weg zurück* (1931; *The Road Back*, 1931).

The Road Back deals with the fate of those who survived the war and their experiences as they attempt to reintegrate into German society. The majority of the characters find reintegration not just difficult but impossible. In the turbulent world of postwar Germany, what was heralded as the comradeship of the trenches becomes a much more questionable entity, not least of all in the new, militarized youth (a clear reference to the Nazi Party and an anticipation of the future conflict).

Still, it was not until the 1980s that a real revival of interest in *All Quiet on the Western Front* began. An advertisement for an edition of the novel in the newspaper *Die Zeit* on April 12, 1984, comments:

> The book experienced a renaissance after the Second World War that is being repeated nowadays under the increasing threat of war. For the horrors of the 1st. World War are the horrors of all wars even if the possibilities of destruction have become more radical in the meantime.

On March 22, 2003, Ulrich Baron published an article in the newspaper *Die Welt* titled "Birth of the Generation Gulf War." The article, alluding to September 11, 2001, focuses on how the experiences of new European generations who have never known war differ from those generations in Iraq for whom war is a reality. Baron draws attention in particular to the notion of the "lost generation": "Far more telling than the rather underplayed pacifist tendency of his book, is the invocation of a lost generation."

Peter von Becker starts his article in the *Tagesspiegel* of August 6, 2006, with this simple observation: "It was a book of the century and novel of the hour. It is exactly the same now." Ranging widely over historical and more contemporary conflicts, Becker considers various modes of representing war, including film and the television coverage of the Balkan conflict, Israel and Lebanon, the Gulf War, and the Iraq War. He observes in the modern media reports and records a kind of impersonality and the absence of the perspective of the common soldier. While the effects of war, particularly on civilians are vividly portrayed, these remain what he calls "pictures from the outside." For him, "The complex system and the barbarically brutal effect of modern war can scarcely be depicted with more insight, scarcely more appeal to the sensual imagination, than in Remarque's novel."

The year 2009, the eightieth anniversary of the publication of *All Quiet on the Western Front*, witnessed a further flowering of interest in Remarque's text. However, few new insights or connections emerged in the many newspaper and magazine articles devoted to discussion of the novel. Rather, media coverage tended to rehearse and repeat the kind of connections made from the 1980s onward between the experience of World War I and the many other conflicts, of greater or smaller proportion, that are still a reality in the late twentieth and the early twenty-first centuries.

Much of the academic engagement with Remarque has been colored by his success, at the time of publication and subsequently, with *All Quiet on the Western Front*. There is a kind of sometimes suppressed, sometimes explicit, premise that a best seller such as *All Quiet on the Western Front* is somehow inferior to and different from other works of literature. Equally, Remarque's general lifestyle and career—his love of fast cars; his relationships with Marlene Dietrich and, subsequently, Paulette Goddard; his fondness for alcohol; his involvement with Hollywood; and his early career as a journalist and advertising copywriter—all give rise to a degree of suspicion toward his status as an author.

One of the earliest scholarly engagements with *All Quiet on the Western Front* is to be found in J. Knight Bostock's *Some Well-Known German War-Novels, 1914-1930*, which was published in 1931. Bostock engages with the phenomenal success of the novel:

> There is no doubt that Remarque's methods and personal character, as revealed by Mynona's muck-rake, are dubious; nevertheless we cannot in consequence dismiss *Im Westen nichts Neues* as sheer humbug. We have to explain both the *phenomenal* success of the book and the extraordinary controversy that it aroused. . . . If *Im Westen nichts Neues* is humbug, it is clearly humbug of no ordinary kind. (7)

Bostock identifies "the black depression which dominates the book to an extent previously unheard of in literature"(8) and attributes this tone precisely to the novel's failure to mediate a particular political or social position and to the limited perspective of Remarque's narrator, who has no understanding of the origins and causes of the horror in which he is caught up: "No one has any genuine idealism, or knows what he is fighting and suffering for. They do their duty as soldiers should, but purely by instinct. It is pessimism unrelieved, complete and universal intellectual bankruptcy" (8). Stylistically, Bostock also discerns a kind of negativity in Remarque's short, disjointed sentences and his appeals to his reader's imagination with skillfully chosen words and hints. Bostock's conclusion is fairly stark: "It is clever journalism, but it is not great literature, and if the book is re-read deliberately after the first flush of excitement has passed, it appears to be very dull" (9).

A further example of the British reception comes from Herbert Read in his brief essay "The Failure of War Books," written around the time of the end of World War II. Read observes that young writers returning from the trenches wanted not only to describe the horrors of war but also to warn future generations; while war novels may appeal to the imagination with their vivid descriptions, they do not communicate an underlying reality:

> But war acquires its reality from psychological and economic forces, and it is useless to protest against war unless at the same time there is some understanding of the workings of these primary forces and some attempt to control them. But there was no such understanding. (73)

Hence, for Read, it is then relevant to make the simple point that, ten years after the publication of *All Quiet on the Western Front*, the world was once against at war. He also mentions a recurrent issue in criticism of the novel, the charge of sentimentality: "To some extent the criticism is true, but sentimentality was not, for effectiveness a fault" (74). He points to *Uncle Tom's Cabin* as a more sentimental text, yet notes that that novel played a pivotal role in the abolition of slavery.

An overview of the scholarly secondary literature reveals a pattern that is strikingly similar to the novel's more popular reception. The volume of criticism shows that scholarly interest in Remarque generally and in *All Quiet on the Western Front* particularly has grown exponentially since the late 1970s. Nevertheless, the two early pieces cited make interesting points. Bostock's judgment of the text as "dull" has been countered by the reading public's continuing interest in the book and is now being overturned by the weight of academic engagement with the text. On the other hand, Read's title, "The Failure of War Books," has sadly proven to be only too prophetic.

Works Cited

Andersch, Alfred. *Winterspelt*. Zurich: Diogenes, 1974.

Baron, Ulrich. "Birth of the Generation Gulf War." *Die Welt* 22 Mar. 2003.

Bostock, J. Knight. *Some Well-Known German War-Novels, 1914-1930*. Oxford: Blackwell, 1931.

Dyson, Freeman J. Rev. of *Einstein in Berlin*, by Thomas Levenson. *Nature* 24 Apr. 2003: 812.

Erbelding, E. *Im Westen doch Neues*. Munich: Ebering, 1930.

Hall, Mordaunt. Rev. of *All Quiet on the Western Front* (film). *New York Times*, April 30, 1929.

Klietmann, Franz Arthur. *Im Westen wohl was Neues*. Berlin: Nonnemann, 1931.

Kropp, Peter. *Endlich Klarheit über Remarque und sein Buch "Im Westen nichts Neues."* Hamm: Author, 1930.

Müller-Scheld, Wilhelm. *"Im Westen nichts Neues" eine Täuschung*. Idstein im Taunus: Grandpierre, 1929.

Mynona [Salomo Friedländer]. *Hat Erich Maria Remarque wirklich gelebt?* Berlin: Steegemann, 1929.

Nickl, Gottfried. *"Im Westen nichts Neues" und sein wahrer Sinn. Betrachtungen über den Pazifismus und Antwort auf Remarque*. Leipzig: Stocker, 1929.

Otto, Carl. *Im Osten nichts Neues*. Zirndorf: Sanitas-Verlagshaus, 1929.

Pym, John. Rev. of *All Quiet on the Western Front* (television film). *Monthly Film Bulletin* May 1980.

Read, Herbert. "The Failure of War Books." *A Coat of Many Colours*. London: Routledge, 1945.

Requark, Emil Marius [Max Joseph Wolff]. *Vor Troja nichts Neues*. Berlin: Winckler, 1930.

Road, Alan. Rev. of *All Quiet on the Western Front* (television film). *Observer Magazine* 11 Nov. 1979.

Rüter, H. *Remarque "Im Westen nichts Neues." Ein Bestseller im Kontext*. Paderborn: Schöningh, 1980.

Smith, Helen Zenna [Evadne Price]. *Not So Quiet . . . : Stepdaughters of War*. London: A. E. Marriott, 1930.

Tucholsky, Kurt. "Hat Mynona wirklich gelebt?" *Gesammelte Werke*. Ed. M. Gerold-Tucholsky and F. Raddatz. Reinbek bei Hamburg: Rowohlt, 1975. 7:282-86.

Partial Accusation?
Stylistic and Structural Methods
in *All Quiet on the Western Front*_____

Peter Hutchinson

Because of its undemanding language, Erich Maria Remarque's best-selling novel *All Quiet on the Western Front* may give the appearance of being an "easy read," of being a swift succession of easily digestible episodes from which only a single theme emerges: the horror of war. This external simplicity is deceptive, however; the novel's linguistic range, careful structuring, irony, and extended network of ideas all work together to treat sensitively the story of a confused young man, warfare, and suffering and loss.[1]

Remarque's subtle, indirect method is evident even in the brief lines that preface the novel:

> This book is intended neither as an accusation nor as a confession, but simply as an attempt to give an account of a generation that was destroyed by the war—even those of it who survived the shelling.

This stark sentence (and the translation adheres perfectly to the tone of the original German) is couched in the same tone and register as much of what follows; it is simple, restrained, unemotional, and it claims only to "give an account." Superficially, it makes a promise that may seem to be largely fulfilled in the novel. Although a small number of direct "accusations" are made against certain individuals in positions of command, even those who may be accused of bullying those over whom they have control are later seen more sympathetically when they too are sucked into the war. So, too, the patronizing hectoring and patriotism of former teachers is seen to be misguided rather than culpable, and blunt allegations, such as the claim that wealthy factory owners must have profited from the slaughter, are isolated. Nor does there seem any true "confession" in the narrator's approach. A confession would involve a sense of regret or guilt, and, although there may be brief moments of remorse, they are quickly forgotten, not dwelt upon. The novel, then, might seem one that goes out of its way to be impartial and unemotional, to be one of understatement and personal candor.

Yet the issue is not, however, quite so straightforward, and I feel the author is being slightly disingenuous in these opening lines. The use of potentially emotive words ("accusation," "confession") alerts us to other ways in which the novel could be read, if we so wished. The verb "destroyed," too, is emotionally powerful and blunt, and there is an unexpected subordinate clause following the dash. We might well have expected the sentence to stop after "destroyed by the war," but it goes on to make the point that trauma is not always simply physical. We are promised, then, a novel not just of slaughter but also of psychological destruction. Any reader is bound to respond, both emotionally and intellectually, to such subject matter, and Remarque's preface can therefore be seen as a signal, or even a provocation, for us to react against the author's understatement, for us to see the implications behind what he describes so factually, to see forms of accusation, even if they are partial and suppressed. Such a purpose, as we will see, is particularly evident in the novel's repeated lament that war has not just hardened, but brutalized, a generation.

The unconventional structure and tone of Remarque's novel results from his narrator, an unpretentious, candid, but confused and partially immature young man, who semi-innocently attempts to describe events exactly as they occur. The first-person narration allows Remarque to move through the story erratically, offering snapshots, from a period of probably a little over two years, of attacks, meals, arguments, and reflections—and the emotions aroused by them. This constant movement gives the impression of a simple mind that flashes this way and that, at times concentrated on the moment but at other times, when not under pressure, distracted into thoughts of the past and, occasionally, of the future.

The form of the novel is almost like that of a diary or journal, with a number of moments giving a sense of reportage. The chapters are of very unequal length, and each is subdivided into a number of short sections, some of which cover only half a page while others stretch over three or four. Further, the paragraphs are regularly brief: those comprising less than half a dozen lines far outnumber the longer ones. And the lexis is generally simple, placing few demands on the reader. Apart from the technical vocabulary of the battlefield, the words are usually plain, the sentences very short, the direct speech curt and colloquial.[2]

The first chapter can be seen as structurally typical. It is only thirteen pages in length and comprises four short sections, each one dealing with a completely different subject. The first begins almost leisurely with a description of the enormous meal and generous rations the hero's company have been allotted. But the sense of security and satisfaction is quickly seen to be false: the meal is so ample because the cook had been preparing for 150 men—he had not heard that almost half of the company had been killed the previous day. The reader will be struck by several features of this opening: the simplicity of the sentence structure; the brevity of many sentences; and the flow from one idea to another, as we are given a clipped but rounded picture of the camp and its inhabitants. Yet the easy movement and the joking attitude of the soldiers, reflected in this relaxed and casual style, disguises a troubling reality: the men may be delighted at the prospect of a good meal, but it has been achieved at the expense of those who are now in a "field hospital or a mass grave" (3). This gulf between the horrific events and the casual way in which the men regard them is the first real form of provocation in the novel, and the narrator's unemotional description of the men's callous attitude may be seen as the first form of "accusation." The soldiers' glee is distasteful; it disturbs us and shows us one way in which war has changed humankind for the worse. This is an important theme, which I would classify as one of indirect and partial accusation, and it has not been brought out fully in earlier studies of the novel.[3]

This first section, then, in a mere four pages, introduces us to one of the distressing ironies of war: one man's loss is another man's gain. The second section, which is only two and one-half pages long, focuses on a completely different form of irony: the way in which war has torn down the men's modesty and inhibitions. They happily defecate together, playing cards and chatting aimlessly as they cheerfully accept the abandonment of propriety that war has forced upon them. Here, too, we may be left uneasy.

There is then a two-page section, a flashback to days at school and the fateful moment when the hero's whole class was bullied into enlisting. Once again, a sense of "accusation" is raised, although it is not developed. Instead, it is glossed over as other factors are taken into account and German teachers as a whole, not just in one school, are blamed not for blind patriotism but for ignorance. Again, however, the reader must infer the implications: the narrator's blame is implicit, indirect. The language changes in this section, too, as it introduces another component that will appear at various points throughout the novel: the reflection on life and war and especially on the disillusionment brought on by, of hopes and beliefs lost to, the harshness of battle. And so we find sociological observations (such as "it was the poorest and simplest people who were the most sensible" [8]), recognition of youthful illusions ("in our minds the idea of authority—which is what they [the teachers] represented—implied deeper insights and a more humane wisdom" [9]), and troubling self-insight ("Suddenly we found ourselves horribly alone—and we had to come to terms with it alone as well" [10]).

The chapter concludes with a visit to the field hospital, where a comrade has had part of his leg amputated. He is in such pain that he is unaware of what has happened, and, placed as he is in a crowded, busy ward, he is not being treated as well as he might be. There is another, more subtle form of accusation within this gloomy scene. As one of the visitors suddenly realizes that if his comrade dies, his excellent pair of boots could be passed down to one of them, we recognize again the loss/gain irony, the way one can be seduced into putting one's own physical needs above all else, including the psychological demands of others. After this hospital visit the first minor outbreak of "shell shock" occurs, as one of the men, Albert Kropp, suddenly starts swearing and stamping madly on his cigarette. The precise reason for this is unclear, however, and it is left to the reader to decide whether this irrational behavior is caused simply by the "strain of being at the front" (13) or whether the clever, sensitive Kropp is disturbed by more general aspects of life and death. The event passes quickly, but it foreshadows several more, as well as the way in which shell shock is handled and punished.

The structure and style of this first chapter, then, prepare us for a story that is far from uniform and that moves, often abruptly, from one scene to the next. There is no conventional plot, and we are only vaguely aware of where the action might be taking place or what year it might be. More important are intense single events, ranging from moments of hardship and comradeship to those of fear, disgust, or comedy and those of sad reflection on what war has made of young men. Again, this range is easy to achieve given the way in which Remarque structures his novel. It is a first-person, contemporaneous account, with a narrator who is young, still often impressionable, and with a quick-moving mind, and this structure allows Remarque to compress various quite different elements into surprisingly short passages.

There are, however, certain sections that stand out from the rest because of their differences in tone and style, although they also, significantly, manifest suppressed accusations. The most important of these are the sexual encounter with the French girls, Paul's first trip home, and his mortally wounding the Frenchman in the shell hole.

The night swim across the river in the hope of sexual thrills is the first real respite from camp life and the intensity of battle, and the episode introduces new language and prose rhythms to the novel. The prelude to the adventure is already different in mood: Paul admits they are all in a "state of great excitement" (105), and livelier sentences suggest anticipation and bravado, but these then give way to more sober lines as the soldiers swim with difficulty across the river, carefully carrying their "presents"—sausages and loaves of bread. The rhythms then suggest the awkward initial encounter with the girls, the feeling that "we all become a bit embarrassed" (106), and there is a sense of uncertainty as the outcome of their meeting falls into doubt. But, as it becomes clear sexual gratification is imminent, the length of the sentences becomes far longer and Paul drifts into a completely different emotional world. He becomes far more private and intimate, and a new aspect of his personality emerges—his sexual shyness and fear. There is a brief reference to the fact that he has visited brothels for "other-ranks" (108), where one must line up and wait one's turn, but the memories are unfulfilling and distasteful to Paul, and he urgently tries to suppress them. The liaison with the French woman, however, quickly takes on an element of the mystical, and minimal description is provided of the physical side. This event transcends everything Paul has hitherto experienced, and the reader is likewise taken out of the less pleasant aspects of what has preceded—the furtive swim, the embarrassing difficulties of communication, the clear hunger of the women. Remarque demonstrates his ability to work on a completely different stylistic plane here and to suggest fulfillment and spiritual peace.

Yet the hopes raised here are soon undone. Back in camp, Paul learns that he is to be given leave, another uplifting event, but this means that the second visit to the French girls is very different. Paul manages to convey to the woman he is about to sleep with that he will be going away, although not to the front, and he is disturbed by the woman's seemingly blasé reaction. His response to this is devastating: "Well, she can go to hell with her whispering and her words. You believe in a miracle, but really it just comes down to loaves of bread" (110). The hopes of the previous evening are destroyed at a stroke. Remarque bluntly returns to the world of materialism and disillusionment, a world in which the young do indeed seem to have been turned into animals, concerned mainly with survival and primitive pleasures. It is not difficult for the reader to see a form of accusation in this semiprostitution that the war has produced. (And the fact that there is a total of three references to brothels in the course of the novel will certainly represent to many another form of accusation.)

The image of the tough, insensitive soldier may here be restored, but it is undermined in the very next section of this chapter, the extended description of Paul's leave (110-32). Here, there are several outbursts of human emotion, which deny the motif that all soldiers are animals, or "automata" (83), incapable of relating to their fellow human beings. The section begins with the discomfort and frustration of traveling in wartime, but then Remarque slowly suggests the nostalgia that comes over the narrator as he draws closer to his hometown. A sense of calmness descends as Paul experiences the peace of nature, especially the trees, "one behind the other and far away, made out of shadow, light and longing" (111), the sounds of the prose become softer (this is slightly more marked in the original German), and Paul is almost overcome by memories of his youth. As he opens the door to the block in which his family lives, he is having to force himself onward, "my eyes can't see clearly any more" (112), and then, as he hears his sister call out to their mother, there is an uncontrollable flood of tears and inability to move. This sense of helplessness is reflected in the hypotactic sentence structure, with its succession of connectives: "And so I stand there on the stairs, wretched and helpless, horribly paralysed and I can't help it, and tears and more tears are running down my face" (113). Paul's embarrassed crying, against which he vainly tries to fight, suggest the potential for emotion still within him, and at points the imagery employed in this section, in contrast to the violent descriptions of the battlefield, is almost poetic: "the world as soft as rubber and my veins as fragile as tinder" (116). This idea of hypersensitivity is repeated in the final night at home, when his mother holds a form of vigil by Paul's bed until he pretends to wake up and they "talk." Here, the tortured Paul is actually proving what he had earlier chosen to deny, that strong emotions remain within him. He is not fully an adult; he has retained childlike feelings of helpless filial devotion. To my mind this section is as powerful as any other, but in a very different way, focusing as it does on a completely different side of war. It is also a stark reminder of the privations and sorrows of the "home front," and that the occasional accusations of sentimentality that critics have made against Paul's moments with his mother are not well founded. Here, as throughout the novel, emotions are presented forcefully and honestly.

Paul's agonizing night and day with the wounded Frenchman is another exceptional event, to which several pages are devoted. Stylistically, this section is quite different from most of the novel, especially in the flexibility in the lengths of sentences: the majority are short and bring out the constant sense of fear and the threat of death that accompany battle; longer ones are employed for the self-analysis that Paul undergoes. The section begins dramatically as Paul, out on a reconnaissance mission, is cut off from the others in his party following a surprise attack. This attack is repelled, but in his retreat, an enemy soldier lands on top of Paul in the shell hole in which he has taken cover. Instinctively lashing out, Paul stabs the French soldier, who slowly—over the course of the night and most of the next day—dies in agony and fear. The description here is detailed: of the man, of his wounds, of the frightening, gurgling noise he makes, of Paul's futile attempts to relieve his suffering. And equally important are Paul's constant flitting among his own pain, guilt, remorse, despair, and instinct for self-preservation; his reflections on the pointlessness of it all; his humanitarian feelings toward the dying man; and then his sudden determination, once the man is dead, to try to do something for his family. But, as in the case of the episode with the French girls, the idealism engendered by his encounter with death is swiftly replaced by the realism of the battlefield. Remarque shows the movement from anguish to pragmatism and the planning for survival, and he allows the reader to see the way in which war repeatedly drains soldiers of their compassion. For Paul recovers all too quickly from this worst of his experiences and realizes that he will never make good on his promise to help the dead man's family. Some unease remains with him until the following day, when he is able to tell his comrades the details of what has happened; but after discussing it with them, we have a full, devastating return to "normality": "What sort of rubbish did I dream up in that shell hole?" (161).

This movement from pity and a deep concern for a fellow human being to a detached, indifferent attitude, and then to an actual rejection of the initial emotions, is anticipated early in the novel. In Paul's first reflection in chapter 1 on how the war has transformed his generation, he tries to pinpoint a key change: "In some strange and melancholy way we have become hardened, although we don't often feel sad about it any more" (15). The idea that an individual would *not* regret the hardening of his emotions may come as a surprise at this early point of the novel, but Remarque produces a sequence of events to convince us of how self-interest must regularly prevail over emotion and how there need be no guilt attached to the suppression of one's feelings. As we reach the first direct experience of the front itself, there is another laconic summary of how man is forced to change: "We reach the zone where the front line begins, and we have turned into human animals" (40). Yet these repeated claims that war makes men into animals are not, in fact, fulfilled. War may *attempt* to turn humans into savages—a key indictment—but it ultimately fails to do so. Even on the battlefield we see powerful acts of loyalty and compassion, belying the idea that man can remain a beast for long. Furthermore, acts of bravery are born from these emotions, and especially from that of friendship. Paul's heroic carrying of the wounded Katczinsky is a prime example, and there are several other moments of men risking their lives for others—and even for a dog.

The twin themes of loyalty and friendship—and the way warfare both creates and destroys such bonds[4]—are important ones in the novel, but Remarque also develops several other ideas, many of which are interrelated and linked to the issue of indirect accusation. The first is obviously the cluster of themes around life at the front, such as the horrific aspects of bombardment and close-range fighting; the sickening nature of the wounds incurred; the shocking number of sometimes agonizing and protracted deaths; and the permanent sense of unease, even when the front is quiet. The omnipresence of death is also regularly emphasized: when marching to and from the front, bits of bodies and of uniforms can be seen hanging in the trees; stretcher bearers are constantly at work; and there are even regular deaths at the prisoner-of-war camp for Russians that Paul briefly has to guard. Motifs associated with death and mutilation are evident away from the front line too: the soldiers' fear of amputation and being gassed, as well as their dread of army doctors, and some men even determine that they would rather commit suicide than survive as an amputee. Paul's stay in the hospital ward is among the most depressing episodes. There may be respite from the fear of the front, but there are fears of a different sort: the prospect of an operation; the anxiety that one might soon be destined for the "Dying Room"; the mixed feelings associated with having too serious a wound to be declared fit again for the front or being so badly wounded that one is fit only to be shipped back home, where there will be no new life waiting for them. And so a musician attempts a grisly suicide, and life seems to drain away from the characters who fear that there is, indeed, nothing ahead. Death is sometimes seen as a welcome escape—and this is certainly one possible reading of the final lines of the novel.

Death is not just to be seen among human beings, of course. It is also among a good number of animals—geese, piglets, and horses, as well as lice and rats, are disposed of in particularly uncomfortable ways. Even the starving Russians are like "sick storks" (136), scavenging like desperate animals. And there are distressing noises associated with all these creatures, as the author stresses the acuteness of the soldiers' sense of hearing (and vision). The most powerful moment here, one that has attracted widespread comment, is the screaming of severely wounded horses, which distresses some even more than the cries of their comrades.

Returning to the need to suppress one's feelings—a theme that, to my mind, is slightly forced and sometimes too bluntly conveyed—we can see this, too, as an indictment of the unnatural attitudes created by war. As previously mentioned, early in the novel three friends go to visit a comrade in the hospital; they know he has a leg wound and that he is most likely to be returned to Germany. Upon seeing him, however, they immediately realize that he is more likely to die than to return home, and so one of them takes an interest in his fine boots. Paul is slightly embarrassed by the apparent callousness revealed here, that is, by his comrade's greater interest in acquiring the man's boots than in raising his spirits. Yet, after the visit, he laconically rationalizes the situation, just as he does so many other moments, firmly justifying what had initially seemed to be heartless: "We have lost our ability to see things in other ways, because they are artificial. For us, it is only the facts that count. And good boots are hard to come by" (15). This is a compressed argument. The "normal" way of viewing things is regarded as "artificial," but rather than telling his reader it is "feelings" that inform a "normal" attitude, Remarque leaves it to his reader to deduce what "normal" might be. The punch line clinches the "argument" with a simple return to the factual.

Indeed, there is a steady thread of arguing and questioning throughout the novel, and we as readers are regularly challenged to make deductions. Remarque's narrator philosophizes on the nature and purposes of life, war, and human relations, and his questioning can also often be seen in the soldiers' banter. Why are they fighting? they ask. Who is benefiting from it and why does it not end? These are above all questions for the reader. And they are often generalized, like the novel as a whole. As we have seen, the setting is virtually timeless (1918 is mentioned only on the final page) and spaceless (somewhere in France). Even in Germany, the narrator's hometown is never identified; it is simply somewhere in the north. The narrator often shifts from "I" to "we," and there are various other methods of broadening the relevance of what is suggested.[5] So the hero's questionings, his general musings, his sometimes agonized metaphysical searches, are intended to be seen as that of the common, but representative, German soldier.

These moments of private, sometimes public, and sometimes extended deliberation are part of the structural principle of the work. They often act as periods of calm after more excited moments, but they are not in any way anticlimaxes; rather, they are natural extensions of the emotions aroused by what has preceded them. It is in these sections that we may sense a stronger didactic aim or, at any rate, a desire to draw the reader into comparable reflection. An obvious example is Paul's musing on "chance" (72), which proves to be a motif of the novel as a whole; it is commonly associated with irony, and the last lines of the novel provide the final example. Completely different are Paul's analysis of how the human body reacts to being under fire and his lyrical outburst in praise of the earth, onto which one flings oneself for protection. In even greater contrast are his idyllic memories of life before the war, of feeling at home with nature and reveling in the silence and peace evoked by the simplest aspects of the countryside. These reflective moments have a broad range, covering such topics as the hierarchy of human institutions and the urge to power; ways of coping with battle, both during and after; deep uncertainty about the sort of life that could follow the experiences they have had to undergo; nostalgia for a former existence. The longest and most intense such section comes toward the end of the novel, at the beginning of chapter 11, where the narrator reflects extensively on the ways in which minds have been changed by the long experience of battle. The register here is different from the rest of the text, and the ideas are presented in more intellectual a fashion. Paul muses, for example, on one of the ironies of war, the comradeship created out of shared suffering:

> It is brotherhood on a large scale, in which elements of the good fellowship you get in folk songs, of the solidarity you find among convicts, and of the desperate clinging together of those condemned to die, are all combined in some strange way to give a form of life which, in the midst of all the danger, rises above the tension and the abandonment of death, and leads to a fleeting and quite dispassionate grasping at whatever time we can gain. It is heroic and banal, if you really think about it—but who does? (192)

Although there have been earlier reflections on comradeship, life, war, and human relations, this chapter contains far more than any other. Paul's broad generalizations lift us into a different, spiritual world but, typically, we are brought back to reality in his final, rhetorical anticlimax. In this section too there are also poetic touches in the imagery, which is far more imaginative than that used hitherto, noticeably in the idea that the soldiers are all like coins from different countries that have been melted down and then restruck. The ideas are also presented in a more formal, controlled language, and in carefully constructed paragraphs. The leaps and bounds of idea and activity we encounter elsewhere are absent; there is a clearer, more logical progression, and insights into human character are conveyed in appropriately calm and rational tones (for example, "the differences brought about by education and upbringing have been almost completely blurred and are now barely recognisable" [191]). This restrained, fatalistic, but at moments lyrical section proves to be a calming prelude to the fate of several who have been close to the narrator for long and, of course, to Paul's own death. It is also the final extended section of indirect accusation, the partial indictment of a world that has destroyed both bodies and minds.

One might imagine that the subject matter of this novel would preclude humor, but in fact it is a regular phenomenon, its range is broad, and it, too, is often linked with Remarque's purpose of provoking his reader into questioning. Some of this humor would be appropriate in any situation, such as soldiers preferring dripping to cans of lobsters, or young men who are quite at ease defecating alongside one another being too embarrassed to ask a nurse for a bottle in which to pass water. But then there is more sinister humor, such as the Germans losing the war because they have had to spend so much time practicing saluting, and humor that verges on the grotesque, such as a doctor declaring a wounded man fit to return to the front even though he has a wooden leg (and the man's comment that he will indeed return to the front, have his head blown off, then come back and get a wooden one so that he too can become a staff doctor). The narrator himself makes the point that the horror of the front fades once one has left it, and one can then "attack it with coarse or black humour" (101). Such humor is one means of relieving the darkness of the novel, but it is also a reflection of how soldiers did in fact cope with war: not just through blasphemy and vulgarity but also through understatement, euphemism, and making jokes out of their despair. Still, the reality of the front was much different from that presented by Remarque, for he clearly sanitizes the coarse language of true army life. This is one of the many ways in which the novel is clearly fiction rather than documentary or autobiography.[6]

All Quiet on the Western Front is not just a rejection of the patriotic, more idealized presentation of the trench morale that was popularized in Ernst Jünger's highly successful novel *In Stahlgewittern* (1920). There may, indeed, be a subtle allusion to Jünger in Paul's description of the hail of bullets that prevents him from moving from a shell hole—a "mesh of steel" (154). That phrase must have alerted many to the title of Jünger's novel, which translates literally as "in storms of steel." But Remarque's work is more general than this, and its honesty and directness may also be seen as a response to, and a rejection of, the avant-garde of the period: a rejection of the experimental and highly self-conscious novels of the 1920s, such as Thomas Mann's *Der Zauberberg* (1924; *The Magic Mountain*, 1927) and Hermann Hesse's *Der Steppenwolf* (1927; *Steppenwolf*, 1929). In both these works there is a strong tendency toward playfulness, to play with subject matter and, equally important, play with the reader. Remarque has nothing to do with such techniques: his novel is not intended for intellectuals, and its author has no desire to entertain or provoke in a learned or academic manner. With the work's striving for realism—evident partly in its seeming formlessness and its strong sense of immediacy—it is aiming above all at the simple, unsophisticated reader, who will react directly and without excessive reflection. But even to such common readers, it points out fairly clearly—and it quietly, indirectly condemns—the multiple trauma of warfare.

Notes

1. The stylistic strengths of the novel are regularly passed over. The closest reading of the author's care with detail is provided by Murdoch in "Narrative Strategies in Remarque's *Im Westen nichts Neues*."

2. For brief comments on language, see Bekes's *Erich Maria Remarque* (41-43).

3. The general theme of "brutalization" is, however, one that has been treated extensively. The best short survey, with numerous key quotations, is provided by Richard Littlejohns in "'Der Krieg hat uns für alles verdorben': The Real Theme of *Im Westen nichts Neues*" (90-93).

4. For further details, see Murdoch's *The Novels of Erich Maria Remarque* (38). See also Gordon's *Heroism and Friendship in the Novels of Erich Maria Remarque* (esp. 130-31).

5. Murdoch has presented sensitive analysis of the intriguing shift from the emphasis on "we" to the emphasis on "I" (see *The Novels* 35 passim; "Narrative Strategies" esp. 186-87, 190-94).

6. For more details on this aspect, see Bance's "*Im Westen nichts Neues*: A Bestseller in Context" (363).

Works Cited

Bance, Alan F. "*Im Westen nichts Neues*: A Bestseller in Context." *Modern Language Review* 72 (1977): 359-73

Bekes, Peter. *Erich Maria Remarque: "Im Westen nichts Neues."* Munich: Oldenbourg, 1998.

Gordon, Haim. *Heroism and Friendship in the Novels of Erich Maria Remarque.* New York: Peter Lang, 2003.

Littlejohns, Richard. "'Der Krieg hat uns für alles verdorben': The Real Theme of *Im Westen nichts Neues*." *Modern Languages* 70 (1989): 89-94.

Murdoch, Brian O. "Narrative Strategies in Remarque's *Im Westen nichts Neues*." *New German Studies* 17 (1992-93): 175-202.

_____. *The Novels of Erich Maria Remarque*. New York: Camden House, 2006.

Remarque, Erich Maria. *All Quiet on the Western Front*. 1929. Trans. Brian O. Murdoch. London: Jonathan Cape, 1992.

Love and War in *All Quiet on the Western Front* and Hemingway's *A Farewell to Arms*_____

Matthew J. Bolton

More than a decade after World War I ended, 1929 saw the publication of two of the most powerful depictions of the war, Erich Maria Remarque's *All Quiet on the Western Front* and Ernest Hemingway's *A Farewell to Arms*. Both novels provoked strong reactions in their own time—they were lauded in some quarters and banned in others—and both are canonical and widely read today. For many readers, these two novels are the definitive literary representations of World War I. In a now-classic essay that is frequently anthologized in critical guides to *All Quiet*, Helmut Liedloff compares Remarque's and Hemingway's depictions of the war at some length. Liedloff notes that both works "stress that side of the war which was, at that time [1929], not the official one: the unheroic, dirty, painful, bloody side of it" (404). Yet Liedloff identifies several differences between the two novels. War is only part of Hemingway's novel, for his protagonist, Frederic Henry, is able to escape from the front in a way that his counterpart in *All Quiet*, Paul Bäumer, cannot. Moreover, Liedloff finds that Hemingway's novel "makes extensive use of symbolism, whereas *Im Westen* [*All Quiet*] employs comparatively little" (391). The comparison is a valid one, and Liedloff's essay has no doubt directed many readers of Remarque to see in his work strong parallels with that of Ernest Hemingway.

Yet in stressing the difference between Hemingway's use of symbolism and Remarque's refusal to move beyond concrete description, Liedloff risks missing the forest for the trees. Symbolism in Hemingway's novel is not merely a gloss on concrete description nor should it be read as evidence that *A Farewell to Arms* is necessarily greater or more ambitious in scope than *All Quiet*. Rather, this difference in language indicates a more fundamental difference in genre, plot, and theme. Remarque and Hemingway both depict the war, but they do so in the context of two very different literary modes. For Hemingway, war is inextricably bound up with love, and his war story quickly modulates into a romance. In fact, this romantic impulse runs not only through this novel but also through most of Hemingway's depictions of war. He tends to present combat as a rite of passage and an initiation for a young man who will eventually find love. Remarque, on the other hand, raises the possibility of romantic love only to underscore how impossible such a fiction is to maintain in the face of war. The starkest difference between the worldviews of these two novelists may therefore be found not in their respective use of symbolic language and patterns of imagery but in their depictions of women and in the very different conclusions that each draws about whether romantic love can offer a means of escaping the hardships of war.

An American who has volunteered as an ambulance driver in the Italian Army, Frederic Henry enters World War I in advance of his country. When a British nurse asks him why he joined the Italians, he responds laconically, "I was in Italy . . . and I spoke Italian" (22). But this hardboiled response does little to explain the sense of duty or purpose that prompted Henry to volunteer. As is typical of the Hemingway protagonist, he must be judged by his actions rather than by his words. Henry's voluntary service in an army with whose cause he agrees is the first and surest sign of his romantic disposition. Like Byron fighting for Greek independence a century earlier, Henry has followed the dic ates of his conscience. Remarque's Paul Bäumer, on the other hand, enlists in his native German army because his classmates and his schoolmasters, particularly the patriotic Kantorek, expect it of him. Caught up in a wave of patriotism, he is too youthful, dutiful, and self-conscious to make a decision on his own terms. At the front, Paul soon finds that the romantic sentiments of his schoolmaster are entirely at odds with the grotesque and dehumanizing reality of modern warfare.

This gap between the schoolmaster Kantorek's romantic vision of war and the stark realities of the trenches may help to explain why

Paul—and behind him—Remarque, refuses to let his descriptions of the front take on symbolic resonances or overtones. Kantorek, and other civilian patriots, may see the world as charged with metaphysical significance, but Paul is keenly aware of the physical reality of the front. When Paul goes on leave and reencounters his schoolmaster, Remarque writes large this difference between what the civilian imagines and what the soldier experiences. Paul and his classmate Mittelstaedt find that Kantorek, who had compelled them both to enlist, has himself been conscripted. Since Mittelstaedt outranks his former schoolmaster, he subjects Kantorek to all manner of hardship and humiliation. Mittelstaedt's treatment of Kantorek might be read as the triumph of realism over romanticism, as the young man who has been at war punishes the older man who so grossly misrepresented a phenomenon he had never himself experienced.

Paul's subsequent encounter with his former headmaster amplifies this difference. The headmaster and schoolmasters whom Paul runs into in a beer garden have their own preconceived notions of war and combat. When Paul offers something of his own experience, the headmaster suggests that the direct experience of a soldier lacks the wider view of a strategist. Paul understands "the details, yes," according to the headmaster, "but this relates to the whole. And of that you are not able to judge. You see only your little sector and so cannot have any general survey" (167). Paul cannot make these men of the older generation see the gap between what is actually happening at the front and the lofty, romanticized vision of war to which they still subscribe. Paul leaves the beer garden with a profound sense of alienation: "I find I do not belong here anymore, it is a foreign world" (168).

It would be a mistake to place Hemingway and his protagonist on the side of the schoolmasters. Yet Hemingway's vision of war is by no means as stark or as radical as Remarque's. He has some measure of Kantorek's romantic vision of war. For Frederic Henry's life, unlike Paul's, can accommodate more than just the war, and Hemingway's novel accommodates more than just a war story. In the novel's earliest scenes, Henry returns from leave and recounts a trip through Italy that he undertook with all the abandon of a civilian of a previous generation making the grand tour. Henry's experience of the war is fundamentally different from Paul's in part because the town in which he is stationed in not on the front lines in the same way that Paul's trenches are. In northern Italy, there is still a semblance of civilian life, with cafés and commerce and intact and inhabitable houses. And, perhaps more important, there are women in this town and hence the possibility of romance.

Within the first fifteen pages of *A Farewell to Arms*, Henry's eventual love interest has made her appearance. On his return from touring Italy, Henry hears from his friend Rinaldi about the new English nurses in the village, and in particular about Catherine Barclay. Like Paul Bäumer, Henry has strong bonds with his fellow soldiers. Rinaldi and Kat, for example, stand in much the same relationship to their novel's respective protagonists. Yet over the opening chapters of *A Farewell to Arms*, Henry begins to move from a world of men to a relationship with a woman. When he is wounded by a trench mortar and hospitalized, this movement is made explicit. The hospital in Milan is the realm of Catherine and the other nurses, and Henry is no longer a soldier in the company of men but a patient in a hospital staffed and managed by women.

Henry's relationship with Catherine feels more than natural; it is, in the context of Hemingway's novel, inevitable. Henry has always been an outsider in the Italian army. He is liked, respected, and perhaps even loved, but he is also an object of puzzlement and curiosity. Catherine, on the other hand, speaks his language and shares his status as an expatriate. Moreover, neither one of them has any illusions about the nature of the war in which they are engaged. Catherine describes the romantic notion she once subscribed to when her fiancé joined the army and she volunteered as a nurse:

I remember having a silly idea that he might come to the hospital where I was. With a sabre cut, I suppose, and a bandage around his head. Or shot through the shoulder. Something picturesque. . . . People can't realize what France is like. If they did, it couldn't all go on. He didn't have a sabre cut. They blew him all to bits. (20)

Henry, too, has seen action and knows that the trench and the machine gun have destroyed the romantic image of war to which a previous generation subscribed. He predicts of the front on which Paul Bäumer fights, "We'll crack. We'll crack in France. They can't go on doing things like the Somme and not crack" (20). Yet while they hold no romantic illusions about war, Catherine and Henry still see the possibility of romantic love. The second time they meet, Catherine asks Henry if he loves her, and he thinks she "was probably a little crazy" (30). Yet when he sees her in the Milan hospital after being wounded, he finds that he, too, is suddenly in love. The couple has no illusions about war and the front, but regarding their own relationship, each is ardently romantic. At times, in fact, the war seems like little more than a picturesque background for Henry and Catherine's affair.

Paul Bäumer is fighting on the French front where Catherine's fiancé was blown "all to bits," and he experiences the hardship that Henry says will "crack" one of the two armies. There is little semblance on the French front of the civilian life that Henry and Catherine can still enjoy in Italy. When Paul and his comrades are pulled back from the front lines, however, they are able to interact with civilians in the territory that the Germans have recently occupied. In one memorable encounter, Paul and his companions swim across a river to visit a house inhabited by three French women. They bring with them bread, sausages, and other rations, and, in trading food for sex, the transaction might be considered a form of prostitution. Certainly the men would not have been welcomed so readily had they arrived empty-handed. Paul spends the night with one of the women, but realizes early on that she holds some of the romantic notions of war that he has long since abandoned. He thinks:

If I were going up to the front, then she would have called me again '*pauvre garçon*'; but merely going on leave—she does not want to hear about that, that is not nearly so interesting. May she go to the devil with her chattering talk. (153)

The woman may be suffering hardship and deprivation due to the war, but it seems not entirely to have dispelled the aura of bravery and gallantry that she sees the soldier as possessing. She would feel more passionate about a young man going to fight on the front lines than about one going home on leave. In fact, it is only Paul whose illusions are dispelled during this visit; he laments, "A man dreams of a miracle and wakes up to loaves of bread" (153). Paul hopes to find in his sexual, physical encounter with this woman something beyond the physical. What he wants is not merely sex, but romance; he hopes that a woman can provide him with some viable alternative to war and violence. He hopes that her kiss will have some restorative power: "But then I feel the lips of the little brunette and press myself against them, my eyes close, I want it all to fall from me, war and terror and grossness, in order to awaken young and happy" (150).

Ultimately, Paul's visit to the French woman never ushers in an alternative to the world of war and of men that he inhabits. He visits the women in the company of his friends, and at the end of the night he leaves again with them. The last image in the chapter is of the three young men laughing that their fourth companion, whom they plied with drinks and left sleeping back at their camp, has awoken and made his way across the river. As they watch him make his way to toward the farmhouse in which the three women live, neither Paul nor any of his friends feel a sense of propriety or jealousy. They come away from the night bonded more closely to each other rather than to any of the women. In *A Farewell to Arms*, it is possible to leave the world of men for that of women, but such a movement would be mere fantasy on Remarque's western front. The fantastic nature of romantic love is summed up in the image of Paul standing in front of a tattered poster advertising an old theatrical production. Staring at the poster, he thinks, "The girl on the poster is a wonder to us. We have forgotten that there are such things, and even now we hardly believe our eyes. We have seen nothing like it for years, nothing like it for happiness, beauty, and joy" (141). The image of a beautiful girl, living in a peacetime world of regular meals and baths, fancy clothing, and trips to the theater, has become an entirely alien concept to Paul.

One of the most striking contrasts between Hemingway's and Remarque's depiction of women and of romantic love comes when the protagonist of each respective novel is wounded and hospitalized. Injured by an explosion at the front, Frederic Henry finds himself hospitalized in the same institution in which Catherine Barclay will be serving as a nurse. Here at the novel's midpoint, the war plotline gives way to the romance plotline. Indeed, so ingeniously does Hemingway structure his novel that the reader may not have realized until this point that it is constructed around a double plotline. After the retreat from Caporetto, in which Henry narrowly escapes being shot as a deserter, he will make his eponymous farewell to arms, running away to neutral Switzerland with Catherine. But it is in the hospital that his allegiance to war and to the Italian army first falters. In moving from the barracks and the battlefield to the hospital, Henry moves from a world ruled by men to one ruled by women. Suddenly, he answers to the head nurse and, to a certain extent, to Catherine herself. Henry has now fully entered her domain, and the power dynamic between them shifts so that he is in a very real sense subordinated to her. Henry emerges from the hospital with a new allegiance; he is now first and foremost bound to Catherine rather than to his adopted army.

Like Frederic Henry, Paul Bäumer is wounded and evacuated to a hospital. Yet his experiences are fundamentally different from those of Henry. Though he too is now surrounded by female nurses, nuns, and volunteers, his allegiance remains with his fellow soldiers. He sticks close to his wounded comrade, Kropp, even faking a fever so that he can get off the train at the same station as his sick friend. In the ward, too, the men band together. When the nuns leave the door open during their prayer sessions, for example, the men present a united front in demanding that the door be closed so that they may sleep. Likewise, the men work together to allow one patient to enjoy a conjugal visit with his wife. Paul may be living in an institution staffed by women, but there seems to be no opportunity or incentive for him to escape from war into a relationship with a woman. The hospital and the company of women offer no viable alternative to a return to the front.

It is interesting to speculate about how a Hemingway hero would have acted in Paul's place—or, perhaps more tellingly, how the situations in which Paul finds himself might play out differently were Hemingway writing them. Paul actually has several encounters with women, including the French woman with whom he presumably sleeps, a volunteer who gives him coffee when he comes home on leave, the young sister attending to him on the train ride to the hospital, the girls who frequent the Soldiers' Home, and the various nurses and volunteers who interact with him during his convalescence. Yet none of these encounters blossom into a romantic plotline. This is in part because Paul himself remains impassive and observational, as in this description of the Soldiers' Home:

> I go through the routine mechanically. In the evenings I generally go to the Soldiers' Home, where the newspapers are laid out, but I do not read them; still there is a piano there that I am glad enough to play on. Two girls are in attendance, one of them is young. (187)

Paul notes that one of the girls is young, but her youth seems to elicit no emotional response or romantic impulse in him. He responds to her as "mechanically" as he does everything else at this point in his life. In contrasting Henry and Paul's experiences with women behind the lines, one might conclude that Hemingway and Remarque are operating in two very different genres or sets of narrative possibilities. Or, to be more exact, Hemingway's novel skillfully juxtaposes two plot-lines—those of the war story and of the love story—whereas Remarque's novel allows for only one. In this sense, Henry is able to escape from one genre into another, whereas Paul Bäumer is offered no such alternative. Neither his own inclinations nor the world he inhabits make possible the romantic intrigues that confront Frederic Henry.

Hemingway and Remarque therefore hold substantively different attitudes toward war. In Remarque's novel, war is presented as so overwhelming a force as to allow for no alternative or means of escape. It is hard to imagine the warfare of *All Quiet* being successfully integrated into any secondary plot or genre; so devastating are the effects of four years on the front that Paul himself cannot imagine any alternative way of living. He muses:

> Had we returned home in 1916, out of the suffering and the strength of our experiences we might have unleashed a storm. Now if we go back we will be weary, broken, burnt out, rootless, and without hope. We will not be able to find our way anymore. (294)

Pushed beyond a certain point, a man experiences more trauma than he can reasonably cope with or integrate into the rest of his life. And in point of fact, Paul will not have a life after the war, for he dies during its final days.

In comparison, Hemingway's vision of war seems less absolute. He certainly acknowledges the horrors of modern warfare—Catherine's comment about her fiancé's death speaks to the grotesque suffering that World War I inflicted on the soldiers who fought in it. Yet in so many of his depictions of soldiers, Hemingway treats war and love as closely allied fields. Jake Barnes of *The Sun Also Rises*, Frederic Henry, and Robert Jordan of *For Whom the Bell Tolls* are all fighters and lovers. War is still something of a rite of passage for Hemingway and for his protagonists. He can see warfare steadily enough to recognize how terrible it is, and yet it still holds a fascination for the author that can shade into a romanticizing of both war itself and of the character that war develops in the men who wage it.

Hemingway and Remarque's different attitudes toward war may be a reflection of their very different experiences in World War I. In some respects, one might read both Frederick Henry and Paul Bäumer as versions of their author's younger, wartime selves. Like Henry, Hemingway volunteered for a war that his country had not yet entered. As a volunteer for the Red Cross, he served briefly in Italy, and in 1917 he was wounded in the leg by a piece of shrapnel while distributing chocolate and cigarettes to soldiers. He was taken to an Italian hospital, where he had an affair with the English nurse who cared for him. In some respects, then, Henry's war experience echoes that of his author. Yet Hemingway often seemed compelled to elaborate on his experience in the war. The author's note that was appended to his first collection of short stories, *In Our Time*, described him as an ambulance driver—a more glamorous wartime role that he would later ascribe to Frederic Henry. Over the years, Hemingway's references to his wartime service and to the circumstances under which he was injured would change and expand in scope. War, like his subsequent avocations of boxing, bullfighting, hunting, and fishing, fit into Hemingway's code of masculine conduct. He knew how horrible the modern battlefield is, but he was also fascinated by war and by the soldiers who survived it. On some level, Hemingway seems to have regretted that he himself had not been one of these soldiers. Frederic Henry's story therefore serves as an amplification of Hemingway's own war experience, and one might read it as an instance of authorial wish fulfillment. Like the early Jake Barnes and the later Robert Jordan, Henry is an idealized version of Hemingway himself.

Hemingway lends his own war injury to two of his most memorable protagonists, Jake Barnes and Frederic Henry, and for both characters their war service and their battlefield wounds serve as markers of a certain kind of masculinity. For Barnes and Henry alike, war serves as a rite of passage and as a prelude to love. Rendered impotent by his injury, Jake carries on a platonic affair with Brett Ashley; in a sense, the war is always present for these two, since Jake's wartime disability stands between their being together. But as Jake says, getting the novel's last word, "Isn't it pretty to think so?" (247). In point of fact, it is Jake's sexual unavailability that makes him a continued source of fascination for Brett. She wants him because she cannot have him, and so the romance of their relationship is bound up with Jake's war service. His debilitating injury has moved him out of the realm of postwar sexual politics, in which men and women may sleep together freely. Instead, Jake and Brett have a tragic and chaste relationship that would not be out of place in a medieval romance. Ironically, modern warfare has knocked Jake out of step with modernity itself. Surrounded by prostitutes, open relationships, and all manner of sexual liberation, Jake subscribes instead to an enforced chastity that makes him resemble a modern-day Gawain or Galahad.

Henry's romance, too, begins with his being wounded at the front. Upon being injured, he moves from the world of men to that of women, and to his de facto marriage to Catherine. Yet by novel's end, he will be entirely alone, having survived both the war and a love affair that ends tragically and abruptly. In this respect, the role of the Hemingway protagonist in these early great novels seems to be that of the rugged veteran who survives both war and love to emerge as a stoic, tragically solitary figure. The Hemingway hero suffers and survives both the horrors of war and the heartaches of love. In this respect, Hemingway has a contradictory interest in portraying modern warfare as both a terrible ordeal and as an experience that the right kind of man can endure and overcome. There is an inherent tension between Hemingway's understanding of the horror of war and his tacit acceptance of war service and the war injury as a mark of a man's true character.

In his third great war novel, *For Whom the Bell Tolls*, Hemingway again will intertwine a war story with a love story. Robert Jordan is yet another American volunteer, a bomb maker fighting for the republican partisans in the Spanish Civil War. The guerrilla band to which Jordan attaches himself is made up of both men and women, and he soon finds himself carrying on a love affair with the beautiful, traumatized Maria. Jordan's lover is also a fighter, and so the war plot and the love plot in this novel are inextricable. Yet in the context of Hemingway's other novels, it is almost absurdly predictable that the unit Jordan joins would contain an attractive and available young woman. It is as if Hemingway cannot think of war without immediately thinking of romance. Jordan, too, will suffer a grievous injury, and will, by novel's end, make a sacrifice that might be read as a quintessentially romantic portrayal of warfare.

Remarque had a very different war experience and emerged from the trenches with a far less conflicted attitude toward combat. A veteran of the German army, Remarque fought on the western front—the border between Germany and France—where he was wounded. He could boast of the war experience that Hemingway seems so often to envy. And, perhaps because of the nature of his service, he became a pacifist. Remarque records the horrors of war in *All Quiet* and elsewhere in his writings, but he seems not to share Hemingway's fascination with the soldier's life or his readiness to make war stand for something other than itself. This certainly ties into Liedloff's point that Hemingway gestures toward the symbolic in a way that Remarque does not. But it also helps to explain why Remarque's novel focuses so exclusively on the war experience. There can be no second plot or romantic component to the novel, because war is too all-encompassing to allow for any elements of beauty. Hemingway's characters survive the war and their war injuries, which become for each a "red badge of courage" marking out inherently masculine qualities. Hemingway could never truly be a pacifist, for he would always see war as a rite of passage and as a prelude to other phases of life. Paul Bäumer, however, will die before the war ends, and war is therefore not presented as an experience that a man can integrate into the rest of his life. Paul goes to war instead of having the kinds of experiences in love and in civilian life that Hemingway's veterans will enjoy. At different points in his narrative, Paul expresses an awareness that his years in the trenches will be the defining experience of his life and that, whether he survives or not, the war will claim both his youth and his adulthood. So whereas Hemingway gives his protagonists an amplified version of his own war experience, making his Americans volunteer as soldiers, ambulance drivers, and bomb makers, Remarque creates in Paul Bäumer a more fragile version of himself. After all, Remarque actually survived fighting in the same theater of war in which Paul dies. So convincing and moving is the narrative voice of *All Quiet* that readers may have to remind themselves that this is not a posthumous work. Remarque survived the war that his protagonist does not.

The differences between *All Quiet* and *A Farewell to Arms* are located in more than just their respective uses of symbolic language or in the fullness of their respective treatments of war. Rather, Hemingway's novel is animated by a strain of romanticism that is absent from Remarque's. War still holds a fascination for the American author that it does not for his German counterpart, and, as a result, Hemingway is ready to integrate a war plot and a romance plot in a way that would be entirely out of place in *All Quiet*. The two novels therefore differ on the most basic of levels: those of genre, plot, theme, and character. For Hemingway, the most admirable of men is the laconic veteran of World War I, one who bears the scars of combat but still perseveres and endures. The Hemingway protagonist makes "a separate peace" with the war and creates for himself a new identity in relation to the woman he loves. Yet love, too, is a harrowing experience from which a man must eventually emerge. In the final analysis, the Hemingway protagonist stands alone, a survivor of war and love alike. For Remarque, himself a survivor of the trenches, war's effects are far less easy to shrug off or to integrate with the rest of one's life. It may be that Remarque saw some part of himself, and some part of every soldier who sees combat, as lying fallen in the mud with Paul Bäumer.

Works Cited

Hemingway, Ernest. *A Farewell to Arms*. New York: Charles Scribner's Sons, 1929.

_____. *The Sun Also Rises*. New York: Charles Scribner's Sons, 1926.

Liedloff, Helmut. "Two War Novels." *Revue de Littérature Comparée* 42 (1968): 390-406.

Remarque, Erich Maria. *All Quiet on the Western Front*. New York: Ballantine, 1929.

CRITICAL
READINGS

The End of War?

Erich Maria Remarque and Ian Hamilton

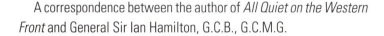

A correspondence between the author of *All Quiet on the Western Front* and General Sir Ian Hamilton, G.C.B., G.C.M.G.

To the historian, the year 1929-30 will be chiefly remarkable as that in which men's emotions first began to turn vigorously against the idea of war. It may seem strange that such an emotional change should have been so long delayed, but the fact is that men can only bear to examine painful events which have receded a little into the past, and there is natural unwillingness to disparage military glory while bereavement is fresh. Symptoms of this change of attitude are cropping up on every hand. One of them is the sudden and unexpected revival of interest in the actualities of war all over Europe. Books which a year or so ago no publisher could hope to sell, either in this country or in any other, are now read eagerly by hundreds of thousands. Of these, England has contributed a notable one, *Undertones of War*, by Edmund Blunden. But *All Quiet on the Western Front*, by Erich Maria Remarque, has made the deepest and widest impression of any. The following number of copies have been sold (the figures are some months old):

Germany	850,000
Denmark and Norway	60,000
America	215,000
Finland	5,000
France	300,000
Holland	50,000
Rumania	6,000
Sweden	50,000
Spain	25,000
Czecho-Slovakia	20,000
England	300,000

That in France more copies should have been sold than in America is significant, though this may be partly due (the Americans appear to be the world's worst translators) to the inferiority of the American version.

Although the great majority of those who have read *All Quiet on the Western Front* have regarded it as a most salutary book, strengthening aversion from war, others have suspected the author of a desire to exploit horrors for their own sake. Messrs. Putnam, its publishers over here, have shown me a huge packet of press-cuttings. Among them are passages from Service magazines translated from derogatory comments published in Germany, a pleasing example of professional solidarity. These were sent to Herr Remarque, and it is interesting to see the way he has taken them. Writing on September 15th, from Berlin, he says:

I thank you for the Press notices sent to me, which contained several things new to me. I learned from the interview in the *Observer*, of 8th September, that Herr Moissi pretends to have known me well, and to have said that I am twenty-six years old. I have not the slightest acquaintance with Herr Moissi and am unfortunately five years older than that.

Again I find gossip-paragraphs in various papers, about which I have been asked questions sometimes by the Berlin correspondents of English publications. To this I can only say that I consider it really unnecessary to take any notice of tittle-tattle which is due to ignorance, envy, hatred, or love of sensation. In Germany, no one would see the point of my doing so because here everyone understands where it all comes from. This little group of dissatisfied people, reactionaries, war-worshippers, is no longer Germany, in spite of the noise which they delight to make. Germany to-day stands for work, reconstruction, sympathetic understanding, diligence, and peace.

When I see what the petty Press and Diehard societies make of me I could sometimes fancy myself a monster. My age, for instance, varies between twenty-two and fifty-five years, and I can hardly keep count of the different names I am supposed to bear, or to how many different regiments, brigades, or divisions I am supposed to have, or *not* to have, belonged. I am said, in the same breath, to have stolen my manuscript from a dead comrade, to have cribbed from other war-books and to have written it as a commission from the *Entente*. The latest information about me changes from day to day. All I can say in reply is, that I wish these people were right at any rate about one point: that I never had been a soldier. Then, indeed, I could be sure to-day that I am a really good writer, of which I have still to convince myself. Besides, in my opinion, an author should have said the last word about his book when he wrote the last word of it. If it is good, it can hold its own against hostile criticism; if bad, all subsequent justification is useless.

Injured vanity and injured self-esteem would be the main motive for replying to personal attacks. *Amour propre*, however, is only permissible after one has turned seventy and completed one's life-work. But I am young and only at the beginning of it. I should be ridiculous in my own eyes were I to take for granted, on the strength of a single book, that I am a good writer. I must first take the measure of my abilities; and to that end I must work. Work—not talk and quarrel. I am the less inclined to talk since all the nonsense which has been gossiped about me was inaccurate and false, and moreover so clearly malevolent and crazy that in Germany every one shrugs his shoulders at it.

Not all soldiers, however, have taken his book in that spirit. The publishers sent an advance copy to General Sir Ian Hamilton, and his letter, forwarded to the author, drew from him that criticism of his own work which we now publish. During all the hubble-bubble over his book, Herr Remarque has hitherto remained silent. This is the first time he has explained what it is he really cares about in his own work. We print the complete correspondence because it is interesting that a distinguished English soldier should, by his comments, have divined so nearly the author's main intention that they have persuaded him to break that silence.

April 2nd, 1929

My Dear Huntington,

Thank you for the advance copy of *All Quiet on the Western Front*: I am glad you have found so capable a translator, clever enough to pick up Remarque's bomb and fling it across the Channel. We here just needed this bit of wakening up.

The tale is that of a generation who have been destroyed by the war: we who fought 'are forlorn like children, and experienced like old men, we are crude and sorrowful and superficial—I believe we are lost'; or, more tersely, 'the war has ruined us for everything'.

This is the keynote of the diary—in which form the revelations are cast: it is struck firmly in the opening half-dozen lines and recurs again and again, until, at the end, the last chord dies softly away into the unknown.

There was a time when I would have strenuously combated Remarque's inferences and conclusions. Now, sorrowfully, I must admit, there is a great deal of truth in them. Latrines, rats, lice; smells, blood, corpses; scenes of sheer horror as where comrades surround the deathbed of a young *Kamerad* with one eye on his agonies, the other on his new English boots; the uninspired strategy; the feeling that the leaders are unsympathetic or stupid; the shrivelling up of thought and enthusiasm under ever-growing machinery of an attrition war; all this lasting too long—so long indeed that half a million souls, still existing in our own island, have been, in Remarque's own terrible word, 'lost'. Why else, may I ask, should those who were once the flower of our youth form to-day so disproportionate a number of the down and out?

All the same, this German goes too far. As there is more in Easter than hot-cross-buns, so there is more in Patriotism than 'beans and bacon'. Even in the last and most accursed of all wars—the war 'on the Western Front'— was there not the superb leading of forlorn hopes; the vague triumphs, vague but real, of dying for a cause? Was there not also that very patriotism which Remarque treats much as he treated the goose his hero murdered in the officers' mess? Above all, is there not the victory of those, and they were many, who survived everything; profited even by Passchendaele; and afterwards still found courage enough to turn themselves to making the world a better place for themselves and everyone else, including their ex-enemies?

Remarque seems to me a writer who could do anything. He says some incredibly coarse things, but he lets slip sometimes, as if by accident, astonishingly true things hitherto unsaid. As, for instance, his answer to those who with their clumsy questions grope and rummage about his heart, seeking for his innermost feelings upon the happenings of the Western Front: 'a man cannot talk of such things; I would do it willingly, but it is too dangerous for me to put these things into words. I am afraid they might then become gigantic, and I be no longer able to marshal them'.

Im Westen Nichts Neues is a masterpiece of realism, but not a perfect war book; for war, as well as life, holds something more than realism.

Yours sincerely,
(*Signed*) Ian Hamilton.

II[1]

June 1st, 1929

Dear Sir Ian Hamilton,

An extract from your letter to Mr. Huntington concerning my book, *All Quiet on the Western Front*, was very kindly sent on to me by the publishers, Messrs. Putnam. I intended to write to you about it at once, but was prevented from so doing during long weeks of illness which denied me the quiet hour I needed for my reply.

I cannot even now tell you which feeling was uppermost in me on receipt of your letter—whether that of personal pleasure, or of amazement and admiration at having been so clearly, so completely, so justly understood. Probably both were equally strong. You will be able to appreciate that I was entirely unaware what effect my work might produce outside Germany—whether I should have succeeded in making myself intelligible to all, or not.

A book on the war is readily exposed to criticism of a political character, but my work should not be so judged, for it was not political, neither pacifist nor militarist, in intention, but human simply. It presents the war as seen within the small compass of the front-line soldier, pieced together out of many separate situations, out of minutes and hours, out of struggle, fear, dirt, bravery, dire necessity, death and comradeship, into one whole mosaic, from which the word Patriotism is only *seemingly* absent, because the simple soldier never spoke of it. His patriotism lay in the *deed* (not in the *word*); it consisted simply in the fact of his presence at the front. For him that was enough. He cursed and swore at the war; but he fought on, and fought on even when already without hope. And of this there is, I believe, for those who can read, enough in my book.

But you, Sir Ian, have in a few words, exposed the very heart of my book, namely, the intention of presenting the fate of a generation of young men, who at the critical age, when they were just beginning to feel the pulse of life, were set face to face with death. I thank you for that most sincerely, and am delighted to hear these words from a man of high military rank. Your words are prized by me as those of a voice speaking clearly from England. In Germany it has never been forgotten how *fair* the English were, even in the midst of the battle, and so I am particularly pleased to find it confirmed in letters from English soldiers and English officers, that the background, the little things, but things so important for the individual soldier, were apparently similar on all the fronts.

I have not felt myself called upon to argue about the war. That must be reserved for the leaders, who alone know all that it is necessary to know. I merely wanted to awaken understanding for a generation that more than all others has found it difficult to make its way back from the four years of death, struggle and terror, to the peaceful fields of work and progress. Thousands upon thousands have even yet been unable to do it; countless letters from all countries have proved it to me. But all these letters say the same thing: 'We have been unable, because we did not know that our lethargy, our cynicism, our unrest, our hopelessness, our silence, our feeling of secession and exclusion arose from the fact that the regenerative power of our youth had been dissipated in the war. But now we will find the way, for you in your book have shown us the danger in which we stand, the danger of being destroyed by ourselves. But the recognition of a danger is the first step towards escape from it. We will now find our way back, for you have told us what it was that threatened us, and thereby it has become harmless.'

You see, Sir Ian, it is in this vein that my comrades write to me, and that proves that my book is only *seemingly* pessimistic. In reality, as it shows how much has been destroyed, it should serve as a call to them to rally for the peaceful battle of work and of life itself, the effort to achieve personality and culture. For the very reason that we had so early to learn to know death, we now want to shake off its paralysing spell—for we have seen it eye to eye and undisguised—we want to begin once again to believe in life. This will be the aim of my future work. He who has pointed out the danger, must also point out the road onward.

I have as yet never spoken my mind so fully; but your charming, appreciative letter compelled me to take up the pen in order to emphasize the two things in my book which, though not there in any very explicit way, are nevertheless there implicit—I mean, in the first place, the quiet heroism of the simple soldier, which lay precisely in the fact that he did not speak of it, that he did not perhaps so much as once realize it himself—speaking only of 'beans and bacon,' while all the time so much more lay behind that was other than this; and secondly, the fact that my book does not desire to preach resignation but rather to be an S.O.S. call.

You are right, Sir Ian, my book is not a 'perfect war book'. But such a war book, in the comprehensive sense, may not be written for yet another ten, perhaps even another hundred years. I restricted myself to the purely human aspect of war experience, the experience through which every man who went up to the front had to make his painful way: the fighting, the terror, the mastery, the power, the tenacity of the vital forces in the individual man faced with death and annihilation.

I like to regard that as the universal, fundamental experience; and I have aimed at describing without rhetoric and without political exploitation, this fundamental experience alone. And to this, I believe, may be attributed the success of my book, which in Germany has been read not merely in literary circles, but by those also who almost never take a book in their hands—by artisans, labourers, business people, mechanics, postmen, chauffeurs, apprentices, and so on; for many hundreds of letters all say: '*It is my own experience*'. The *outward* experience was, perhaps, in each case merely similar (though, as far as possible, I described only typical, standard situations, such as constantly recurred), but the decisive factor undoubtedly was that the book represented a part of the *inner* experience—Life confronting and fighting Death.

In conclusion, Sir Ian, allow me to thank you once again for your letter, and you may judge from the length of this how highly I valued it. I am happy to have met with such appreciative understanding.

Yours sincerely,
(*Signed*) Erich Maria Remarque.

III

June 19th, 1929

Dear Mr. Remarque,

Yours of June 1st has given me much pleasure. I can well imagine the postman pouring out the best part of his heavy bag whilst you look at the pile of letters in despair, saying to yourself: 'So, because I have written well I must go on writing for ever!' All the more then am I grateful to you for having found time to write so fully and indeed so important an epistle to an ex-enemy commander.

I fear I have been a long time in answering, and one reason is that I have so much work on my hands as President of the British Legion in London and in trying to help old soldiers who fought under me in the war. You see, in England we have over one million unemployed. More than half of these are old soldiers. When they went to the war they were the flower, not the dregs, of our people. Always I have tried to rouse them and stir them up by explaining to them the reason; namely, that education is most valuable from the age of eighteen to twenty-two and that, just during those very years, when the stay-at-homes were mastering their trades, they were standing in mud under a rain of shells. Therefore, when they came back they were at a disadvantage. Therefore, when trade was slack they were the first to be discharged. But all this lost ground, I have been careful to add, could be, by courage and perseverance, recovered. First of all the Legionaries must bind themselves into a body professing, as such, no politics, so that they must carry weight with any Government. Secondly, they must work to save their old comrades and the widows and orphans of their late comrades. Thirdly, they must strive for some high ideal, the highest being peace: for this, as ex-service men they could do with far better grace than professed pacifists: especially they could work wonders for the cause of peace by holding out the hand of friendship to ex-enemy associations of soldiers. For all the people of the world would then say to one another: 'Surely, if these soldiers who threw bombs at one another can shake hands, we, who never struck or were stricken in our own persons can also afford to be friends!'

These things I tell you not (I hope) from conceit, but because you should thus understand better how your work has appealed to me. For you have explained to your war heroes (no longer *die Gemeine*) that the war not only robbed them of their education, but actually burnt up in its fiery furnace the energy and regenerative power which was intended by God to see them through the early struggles of their careers as citizens.

But when we come to practice, how difficult! Easier it will be to put a hook into the nose of leviathan than to draw the Stahlhelms and the Reichsbanner into one non-political Legion for the battle against war.

Five years ago, I was almost voted out of the Presidency of the Legion in London because I wanted them to shake hands with the Germans, and because I pointed out that they would thus show the way to the timorous, manœuvring politicians and *Beamten* at Geneva, who depend for their livelihood upon the absence of the peace they are paid heavy sums to secure.

Yet still the pen is mightier than the sword. So write another book, my dear Mr. Remarque. As one who has served in eight campaigns, I say, take up thy pen and write. For you possess the gift of genius and you may not wrap it up in a napkin. That magical scene where you sit in your old room and pray in vain to your old gods, the books. That unforgettable moment when you breathe in again the acid smell of the cold water of the Mill—*In einem kuhlen Grunde!* Yes; you have the touch; the sure touch, and you can do it as no other can. But you will need all the power of your persuasive pen. For great and terrible is the counter-power of the romance and beauty of war, to which you wisely make no reference in your book. But there it is—entrenched somewhere—latent in your soul. Have you seen a German army corps, colours flying, march past, the earth shaking to the tramp of the parade step? Lord Roberts told me in his old age, that the most superb picture he preserved in his mind's eye was that of two Highland battalions, in their kilts and feather bonnets, advancing in perfect line against the walled city of Lucknow, the round shot hopping and skipping over the plain, sometimes over them, sometimes into them, yet all keeping step as on an inspection parade. These are the legends and illusions you have got to transfix very quickly with your pen.

For the boys of to-day are just the same as you were twenty years ago, and as I was sixty years ago.

Yours very truly,
(*Signed*) Ian Hamilton.

From *Life and Letters* 3, no. 18 (November 1929): 399-411. Copyright © 1929 by New York University Press. Reprinted with permission of the Estate of the Late Paulette Goddard Remarque.

Note
1. Translated by A. W. Wheen.

All Quiet on the Western Front_____

Hilton Tims

Germany's bookshops were awash with novels and memoirs of the war and by the end of the decade there was a perception in the publishing business that the book-buying public was satiated. In those ten years following the armistice more than 200 war-related titles with respectable sales had appeared, twenty-four of them in the twelve months of 1927/28 alone.

Remarque made no attempt to submit his manuscript. His reluctance remains a mystery he never publicly clarified. Involved as he was in publishing, he may have discerned the prevailing trend, or merely regarded his book as a personal rite of exorcism, for private consumption only. More likely, his chronic lack of confidence prevented him from gauging the true measure of its merits and potential. Billy Wilder allegedly warned him while he was writing it that nobody would want to read 'a grim piece of anti-war realism' and urged him not to jeopardize his job.[1]

At least Jutta had faith in it. Remarque welcomed her comments as he wrote and passed the pages to her for correction and editing. There is evidence that he ultimately made her a gift of the original manuscript. When it mysteriously surfaced for auction at Sotheby's in London in 1995, the anonymous vendor was rumoured to have acquired it from Jutta's estate following her death twenty years earlier.

The manuscript lay undisturbed in Remarque's desk drawer for six months until, pressed by Jutta and others, he decided to seek a publisher. Tactfully—though with negative consequences later—he discounted his own employers. The Hugenberg organization with its increasingly Fascist stance had no sympathy for anti-war sentiment. Only that year its owner Alfred Hugenberg had been elected leader of the German Nationalist People's Party and would throw in his lot with Hitler five years later.

Instead Remarque sent the manuscript to the Berlin house of

S. Fischer Verlag, publisher of Thomas Mann's *Buddenbrooks*. Their reaction to it foreshadowed the impact it was to make. One of the firm's directors Bermann Fischer read the novel at a single sitting, passed it on to his brother and company chairman Samuel Fischer the following morning and urged him to read it at once and draw up a contract with the author without delay 'before any other publisher got sight of it'.[2]

The response of the all-powerful Samuel Fischer was more cautious. He hedged his bets by suggesting they would take the book if no other publisher was prepared to accept it, on the grounds that sales were questionable because nobody wanted to read about the war any more. Privately he felt the novel's style and content did not accord with the Fischer house-image of publishing 'literature' by established authors, a view he maintained even after its spectacular success.

If Remarque was disappointed, Bermann Fischer's enthusiasm compensated and spurred his determination. He promptly sent it to Propyläen Verlag, the book arm of the vast Ullstein publishing company. There have been many versions of the chain of circumstances that turned an unsolicited manuscript into one of the publishing sensations of the twentieth century—and just as many claimants to the honour of 'discovering' it. In a 1963 Berlin television interview—the only one he ever gave—Remarque recollected that a friend, Dr Fritz Meyer, who had contacts with Ullstein, asked his permission to show it to Fritz Ross, one of the firm's editors. 'That did it. I received a letter from Ullstein. Would I like to go along to them?' he said.

But other accounts suggest it was not quite so straightforward as that. Fritz Ross was certainly among the first to read it and recommend buying it. Where the legends diverge is in what happened next. According to some eye-witnesses, Ross's superiors did not share his enthusiasm and it lay, unheeded, on various readers' desks until the production manager Cyrill Soschka, leaving the office one evening, randomly took it home as something to read that night.

The next morning he thrust it to the editorial team, saying: 'I know war, and this is the real war, the truth about war, naked and honest.' And he vowed that if no publisher was prepared to take it, he would found his own company to publish it.

Not without some of Samuel Fischer's trepidation, Ullstein offered Remarque a contract, paying him 24,000 marks in monthly installments of 1,000 over two years, with a proviso that if the book failed to cover the publishing costs the author would be required to cover the deficit by submitting further writings without payment. Unofficially, however, they signalled a vote of confidence in the book's quality by not demanding any alterations or corrections.

Until the 1995 Sotheby's auction, it was generally believed that *All Quiet on the Western Front* had been originally published exactly as Remarque had written it. In fact the rediscovered autograph manuscript revealed a previously unsuspected opening chapter in which the protagonist Paul Bäumer described his home life and family.

Susan Wharton, Sotheby's specialist in continental manuscripts, said: 'This manuscript shows how it was originally envisaged . . . his second thoughts were really much better than his first.'[3]

* * *

While the book was being typeset Cyrill Soschka had galley proofs pulled and sent to the editors of twelve newspapers and periodicals in the Ullstein group, inviting them to bid for serialization rights. Only one responded, Monty Jacobs, the editor of the leading liberal daily *Vossische Zeitung*, the favoured reading of Berlin intellectuals and affectionately known as *Tante Voss* (Auntie Voss). Pre-publication serialization was scheduled to start in November. Ullstein, sensing the expectation that was building up in a book they had been so hesitant about taking, began to plan a promotional campaign unprecedented in German publishing. From press advertising and street hoardings the public quickly became aware that a literary event was in the offing. Booksellers received publicity window displays.

As always, Remarque's reaction was ambivalent: elated by the growing excitement and the justification of his abilities as a writer, enjoying the putative aura of celebrity, yet dismayed by the reality of the media interest it was focusing on him personally. He would later claim to have had no preconception of the book's success.

He had already started work on a so-called sequel *The Road Back* (*Der Weg zurück*) dealing with the immediate post-war problems—loosely his own—that confronted the young veterans of the trenches returning to civilian life in a defeated homeland. But in the run-up to publication of *All Quiet on the Western Front* he found it impossible to write in Berlin and decided to return to Osnabrück. Not, however, to the family home. His advertisement for lodgings in an Osnabrück newspaper brought a reply from a Frau Maria Hoberg, a well-to-do war widow, who would briefly assume the near-status of a surrogate mother to him.

The rooms she offered him in her house on Süsterstrasse were perfect for his writing requirements and state of mind: spacious, quiet, with a terrace fronting a peaceful garden which he could look out on from his desk in the window. Ironically, a neighbour on the opposite side of the street was one of the Vogt brothers who had employed him five years before. Leaving Jutta in Berlin, he moved in on a four-week rental—the period during which his book was appearing in *Vossische Zeitung*. Karla Hoberg, his landlady's daughter, later recalled that he seemed to be in a state of deep depression.

* * *

The circulation of *Vossische Zeitung* shot up threefold during the serialization. The installments carried the title *Nichts Neues im Westen*, a sardonically bitter annexation of the phrase used in official war bulletins meaning 'nothing new on the Western Front'. In the weeks preceding the book's publication Ullstein reversed the words to the sharper, more mellifluous *Im Westen nichts Neues*. The initial print-run was to be 30,000, unusually large for a 'first' novel by an unknown author, but as serialization continued, booksellers' orders increased to avalanche proportions. Another 20,000 copies were added to the run.[4]

Five days after the first instalment appeared Remarque was summarily fired from his job with *Sport im Bild*. Not only had he flouted Hugenberg house rules by failing to give them first refusal on the novel and serialization rights, but the tone of the book was anathema to the company's political ethos. It was a minor indignity in the context of what the future held for him.

By publication day, 31 January 1929, Germany was engulfed in *All Quiet* fever. No book until then in the history of literature had created such excitement. The first print run sold out on the first day. The mighty Ullstein, unable to cope with the printing demand, was forced to sub-contract six outside printers and ten book-binding firms. In the first few weeks sales were estimated at 20,000 a day. By the end of 1929 nearly 1 million copies had been sold in Germany alone.

The pattern, though less frenzied, was repeated abroad. *All Quiet on the Western Front* became an international publishing phenomenon, selling in its first year 300,000 in both Britain and France, 215,000 in the United States and proportionate numbers in smaller markets such as Spain, Italy and the Scandinavian countries.

In Germany, however, the book, unlike elsewhere, quickly became a literary and political *cause célèbre*, polarizing opinion and drawing aggressive critical fire from 'old school' nationalists and military traditionalists for what they perceived as its defeatist, inglorious depiction of German soldiery. Remarque had portrayed life in the trenches as he had observed it, in harsh realism and cryptic neo-documentary sentences. The style of writing, raw, stark and uncompromising, frequently shocking, was unprecedented in fiction. In many respects it prefigured the idiosyncratic style Ernest Hemingway was developing with his First World War novel *A Farewell to Arms* published nine months later in the United States. Even after seventy years Remarque's descriptions of battle and the physical and psychological wounds of its victims still convey a disturbing, piteous immediacy. It speaks for all common soldiers in all warfare and it was this universality that commended it to readers of all ranks and classes.

It was this aspect, too, which determined its impact among politically motivated critics as subversive. They came not only from the right wing. Leftists, too, found cause to attack the book and its author for failing to take an overtly political stance or challenge the social and economic agenda of the ruling classes.

Overwhelmed by the scale of his success, Remarque was totally unprepared for the ensuing controversy, the vehemence of the attrition directed at him personally, not least from fellow authors, impelled no doubt by professional jealousy. Count Harry Kessler noted in his diary the reaction of the left-wing pacifist Arnold Zweig, himself the author eighteen months earlier of a bestselling novel about the war, *Der Streit um den Sergeanten Grischa* (*The Case of Sergeant Grischa*). Zweig 'was venomous about Remarque', Kessler wrote, dismissing the upstart as 'slapdash' and 'a good amateur' who had failed to see the angle from which he should have tackled his subject.

In Remarque's depressive state of mind the onslaughts outweighed the approbations. 'When this success suddenly came upon me last spring, it led to an almost annihilating crisis,' he said later that year, 'I felt that I was finished, vanquished for good. I thought, whatever I write from now on, I would always remain the author of *All Quiet on the Western Front*. And I knew only too well, this book could just as well have been written by anyone else. It was no achievement of mine to have written it.'[5]

More than thirty years later, asked what his reaction had been, he would still remember: 'The feeling of unreality. It never left me . . . I found it to be totally out of proportion. And that it was! Fortunately I always realized this and it prevented me from developing delusions of grandeur. On the contrary, I became insecure.'[6]

The Press clamoured to interview this new literary lion. Veterans organizations and literary groups inundated him with speaking invitations. Remarque went to ground. He had tried to co-operate all he could in Ullstein's pre-publication publicity but the resulting furor cowed him. There was to be no let-up in the months ahead, nor, indeed, were his perceived transgressions to be forgotten in the years to come. The author of the world's most famous anti-war novel was to be hounded by it, sometimes perilously and once shockingly, into middle age. His book became the catharsis of the contradictions in his character: the celebrity and material rewards he revelled in duelling with his lurking sense of inadequacy and instinct for anonymity. He recoiled from the invasion of privacy his sudden fame now triggered.

'I wrote *All Quiet on the Western Front* to escape from something that was depressing me, and when I had finished it I felt free of a dreadful weight of those experiences,' he told an English journalist. 'But now this new terror is hanging over me. I cannot escape from this interest in my own person. People . . . manuscripts . . . the postman . . . everybody I meet, everywhere I go.'[7]

The National Socialists were on the rise and one of the most scurrilous attacks on him was mounted by Hitler's mouthpiece newspaper, the *Völkischer Beobachter*, averring that his real name was Kramer—Remark spelt backwards—and that he was Jewish. It was a myth he tried half-heartedly to correct but which would persist even into some of his obituaries nearly half a century later. Another, with marginally more basis in fact, was that he had never served on the front line and his depiction of conditions and attitudes of the troops there were a falsification.

This touched a nerve. 'The details of my book are real experiences in spite of all the rumours spread to the contrary, which I will not take the trouble to contradict. I was at the front long enough to have experienced personally just nearly all I have described,' he insisted.[8]

He was somewhat placated by the reviews from London when Putnam published A.W. Wheen's superlative English translation in March. Unconcerned with internecine German political polemic, the British Press judged the novel according to Remarque's own ethos, as a commentary on the ordinary soldier in combat, and hailed it as a masterpiece. 'It has marks of genius which transcend nationality. There are moments when the narrative rises to heights which place it in the company of the great,' observed *The Times*. 'So dreadful that it ought to be read by every man and woman who is doubtful about the need for preventing the Next War,' was the prescient advice of the Manchester *Evening News*.

The distinguished critic Herbert Read wrote: 'It is terrible, almost unendurable, in its realism and pathos. But it has swept like a gospel over Germany and must sweep over the whole world because it is the first completely satisfying expression in literature of the greatest event of our time. It is a superb piece of construction.' Demand for the book in Britain necessitated no fewer than eight reprints in the first month and more than twenty by the end of the year.

In the United States some passages in the Wheen translation, mainly referring to bodily functions, were deleted by the publishers Little, Brown to satisfy demands of a lucrative Book-of-the-Month Club contract which they would otherwise have lost. Although the novel has never been out of print in America, the cuts were not restored until 1978 for a new paperback edition.

The world's Press announced in July that the film rights had been sold to Hollywood for $40,000, a record sum for that time. 'A talking film based on the book is to be produced, partly in Germany and partly in Hollywood, in two versions, German and English,' reported *The Times*. In the event it was filmed entirely in California.

Carl Laemmle, the German-born head of Universal Studios, travelled to Berlin to clinch the deal with Ullstein and persuade Remarque to work on the screenplay. Legend has it that he also wanted the author to star in the film as Paul Bäumer. Remarque reluctantly agreed to prepare a treatment but after a half-hearted attempt abandoned the project.

* * *

A sequence of coincidences at this point produced a curious align-ment of interests and frustrated cross-purposes between the authors of the two great classic works from opposing sides of the First World War.

On 21 January 1929, ten days before *All Quiet on the Western Front* was published in Germany, *Journey's End*, a play depicting a group of British army officers in the Flanders trenches, opened in London at the Savoy Theatre. Its author R. C. Sherriff, like Remarque, was unknown before overnight success thrust him into the public eye. So was its lead-ing actor, Laurence Olivier. Robert Cedric Sherriff was two years older than his German counterpart but they shared a June birthday.

On its opening night, the play was acclaimed for its realism and anti-war credo, and mirrored the excitement in Germany over Remarque's novel. It was translated into every European language and through countless revivals since has established itself as one of the definitive English-language dramas of war.

Productions of *Journey's End* quickly followed throughout Europe and the United States. Remarque, in the first flush of celebrity, was ap-proached to adapt it for the German stage under the title *Die andere Seit* (*The Other Side*) even though he did not speak or read English. He declined. 'I read it and felt it agreed completely with my own attitude,' he explained, 'But I don't want to be identified with the war and books and plays the war has brought about. I can't escape from my own book.'[9]

Meanwhile Sherriff, in New York for the July premiere of his play, was being approached to write the screenplay for *All Quiet on the West-ern Front*. Following Remarque's aborted effort, he was the first writer to be considered.

'It was a tempting offer . . . what lured me was the magic spell of Hollywood, a spell I'd been under since my schooldays,' he wrote in his autobiography,

But there was something pulling harder in a different direction. I was longing to get home. Before I'd sailed we had decided to give the house a face-
lift. It was a big old place and we'd never had much to spend on it, but now
I'd given my mother a free hand, and all the money she needed. . . . I had
promised to be home in three weeks and my mother had promised to have
everything done and ready for my return. It would be a bitter disappointment for her if I cabled to say I was going to Hollywood instead. So I sent
my regrets to Carl Laemmle and booked a passage on the *Mauretania*, sail-
ing the following night.[10]

Two years later he would finally be lured to Hollywood to work on the
screenplay of Remarque's *The Road Back*, launching his distinguished
career there as a screenwriter.

The two writers were never to meet or communicate with each
other, although Sherriff was in Berlin for the German premiere of
Die andere Seit in the summer of 1929. Years later Remarque hinted
that he had regretted turning down the offer to adapt *Journey's End*.
'Had I done it at that time, I would probably have written further
theatre pieces, for the theatre fascinates me,' he admitted. So why did-
n't he? 'Because I thought to rebel. From all sides I was being abused
for doing this and that to the poor German soldier. I didn't want to
make a business of the war and write about it a second time. Quite
stupid!'[11]

Over the years he would attempt and abandon a number of plays before finally making it to the Berlin stage with *Die letzte Station* in 1956.

* * *

As income from *All Quiet on the Western Front* soared to unimag-
ined levels, a grateful Ullstein presented Remarque with a bonus—a
grey six-cylinder Lancia Cabriolet convertible. Nothing could have
pleased him more. It was a dream car. He called it Puma, a pet-name he
would recycle in the future.

At Ullstein's insistence he reluctantly submitted himself to a number of Press interviews during the summer months, but avoiding public scrutiny took on a near-paranoid urgency for him. 'I think I should like to disappear, grow a beard and begin a new kind of existence altogether,' he told a journalist that summer.[12] Cars, especially fast cars like the Lancia, became even more central to his life, subconsciously representing, perhaps, a speedy means of escape. 'I spend my free time trying out cars. That's something I do understand. Cars and dogs and fish . . . .'[13] He had privileged access to the Avus race-track where he could test-drive various models and where in early 1930 he survived the first of many serious motoring accidents.

In the weeks following publication he and Jutta fled to Davos in Switzerland where she frequently underwent treatment for her tubercular condition. Later he picked up his old friend Georg Middendorf in Osnabrück for an away-from-it-all driving tour through France from Brittany to the Pyrenees, covering 3,750 miles.

But there was no escape from the shockwaves that his book continued to create. It was banned in Italy, already a Fascist dictatorship under Mussolini. In August the Austrian Minister of Defence ordered its removal from all army libraries and 'prohibit[ed] its dissemination anywhere within the precincts of a cantonment'.

Another flurry of controversy followed reports in September that Remarque was to be nominated for the Nobel Prize, with some confusion as to whether it would be in the categories of Literature or Peace. The German Officers' Union promptly announced that it had 'addressed to the Nobel Prize committee an indignant protest against what can only be regarded as an insult to the Army', adding that the book was 'a feeble attempt to misrepresent and discourage the heroic struggle of the united German stock during four years of war.'[14]

Remarque found this rebuke particularly wounding. '[It] makes it difficult for me to imagine how any German officer can really have read into my book an accusation against the heroic spirit Germany showed,' he said. 'The war certainly gave us enough heroes and the only officer I mention is a splendid one who sacrificed his life for his men.'[15]

Like most Germans, he was unaware that the armed forces (*Wehrmacht*), and especially the new younger element of the officer class, was being subtly infiltrated by National Socialist ideology. Such was official concern that General Wilhelm Groener, the Minister of Defence, found it necessary in January 1930 to issue an order of the day. The Nazis, it said, were greedy for power. 'They therefore woo the *Wehrmacht*. In order to use it for the political aims of their party, they attempt to dazzle us [into believing] that the National Socialists alone represent the truly national power.' Soldiers were enjoined to refrain from politics and remain 'aloof from all party strife'.[16]

Far from enjoying his success, Remarque was becoming increasingly soured by it. 'I know nothing of politics and I can only say that the atmosphere of political recrimination which is that of Germany today is hateful to me.'[17]

Notes

1. Maurice Zolotow, *Billy Wilder in Hollywood* (New York: Proscenium Publications, 1987).

2. P. de Mendelssohn, *S. Fischer und sein Verlag*, cited in Christine R. Barker and R. W. Last, *Erich Maria Remarque* (London: Oswald Wolff, 1979).

3. *Daily Telegraph*, London, 30 October 1995.

4. C. R. Owen, *Erich Maria Remarque: A Critical Bio-Bibliography* (Amsterdam: Rodopi, 1984).

5. EMR interview with *Kölnische Zeitung*, 6 November 1929, cited in Owen.

6. EMR interview in *Die Welt*, 31 March 1966, cited in Barker and Last.

7. EMR interview in the *Observer*.

8. *Ibid.*

9. *Ibid.*

10. R. C. Sherriff, *No Leading Lady* (London: Victor Gollancz, 1968).

11. Television interview, *Das Profil*, Berlin, 1963, transcribed in Erich Maria Re-

marque, *Ein militanter Pazifist. Texte und Interviews 1929-1966*, ed. Thomas F. Schneider (Cologne: Kiepenheuer and Witsch, 1994).

12. EMR interview in the *Observer.*

13. *Ibid.*

14. *The Times*, London, 16 September 1929.

15. *The Observer.*

16. William L. Shirer, *The Rise and Fall of the Third Reich: A History of Nazi Germany* (New York: Simon & Schuster, 1960).

17. *The Observer.*

Im Westen nichts Neues:
A Bestseller in Context_____

Alan F. Bance

It fell to Erich Maria Remarque, born Erich Paul Remark, to write the best-known war book to emerge from the First World War in any country. *Im Westen nichts Neues* also represents a unique publishing event. And yet, perhaps because of its phenomenal commercial success, it has received relatively little serious discussion. No one would want to claim for the novel a place in the ranks of first-class literature, but nonetheless a work so powerful in its effects deserves some appraisal. Seen in the context of its time, as an expression of Weimar Germany and as the popular European war-book *par excellence*, it is an intriguing subject still. The reasons for its success, both domestic and foreign, are not the least part of the book's interest for us today.

Im Westen nichts Neues appeared in the *Vossische Zeitung* as a serial from 10 November to 9 December 1928, and was issued in book form by the Propyläen Verlag on 31 January 1929. Its initial domestic success might be thought to be adequately explained by publicity. The house of Ullstein laid on a sales campaign unprecedented for the time, enormous numbers of review copies being sent out and all the resources of the great publishing house put at Remarque's disposal. Within twelve weeks of its appearance, its German sales had already reached half a million copies,[1] and by then it had been translated into fourteen languages. Within a year of publication the figure of a million sales in Germany alone had been achieved.[2] The intensive sales campaign did not slacken: the first two thousand of the second million of the German edition were printed in Braille, and presented to blinded ex-soldiers in May 1930. By this time the number of translations had risen to twenty-three, and the total circulation, excluding pirated editions produced in Soviet Russia, Turkey, Yugoslavia, and China, was estimated to have reached three million. The Italian version was banned by Mussolini.[3] The film version which quickly followed publication obviously did nothing to harm sales, especially as the premiere in December 1930 was turned into the occasion for a curiously juvenile set-piece demonstration by the Nazis, who 'under Goebbels's leadership, led riots against the film, invaded the theatre, throwing stink bombs and letting loose mice, and finally succeeded in having the film banned' (Peter Gay, *Weimar Culture* (London, 1969), p. 137). The notoriety of the novel was a publisher's delight, and Remarque, intentionally or not, seems to have aided it by playing the part of the mystery man. He declared that he had written *Im Westen* in order to free his mind from an oppression; that he never imagined it would become famous; that he would not discuss it or supervise the filming of the story; and that he might never write again.[4] An anti-Remarque industry sprang up in the wake of the novel. In 1930 one Peter Kropp wrote a book entitled *Endlich Klarheit über Remarque und sein Buch 'Im Westen nichts Neues'* (Hamm, Westf.), and Emil Marius Requark sold twenty thousand copies of his reputedly feeble skit *Vor Troja nichts Neues* (Berlin, 1930). No doubt all this, too, was grist to the publicity mill.

Remarque certainly shows all the popular novelist's facility for smoothing the reader's path, in this case by means of a setting evoked with sufficient realism, yet not stretching the reader's imagination too much; a varied pace created by stirring events alternating with restful periods of calm (as the story progresses to its climax, action dominates increasingly); and certain easily-recognized stereotype characters. But commercial luck and acumen do not exclusively account for the success of Remarque's novel. Apart from any intrinsic merits it may have, the date of its appearance played an important part. In 1928 nearly all nations officially renounced war through the Kellogg-Briand Peace Pact. Anti-war sentiment had reached its climax. At the same time there was a tide in the psychological affairs of men that brought a renewal of interest in the Great War. The public was ready to read about it, and writers to respond. Although the legend of 'die Verspätung der

Kriegsliteratur' [the lateness of the war books] has now been substantially revised,[5] it is true to say that it was not until a decade after the end of the fighting that many writers, with a strange unanimity, began to turn their war experience into literary form. After 1927 an international crop of war books appeared. In defeated Germany it was, on the whole and for complex reasons, the writers of a pacifist disposition who were slower to make their mark. The successful early war books (e.g. those of Walter Flex and Ernst Jünger) had been predominantly 'heroic' or militarist in outlook, in contrast to the pacifism of, for example, the best-known early French products such as *Les Croix de Bois* by Roland Dorgelès (1919) and Barbusse's *Le Feu* (1916). But by 1927 the balance began to be redressed in Germany. Although war books of the Right continued to appear (and may even have received some impetus from works like *Im Westen nichts Neues*), the more pacifist novel came into its own, with Arnold Zweig's *Der Streit um den Sergeanten Grischa* (1927), Ludwig Renn's *Krieg* (1928), *Im Westen* in 1929, Theodor Plivier's *Des Kaisers Kulis* and Edlef Köppen's *Heeresbericht* (1930).

Remarque's statement that he only wrote *Im Westen* in order to free himself from an obsession has a familiar ring. There is probably little reason to doubt its sincerity.[6] So many writers struggled ten years to assimilate the war experience, and the phenomenon is one that ignores frontiers. Richard Aldington in the dedication to his *Death of a Hero* (London, 1929) reports that he began the novel immediately after the Armistice, while he was still in Belgium, but that he 'threw it aside, and never picked it up again'. He goes on to say: 'The attempt was premature. Then, ten years later, almost day for day, I felt the impulse return, and began this book' (p. ix). The preface to Edmund Blunden's *Undertones of War* (London, 1928) tells a similar tale: 'I tried once before. . . . But what I then wrote . . . was noisy with a depressing forced gaiety then very much the rage' (p. vii).

One characteristic which distinguishes Remarque's novel from the rest is the thoroughness with which he assimilated his war-obsession to fictional form. Robert Graves's experience is probably more typical. According to *Goodbye to All That* (London, 1929) Graves was haunted by daydreams of the trenches until well into 1928, and when he did write his war-book he was unable to find a fictional medium that did not seem to him a betrayal of the truth:

> I made several attempts during these years to rid myself of the poison of war memories by finishing my novel, but I had to abandon them . . . ashamed at having distorted my material with a plot, yet not sure enough of myself to retranslate it into undisguised history. (p. 410)

Graves's difficulty in finding the right fictional form for a war-book illuminates the general problem of achieving sufficient distance from experience to produce ambitious fiction, and the guilt that is associated with the attempt to do so. Almost universally, the need to wring from the war a clear moral message seems to conflict with the demands of fiction.[7] Remarque stepped in where angels feared to tread. The time was ripe for a pacifist war-book and the public was clearly grateful for the simple fictional form he created.

For *Im Westen* is undeniably fiction.[8] The novel is not autobiographical to any marked degree,[9] and it is remarkably free from the obligation to the documentary that is common to most war-books. Dates and places are hardly mentioned. The war does not fall into individual battles (Verdun, the Somme) but is a continuous undifferentiated process, like a conveyor belt. There is no indication of a strategic awareness of the hostilities as a whole, and no analysis of the causes or deeper significance of the war as a historical event, such as can be found in almost any other war-book.[10] These very limitations, we would suggest, have contributed to the novel's lasting success and universal appeal.

Remarque capitalizes on the bare *Fronterlebnis*, for the authenticity which this experience lends his novel needs no further embellishment. There is an interesting parallel with the way that Hitler's speeches and career capitalized on his front-line experience as the ultimate legitimation of his message, superseding politics, for: 'are not feelings, unlike the complexities of economics or politics, something Everyman can understand and judge and share?'[11] In these terms, lack of documentation means a *greater* authenticity in the novel, not less, and paradoxically the documentary obsession of other war-writers can be seen simply as obscuring the authenticity of their personal statements. There is very little in *Im Westen* to inhibit the reader's response; the lowest common denominator is invariably found. Paul Bäumer, the hero, though not lacking in educational background (and the conventional artistic aspirations of the *Abiturient*) deliberately assumes and even exaggerates the ignorance of the humblest ranker. Remarque reduces him totally to the passive object of official decisions. There is a great deal of popular attraction, as well as some truth, in the view of the war as a social leveller.[12] In the front line, education and class confer few advantages. There are not many other successful works which exploit this aspect of the war so thoroughly.

Among the list of well-known war-books given by George Orwell in 'Inside the Whale' (1940) we find none which adheres so strictly to the limited point of view of the private soldier as *Im Westen*.[13] The *poilus* in *Le Feu* are infinitely more sophisticated than Paul Bäumer and his friends, and have only too clear an insight into their situation. The British or American novels that Orwell mentions are written by or about officers or combatants who are officer-material (Hemingway's *A Farewell to Arms*, Graves's *Goodbye to All That*, Sassoon's *Memoirs of an Infantry Officer*, and *A Subaltern on the Somme* by 'Mark VII', i.e. Max Plowman). In comparison with other German war-books, too, Remarque's vision is severely reduced. Certainly this does not preclude discussion of the war and war-aims among his soldiers (whereas in the British books, by contrast with the continental ones, such general discussions are comparatively rare). But the discussion is vague and ill-informed, and amounts to little more than grumbling between offensives. Its naïveté emphasizes the helplessness of the serving man.

It may well be that the undocumentary vagueness that characterizes *Im Westen*, the reduction of vision to the immediate moment, was favourably received in 1929 because the essential aspects of the war which it conveys correspond quite closely to the surviving European folk-memory of trench warfare. In other words, *Im Westen* was the Great War *comme il faut*.

The structure makes few demands; it is an episodic series of anecdotes typifying the experience of the war generation as Remarque sees it: from school to basic training; the first taste of the front with a working party; the retreat to the rear; the front line again in all its horrors; the comic relief behind the lines when the hero and friends make their conquest of some local ladies; going on leave; the return to the front; being wounded, convalescent, and sent back to the fighting again; the increasing despair, apathy and perverse pride of the veteran, etc. Remarque knows how to emphasize by selection: we learn surprisingly little in detail about life in the trenches.[14] As Pfeiler pointed out, 'in a book which claims to be a report of the front by a front soldier, of 288 pages of text only about 80 pages deal with situations at or right behind the front, and even they are heavily interspersed with reflections' (p. 142). Strong emphasis is therefore thrown on to those aspects of the front which *are* mentioned, and from a documentary point of view certain exciting elements of 1914-18 warfare are dramatized unduly. There is the apparent frequency of the attacks (when much of front-line life consisted in reality of tedious and uncomfortable inactivity,[15] with the occasional patrol into no-man's-land or raid on enemy lines); there is hand-to-hand combat and the sight of the enemy dying slowly at your hands, in contrast to the dealing of death at long distance which was much more typical of the war.[16] There are the fits of berserk bloodlust that descend upon the attacker during an offensive.[17] None of the war-books avoids horrors, but Remarque heaps them up unmercifully (see the catalogue on p. 137). He is given to sensational touches and macabre effects to intensify the horrors of war: the screaming of the wounded horses (p. 66) is a sentimental and gruesome motif that became a feature of many a war-novel after *Im Westen* (see Bostock, p. 20). The first full-length description of action sets the scene in a church-yard where the hero cowers beneath a heavy artillery bombardment combined with a gas attack, while coffins fly through the air around him (p. 72). The elimination of each member of the small group of comrades by turn, until only the hero is left, is a conventional but effective technique, and the death of Bäumer at the eleventh hour, in the last days of October 1918, after he has survived the worst years of the war, is a somewhat sensational and contrived, though not impossible, dénouement.[18] The breach of narratorial discipline involved in the abrupt and unexplained change from the first person perspective and from historic present to the past tense in the final short paragraph, following Bäumer's death, is in keeping with the unself-conscious presentation of the story throughout.

Yet the book's limited vision is effective, taken on its own terms. For example, the strongly developed sense of living in the moment and the blurring of the passage of time in the trenches reflect the dehumanizing effect of a war which turned the ordinary soldier into an automaton, a part of the war-machine:

Vergehen Wochen—Monate—Jahre? Es sind nur Tage. Wir sehen die Zeit neben uns schwinden in den farblosen Gesichtern der Sterbenden, wir löffeln Nahrung in uns hinein, wir laufen, wir werfen, wir schießen, wir töten, wir liegen herum, wir Bind schwach und stumpf. . . . (p. 136)

[Is it weeks that pass—or months—or years? It is only days. We watch how time disappears before our eyes in the ashen faces of the dying, we shovel food into ourselves, we run, we throw, we shoot, we kill, we hurl ourselves down, we are weak and dulled. . . .]

It suits Remarque to depict his heroes as 'puny creatures at the mercy of inhuman technology'.[19] The point becomes clear if we compare almost any other war-books and the relative sovereignty of their heroes.

For officers on both sides, relief from the front was much easier to achieve than for other ranks (although, of course, the casualty rate among officers was much higher). It is not surprising then to find that in the British books the hero still has to some degree a sense of being master of his own fate.[20] The same holds true for Jünger in *In Stahlgewittern* (for example, p. 75). But the sharpness of this contrast signifies more than a mere discussion of rank: it reminds us that *Im Westen* is a novel of Weimar Germany. Commentators have noted that in the last years of Weimar the individual became fully aware of his limited freedom of action in the face of social, industrial and political forces. Egon Schwarz sees the expression of this loss of identity as the chief function of *Neue Sachlichkeit* literature, namely 'das Augenmerk auf jene gigantischen und doch im Verborgenen wirkenden Kräfte zu richten, denen gegenfiber die Bewegungsfreiheit des Einzelnen zu einer *quantité négligeable* zusammengeschrumpft war' ['to focus upon that gigantic but nevertheless concealed force, in the face of which the freedom of action of an individual had shrunk to a *quantité négligeable*'].[21] The war in its later phase, the *Materialschlacht*, is highly symbolic of the mass industrial age voraciously devouring men and materials in a self-perpetuating system.[22]

In *Im Westen* this statement is always implicit, however, never enshrined in formal political utterances which might deter the reader. The characters of *Im Westen*, like so many created by the pacifist wing of *Neue Sachlichkeit*, are apolitical. The novel presents a very generalized pacifism, not a detailed programme but something akin to a pious wish for international amity, unlikely to arouse much resistance. Even then, the pacifism is diluted (certainly when compared to *Le Feu*!). After spending a night of profound penitence pinned down in a shell crater with the body of the Frenchman he has killed in hand-to-hand combat, Bäumer makes the dead man a promise he knows even at the time he cannot keep:

Aber wenn ich davonkomme, Kamerad, will ich kämpfen gegen dieses, das uns beide zerschlug: dir das Leben—und mir—? Auch das Leben. Ich verspreche es dir, Kamerad. Es darf nie wieder geschehen. (p. 225)

[But if I get out of all this, pal, I'll fight against the things that wrecked it for both of us; your life, and my—? Yes, my life too. I promise you, pal, it must never happen again.]

These thoughts, like a reversion to prayer in moments of danger, can be dismissed when 'normal' conditions are resumed.

Bäumer is kind to the Russian prisoners of war in his charge, and at one point his thoughts dwell on the process by which international treaties artificially create hostility between private citizens of different nations who bear each other no personal grudge (p. 194). But the front line is no place for such thoughts and they are banished to the margin for the duration: 'hier darf ich nicht weiterdenken. Dieser Weg geht in den Abgrund' ['I mustn't think along those lines any more. That path leads to the abyss']. No doubt the implication is that the 1929 reader should be taking up this cause. Such pacifism seems today utterly banal.[23] The emotional appeal is simple and commits no one to action or the sacrifice of his personal interests. It even exists comfortably alongside the thrill of battle, the pride of the veteran soldier, and the assertion of Germany's undefeated military efficiency 'wir Bind nicht geschlagen, denn wir Bind als Soldaten besser und erfahrener' ['We haven't been defeated, because as soldiers we are better and more experienced'] (p. 280). For many Germans in 1929, this must have offered a very acceptable package to fill (however momentarily) the moral vacuum experienced by the Weimar generation.[24] The message is delivered with a fervency which contrasts with its innocuous content:

Mein Herz klopft: ist hier das Ziel, das Große, das Einmalige, an das ich im Graben gedacht habe, das ich suchte als Daseinsmoglichkeit nach dieser Katastrophe aller Menschlichkeit, ist es eine Aufgabe für das Leben nachher, würdig der Jahre des Grauens? (p. 194)

[My heart is pounding. Could this be the goal, the greatness, the unique experience that I thought about in the trenches, that I was seeking as a reason to go on living after this universal catastrophe is over? Is this the task we must dedicate our lives to after the war, so that all the years of horror will have been worthwhile?]

The very modesty of Remarque's pacifism, such as it is, is highly appropriate to the nature of Weimar society, which, for all its cultural and artistic ferment, had in the main few ambitions in the direction of radical reform, and sought security rather than political revolution.

In the same way that Remarque discovers a formula that promises the least possible resistance to the idealistic content of his novel, so does he attempt to represent the fate of a whole generation through characters whose individuality is minimal. Jost Hermand has rightly remarked that Paul Bäumer is 'eine genau durchdachte Typisierung' ['a type which has been precisely thought through'] who, despite the apparently individualized treatment, has no 'psychologisch erfaßbare Privaterlebnisse' ['psychologically identifiable private experiences'] (*Die sogenannten zwanziger Jahre*, p. 223). He is the Everyman subsumed in the first person plural of Erich Kästner's poem on the lost generation, 'Jahrgang 1899' (Remarque was born in 1898):

> Wir haben der Welt in die Schnauze geguckt,
> anstatt mit Puppen zu spielen.
> Wir haben der Welt auf die Weste gespuckt,
> soweit wir vor Ypern nicht fielen

Man hat unsern Körper und hat unsern Geist
ein wenig zu wenig gekräftigt.
Man hat uns zu lange, zu früh und zumeist
mit der Weltgeschichte beschäftigt!

[We looked the world in the teeth
rather than playing with dolls.
We spat on the world's jacket
insofar as we weren't killed at Ypres.

Our bodies and our souls
were offered a trifle too little support.
What we were given was history—
for too long, too early, and too much.]

Pfeiler points out (p. 142) that the factual evidence (the war-letters of students, the work of Walter Flex, etc.) shows that Remarque's heroes are not truly representative of a whole generation, but only of a certain type. But what may not be quite true of the war generation may be more appropriate to Weimar Germany, its despair and loss of direction. Remarque's tendency to claim homogeneity for his generation conforms to the well-known collectivism, 'der Zug ins Kollektivierende' [the urge towards collectivism] (*Die sogenannten zwanziger Jahre*, p. 214) that characterizes Weimar Germany and its literature which, in the latter phase, tends towards the panoramic reflection of mass culture. (Examples are war-novels like Arnold Zweig's *Der Streit um den Sergeanten Grischa*, and Ludwig Renn's *Krieg*; factory-novels like Erik Reger's *Union der festen Hand* (1931); metropolitan novels like Dublin's *Berlin Alexanderplatz* (1929); novels of the Depression like Leonhard Frank's *Von drei Millionen drei* (1932), etc.; compare *Die sogenannten zwanziger Jahre*, p. 216.) By contrast, the society that is reflected in the British war-books—both that of 1914-18 and that of the late twenties and thirties—is clearly intact and unified to a degree un-

---

known in Weimar Germany. For that reason, the heroes are too individ-ualistic and too wrapped up in the intensity of their own private experi-ence to consider themselves as part of a collective called a 'generation'.[25]

Remarque's generation is the one that was just old enough at the be-ginning of the war to go straight from school into the trenches. Its expe-rience, Remarque claims, is more shattering, its fate more pathetic than that of others slightly older or slightly younger (the former had already established the basis of an existence before the war, the latter escaped the same total exposure to it). In other war novels, characters are re-vealed, and perhaps warped, but not, as in *Im Westen*, entirely formed by the war situation. For Remarque's youngsters the war is a total ex-perience, it is *the* experience (again we are reminded of Hitler's speeches) which imprints itself on a *tabula rasa*. War becomes the only point of reference in a world that is otherwise totally incomprehensi-ble. This sensational and monumental totality may be another source of the appeal of *Im Westen*. But it is interesting to speculate also what part of its appeal, in Germany at any rate, was due to its continuation of the theme of rebellion of the school-pupil against a rigid and despotic, but essentially hollow caste of pedagogues. Wedekind's *Frühlings Erwachen* or Robert Musil's *Törless*, Thomas Mann's *Buddenbrooks* or Heinrich Mann's *Professor Unrat* reveal the moral bankruptcy which the German pedagogue disguised in a zealous rectitude. There is a whole generation of *Schulromane* contemporary with *Im Westen*, such as Walter Harich's *Die Primaner* (1931), Franz Werfel's *Abituriententag*, Ernst Glaeser's *Jahrgang 1902* (1928), and Friedrich Torberg's *Der Schüler Gerber hat absolviert* (1930), which explore the betrayal of the 'lost generation' by its elders. The picture of the educational failure of the pre-war German schools that emerges is a dual one: on the one hand the pupil was overburdened by the sheer weight of subject-mat-ter, so that the problem of examinations assumed monstrous propor-tions; on the other, despite lip-service to a fine old tradition of *Bildung*, German schools were austere places of instruction rather than of education in the wider English sense, and the efficient Prussian autocracy of the Hohenzollerns gave rise to the conception of an efficient citizen-subject, well instructed, obedient, trustworthy, and a loyal instrument of the state.

In *Im Westen* the old culture collapses at the first shot: 'Das erste Trommelfeuer zeigte uns unseren Irrtum, und unter ihm stürzte die Weltanschauung zusammen, die sie uns gelehrt hatten' [Our first experience of heavy artillery fire showed us our mistake, and the view of life that their teaching had given us fell to pieces under that bombardment] (p. 18). If we compare the British war-books we see that the manly, anti-intellectual and games-centred ethos of the English public school could be transferred with great ease to the front-line situation. There is a verse by R. E. Vernède which neatly expresses the point:

> Lad, with the merry smile and the eyes
> Quick as a hawk's and clear as the day,
> You who have counted the game the prize,
> Here is the game of games to play.
> Never a goal—the captains say—
> Matches the one that's needed now:
> Put the old blazer and cap away—
> England's colours await your brow.[26]

One public-school quality in particular, the phlegmatic self-control implied in the understatement of Blunden's title, *Undertones of War*, was undoubtedly useful in a static war of attrition.[27]

German *Bildung* (as reflected in *Im Westen* and other works) is more pretentious in its claims, based on precept rather than example, divorced from everyday practicality, and (in the worst sense) idealized. In *Im Westen* the effect of a brutal confrontation with the reality of warfare is that all established values are immediately wiped out. *Bildung*, with its strong insistence on respect for authority, is revealed as a preparation for slaughter. The adolescents reply by creating a kind of alternative society. Moral law is rewritten on the battlefield. If a badly wounded man is going to die in any case and is suffering unbearable agony, the question is whether one is justified in shooting him for mercy's sake, and the answer is yes (though it remains a hypothetical answer).[28] The old rules are now irrelevant, like the academic education of the pre-war German schools. Other rules are developed, such as that which forbids a saw edge on one's bayonet, for fear of an unpleasant death at the hands of the enemy if one is captured. A new practical education for survival is required, like a grotesque parody of Baden-Powell's *Scouting for Boys*: you must not only know how to light a fire with wet wood, but also how to stick the enemy with your bayonet without getting it irretrievably fixed.

Despite the pacifist message, much of this must inevitably contain a certain glamour for the youthful mind. By the same token, much of the novel exploits the attractions of a juvenile rude gesture to the adult world. The greatest bliss behind the lines is a communal visit to the latrines in one-man open cabins drawn into a sociable circle (p. 13). 'Dem Soldaten ist sein Magen und seine Verdauung ein vertrauteres Gebiet als jedem anderen Menschen. Dreiviertel seines Wortschatzes sind ihm entnommen . . . Unsere Familien und unsere Lehrer werden sich schön wundern, wenn wir nach Hause kommen. . . .' ['A soldier is on much closer terms with his stomach and digestive system than anyone else is. Three-quarters of his vocabulary comes from this area. . . . Our families and our teachers will be pretty surprised when we get home.'] (p. 14). Nothing is more important than eating, drinking, and sleeping. It was long ago pointed out that there is a good deal of juvenile wish-fulfilment in *Im Westen*.[29] The revulsion against authority is concentrated on two symbolic figures, the schoolmaster Kantorek, who patriotically inspires his whole class to enlist, and Corporal Himmelstoss, a postman in civilian life, who sadistically persecutes his recruits in their early army training. (It is significant that the limits of military authority encountered in the book are set for the most part at N.C.O. level: once again there is the avoidance of wider issues such as class-friction—contrast *Erziehung vor Verdun*—or the efficiency of the command, a question raised as a matter of course in many of the British works.)

Acting as convenient foci for the resentment of Bäumer's generation, these two men are discussed and hated throughout the book, and their ultimate defeat is lingered over with affection. In the case of Himmelstoss, victory comes in three installments, culminating in the corporal's final humiliation on the field of battle, where by a satisfying reversal of roles the boy-heroes are now the veterans and Himmelstoss the novice. The process of revenge takes us up to page 135, and only after the last drop of enjoyment has been wrung from the theme does the humiliation of the schoolmaster Kantorek take over to maintain this line of interest. He is reduced (like Professor Unrat) to a wreck, by the very methods applied by Himmelstoss against the boys themselves in basic training. But there are indications of the self-destructiveness of such a revenge-obsession for the adolescent mind. The child who apparently takes a delight in destroying the authority set over him is basically disturbed by his inability to put anything in its place. Here we touch on a theme central to Remarque's book and possibly central to the German experience of the destructiveness unleashed by the war: the vacuum that is left in the place of a discredited authority, and the unbearable responsibility for one's own future, cause a suffering as great as the physical horrors of war. If the lessons learnt at school do not apply at the front, it is equally true that the war has filled Remarque's soldiers with a knowledge that will alienate them totally from civilian life.

Appropriately, in view of the later course of German history, a sense of post-war purpose is conceived in no other terms but those of aggression against somebody or something. Most revealing of conditions in Germany in 1929 is the picture of resurrection after the war (p. 143). The dead will march alongside the survivors to a new goal, but the vision collapses on the question, 'Marching? Against whom?'—'gegen wen'? The heroes' youthful antics can be seen as desperate attempts to

assert individual freedom of action within a condition of total helplessness, which in turn could serve as a paradigm for the plight of the individual drawn along in the career-course of political developments in
Weimar Germany.

In the war situation individuality is suspended; in *Im Westen* this
point is made directly through the sheer size of military operations,
demonstrated by terrible statistics and the masterly organization required to keep the war going.[30] Indirectly, at the moment of death, loss
of individuality is sketched in with reminders of particular human personalities, about to be obliterated for ever. Remarque's warriors have a
kind of typical individualism, as inalienable from them as a finger-
print and just as unremarkable. As annihilation threatens, one token
characteristic serves as a reminder of the individuality which has been
forfeited in war: 'Leer . . . verblutet rasch, niemand kann ihm helfen . . .
Was nützt es ihm nun, daß er in der Schule ein so guter Mathematiker
war' ['Leer . . . bleeds to death very quickly and no-one can help him . . .
What use is it to him now that he was so good at mathematics at
school?'] (p. 278). Of another dying comrade, Kemmerich, it is said,
'Zigaretten konnte er nicht vertragen' [he could never stand ciga-
rettes] (p. 34). The situation which, rationally speaking, makes nonsense of individuality, in fact emphasizes the value of individual existence. (Hitler, too, was able to turn the helplessness of the 'armes
Frontschwein' ['poor bloody infantry'] into a validation of existence.)
Modern man, who *knows* his own individuality despite all the evidence
of his reduction to collective anonymity, will be quick to take the point
Remarque is making. In battle, the threat of death heightens the sense
of individual life unbearably. Remarque injects a strong sensuality into
the determination to survive, and much of the appeal of the novel is
surely drawn from this vitality. There is an almost ecstatic feeling for
the earth itself as the soldier under fire attempts to fuse himself with it
(p. 59). Again and again after the trenches the hunger for life is reborn.
When the hero returns home on leave, his personal likes and dislikes
suddenly become important again. The contrast with the impersonality

of the front is too much for him, and he breaks down into a childish weakness. The war and his insignificance in the face of its vastness have literally been brought home to him.

Just as the sensation of threatened individuality is an experience common to the trenches and to life in Weimar Germany (though of course with a difference of acuteness), so the attempt at a solution, too, is shared. In *Im Westen, Kameradschaft* is raised to the level of a cult: and for many suffering from the dissensions, the lack of social cohesion, and the bewildering political diversity of Weimar, the comradeship of the war was indeed the object of a cult, especially for those at the extreme ends of the political spectrum. From the example of the moderate Remarque, however, it can be seen that extremes meet on this territory:

> Der Krieg hatte . . . die Erfahrung einer realen Gemeinschaft gebracht. für einen großen Teil der Soldaten war these 'Kameradschaft' Lebensbasis geworden. Im Nachkriegsdeutschland, in dem wieder jeder auf sich gewiesen blieb, unter wirtschaftlich and politisch schwierigen Bedingungen, sehnten sich viele nach der Sicherheit der 'Kameradschaft' zurück, bauten sogar ihre Staatsvorstellung auf dem Verlangen nach ihr auf.[31]

> [The war brought in the experience of a real community. For a large proportion of the soldiers, this "comradeship" became their whole basis for living. In Germany after the war, where everyone had to rely again on themselves in economically and socially difficult conditions, many longed to get the security of that "comradeship" back, and even constructed their views of the state upon the demand for it.]

(This theme is taken up specifically in Remarque's own later novel *Der Weg zurück* (Berlin, 1931).) In *Im Westen* comradeship reaches an almost mystic intensity, to which is added a measure of adolescent hero-worship in Bäumer's reverence for his older comrade and mentor, 'Kat'. (There is even a hint of latent adolescent homosexuality, for example in the disappointment in women experienced by the hero after his first sexual encounter, which implicitly serves merely to reinforce his love of his comrades (p. 155); yet the disillusionment with females has an adolescent illogicality, too, since the women concerned are bought for the price of a loaf of bread, and their status as consumer objects is brought out by the pre-war advertising poster depicting a desirable young lady, which first whets the comrades' appetite for female company.)

Parallels to this *Kameradschaft*-cult are hard to find in the British war-books. It is clear that in *Im Westen*, *Kameradschaft* bears the full weight of the soldiers' frustrated potential for idealism. Once again, the observation is as appropriate to Weimar as it is to Remarque's war.

Because of his characters' total immersion in war and lack of counterbalancing experience, Remarque clearly feels the need to supply certain safety valves to take off the pressure for his reader. Apart from the *Galgenhumor* of the troops, the main source of relief is the novel's overt sentimentality, as in the treatment of the hero's dying mother (Chapter 8; also p. 198) and the passage in which Bäumer describes himself as 'ein kleiner Soldat in der Frühe' [a little soldier in the early morning] (p. 101). Before dismissing the latter as part of Remarque's bid for popular success, it would be apposite to remember that the novel conforms in this respect, as in so many others, to a characteristic tendency of *Neue Sachlichkeit*, described by Siegfried Kracauer in his influential book *Die Angestellten*: 'Nicht schlagender könnte sich das Geheimnis der neuen Sachlichkeit enthüllen. . . . Nur einen Schritt in die Tiefe, und man weilt mitten in der üppigsten Sentimentalität' ['The secret of the New Objectivity could not be revealed more strikingly. . . . Just one step in, and there you are, right in the middle of the most florid sentimentality.'].[32] Kracauer puts his finger on a 'popular' element which *Im Westen* possesses in good measure. But in the Weimar context sentimentality can be seen as a deliberate flouting of the pre-war aesthetic canon in the interests of democracy, related to the attack of *Neue Sachlichkeit* on authority in general.

Furthermore, in pragmatic terms, sentiment travels better than all but the best profundity. This brings us to the international, as against the internal, success of *Im Westen*. Partly it can be explained in rather crude terms: the novel represented the German soldier as a human being. In 1929 Germany was still an enigma to the outside world, and therefore an object of fear. By 1929 the British at least were beginning to try to understand their former enemies, to look for the common denominator and the definition of some area of agreement upon elementary and indisputable facts. The novel was increasingly regarded as a way of understanding the Germans, and by 1929 there was (in complete contrast to the pre-war dearth of translations) a score or so of German novelists whose work could be sampled in English.[33] None was as successful as Remarque in establishing the common denominator. One wonders, in fact, what part was played by this one book alone in creating that willingness to give the Germans one more chance to show that they were, after all, *human*, which ultimately led to Munich. Remarque may, in other words, have been influential in lulling his foreign readership into a false sense of security.

Remarque's novel possesses an unemphatic internationalism, largely by virtue of what it does *not* say.[34] It sets up few barriers to acceptance in translation. This is not to say that it is in any sense an un-German book: it accurately reflects, as we have seen, German pride of arms as well as certain aspects of Weimar society. But, for example, no chauvinism is apparent in attitudes to the enemy. Indeed, no attitude is apparent except the practical kill-or-be-killed approach which survival dictates. The other side is simply 'die drüben' [those over there]: rarely is the nationality of the opposing troops identified.[35] The shadowiness of the enemy contributes to the impersonality of Remarque's war, but at the same time it offers no hindrance to the willingness of a wide international readership to identify itself with Bäumer and his comrades. Even the aspects of trench life which are specifically German will tend to increase the sympathy of the foreign reader, rather than stand in its way. The German soldier (see p. 40) was far worse fed and worse supplied than his Allied counterpart. At one point we are told that the corned beef and butter and white bread to be captured in the Allied trenches are now the major reason for pressing forward to the attack, and no one will fail to understand a half-starved man in the front line who attacks to eat (p. 121). Even the claim put forward by Remarque's narrator that Germany was not defeated, but simply overwhelmed by the Allies' wealth of men and material, need not have the effect of alienating the non-German reader, since it is a fair statement of well-known facts,[36] and a corrective to the dangerous contemporary propaganda, the so-called *Dolchstoßlegende*, which holds that Germany could have won but for the treachery of her politicians.

In the lack of differentiation of attitudes to enemy soldiers we strike against one of the limits of Remarque's documentation. Discussion of such matters certainly took place in all armies and is a commonplace in most other war-books.[37] But whatever the reason for the failure to record some aspects of the war, the result is to increase the universality of the book's appeal. The analysis of German civilian society is equally undelineated (apart from Remarque's obvious hatred of the medical profession). The nature of Weimar society (artistic and cultural life apart) being essentially conservative, Remarque's German readers would not in any case have thanked him for an analysis which specifically demanded changes in their own social arrangements. His social criticism is confined almost entirely to exceptional wartime conditions and lacks any kind of *Appellcharakter*, or demand for action. There is the familiar lack of comprehension of the civilian for the front-line soldier, to be found in the majority of First World War books. There is the hatred of *Etappenschweine* and non-combatant soldiers. There is the sentiment, heartily endorsed in other war-books by veterans of both sides, that 'the wrong people are fighting here' (p. 46). There is bitter criticism of the people sitting safely at home talking of the need for a breakthrough. Equally familiar, and even more bitter, there is criticism of the industrialists growing fat on the profits of the war. The title of the novel itself, strikingly echoed in Aldington's *Death of a Hero* (pp. 323,

353), is equally international, encapsulating as it does the soldiers' awareness of the loss of interest among those at home as the war settles down into an 'uneventful' stalemate ('all quiet on the Western Front' is the familiar newspaper report of the later war years). Tacitly it suggests the solidarity of the fighting man in all armies against his real enemy, the civilian authority and civilian society—including the soldier's own family—in so far as it supports authority; which, in general, it blindly does. (See the 'Nutwood Manor' section of Sassoon's *Memoirs of an Infantry Officer* for an example of the complete gulf between the front-line soldier and the society of which he was formerly a complaisant member.)

Towards the end of *Im Westen* (p. 286) the moral collapse of authority becomes so obvious to the soldier—and here the German experience is closer to the French than to the British—that there is vague talk of making an end to the war and of revolution of an unspecified nature. This belongs mainly to the experience of the losing side, of course. It is a feature which, like Remarque's pacifism, can have done little to disturb the equilibrium of the average bourgeois reader. It is an illogicality, but a very human one, that even if we concede that war is meaningless at any time, it appears infinitely less meaningful when defeat becomes inevitable. Though in rational terms pacifism is more convincing in the victor, it is emotionally more acceptable in the defeated.

Im Westen nichts Neues comes close to being all things to all men. It is a pacifist novel, yet it could be seen and has been seen as a glorification of the German soldier and of the war.[38] The war was distant enough in 1929 to be discussed and thought about again; and yet it was not decent for it to be depicted without reservation as heroic and exemplary. One can imagine that the pacifist framework of *Im Westen* salved the conscience of the crypto-militarist or the prurient reader reliving the horrors of 1914-18. Looking at the book in a different perspective, however, we see that through its democratic interest in the small man whom the war devours, the novel says a good deal about Germany in the late twenties. Indeed, since the society of Weimar Germany, of which it was a product, was a forcing-ground for many developments of twentieth-century European society, the very indebtedness of the book to its origins may have helped to make it something of a monument, and contributed to its lasting reputation.

Notes

1. See J. Knight Bostock, *Some Well-Known German War Novels 1914-30* (Oxford, 1931), p. 3.

2. See D. R. Richards, *The German Best Seller in the Twentieth Century* (Berne, 1968), p. ii.

3. Bostock, p. 3.

4. See '*All Quiet on the Western Front*, Why it was written. Interview with Erich Remarque', *The Observer*, 13 October 1929, pp. 17-18; and also 'The End of War? A Correspondence between the Author of *All Quiet on the Western Front* and General Sir Ian Hamilton, G.C.S., G.C.M.G.', *Life and Letters* (edited by Desmond MacCarthy) 3 (November, 1929), 399-408. In the *Observer* interview, Remarque supplied a colourful list of his varied activities after the war, which can only have increased the mystery surrounding him: among other things, he was a sporting journalist, a pedlar, an agent for a monumental mason, and organist in a lunatic asylum.

5. See Walter Schiffels, 'Formen historischen Erzahlens in den zwanziger Jahren', in *Die deutsche Literatur in der Weimarer Republik*, edited by Wolfgang Rothe (Stuttgart, 1974), pp. 204, 208.

6. But Bostock (p. 4), who is very sceptical about Remarque's integrity, finds almost all his statements suspect, 'too conventional to be quite genuine'.

7. On the whole, First World War books are most successful when they are autobiographical and documentary, and most of the authors can easily be identified with their narrators: Ludwig Renn in *Krieg* and Peter Riss in *Stahlbad Anno 17* even give their heroes their own names (in Renn's case his *nom de plume*). Very few successful fictional treatments of war themes come to mind. Richard Aldington's literary quality in *Death of a Hero* certainly does not lie in his plot or his characterization. The success of his novel as a best-seller of 1929 must surely have been due to its descriptive and documentary qualities; the disclaimer in his dedication ('this book is not the work of a professional novelist') is borne out by the quality of the fiction. Likewise, C. E. Montague's novel *Rough Justice* is embarrassing as war-fiction, whereas the same author's documentary *Disenchantment* (1922) is one of the most powerful of all literary indictments of the war. Arnold Zweig's *Erziehung vor Verdun* (1935), which is more exclusively concerned with an account of front-line fighting than his

Der Streit um den Sergeanten Grischa (1927), suffers as fiction from looseness of structure.

8. William K. Pfeiler makes the same observation as a negative criticism of Remarque, thus illustrating the general suspicion of fictionality in war-books: '. . . it may be characteristic [of *Im Westen*] that the actual life at the front is described in general terms without ever a definite location given, while scenes behind the front, at hospitals, at home, in the barracks etc., are given in a more clearly outlined realism. The implication is obvious; *it leaves little doubt that many of his situations are fictitious*' (my italics): *War and the German Mind: The Testimony of Men of Fiction who Fought at the Front* (New York, 1941), p. 142.

9. This is not to deny that Remarque had indeed been at the front. As he said in the *Observer* interview (see note 4 to p. 359 above), 'the details of my book are real experiences, in spite of all the rumours to the contrary, which I will not take the trouble to contradict. I was at the Front long enough to have experienced personally just nearly all I have described. I was wounded twice. . . .' The rumours were obviously provoked, however, by the general and typical quality of Remarque's observations about the front. Furthermore, it is understandable that Remarque was defensive about his frontline experience, for there is some evidence that it was not very broad. According to Kropp (see p. 360 above) Remarque received a slight wound in the leg, and when it had healed he became a clerk in the hospital (Bostock, pp. 5-6).

10. See for example the division of the war into three phases in Ernst Jünger's *In Stahlgewittern* (1920): *Werke, Tagebücher* 1 (Stuttgart, 1960), p. 78.

11. J. P. Stern, *Hitler: The Führer and the People* (London, 1975), p. 26.

12. See *Im Westen nichts Neues*, first edition (Berlin, 1929), pp. 266-7. All subsequent page references are to this edition.

13. One of the few records of the war by a genuine other-ranker is Frank Richards's *Old Soldiers Never Die*, described by Robert Graves, who sponsored its publication, as 'the only veracious and unvarnished record of the First World War by a regular private soldier—twelve years with the Colours'.

14. Compare other war-books: Graves, Blunden, or Jünger (e.g. pp. 56-8 of *In Stahlgewittern*). We also learn very little from Remarque about the sufferings of the alien civilian population, a lack which is surprising in a supposedly pacifist novel whose hero is based for three years on occupied territory. Once again, it forms a contrast to Jünger's *In Stahlgewittern*, where there is frequent and sympathetic mention of the French civilians (e.g. pp. 190, 221). See also Arnold Zweig's *Erziehung vor Verdun* (1935; new edition, Berlin and Weimar, 1974), p. 76.

15. Compare Jünger, *In Stahlgewittern*: 'Statt der erhofften Gefahren hatten wir Schmutz, Arbeit und schlaflose Nächte vorgefunden, deren Bezwingung ein uns wenig liegendes Heldentum erforderte. Schlimmer noch war die Langeweile, die für den Soldaten entnervender als die Nähe des Todes ist' [Instead of the dangers we had hoped for we got pain, hard work and sleepless nights, and overcoming them called up a kind of heroism that didn't mean much to us. What was worse was the boredom, which for a soldier is more damaging than the closeness of death.] (p. 19). See also p. 189: 'Wieder machte ich die Erfahrung, daß kein Artilleriefeuer die Widerstandskraft so gründlich zu brechen vermag wie Nässe und Kälte' [Once again I

discovered that no artillery fire is as good at breaking down your resistance as the cold and the wet].

16. See C. E. Montague, *Rough Justice* (London, 1926): 'not many men died by the bayonet, in the whole of the war' (p. 340), and his *Disenchantment* (London, 1922), p. 157. Also Aldington's *Death of a Hero*, (London, 1929), p. 292: 'The fighting was so impersonal that it seemed rather a conflict with the dreadful hostile forces of Nature than with other men. . . . Actual hand-to-hand fighting occurred, but it was comparatively rare. It was a war of missiles, murderous and soul-shaking explosives, not a war of hand-weapons'.

17. Compare *In Stahlgewittern*, where Jünger reports of an attack: 'Der ungeheure Vernichtungswille . . . verdichtete sich in den Gehirnen und tauchte sie in rote Nebel ein' [The monstrous will to annihilate . . . settled itself in our brains and filled them with red mist] (p. 250). If this phenomenon was known on the British side, it has left very little record in the war-books, though we certainly find the same fighting fury in Barbusse's novel *Le Feu*. C. E. Montague specifically takes Barbusse to task for what he calls the 'doctrinaire fire' which makes the Frenchman pervert and exaggerate the 'thrill of drastic passion' (*Disenchantment*, p. 52). This response is typical of British writers' reaction to Barbusse's 'lack of restraint'! For Montague, the offensive is usually characterized by bathos, confusion, muddle, and 'the queer flashes of revelation, in contact with individual enemies, of the bottomless falsity of the cheaper kind of current war psychology' (p. 53).

18. Aldington's novel ends on the same note: in the very last days of the war, the hero practically throws his life away.

19. See Helmut Gruber, 'Neue Sachlichkeit and the World War', *GLL*, 20 (1967), 139.

20. Officers were frequently seconded from the front for special courses of instruction: see Edmund Blunden, *Undertones of War* (London, 1928), p. 251: 'It was wonderful to be promised an exeat from war for weeks, but I . . . felt as usual the injustice of my own temporary escape . . .'. Blunden is eventually blessed with six months' duty at a training centre in England, which effectively takes him out of the war altogether. Sherston in *Memoirs of an Infantry Officer*, recovering from a wound in the protective hospitality of Nutwood Manor, has the choice of taking an army job in England rather than returning to the front for the third time. Graves is offered a similar choice: 'In December I attended a medical board. . . . The president wanted to know whether I wanted a few months more home service' (*Goodbye to All That* (London 1929), p. 293).

21. See *Die sogenannten zwanziger Jahre*, edited by Reinhold Grimm and Jost Hermand (Bad Homburg, 1970) p. 139.

22. That the war can be seen in quite a different light is demonstrated by Ernst Jünger, who stresses the scope for individualism granted to an officer in wartime: 'Eines der Vorrechte des Führers liegt darin, daß er in dieser Zeit der Massenbewegung allein gehen darf' ['One of the rights afforded to a leader is that in this time of mass movement, he is permitted to walk alone'] (*Das Wäldchen* 125, in *Werke, Tagebücher* I, p. 371). Much closer to Remarque's tone is Arnold Zweig's version of war as an expression of the industrial society continued by other means: 'Die Infanteristen hier . . . sahen aus wie die abgetriebenen Herden des Todes, Fabrikarbeiter der Zerstörung; sie

hatten alle die Gleichgültigkeit, die Industrie und Maschine dem Menschen auf-pressen' ['The infantrymen here . . . looked like the driven herds of death, factory workers of destruction; they all had the same indifference which industry and machin-ery forces upon the human being.'] (*Erziehung vor Verdun*, p. 174).

23. Yet we should bear in mind the violent response of many Germans to this harm-less message at the time of the novel's appearance.

24. The sense of a vacuum manifested itself particularly in the search for a myth (in the broadest sense) by which to live: see the use of the term 'leerstehende Struktur' to express the post-war receptivity to myth in Germany, in Theodor Ziolkowski's essay 'Der Hunger nach dem Mythos', in *Die sogenannten zwanziger Jahre*, p. 198; and compare the term 'Leerformel' in Hans Schuhmacher's 'Mythisierende Tendenzen in der Literatur 1918-1933', in *Die deutsche Literatur in der Weimarer Republik*, p. 286.

25. However, the stereotyped Oedipal aspect of this generation-bitterness is found, exceptionally, in the words of Winterbourne in *Death of a Hero*: 'He resented it, re-sented it bitterly, but the doom was on him as on all the young men. When "we" had de-termined that they should be killed, it was impious to demur' (p. 259).

26. See 'The Call', in *War Poems and Other Verses* (London, 1917), p. 32.

27. The public-school 'stiff upper lip' and leadership qualities are personified in Ev-ans, the brave but rather limited archetypal British officer in *Death of a Hero*: 'Evans possessed that British rhinoceros equipment of mingled ignorance, self-confidence, and complacency which is triple-armed against all the shafts of the mind. . . . He was exasperatingly stupid, but he was honest, he was kindly, he was conscientious, he could obey orders and command obedience in others, he took pains to look after his men. He could be implicitly relied upon to lead a hopeless attack and to maintain a des-perate defence to the very end. There were thousands and tens of thousands like him' (p. 331).

28. Bostock objects to this faint-heartedness in Remarque: 'it was weak . . . to let Katczinsky be interrupted when on the point of putting the mortally wounded man out of his pain' (p. 8).

29. Karl Hugo Sclutius, 'Pazifistische Kriegspropaganda', *Die Weltbühne*, 25 (2 April 1929), 517, quoted in Gruber, p. 146. What could be finer (as Sclutius points out) than going for weeks without washing, and bouts of Gargantuan feasting?

30. See, for example, p. 260. Both Aldington and Remarque use what is essentially the same motif to characterize the war-machine: their soldiers note the crosses or cof-fins stacked ready for use after the battle. See *Im Westen*, p. 102, and *Death of a Hero*, p. 359.

31. Wolfgang Wendler, 'Die Einschatzung der Gegenwart im deutschen Zeit-roman', *Die deutsche Literatur in der Weimarer Republik*, p. 173. Significantly, one positive aspect of the war to emerge for the hero Bertin in Arnold Zweig's *Erziehung vor Verdun* is the integration of German society; a sad irony on the part of the novel's Jewish author. See p. 174, and especially p. 176.

32. New edition (Allensbach and Bonn, 1959), p. 90.

33. See the *Times Literary Supplement*, 18 April 1929, Recent German Literature Number (appearing in the very week of publication of *Im Westen* in English transla-

tion!). The leading article in the special number concerns itself with the 'German Enigma'. See also p. xx, 'Some Novels and Novelists'.

34. Remarque does not, for example, reproduce war-time German propaganda against the enemy. Official propaganda as reported in the novel is more concerned to lie about the high morale of the German troops in the field than to smear the other side (p. 142).

35. A rare exception occurs on p. 115: 'Wir erkennen die verzerrten Gesichter, die flachen Helme, es sind Franzosen' [We recognize the distorted faces, the flat helmets—they are French]. Jünger, by contrast, is punctilious to a fault in identifying the opposing troops: 'An den englischen Mützenschildern stellten wir an diesem Tage fest, daß uns das Regiment Hindostan-Leincestershire [sic] gegenüberlag' [That we were able to tell from the English cap-badges that it was the Hinostan-Leicestershire Regiment that was facing us] (In Stahlgewittern, p. 65).

36. Compare Graves, Goodbye to All That: 'Now that the war was over and the German armies had been beaten, it was possible to give the German soldier credit for being the best fighting-man in Europe. I often heard it said that it was only the blockade that had beaten them; that in Haig's last push they never really broke, and that their machine-gun sections had held us up for as long as was needed for the withdrawal of the main forces' (p. 363).

37. See, for example, Graves, p. 241: 'Newspaper libels on Fritz's courage and efficiency were resented by all trench-soldiers of experience.'

38. Bostock (p. 9) reports that 'one reviewer thought it was subtle propaganda in favour of militarism'. Remarque himself was so well aware of the seductiveness of his theme that he felt obliged to make Paul Bäumer die, because otherwise 'people might have said, "What an interesting time this young Bäumer had. . . ." That would have made war seem a great adventure. And war really is a great adventure—when one comes back again' (The Observer, 13 October 1929, p. 18).

Memory

Modris Eksteins

We who have known war must never forget war. And that is why I have a picture of a soldier's corpse nailed to the door of my library.

—Harry Crosby

Soyons, à notre tour, le printemps qui reverdit les grises terres de mort, et de notre sang versé pour la justice, faisons après les veilles d'horreur surgir des lendemains de beauté.[1]

—José Germain, 1923

At school, and in books written for boys, one was so constantly reminded that we had won the war that my school friends and I found our curiosity excited by those who had lost it. Losing seemed much more original and stimulating than winning.

—Richard Cobb, 1983

Qui aurait pensé, il y a dix-sept ans, qu'on pourrait louer l'harmonie du *Sacre*? C'est un fait. On ne songe plus à ses audaces, on admire ses perfections.[2]

—André Rousseau, February 1930

War Boom

Erich Maria Remarque's *Im Westen nichts Neues*, or *All Quiet on the Western Front*, as the English translation would be entitled, was published first in Berlin by the house of Ullstein at the end of January 1929. Twenty months later, in October 1930, the *Nouvelles littéraires* in Paris would refer to Remarque as the "author today with the largest audience in the world."[3]

When the book was published, accompanied by an advertising campaign larger than any ever before launched by a German publisher, about ten thousand advance orders had been placed. For weeks Berlin's advertisement pillars had been plastered with posters, each week a different one. First week: "It's coming." Second week: "The great war novel." Third week: "All Quiet on the Western Front." Fourth week: "By Erich Maria Remarque." The novel had by then appeared in serialized form in Ullstein's most distinguished newspaper, the *Vossische Zeitung*, from November 10, the day before the tenth anniversary of the Armistice, to December 9. While the paper's circulation did not skyrocket dramatically, as some have claimed, sales did rise slightly and daily editions usually sold out.

But now, after publication, the rush began. Within three weeks 200,000 copies were sold. The sale of 20,000 copies in one day was not unusual. By early May, 640,000 copies had been sold in Germany. English and French translations were hastily prepared. The English edition appeared in March, the American at the end of May, and the French in June. The American Book-of-the-Month Club selected the novel as its choice for June and ordered 60,000 copies for its 100,000 subscribers. The Book Society, a comparable book club in Great Britain, "recommended" the novel to its members. By the end of the year sales neared a million in Germany, and another million in Britain, France, and the United States together. In Germany the Ullsteins were using six printing and ten bookbinding firms to try to keep abreast of demand. In Britain the Barrow public library announced to its members in November that *All Quiet* had been reserved in advance for two years! Within the year the book had been translated into about twenty languages, including Chinese and Esperanto, and the Ullsteins, in their remarkable promotional effort, even had a German Braille edition prepared and sent without charge to every blind veteran who requested it.[4]

Almost overnight Remarque's novel had become, as one comment put it, "the postwar phenomenon of book-selling." That was an understatement. Remarque's success was unprecedented in the entire history of publishing. In England and Germany the book trade, which had suffered throughout the decade but now was in even worse straits because of the general downturn in the economy in 1928-1929, gave thanks. "Remarque is our daily bread," quipped booksellers in Berlin.[5]

Remarque's spectacular success brought on a flood of war books and other material dealing with the war and ushered in what came to be known as the "war boom" of 1929-1930. War novels and war memoirs suddenly dominated the lists of publishers. Robert Graves, Edmund Blunden, Siegfried Sassoon, Ludwig Renn, Arnold Zweig, and Ernest Hemingway, among others, became familiar names. They were so in demand, as public speakers and radio performers, that they could not cope with the glut of invitations. The sudden public interest in the war meant that moldy manuscripts, previously rejected by wary publishers who thought that the war would not sell, were now rushed into print. New books, too, were quickly commissioned and quickly written.

Translators were in great demand. The stage readily made room for war drama, and R. C. Sherriff's *Journey's End*, in which Laurence Olivier played the lead in the latter part of the London run, became an international hit. By November 1929 it was being staged in twelve foreign countries. The cinema, which had not been quite as reluctant as the publishing industry to deal with war material—Hollywood had started a small wave in 1926 with films like *What Price Glory?*, *The Big Parade*, and *Wings*—the cinema now joined in with a rash of war films. Galleries exhibited paintings and photographs from the war. Newspapers and periodicals gave much space to discussions about war, past and future. What some felt to have been a deliberate silence about the war was now shattered with a vengeance.

What provoked the sudden revival of interest in the war at the end of the twenties? And what did the war boom reveal? A look at the motivations of Remarque in writing his novel may yield some clues.

Life or Death

Until the publication of *All Quiet*, Erich Maria Remarque had led a moderately successful, though unsettled, life as a dilettante intellectual and aspiring author. He was born on June 22, 1898, in Osnabrück, the son of a Catholic bookbinder, Peter Franz Remark, and his wife, Anne Maria. Christened Erich Paul, he adopted a pen name after the war by dropping the Paul—the main character in *All Quiet* is named Paul and dies toward the end of the war—adding his mother's name, and Gallicizing his surname. Remarque did not have a happy childhood. His lower-middle-class milieu apparently depressed him. He was, he said later, deeply moved as a youth by the sorrows of Goethe's sensitive and splenetic Werther; he professed to be a romantic; and he often toyed with the idea of suicide. This mood of existential doubt was never to leave him. It pervades his entire *oeuvre*. In public, though clearly craving recognition, he always assumed the manner of a recluse. Even though he would marry Paulette Goddard, the film star and former wife of Charlie Chaplin, live extravagantly in New York, and surround himself with the trappings of success, he would remain—so it appeared—desperately unhappy, a chain smoker, a heavy drinker, fixated by fast cars, speedboats, and escape.

Remarque's class background bears emphasis. He was the product of a social group strongly affected by technological and social change. John Middleton Murry, who also suffered in his youth from an intense anxiety born, he suspected, of his social background, called the urban lower middle class "the most completely disinherited section of modern society."[6] It was a stratum that the war and especially the economic instability of the twenties would assault with ferocity.

Considerable mystery surrounds Remarque's war experience. Aged sixteen when war broke out, in August 1914, he was conscripted two years later, in November 1916, while training as a teacher, and he first saw front-line action in Flanders in June 1917. At the front he was wounded, according to his own testimony, either four or five times, but according to other evidence, only once seriously. The German army minister, General Groener, was to inform his cabinet colleagues in December 1930 that Remarque had been wounded in the left knee and under one arm on July 31, 1917, and that he had remained in a hospital in

Duisburg from August 3, 1917, to October 31, 1918. The minister dismissed as false the reports that Remarque had been either decorated or promoted.[7]

Little else is known about Remarque's days as a soldier. After he was catapulted to international fame, he proved reluctant to give interviews, let alone precise information about his war career. He showed little interest in countering any of the scurrilous rumors that circulated about his earlier life, and many of his critics found his aversion to publicity suspicious. There was a sustained attempt in 1929 and 1930 to uncover the "real" Remarque, especially to disprove the claim of his publisher, Ullstein, that he was a seasoned soldier. A man named Peter Kropp maintained that he had spent a year in a hospital with the author during the war and that one of the characters in *All Quiet*, Albert Kropp, was modeled on him. The leg wound that hospitalized Remarque, Kropp alleged, was self-inflicted, and he insisted that once the wound healed, Remarque had become a clerk in the hospital. In the end, argued Kropp, Remarque had no special qualifications for representing the feelings and behavior of the front soldier.[8] While many of the allegations of Remarque's critics and opponents were malicious and prompted by envy, opportunism, and political intent, there do appear to be grounds for suspecting that Remarque's war experience was not as extensive as his successful novel, and particularly the promotional effort surrounding it, implied.

After the war Remarque returned briefly to the Osnabrück Catholic seminary for teachers, and early in 1919 he became a village schoolmaster. He soon abandoned this occupation and took up freelance journalism and odd jobs to meet financial necessity. He published articles on cars, boats, cocktail recipes; he worked for a while for a tire-manufacturing company in Hanover, writing advertising jingles; and eventually he became a picture editor in Berlin for a publication owned by the right-wing firm Scherl. The glossy, high-society magazine *Sport im Bild* was a German version, despite its misleading title, of *The Tatler*. All the while, he tried to write seriously, working on novels, poetry, and a play.

Two of his novels were published, *Die Traumbude*[9] in 1920 and *Station am Horizont*[10] in 1928, but he seems to have derived little satisfaction from them. Trite sentimentality relegated the first work to the rank of pulp fiction. Of *Die Traumbude* Remarque was to say later:

> A truly terrible book. Two years after I had published it, I should have liked to buy it up. Unfortunately I didn't have enough money for that. The Ullsteins did that for me later. If I had not written anything better later on, the book would have been a reason for suicide.[11]

In 1921 he sent a number of poems to Stefan Zweig for comment and attached a letter of near despair: "Remember that this is a matter of life or death for me!" An attempt to write a play left him in deep depression.[12]

The death motif here is striking: thoughts about suicide in his youth and threats of it as an adult. Together with the derivative romanticism and the itinerant existence the motif points to a deeply disconsolate man, searching for an explanation for his dissatisfaction. And in his search Remarque eventually hit upon the *Kriegserleben*, the war experience.

The idea that the war was the source of all ills struck him suddenly, he admitted. "All of us were," he said of himself and his friends in an interview in 1929, "and still are, restless, aimless, sometimes excited, sometimes indifferent, and essentially unhappy." But in a moment of inspiration he had at least found the key to the malaise. The war![13]

That he was not truly interested, after his "discovery," in exploring the variety of war experience, but that his main purpose was simply to describe the terrible effects of the war on the generation that grew up during it, is revealed in a review he wrote of war books by Ernst Jünger, Franz Schauwecker, and Georg von der Vring, among others, for *Sport im Bild* in June 1928. It is even possible that these books were the source of his inspiration. Jünger's exuberant, intoxicating vitalism and brutal grandeur, Schauwecker's breathless, mystical nationalism, and von der Vring's lyrical simplicity were lumped together in a rather bland discussion that displayed little appreciation for these distinctive interpretations of the war experience.[14] Remarque was, one must conclude, more interested in explaining away the emotional imbalance of a generation than in a comprehensive or even accurate account of the experience and feelings of men in the trenches. Many of the metaphors and images that Remarque used in his book are strikingly similar to those used by the authors he had discussed, Jünger in particular, and it is not unreasonable to suggest that he took many of his ideas from these sources.

In July 1928 Remarque published another article in *Sport im Bild* that throws more light on his frame of mind at the time. This was a short, rather ingenuous piece about modern photography, in which he regretted the injustice that most professional photographers did to reality. By isolating their subjects from a wider context, by turning the world into a neat and rosy "9 × 12 or 10 × 15 format," photographers created an illusionary world.[15] The point was a simple and honest one, but coming from a picture editor of a snobbish and expensive magazine, it had a pathetic poignancy; it indicated how unhappy the author was in his work and environment.

Having fixed upon the "war experience," Remarque sat down in mid 1928 to write. Working in the evenings and on weekends, he completed his book, so he claimed, in six weeks. The suddenness of the inspiration, the speed of composition, and the simplicity of the theme all indicate that Remarque's book was not the product of years of reflection and digestion but of impulse born of personal exasperation.

Remarque stated the purpose of *All Quiet* in a brief and forceful prefatory comment:

This book is to be neither an accusation nor a confession, and least of all an adventure. . . . It will try simply to tell of a generation of men who, even though they may have escaped its shells, were destroyed by the war.[16]

The story then recounts the experiences of Paul Bäumer and his schoolmates, who move from the classroom to the trenches, bursting with energy and conviction, enthusiastic knights of a personal and national cause. One by one they are ripped apart at the front, not only by enemy fire but also by a growing sense of futility. The war is transformed from a cause into an inexorable, insatiable Moloch. The soldiers have no escape from the routinized slaughter; they are condemned men. They die screaming but unheard; they die resigned but in vain. The world beyond the guns does not know them; it cannot know them. "I believe we are lost," says Paul.

Only the fraternity of death remains, the comradeship of the fated. At the end Paul dies, forlorn yet strangely at peace with his destiny. Peace has become possible only in death. The final scene of the American film version of the novel was to be a masterly evocation of the mood of Remarque's work: a sniper's bullet finds its mark as Paul is reaching from the trench to touch what the war had rendered untouchable, a butterfly. All the shibboleths lose their meaning as the men die violent deaths—patriotism, national duty, honor, glory, heroism, valor. The external world consists only of brutality, hypocrisy, illusion. Even the intimate bonds to family have been sundered. Man remains alone, without a foothold in the real world.

The simplicity and power of the theme—war as a demeaning and wholly destructive, indeed nihilistic, force—are made starkly effective by a style that is basic, even brutal. Brief scenes and short crisp sentences, in the first person and in the present tense, create an inescapable and gripping immediacy. There is no delicacy. The language is frequently rough, the images often gruesome. The novel has a consistency of style and purpose that Remarque's earlier work had lacked and that little of his subsequent work would achieve.

Despite Remarque's introductory comment and his reiteration of the point in later statements, very few contemporary reviewers noted, and later critics have generally ignored, that *All Quiet* was not a book about the events of the war—it was not a memoir, much less a diary[17]—but an angry declaration about the effects of the war on the young generation that lived through it. Scenes, incidents, and images were chosen to illustrate how the war had destroyed the ties, psychological, moral, and real, between the generation at the front and society at home. "If we go back," says Paul, "we will be weary, broken, burnt out, rootless, and without hope. We will not be able to find our way any more." The war, Remarque was asserting in 1928, had shattered the possibility of pursuing what society would consider a normal existence.

Hence, *All Quiet* is more a comment on the postwar mind, on the postwar view of the war, than an attempt to reconstruct the reality of the trench experience. In fact that reality is distorted, as many critics insisted—though with little effect on the initial acclaim for the novel. Remarque's critics said, that at the very least he misrepresented the physical reality of the war: a man with his legs or his head blown off could not continue to run, they protested vehemently, referring to two of the images Remarque had used. But far more serious than such shoddiness, they claimed, was his lack of understanding of the moral aspects of soldiers' behavior. Soldiers were not robots, devoid of a sense of purpose. They were sustained by a broad spectrum of firmly established values.[18]

Although his publisher did not like such admissions, because they undermined the credibility of the novel, Remarque was prepared to say that his book was primarily about the postwar generation. In an exchange in 1929 with General Sir Ian Hamilton, the British commander at Gallipoli in 1915 and now head of the British Legion, Remarque expressed his "amazement" and "admiration" that Hamilton for one had understood his intentions in writing *All Quiet*:

> I merely wanted to awaken understanding for a generation that more than all others has found it difficult to make its way back from four years of death, struggle, and terror, to the peaceful fields of work and progress.[19]

It was in part the misinterpretation of his purpose that led Remarque to write a sequel to *All Quiet*. *Der Weg zurück* (*The Road Back*), a novel published in 1931, explicitly argued the case of the "lost generation."

All Quiet can be seen not as an explanation but as a symptom of the confusion and disorientation of the postwar world, particularly of the generation that reached maturity during the war. The novel was an emotional condemnation, an assertion of instinct, a *cri d'angoisse* from a malcontent, a man who could not find his niche in society. That the war contributed enormously to the shiftlessness of much of the postwar generation is undeniable; that the war was the root cause of this social derangement is at least debatable; but Remarque never took part in the debate directly. For Remarque the war had become a vehicle of escape. Remarque and his book were, to borrow from Karl Kraus, symptoms of the disease they claimed to diagnose.

Notwithstanding Remarque's opening declaration of impartiality—that his book was "neither an accusation nor a confession"—it was in fact both. And it was more. It was a confession of personal despair, but it was also an indignant denunciation of an insensate social and political order, inevitably of that order which had produced the horror and destruction of the war but particularly of the one that could not settle the war and deal with the aspirations of veterans. Through characters identifiable with the state—the schoolmaster with his unalterable fantasies about patriotism and valor, the former postman who functions like an unfeeling robot in his new role as drill sergeant, the hospital orderlies and doctors who deal not with human suffering, only bodies—Remarque accused. He accused a mechanistic civilization of destroying humane values, of negating charity, love, humor, beauty, and individuality. Yet Remarque offered no alternatives. The characters of his *generazione bruciata*—the Italian notion of a "burned generation" is apt—do not act; they are merely victims. Of all the war books of the late twenties—the novels of Arnold Zweig, Renn, R. H. Mottram, H. M. Tomlinson, Richard Aldington, Hemingway, and the memoirs of Graves, Blunden, Sassoon, to name but a few of the more important

works—Remarque's made its point, that his was a truly lost generation, most directly and emotionally, even stridently, and this directness
and passion lay at the heart of its popular appeal.

But there was more. The "romantic agony" was a wild cry of revolt
and despair—and a cry of exhilaration. In perversion there could be
pleasure. In darkness, light. The relation of Remarque and his generation to death and destruction is not as straightforward as it appears. In
his personal life and in his reflections on the war Remarque seemed
fascinated by death. All of his subsequent work exudes this fascination. As one critic put it later, Remarque "probably made more out of
death than the most fashionable undertakers."[20] Like the Dadaists, he
was spellbound by war and its horror, by the act of destruction, to the
point where death becomes not the antithesis of life but the ultimate expression of life, where death becomes a creative force, a source of art
and vitality. A young Michel Tournier, on meeting Remarque, noted
the paradoxical nature of this modern author-hero: world famous for
his antimilitarism, Remarque, "with his stiff posture, his severe and
rectangular face, and his inseparable monocle," looked like a larger-
than-life Prussian officer.[21]

Many of Remarque's generation shared his apocalyptic post-Christian
vision of life, peace, and happiness in death. George Antheil would,
when appearing in concert to play his own music, carry a pistol in his
evening jacket. As he sat down to play, he would take out the pistol and
place it on the piano. The .25 caliber Belgian revolver that Harry
Crosby used in December 1929 to kill himself and his mistress had a
sun symbol engraved on its side. A year earlier while saluting Dido,
Cleopatra, Socrates, Modigliani, and Van Gogh among others, he had
promised soon "to enjoy an orgasm with the sombre Slave-Girl of
Death, in order to be reborn." He yearned to "explode . . . into the frenzied fury of the Sun, into the madness of the Sun into the hot gold arms
and hot gold eyes of the Goddess of the Sun!"[22]

Success would not mellow Remarque or still his chronic anxiety.
The very vital Countess Waldeck, née Rosie Gräfenberg, who in 1929-

1930 was the wife of Franz Ullstein, later had this to say of the young author at the height of his success:

> Remarque was in his thirties. He had a pretty boy's face with a defiant soft mouth. The Ullsteins thought him a little difficult. But that was merely the result of Remarque's having almost rejected the motor-car with which the grateful firm presented him, because it lacked the travelling luggage which, in his opinion, belonged on the luggage rack. I myself thought this and other traits charmingly childlike in Remarque; he wanted his toy to be exactly as he had imagined it. He was a hard worker. Often he would shut himself up for seventeen hours at a stretch in a room where not even a chaise-lounge was permitted, because it might possibly be a temptation to laziness. He was immensely sorry for himself because he worked so hard—was Remarque.[23]

Fame

According to Remarque, his completed manuscript lay in a drawer for six months. In fact it was probably only a couple of months. His employer, the Scherl firm, an important part of Alfred Hugenberg's right-wing nationalist press empire, could not even be considered a potential publisher of the work. Finally Remarque approached the S. Fischer Verlag, the most reputable literary publisher in Germany, but Samuel Fischer was still convinced that the war would not sell. He turned the manuscript down.

Through an acquaintance word reached Remarque that Franz Ullstein, by contrast, did feel that it was time to publish books on the war. Remarque tried the Ullstein Verlag. There the manuscript was passed around to various editors. Max Krell was "gripped by the unusual tone"; Cyrill Soschka, head of the production department and a war veteran, was convinced that it would be a great success because it told "the truth about the war"—a phrase on which the controversy about the book would turn; Monty Jacobs, *feuilleton* editor of Ullstein's *Vossische*

Zeitung, accepted the novel for serialization. The Ullsteins developed great confidence in the book, and, led by Franz Ullstein, one of the five brothers who ran the large newspaper- and book-publishing operation, they proceeded to launch their flamboyant and expensive advertising campaign.[24]

The initial critical response to Remarque's novel was very enthusiastic, not only in Germany, where the playwright Carl Zuckmayer wrote the first review for the Ullsteins' large-circulation *Berliner Illustrirte Zeitung* and called *All Quiet* a "war diary," but also when it appeared in English and French translations. Remarque's supposedly frank portrayal of human responses to war and the depiction of a pitiful dignity under suffering were praised with gusto. "The greatest of war novels" was a phrase that appeared over and over again in the reviews. Its "holy sobriety" would bring about "the rehabilitation of our generation," predicted Axel Eggebrecht, a well-known and respected German critic. Herbert Read, veteran, poet, and art historian, heralded Remarque's account as "the Bible of the common soldier" and struck, thereby, a religious note that would recur frequently in the commentary. "It has swept like a gospel over Germany," wrote Read, "and must sweep over the whole world, because it is the first completely satisfying expression in literature of the greatest event of our time." He added that he had by then read the book "six or seven times." An American rhapsodized about "its blasting simplicity" and called it the "Book of the Decade": "I should like to see it sell a million copies," concluded Christopher Morley. Daniel-Rops, philosopher, theologian, and historian, shared such sentiments in Switzerland: it was "the book we waited for" for ten years, he said. Bruno Frank, Bernhard Kellermann, G. Lowes Dickinson, and Henry Seidel Canby were other eminent literary figures among the early enthusiasts. Several people suggested that Remarque be awarded the Nobel Prize for literature.[25]

In the initial reviews, then, there was rarely a note of vigorous criticism, and there was near unanimity in the belief that the book presented "the truth about the war," or, as the London *Sunday Chronicle* put it, "the true story of the world's greatest nightmare."[26] The exuberance, especially the extravagant use of superlatives and absolutes, and the shrill insistence that this book told "the truth," indicated how sensitive a nerve Remarque had touched and how completely many people shared his frustration—his postwar frustration. The tone of the novel and the tone of the early reviews were very similar.

But what was this "truth" to which almost all referred? That the war had been a nihilistic slaughter without rationale? That its front-line protagonists and chief victims had no sense of purpose? That, in short, the war had been in vain? Few said so outright, but the liberal left and moderate socialists throughout Europe, and even here and there in America and the dominions, were now inclined to view the war as, in the end, a tragic and futile civil conflict in Europe, one that need not have occurred.

However, as sales mounted through the spring and summer of 1929, an opposition began to organize and to voice its opinions as shrilly as the early supporters. The communist left derided the novel as an example of the sterility of bourgeois intelligence: the bourgeois mind, incapable of locating the real source of social disorder, resorted, in its treatment of the war, to tearful sentimentality and regret. The book was seen as a fine illustration of the "decline of the west" mentality.[27] To those at the other end of the political spectrum, the conservative right, Remarque's work was pernicious because it threatened the entire meaning of postwar conservatism, the idea of regeneration based on traditional values. In the eyes of conservatives in all belligerent countries the war had been a necessity, tragic of course, but nonetheless unavoidable. If the war was now found to have been an absurdity, then conservatism as a set of beliefs was an absurdity. Consequently, *All Quiet* had to be rejected—as deliberately "commercialized horror and filth" and as the outgrowth of a degenerate mind that could not rise above the inevitable horror of war to see "the eternal issues involved," the grandeur of an idea, the beauty of sacrifice, and the nobility of collective purpose.[28]

The fascist opposition to the novel blended often with that of the conservatives and presented many of the same arguments, but there was an essential difference in the reasoning. The fascists sanctified not so much the purpose of the war as the "experience" of the war, the very essence of the war, its immediacy, its tragedy, its exhilaration, its ultimate ineffability in anything but mystical and spiritual terms. The war, as we shall see, gave meaning to fascism. Thus, any suggestion that the war had been purposeless was a slur against the very existence of this form of extremism. It is here, on the extreme right, that the most active opposition to Remarque, and to the whole wave of so-called negative war books, films, and other artifacts, assembled.

Both traditionalists and right-wing extremists were incensed by what they saw as a completely one-sided portrait of the war experience. They objected to the language in the novel, to the horrifying images, to the frequent references to bodily functions, and, especially, to a scene involving a jovial group perched on field latrines. Little, Brown and Company of Boston, the American publisher, actually deleted the latrine scene at the insistence of the Book-of-the-Month Club, cut an episode concerning a sexual encounter in a hospital, and softened certain words and phrases in A. W. Wheen's British translation.[29] The latrine passage, retained in the British edition, was harped on by a large number of British critics, who began to refer to Remarque as the high priest of the "lavatory school" of war novelists. In November 1929, *The London Mercury* felt the need to editorialize on this school.

"Criticism," wrote Anatole France, "is the adventure of the soul among masterpieces." The adventure of the soul among lavatories is not inviting: but this, roughly, is what criticism of recent translated German novels must be. . . . The modern Germans . . . suppose that lavatories are intensely interesting. They are obsessed by this dreary subject, and they are obsessed by brutality.[30]

An Australian, writing in *The Army Quarterly*, asked how British firms could publish "unclean war books"; in his view the translation and publication of "filthy foreign books" was an act of treason.[31]

The denunciation of the book as a piece of propaganda—pacifist, Allied, or German, depending on the critic—was the other main form of attack on the right. Franz von Lilienthal noted in the conservative financial daily, *Berliner Börsen-Zeitung*, that if Remarque did in fact receive the Nobel Prize, Lord Northcliffe, the press baron, would have to be applauded as well, because Remarque had nothing to say that Northcliffe, master propagandist that he was, had not said earlier. To the German military the novel was "a singularly monstrous slander of the German army" and thus a piece of "refined pacifist propaganda." The military everywhere for that matter was inclined to support such a view. In November 1929, the Czechoslovak War Department banned *All Quiet* from military libraries. Outside Germany many conservative critics looked on the novel as part of a clever German campaign of cultural dissimulation. In a speech at Armistice celebrations at Folkestone in 1929, a Baptist minister deplored the tenor of the popular novels and plays on the subject of the war. He certainly had *All Quiet* in mind, as well as Robert Graves's recently published *Goodbye to All That* and R. C. Sherriff's *Journey's End* when he said, "I did not think I should ever live to read books written by my own countrymen which are like the dirty work done by enemy propagandists."[32]

Earlier in the year G. Lowes Dickinson, Cambridge humanist and ardent promoter of the League of Nations, had sensed that Remarque's book might be subjected to this type of attack. Urging all those to read the book "who have the courage and honesty to desire to know what modern war is really like," he added, "They need not fear German propaganda. The book is far above all that. It is the truth, told by a man with the power of a great artist, who is hardly aware what an artist he is."[33]

But J. C. Squire and *The London Mercury* would have none of this. "This is not the truth," they retorted, referring to the work of Remarque and other German war novelists, and warned against the apparent tendency among the British public "to sentimentalize over the Germans" and to neglect the French. Then, with a stunning burst of ferocity, reminiscent of the war itself, they continued:

> We repeat . . . (being cosmopolitans and pacifists, but facers of facts) that the Germans (many of whom were not even Christianized until the sixteenth century) have contributed very little indeed to European culture. . . . In war we exaggerated the defects of the enemy; do not let us, in peace, exaggerate his merits; above all, do not let us, in a wanton reaction, take more interest in the enemy than in the friend. The cold truth is that the Russians, who are still largely barbaric, contributed far more, in music and literature, to culture in the nineteenth century than the Germans, let alone the square-head Prussians, have contributed in hundreds of years. . . . Peace with the Germans, by all means; understanding with the Germans, if possible; but let us not, out of mere sentimentality, concentrate our gaze upon the Germans at the expense of more cultivated, productive and civilized peoples. Let us welcome, by all means, whatever good may come from Germany; but the present tendency is to think that anything that comes out of Germany must be good. "Omne Teutonicum pro magnifico" seems the motto of the publishers and the press: it is a grotesque motto.[34]

Paradoxically, when in February 1930 Wilhelm Frick, the newly appointed Nazi minister of the interior in the state government of Thuringia, banned *All Quiet* from schools in that state, a Nazi paper, announcing the decree, commented, "it is time to stop the infection of the schools with pacifist Marxist propaganda."[35]

Both the critical praise and the scurrility that *All Quiet* provoked had, in the end, little to do with the substance of the novel. As *All Quiet* was a reflection more of the postwar than of the wartime mind, so the commentary, too, was a reflection of postwar political and emotional investments. Yet everyone pretended to be arguing objectively about the essence of the war experience. The critical dialogue was worthy of characters in a Chekhov play. They talked past each other. The wider public response was similar.

Remarque's success came at what we now see was a crossroads in the interwar era: the intersection of two moods, one of vague, imploring hope and the other of coagulating fear; "the Locarno spirit" and a fling with apparent prosperity intersecting with incipient economic crisis and mounting national introspection.

Accompanying the efforts at international détente after 1925 was a wave of humanism that swept the west. A wishful rather than assertive humanism this was, however. In 1927 Thornton Wilder ended his Pulitzer Prize-winning novel, *The Bridge of San Luis Rey*, with the sentence: "There is a land of the living and a land of the dead and the bridge is love, the only survival, the only meaning." Melancholy, sentimentality, and wish constitute the dominant mood here. Two years later, in 1929, the disastrous economic slump brought the underlying doubt starkly to the surface. The popular cultural activities of the twenties as a whole were, more or less, a bewildered salute to a bygone age when the individual had had a recognized social purpose.

The war boom of the late twenties and early thirties was a product of this mixture of aspiration, anxiety, and doubt. All the successful war books were written from the point of view of the individual, not the unit or the nation. Remarque's book, written in the first person, personalized for everyone the fate of the unknown soldier. Paul Bäumer became Everyman. On this level only could the war have any meaning, on the level of individual suffering. The war was a matter of individual experience rather than collective interpretation. It had become a matter of art, not history.

Art had become more important than history. History belonged to an age of rationalism, to the eighteenth and particularly the nineteenth century. The latter century had shown great respect for its historians. The Guizots, Michelets, Rankes, Macaulays, and Actons were read and appreciated, especially by a bourgeoisie bent on expansion and integration. Our century has, by contrast, been an antihistorical age, in part because historians have failed to adapt to the sentiments of their century but even more so because this century has been one of disintegration rather than integration. The psychologist has, as a result, been more in demand than the historian. And the artist has received more respect than either.

It is noteworthy that among the mountains of writing built up on the subject of the Great War, a good many of the more satisfying attempts to deal with its meaning have come from the pens of poets, novelists, and even literary critics, and that professional historians have produced, by and large, specialized and limited accounts, most of which pale in evocative and explanatory power before those of the *littérateurs*. Historians have failed to find explanations to the war that correspond to the horrendous realities, to the actual experience of the war. The spate of official and unofficial histories that issued forth in the twenties was largely ignored by the public. By contrast, Remarque's *All Quiet* became, virtually overnight, the best seller of all previous time. Imaginative, not historical, literature it was that sparked the intense reconsideration of the meaning of the war at the end of the twenties. The historical imagination, like so much of the intellectual effort of the nineteenth century, had been sorely challenged by the events of the war; and it was consistent with the subsequent self-doubt of the discipline that H. A. L. Fisher's 1934 lament, in the preface to his *History of Europe*, should have become one of the most frequently quoted theoretical statements by a historian of our century:

> Men wiser and more learned than I have discerned in history a plot, a rhythm, a predetermined pattern. These harmonies are concealed from me. I can see only one emergency following upon another as wave follows upon wave.[36]

Whether the poems, novels, and other imaginative efforts provoked by the war stand as "great" art is a debatable matter. William Butler Yeats, in his idiosyncratic 1936 edition of *The Oxford Book of Modern*

Verse, omitted Wilfred Owen, Siegfried Sassoon, Ivor Gurney, Isaac Rosenberg, Robert Graves, Herbert Read, and others, on the grounds that passive suffering could not be the stuff of great poetry, which had to have a moral vision. But he was imposing his critical vision on a public that felt otherwise. Ten years after the war, amidst the glut of war novels that appeared during the war boom, the *Morning Post* bemoaned in an editorial that "the great novel of the Great War, which will show all things in a true perspective, has yet to be written."[37] The great war novel, explaining all, was a constant vision among intellectuals in the twenties and even the thirties. Mottram's *Spanish Farm* trilogy, Tomlinson's *All Our Yesterdays*, Aldington's *Death of a Hero*, and, in a different vein but with similar intent, Renn's *Krieg* and Remarque's *All Quiet*, to cite but a few, were motivated by this challenge and quest. "The witness of a hundred thousand nobodies," wrote André Thérive in *Le Temps* in December 1929, "isn't worth the semifiction conceived by a great man."[38] This attitude, that art might be truer to life than history, was hardly a new notion, but never before had it been so widespread, in fact so dominant.

Ironically, during the war French and British soldiers had become the "frontier" personalities identified with the avant-garde and with German *Kultur* as a whole before the war; they were the men who had experienced the very limits of existence, who had seen no man's land, who had witnessed horror and agony, and who, because of the very experience that made them heroes, lived on the edge of respectability and morality. Given the failure of the postwar era to produce the apocalyptic resolution promised by wartime propaganda, the whole social purpose of the war—the content of duty and *devoir*—began to ring hollow. Since the tangible results of the war could never justify its cost, especially its emotional toll, disillusionment was inevitable, and soldiers in the postwar world withdrew from social activity and commitment. Only a minority bothered even to join veterans' organizations. Relatively few were able to articulate their alienation, but the statistics speak loudly: of those unemployed between the ages of thirty and thirty-four in Britain at the end of the twenties, 80 percent were ex-servicemen. The incidence of mental illness among veterans was also staggering. "The worst thing about the war generation of introspects," said T. E. Lawrence,"is that they can't keep off their blooming selves." Aldington talked about the "self-prisons" in which former soldiers had become trapped, and Graves wrote about his "cage-mates."[39]

Yet, while former soldiers suffered from a high incidence of neurasthenia and sexual impotence, they realized that the war, in the words of José Germain, was "the quivering axis of all human history."[40] If the war as a whole had no objective meaning, then invariably all human history was telescoped into each man's experience; every person was the sum total of history. Rather than being a social experience, a matter of documentable reality, history was individual nightmare, or even, as the Dadaists insisted, madness. One is again reminded of Nietzsche's statement, on the very edge of his complete mental collapse, that he was "every name in history."

The burden of having been in the eye of the storm and yet, in the end, of having resolved nothing, was excruciating. The result often was the rejection of social and political reality and at the same time the rejection even of the perceptual self—only dream and neurosis remained, a world of illusions characterized by a pervasive negativism. Fantasy became the mainspring of action, and melancholy the general mood. *Nous vivons une triste époque . . . Tout est foutu–Quoi? Tout un monde . . . Il fait beau, allons au cimetière.*[41] Carroll Carstairs ended his book *A Generation Missing* in 1930 with the words "It's a weary world and the raspberry jam sent me from Paris is all finished now."[42]

What was true of the soldiers was true with somewhat less immediacy and poignancy of civilians. The crowded nightclubs, the frenzied dancing, the striking upsurge of gambling, alcoholism, and suicide, the obsession with flight, with moving pictures, and with film stars evinced on a popular level these same tendencies, a drift toward irrationalism. Of course bourgeois Europe tried to "recast" itself, but it was capable of doing so only superficially. The modern temper had been forged; the avant-garde had won. The "adversary culture" had become the dominant culture; irony and anxiety, the mode and the mood. "The war is breaking us but is also reshaping us," Marc Boasson had written in July 1915. Fifteen years later Egon Friedell, the cultural historian, asserted emphatically, "History does not exist."[43]

All Quiet captured for the popular mind some of the same instincts that were being expressed in "high art." Proust and Joyce, too, telescoped history into the individual. There is no collective reality, only individual response, only dreams and myths, which have lost their nexus with social convention.

In the tormented and degraded German front soldier depicted in *All Quiet*—and he could just as easily have been a Tommy, *poilu*, or doughboy—the public saw its own shadow and sensed its own anonymity and yearning for security. A small number of critics perceived this at the time. "The effect of the book springs in fact," wrote a German commentator,

> from the terrible disillusionment of the German people with the state in which they find themselves, and the reader tends to feel that this book has located the source of all our difficulties.[44]

An American noted, "In Remarque the sentiment of the epoch comes to bloom."[45] *All Quiet* seemed to encapsulate the whole modern impulse as it manifested itself in the postwar world: the amalgamation of prayer and desperation, dream and chaos, wish and desolation.

In each country there was a specific variation on this general theme. In Germany after 1925 one noticed a distinct relaxation of political tension, evidenced by the lowest turnout at the polls in the whole of the Weimar period in the national elections of May 1928, the first since December 1924. The government that was formed in June 1928 was appropriately a "grand coalition," ranging from Social Democrats on the left, who led the government, to the moderate right-wing People's Party of Gustav Stresemann. The government began its life in a conciliatory mood. However, in May 1930 it fell, the victim of revived nationalist and conservative sentiment.

Nineteen twenty-nine was the critical year. That the economic situation deteriorated drastically in a year that marked the tenth anniversary of the Treaty of Versailles was an unfortunate coincidence. Reparations were on the public mind. Alfred Hugenberg, press lord and leader of the right-wing Nationalist People's Party, campaigned for his referendum against the Young Plan, the new Allied proposal for reparations, and accepted Adolf Hitler into his camp. The right, in its spirited new offensive against the republic, blamed Germany's renewed economic difficulties on the draconic peace settlement; and on the blood lust of the Allies. Public demonstrations against the "war guilt lie" grew in number and frenzy through the early part of 1929 and climaxed in a flood of meetings in June. The government declared June 28, the anniversary of the treaty, a day of national mourning: Remarque was able to capitalize on both the remnants of political moderation and the heightened sensitivity to the question of the war.

Remarque blamed the war for his personal disorientation; the German public, too, assumed that its suffering was a direct legacy of the war. *All Quiet* actually raised the consciousness of Germans on the issue of the war as the source of their difficulties.

In Britain, where the economy took a very bad turn in late 1928 and where unemployment dominated the election campaign in the spring of 1929, Remarque's portrayal of the German front-line soldier as a miserable, downtrodden pawn, striving to retain some dignity and humanity, met with sympathy. By the late twenties much of British opinion had become favorable toward Germany. French pettiness and obstreperousness earlier in the decade and then "the Locarno spirit" had drawn the British away from the French and closer to the Germans. "In foreign affairs the psychological drama of British politics is precisely that we like the Germans more, and the French less," *The Fortnightly Review* mused, "but with the first we fall out and the latter we are obliged to accept as partners." However, even this partnership with

France was under question in some quarters. J. C. C. Davidson, confidant of the conservative leader, Stanley Baldwin, spoke about the advantages of loosening the tie with France, a "parochial and highly cynical" nation "whose population is declining and whose methods are so little in harmony with our own." Douglas Goldring, who described himself as a "crusted libertarian and little Englander of ingrained Tory instincts," suggested that some terrible errors had been made by British statesmen: "Any intelligent undergraduate, interpreting the past in the light of recent happenings, would probably arrive at the conclusion that our entry into the war was a blunder. . . . My generation," he concluded, "was betrayed, swindled, exploited and decimated by its elders in 1914." And Robert Graves, in his memoir, *Goodbye to All That*, which he wrote in the spring and summer of 1929, thought it fit to quote Edmund Blunden: "No more wars for me at any price! Except against the French. If there's ever a war with them, I'll go like a shot."[46]

The undercurrent of suspicion and scorn in the Anglo-French alliance naturally did not flow only in one direction. In the twenties Frenchmen were convinced that it was mainly they who had won the war; the British contribution had never been equal to the French. How could it have been? The French had held three quarters of the line on the Western Front. British concerns, moreover, had always been overseas and not in Europe. Even during the war the French were prone to accuse the British of fighting to the last drop of other people's blood. Joffre said of the British in 1915: "I'd never let them hold the line on their own—they'd be broken through. I trust them only when they are held up by us." During the mutinies of June 1917 a French soldier was heard to say, "We have to have the Boches on our side within a month to help us kick out the British." By 1922, even before the Ruhr crisis, when the British failed to back French and Belgian punitive measures against the Germans over reparations, General Huguet, the former French attaché to the British armies, could describe Britain as an "adversary."[47] As the decade wore on the relationship deteriorated further.

So Frenchmen, while generally calmer in their response to Remarque's novel, were nevertheless drawn to a book that portrayed the mutual hell through which the principal combatants, French and German soldiers, had gone. Perhaps the *poilu* and the *boche* were not irreconcilable. The success of *À l'ouest rien de nouveau* brought a flood of French translations of German works on the war, and, appropriately, in the initial phases of the war boom at least, British war books were neglected by French publishers.[48]

The great discovery that foreign readers said they made through *All Quiet* was that the German soldier's experience of the war had been, in its essentials, no different from that of soldiers of other nations. The German soldier, it seemed, had not wanted to fight either, once the emotional decoration put on the war by the home front had been shattered. Remarque's novel did a great deal to undermine the view that Germans were "peculiar" and not to be trusted. Furthermore, *All Quiet* promoted at a popular level what historical revisionism was achieving at an academic and political level: the erosion of the idea of a collective German war guilt. But on this score too "art" was clearly more effective than "history." Remarque alone accomplished much more than all the revisionist historians in America and Europe put together.

Who read *All Quiet* with most interest? Veterans and young people appear to have been the most avid readers of war books as a whole. By the end of the decade the disillusionment of former servicemen with postwar society had matured into vituperative scorn for the so-called peace, not only in the defeated countries but also in the victor states. *All Quiet* and other war books of "disenchantment," as C. E. Montague's early venture in this genre was actually entitled, elicited many a "bravo" from embittered and saddened veterans. Yet there were also frequent denunciations from veterans who regarded the spirit and success of *All Quiet* as a manifestation of the malaise that had engulfed the postwar world, as a symptom of the spirit that had betrayed a generation and its hopes. Where exactly the balance lay is difficult to ascertain. What is clear, however, is that the interest of veterans in the literary protest was based largely on their postwar experience. They were reacting to the disappearance, in the course of the decade, of the vision the war had promised.

Youths who had matured after the war were naturally curious about the war. Many commentators noted that fathers who had survived the front were reluctant to talk about their experience even with their families, which is why young people, wishing to penetrate the silence, constituted a sizable part of the readership. And having grown up in the shadow of the hero-father, they were also fascinated by the "negative" portrayal of the war. The literature of disenchantment offered a less ascetic, more humane, and hence more interesting portrait of the warrior-father.[49] In a straw vote among senior Gymnasium, or secondary school, students in Düsseldorf in January 1930 on favorite authors, Remarque topped the poll, outstripping Goethe, Schiller, Galsworthy, Dreiser, and Edgar Wallace. It is worth noting, however, that alongside war diaries and memoirs, works on economics elicited most interest among the students polled.[50] Obviously the economic insecurity felt by students in depression-ridden Germany and the fascination with accounts of horror and death in the trenches were linked. Youth, too, was prone to blame uncertain employment prospects on the war.

The "real war" had ceased to exist in 1918. Thereafter it was swallowed by imagination in the guise of memory. For many the war became absurd in retrospect, not because of the war experience in itself but because of the failure of the postwar experience to justify the war. For others the same logic turned the war into ultimate experience, again in retrospect. William Faulkner was hinting at this process of metamorphosis when he wrote, in 1931, "America has been conquered not by the German soldiers that died in French and Flemish trenches, but by the German soldiers that died in German books."[51] The journey inward that the war had initiated for masses of men was accelerated by the aftermath of the war.

All Quiet, contrary to the claims of many of its enthusiastic readers, was not "the truth about the war"; it was, first and foremost, the truth about Erich Maria Remarque in 1928. But equally, most of his critics were no nearer "the truth" of which they too spoke. They expressed merely the tenor of their own endeavors. Remarque used the war; his critics and the public did the same. Hitler and National Socialism were to be, in the end, the most obsessive and successful exploiters of the war. The war boom of the late twenties reflected less a genuine interest in the war than a perplexed international self-commiseration.

Cloud Juggler

Hart Crane's elegy for Harry Crosby was called "The Cloud Juggler." The title would have suited Erich Maria Remarque as well. Crosby put a pistol to his head, literally, and pulled the trigger. Remarque did so figuratively, again and again. The paradoxical figure of the vital victim—squirming, twitching, pleading, cursing in the face of annihilation—preoccupied both. For both, art had become superior to life. In art resided life.

Virtually everything Remarque wrote after *All Quiet* was concerned with disintegration and death. Yet virtually everything he wrote was an international success.

The film version of *All Quiet* was a fine effort, directed by Lewis Milestone for Universal Studios, and released in May 1930. It met rave reviews and played to crowded cinemas in New York, Paris, and London and was accorded Hollywood's highest accolade, the Academy Award for best picture of 1930. In Berlin, however, after several performances were disrupted by Nazi hooligans led by Joseph Goebbels, it was banned in December, ostensibly because it slandered the German image but actually because it was a threat to internal security and order owing to the controversy it provoked.[52]

On May 11, 1933, after Hitler's takeover in Germany, Remarque's books were among those burned symbolically at the University of Berlin as "politically and morally un-German." "Down with the literary betrayal of the soldiers of the world war!" chanted a Nazi student.

"In the name of educating our people in the spirit of valor, I commit the writings of Erich Maria Remarque to the flames."[53]

On November 20, 1933, 3411 copies of *All Quiet* were seized at the Ullstein publishing house by the Berlin police, on the basis of the presidential decree of February 4, which was drawn up "for the protection of the German people." In December the Gestapo instructed that these copies be destroyed.[54] On May 15 Goebbels, who had been a mere stripling during the war, had told representatives of the German book trade that the *Volk*, the German people, were not supposed to serve books, but books were to serve the *Volk*; and he had concluded, "*Denn es wird am deutschen Wesen noch einmal die Welt genesen.*"[55]

Erich Maria Remarque had sought refuge in Switzerland in 1930. After a long journey to New York, Hollywood, and back, he would die there in his mountain retreat in 1970, still handsome and still unhappy.

Notes

1. Let us in turn be the spring, which brings green new life to the gray terrain of death, and with the blood we gave for justice let us, after sleepless nights full of horror, give rise to new days of beauty.

2. Who, seventeen years ago, would have ever thought that you could praise the harmony of *Le Sacre*? But that's the case. One no longer thinks of its presumption; one admires its perfection.

3. *Nouvelles littéraires*, October 25, 1930.

4. *Börsenblatt für den deutschen Buchhandel*, June 10, 1930, 540; *Die Literatur*, 31 (1928-29), 657; *Publisher's Weekly*, September 21, 1929, 1332; *Daily Herald*, November 23, 1929.

5. Friedrich Fuchs in *Das Hochland*, 2 (1929), 217.

6. John Middleton Murry, *Between Two Worlds* (London, 1935), 65.

7. Cabinet minutes, December 19, 1930, Reichskanzlei files, R431/1447, 383, Bundesarchiv Koblenz (hereafter BAK).

8. Peter Kropp, *Endlich Klarheit über Remarque und sein Buch "Im Westen nichts Neues"* (Hamm i.W., 1930), 9-14.

9. *Dream Lodgings* (*Die Traumbude. Ein Künstlerroman* [Berlin, 1920]).

10. *Horizon Station* (*Station am Horizont* [Köln, 1928]).

11. *Der Spiegel*, January 9, 1952, 25.

12. In D. A. Prater, *European of Yesterday: A Biography of Stefan Zweig* (Oxford, 1972), 140.

13. Interview with Axel Eggebrecht, *Die Literarische Welt*, June 14, 1929.

14. *Sport im Bild*, June 8, 1928.

15. Ibid., July 20, 1928.

16. I have used the A. W. Wheen translation (London, 1929) for quotations. Wheen was himself a veteran of the war; see R. Church, *The Spectator*, 142 (April 20, 1929), 624.

17. Hanna Hafkesbrink, for instance, called *All Quiet* a "genuine memoir of the war"; see *Unknown Germany: An Inner Chronicle of the First World War Based on Letters and Diaries* (New Haven, Conn., 1948), ix.

18. For examples of the criticism see Jean Norton Cru, *Témoins* (Paris, 1928), 80; and Cyril Falls, *War Books* (London, 1930), x-xi, 294.

19. E. M. Remarque and Gen. Sir Ian Hamilton, "The End Of War?" *Life and Letters*, 3 (1929), 405-406.

20. *Time*, March 24, 1961, in its review of *Heaven Has No Favorites*.

21. Michel Tournier, *Le vent Paraclet* (Paris, 1977), 166.

22. Harry Crosby, "Hail: Death!" *Transition*, 14 (1928), 169-70.

23. R[osie] G[räfenberg], *Prelude to the Past* (New York, 1934), 320-21.

24. The legends about Remarque and *All Quiet* are many. One is that he offered his manuscript to forty-eight publishers. See the obituary in *Der Spiegel*, September 2-8, 1970. For accounts of the publication see Peter de Mendelssohn, *S. Fischer und sein Verlag* (Frankfurt am Main, 1970), 1114-18; Max Krell, *Das gab es alles einmal* (Frankfurt am Main, 1961), 159-60; Heinz Ullstein's version in a *dpa* release, June 15, 1962, as well as his letter to the *Frankfurter Allgemeine Zeitung*, July 9, 1962; and the remarks of Carl Jödicke, an Ullstein employee, in his unpublished "Dokumente und Aufzeichnungen" (F501), 40, Institut für Zeitgeschichte, Munich.

25. Carl Zuckmayer, *Als wär's ein Stück von mir* (Frankfurt, 1966), 359-60; Axel Eggebrecht, *Die Weltbühne*, February 5, 1929, 212; Herbert Read, "A Lost Generation," *The Nation & Athenaeum*, April 27, 1929, 116; Christopher Morley, *The Saturday Review*, April 20, 1929, 909; Daniel-Rops, *Bibliothèque universelle et Revue de Genève*, 1929, II, 510-11.

26. The *Sunday Chronicle* is cited in *The Saturday Review*, June 1, 1929, 1075.

27. See Antkowiak's survey of the communist reviews in Pawel Toper and Alfred Antkowiak, *Ludwig Renn, Erich Maria Remarque: Leben und Werk* ([East] Berlin, 1965).

28. Freiherr von der Goltz, *Deutsche Wehr*, October 10, 1929, 270; Valentine Williams, *Morning Post*, February 11, 1930; *The London Mercury*, 21 (January 1930), 238; and *Deutschlands Erneuerung*, 13 (1929), 230.

29. See the reports in the *New York Times*, May 31, June 1, July 14, July 29, 1929.

30. *The London Mercury*, 21 (November 1929), 1.

31. *The Army Quarterly*, 20 (July 1930), 373-75.

32. *Berliner Börsen-Zeitung*, June 9, 1929; *New York Times*, November 17, 1929; *Daily Herald*, November 12, 1929.

33. *The Cambridge Review*, May 3, 1929, 412.

34. *The London Mercury*, 21 (January 1930), 194-95.

35. Reported in the *New York Times*, February 9, 1930.

36. H. A. L. Fisher, *A History of Europe*, 3 vols. (London, 1935), I:vii.

37. "War Novels," *Morning Post*, April 8, 1930.

38. André Thérive, "Les Livres," *Le Temps*, December 27, 1929.

39. Robert Wohl, *The Generation of 1914* (Cambridge, Mass., 1979), 120; A. C. Ward, *The Nineteen-Twenties* (London, 1930), xii; Robert Graves, "The Marmosite's Miscellany," *Poems (1914-26)* (London, 1927), 191.

40. José Germain, in his preface to Maurice d'Hartoy, *La Génération du feu* (Paris, 1923), xi.

41. We live a melancholy era . . . Everything is screwed up. What? A whole world . . . It's nice out. Let's go to the cemetery.

42. Carroll Carstairs, *A Generation Missing* (London, 1930), 208.

43. Letter, July 2, 1915, Marc Boasson, *Au soir d'un monde* [microform], *lettres de guerre* (16 avril 1915-27 avril 1918) (Paris, 1926), 12; Egon Friedell, *A Cultural History of the Modern Age*, trans. C. F. Atkinson (New York, 1954), III: 467.

44. W. Müller Scheld, *Im Westen nichts Neues—eine Täuschung* (Idstein, 1929), 6.

45. *Commonweal*, May 27, 1931, 90.

46. *The Fortnightly Review*, October 1, 1930, 527; Davidson, in John C. Cairns, "A Nation of Shopkeepers in Search of a Suitable France: 1919-40," *The American Historical Review*, 79 (1974), 728; Douglas Goldring, *Pacifists in Peace and War* (London, 1932), 12, 18; Robert Graves, *Goodbye to All That: An Autobiography* (London, 1929), 240.

47. Joffre, in Marc Ferro, *La Grande Guerre 1914-1918* (Paris, 1969), 239; Guy Pedroncini, *Les mutineries de 1917* (Paris, 1967), 177; General Huguet, *L'Intervention militaire britannique en 1914* (Paris, 1928), 231.

48. See the introductory remarks by René Lalou to R. H. Mottram's *La Ferme espagnole*, trans. M. Dou-Desportes (Paris, 1930), i-iv.

49. Christopher Isherwood, *Lions and Shadows: An Education in the Twenties* (Norfolk, 1938), 73-76, and also his *Kathleen and Frank* (London, 1971), 356-63; and Jean Dutourd, *Les Taxis de la Marne* (Paris, 1956), 189-93.

50. *New York Times*, January 18, 1930.

51. William Faulkner, *The New Republic*, May 20, 1931, 23-24.

52. See my "War, Memory, and Politics: The Fate of the Film *All Quiet on the Western Front*," *Central European History*, 13/1 (March 1980), 60-82.

53. In Henry C. Meyer (ed.), *The Long Generation* (New York, 1973), 221.

54. See the correspondence between the Polizeipräsident in Berlin and the Geheime Staatspolizeiamt, December 4 and 16, 1933, Reichssicherheitshauptamt files, R58/933, 198-99, BAK.

55. Wolff'sche Telegraphen Büro report, May 15, 1933, in the Neue Reichskanzlei files, R43II/479, 4-5, BAK.

The Spokesman of a Generation

Harley U. Taylor, Jr.

In the autumn of 1927 Remarque began the actual writing of a story about the war which had been in the back of his mind since his hospital convalescence at Duisburg. The work originally took shape without any definite expectation that it might have commercial prospects. It was simply a book that he felt compelled to write. Remarque was certainly not breaking any new literary ground by choosing the war as a subject. In Germany Ludwig Renn, Arnold Zweig, and other lesser lights, had already enjoyed moderate success with their books about the "Great War."

In a matter of five weeks Remarque completed the episodic novel which was to become the classic war novel with a message transcending national borders. He was fond of saying that the novel wrote itself. If so, the novel was evidently not subject to the same number of revisions as his subsequent works.

For his war novel Remarque, with characteristic irony, chose the title *Im Westen nichts Neues* (*All Quiet on the Western Front*). The phrase had been a standard German army war communique form. The irony is in the fact that there was nothing significant to report on that October day in 1918 when Remarque's protagonist Paul Bäumer met his death. Paul was one of the last survivors in the class of Gymnasium students who had gone into army service together.

When Remarque wrote his war novel he drew not only on his own experiences but also on those of other comrades and war veterans with whom he had discussed the stupidity and horror of the war. Paul Bäumer's first-person narrative, therefore, transcended Remarque's personal story and Bäumer became a kind of "Everyman" protagonist who spoke for all of the young soldiers of his generation.

Remarque s brief introductory statement for the novel made it clear that he was speaking for more than himself:

"This book is to be neither an accusation nor a confession, and least of all an adventure, for death is not an adventure to those who stand face to face with it. It will try simply to tell of a generation of men who, even though they may have escaped its shells, were destroyed by the war."[1]

In a September 22, 1929, interview with Cyrus Brooks of the *New York Times* he discussed his personal experiences and the growing need he had to express those things he had seen during the war:

> "Coming back to Germany after the war was a terrible experience for every one of us. After the strain and hardships of horror of the war we returned to find the country in a state of disintegration, everywhere hunger, depression and bereavement. My own homecoming was overshadowed by the loss of my mother, which was a great blow to me. I had entered the army as a mere boy and was not one of the few lucky ones with a job to come back to, so I had to turn my hand to whatever offered—school teacher, handworker, journalist. I could not settle down to anything, there was a continual restlessness and dissatisfaction that drove me from one job to another. . . .
>
> "The truth was, there was something on my mind—the weight of horror and suffering I had seen during the war years. It was still there, unexpressed and chaotic, robbing one of peace of mind, making it impossible to settle down to the ordinary avocations of civilian life. At last—I was on the editorial staff of a Berlin illustrated weekly at the time—I realized that I had to get these things straight in my own mind, to get them into focus once for all.
>
> "The idea of my book came as a sort of safety valve. I came home one night from my work and started to write it. For obvious reasons I adopted the fiction form, but what I put down was the truth. I was not writing for any wide audience; my object was to see clearly the experiences I had been through and therefore I wrote with the utmost simplicity and integrity as though I were telling the story to an intimate friend. I avoided all panegyric and let the terrible facts speak for themselves."[2]

Although the writing had been relatively easy, the task of finding a publisher was considerably more formidable. Remarque, with his usual self-assurance, decided to submit his manuscript to the Samuel Fischer Verlag, one of Germany's most prestigious publishing houses. The Fischer Verlag, in a monumental error of judgement, decided not to publish the manuscript. The reason given was that the public was no longer interested in reading stories about the war. Disappointed but undaunted, Remarque next submitted his manuscript to Ullstein's Propyläen Verlag. Ullstein's acceptance produced a financial bonanza for them.

It had been generally thought that Max Krell, a former head reader for Ullstein, had been responsible for the wise decision to publish *Im Westen nichts Neues*. When Krell died in 1962, and obituaries credited him with this decision, a statement of disclaimer and clarification was made by Heinz Ullstein, the Ullstein firm's business manager. Ullstein pointed out that the person responsible for deciding whether or not to publish a book at that time had been Paul Wiegler, not Max Krell. When Remarque submitted the manuscript it was first read by Fritz Ross who enthusiastically recommended to Wiegler that the work be published.

After Wiegler's concurrence it was decided to allow the book to appear first in newspaper serial form in order to build public interest in the prospective book. *Die Vossische Zeitung* ran installments of the story from November 10 to December 9, 1928. These installments proved to be very successful in stimulating reader interest. Remarque's story accounted for the first complete sell-out in the paper's history. Printing of the book began January 31, 1929. By the end of 1929 it had been translated into twelve languages and had sold more than a million and a half copies. It remains one of the greatest commercial successes among German books. At the time of Remarque's death in 1970, 30 to 40 million copies had been sold worldwide.

The initial astonishing success, however, was a very mixed blessing for Remarque. On the positive side, it represented the commercial success and literary recognition that he had always wanted. The lavish praise of such literary luminaries as H. G. Wells, Walther von Molo, William Allen White, Heywood Broun, Christopher Morley, and H. L. Mencken was very heady for the young writer. As a more practical consideration it also meant that anything he wrote for the rest of his life would have a publisher eagerly waiting.

The negative aspects of his newly acquired fame, however, were perplexing and difficult to cope with. In a September 22, 1929 interview with Cyrus Brooks he said: "As for what they call fame, I don't want it. It comes between a man and reality. As soon as you become a celebrity you lose touch with humanity, with life. That is why I live so quietly and keep out of the limelight. I must keep in touch, otherwise I can not write simply and directly for the minds and hearts of ordinary men and women. I want to have a little place in the country and breed dogs."[3]

It was, however, obviously impossible for Remarque to have his wish to avoid the limelight. Besieged with requests for interviews, lectures, and various types of commercial commitments, Remarque, who had even lost the name plate on his door to souvenir hunters, decided to leave Berlin. He sought to gain a much needed perspective on his situation by taking an extensive driving tour of France. It is interesting to note that during this trip he always registered at inns and hotels under a pseudonym and gave his occupation as "dog breeder".

One of the worst aspects of celebrity status for Remarque was the strain it had put on his friendships. This was particularly bitter for the man who said in *Im Westen nichts Neues* in summarizing the effect of the war on his generation: "But by far the most important was that it awakened in us a strong, practical sense of *esprit de corps*, which in the field developed into the finest thing that arose out of the war— comradeship."[4]

In a 1930 interview with the author Friedrich Hirth, Remarque spoke at some length about the change in some of his friends. During the conversation he said: "What actually happened? Before my 'success' my friends used to greet me joyfully, but now if I announce that I am going to visit them I no longer find myself in the cordial intimacy of long ago—they receive me flanked with a group of unknown people to whom I seem like some curious animal.—Formerly when I returned from a six months' journey, all my friends were glad and gave me a party. Today their sensitivity has no bounds and if I neglect one or another of them, he treats me contemptuously."[5]

As vexing as these changes in his personal relationships were to Remarque, they were later to seem less important in comparison with the abuse he suffered as a result of the vitriolic attacks on him and on his book.

Although Remarque wrote that his novel was not an accusation, it is immediately clear that it is replete with accusations against various targets. Those targets are the groups regarded by him as being responsible for the senseless slaughter of his comrades and for the wretched plight of his country as a result of the war. The indictments, directly or by implication, were made against incompetent military and governmental leadership, war profiteers, and the misguided, chauvinistic teachers who deceived Remarque and his classmates regarding the true nature of the war.

However, at no time did Remarque ever deprecate the German soldier or the soldier-enemy he faced. Remarque's interpretation of comradeship was broad enough to encompass even those men who were his enemies on the battlefield because he realized that they were as much the pawns of their own government's policies as he and his comrades were of the German government.

Because Remarque's popular book had generated such an enthusiastic response from German readers it was immediately seen by ultranationalists as a serious threat. The National Socialist Party was violently opposed to the book's anti-war, anti-militarism message. They regarded it as a defeatist document diametrically opposite in tone and content to the propaganda image of the German soldier which they wished to promote.

Almost immediately desperate efforts were made to discredit the book by impeaching the credentials of its author. Groups which had their own reasons for hostility began to spread a number of rumors. One of the stories, which still surfaces occasionally, was that Remarque's real name was Kramer and that he was Jewish. It was also said that he was really 55 years old and had never been at the front. Another rumor claimed that he had reworked the diary of a fallen comrade to produce *Im Westen nichts Neues*. These stories were essentially acts of desperation which did very little to impede the book's progress or lessen its impact. It was true, however, that Remarque's combat experiences were not as impressive as those of his protagonist Paul Bäumer. His credentials, although limited, were nevertheless valid.

The attacks on him persisted. In September, 1929, The German Officers' League, on the basis of a report that Remarque might be awarded the Nobel Prize for literature, wrote to the Nobel Prize Committee to protest in advance any such course of action. Although Remarque was never awarded the Nobel Prize it appears unlikely that the German protest was the sole reason.

Among the most literate and imaginative of Remarque's individual critics was Dr. Salomo Friedländer who, in 1929, wrote a book entitled *Hat Remarque wirklich gelebt? (Did Remarque Really Live?)* This effort was written under his pseudonym "Mynona", a reversal of "anonym" which translates as "anonymous". By selectively quoting persons who had known Remarque, and by using material out of context, he managed to present a distorted view of Remarque and his work which still bedevils Remarque's memory. Friedländer, however, apparently was motivated less by pure malice than by a desire to maintain his position as a popular satirist and devil's advocate. He was able skillfully to exploit much of the ambiguity surrounding the new celebrity.

Other treatments were far more vitriolic. In retrospect it is somewhat difficult to understand how this book, whose message is now almost universally acceptable, could cause such bitter controversy.

However, the book's success left dozens of published attacks in its wake. Among the most interesting were Wilhelm Müller-Scheld's 1929 essay "*Im Westen nichts Neues, eine Täuschung*" ("*All Quiet on the Western Front*: a Deception"), Gottfried Nickl's "*Im Westen nichts Neues*, und sein wahrer Sinn; eine Betrachtung über den Pazifismus und Antwort an Remarque" ("*All Quiet on the Western Front*, and its true meaning; a consideration of pacifism and answer to Remarque"), also written in 1929, and, finally, Peter Kropp's 1930 interesting, but shorter, essay "Endlich Klarheit über Remarque und sein Buch *Im Westen nichts Neues*" ("Clarity at last Concerning Remarque and his Book: *All Quiet on the Western Front*").

Just when it seemed that Remarque's critics had exhausted almost every possibility for abuse, as well as general silliness, the literary periodical *Die Literatur* reported contributions pro and con in the "screaming horse" controversy. The controversy developed when issue was taken with Remarque's description of horses screaming in pain as a result of war injuries. His critics said horses did not scream. The last word, however, was had by a Czech veterinarian, a Dr. E. Januschke, who reported: "In response to my inquiry, several of my veterinarian colleagues, who served in the war as veterinarians or as frontline officers, have told me that they have often heard severely wounded horses scream frightfully."[6]

Among those German authors who had already written books dealing with the war, only one, Arnold Zweig, who had written *Der Streit um den Sergeanten Grischa* in 1927, had his nose put seriously out of joint by Remarque's overwhelming success. Harry Kessler in his book, *In the Twenties*, makes some revealing comments about Zweig's reactions. In Kessler's journal entry for Friday, August 30, 1929 he indicated that "Zweig has accused him (Remarque) of being slapdash, but Zweig's artistry comes between his book and the reader, whereas he (Remarque) is only concerned to get close to the reader."[7] Kessler presents Zweig in a very unflattering light later in the same entry.

"Dinner at the Hugo Simons. Arnold Zweig was there and, pretending to present bouquets, was venomous about Remarque. As if someone had attacked the latter, though everyone was singing his praises, he said, 'No, no it's a good book', the word 'good' being pronounced with condescension. 'Remarque is a "good" amateur and he could even have turned his book into a great novel. His amateurism lies precisely in having failed to see the angle from which he should have tackled his subject. He lit on it, but passed it blindly by. There, where he describes the farmer's lad who can't stand the war any more when he sees the trees in blossom and thereupon runs away. That is where I would have started the story and centered everything else around this boy. Then it would have become a great book.' Altogether Zweig was at pains throughout the evening to prove himself maliciously witty. As he has only the malice and not the wit, the upshot was merely excessively tedious literary tittle-tattle."[8]

Rudolf Binding, another German author who wrote about the war on the basis of his personal experience, also had some reservations about Remarque. Binding had served in combat and as a cavalry officer. His literary treatment of the war gave it a nobility and glory that Remarque's book obviously did not. Binding had the outlook characteristic of the officer corps. Although Remarque's approach was not compatible with his own views, Binding did not really question the overall accuracy of the events depicted. However, he appears to have been quite disturbed by the fact that a man who wrote such trivia items as "Über das Mixen kostbarer Schnäpse" for publisher Paul Steegemann's "snob journal"[9] *Störtebeker* would have the audacity to approach a subject as sacrosanct as the war was for Binding. Binding also was on the side of those Remarque critics who maintained that wounded horses do not scream. Because of Binding's extensive experiences with horses as a cavalry officer, horse breeder, race rider, and paraprofessional veterinarian, his opinion has to be carefully considered. As reported in *Der Spiegel*, Binding stated: "Wounded horses do not scream. With almost closed mouths they moan very dully, and barely audibly, through their noses."[10] Debate on this relatively minor point finally ran its course. It ended with each faction still convinced of the correctness of its original view.

The hostility, or opposition, of writers such as Zweig and Binding, as well as niggling technical criticism, had no perceptible impact on the German reading public which was eager to obtain copies of the new literary sensation. Sales of up to 15,000 per day kept seven printing and binding establishments going full-time.

From *Erich Maria Remarque: A Literary and Film Biography* (2003), pp. 61-69. Copyright © 2003 by Peter Lang. Reprinted with permission of Peter Lang.

Notes

1. *All Quiet on the Western Front* (Boston: Little, Brown, and Company, 1929), unnumbered page before the beginning of the text.

2. *New York Times*, Sept. 22, 1929, 7.

3. *Ibid.*

4. *All Quiet on the Western Front*, 26.

5. *The Living Age*, Dec. 1930, 347-48.

6. *Die Literature*, Vol. 32 (1929-30) 6. My translation.

7. Harry Kessler, *In the Twenties* (New York: Holt, Rinehart and Winston, 1971) 367.

8. *Ibid.*

9. *Der Spiegel*, Jan. 9, 1952, 25.

10. *Ibid.*, Jan. 9, 1952, 25.

Post Mortem:
All Quiet on the Western Front (1929)_____

Richard Arthur Firda

By 1925, Remarque had arrived in Berlin to work in the trade of journalism. The publishing center of the city was the *Zeitungsviertel*, Germany's Fleet Street, dominated by two large giants, *Ullstein* and the *Scherl* publishing enterprises.[1] Remarque's address, along with that of his new bride, Jutta Ilse Zambona, was in the fashionable Charlottenburg area, Kaiserdamm 114, more acceptable and comfortable than the wet concrete unseasoned houses of Osnabrück.[2] Remarque entered into the cultural and social life of the metropolis, by then the undisputed center of the German-speaking world, since the collapse of Austria-Hungary. He began to spell his name with a -que instead of a -k. He was an observer of a fateful year of political change for the capital of the Weimar Republic. President Friedrich Ebert's death had ended effective Socialist control of the central government. Given a choice between another democratic leader and one of conservative persuasion, the German citizen moved to replace Ebert with Marshal Paul von Hindenberg, a living national monument now retired in Hannover, "his home a mausoleum of war relics, battle flags, a silver ax, bronze elks and a large collection of pictures of the Madonna" (Friedrich 184). In September 1925, the musician Schönberg left Vienna to settle in Berlin and established the city as a center of German music. The symbolic meaning of the act did not go unnoticed. German culture would develop in tandem with industrial cartels and the military establishment. Ominously, Hitler was released in 1925 from prison for his activities in the aborted Munich *Putsch*. Four years later, in 1929, Remarque was still in Berlin and Germans were riding the crest of an economic boom, though the "recovery" was a false one. Foreign capitalists, especially Americans, were reinvesting in Germany's future. Wages for the German worker were higher than ever and retail sales were good. German political leadership managed

Post Mortem   **173** to achieve a proposed reduction (the Young plan) in the dreaded repayment of war-time reparations:

> These events made headlines in the Berlin newspapers, but international economic conferences rarely have much effect in the streets and on the beaches. To the ordinary Berliners, the new prosperity meant jobs, and a little extra money after all the years of privation. . . . If they wanted more excitement, they could race along the new Avus Speedway, which ran for more than eleven miles without a curve from the Kurfürstenbamm almost all the way to Potsdam. (Friedrich 279)

The Big Money climate of the 1920's not only set the stage for Germany's notorious inflation, it enabled many Germans to become rich, like Remarque's new employer, Alfred Hugenberg, the owner of the *Scherl Verlag*. Remarque was employed by Hugenberg from 1925 to 1928, serving him as a co-editor of a prestigious journal, *Sport im Bild* (*Illustrated Sport*). *Sport* was a high-class endeavor that kept its readers abreast of the latest changes in automotive technology. It reviewed European car races and annotated articles on the future of Berlin as a traffic metropolis. Remarque's previous experience as a writer of advertising copy for the *Echo Continental* in Hannover came into focus with a series of articles instructing women how to cope with automobile failures and tire blowouts. He wrote on weekend excursions into the Grünewald suburbs. Though some of these articles were exceedingly frivolous, to wit, that "the mystical bridge between Man and Machine is now crossed," Remarque cut his journalistic teeth in 1926 in the pages of the *Sport* (*Sport* 98-99). Like Somerset Maugham, Remarque never forgot the merits of a clearly written sentence and the value of episodic structure for the printed page. Here he learned to write for an educated German audience.

Sport found its readers outside the academic community. In 1927-28, *Sport* serialized the chapters of Remarque's second novel *Station am Horizont* (*Station on the Horizon*).[3] Years later, Remarque noted that this novel hardly represented the working philosophy of a matured writer. Its superficial tone embarrassed him and its theme, centering on the fatal romance between a race car driver named Clerfayt and the beautiful, exquisite Lilian Dunkirk, seemed to have little to do with the world as Remarque claimed to know it. Nevertheless, *Station* fit perfectly into the kind of writing that Remarque was then publishing in the pages of *Sport* and related Hugenberg newspaper, the *Montag*, the Monday edition of the *Berliner Lokal-Anzeiger*:

> Automobiles have became cheaper to buy. Last year prices fluctuated but there have been some reductions. Only in the last few weeks have the average prices moderated. You can buy a car today for 2000DM, the smaller kinds of luxury cars costs between three and four thousand marks, and if you have a few more thousand available, then you can buy a real companion with all the extras. ("Die Dame und der kleine Wagen")

The irony of Remarque's being employed by one of Germany's most typical Weimar Capitalists should not be lost. Hugenberg's opposition to the liberal Weimar Republic existed openly in his position of leadership within the Nationalist Party. He had served as a financial director of the Krupp armament empire. Besides owning a large portion of UFA, which in the 1920's meant the German film industry, Hugenberg made the *Scherl Verlag* a vital part of his financial holdings. This latter acquisition was achieved in 1916 and through it, Hugenberg became a figure in the German communications industry. Hugenberg was now available to surface as one of Germany's most vociferous opponents to the humiliating Versailles Treaty. He used his access to German banking houses to obtain funds for the publication of nationalist literature. This included an ill-fated attempt to join forces with a forty-year-old Adolf Hitler in a common effort to end reparations to the Allies for the defeat suffered in World War I.

There have survived several episodes of Remarque's status as an editor and his role as a socialite in Weimar Berlin. One of these, perhaps the most telling, gives us an idea of the young, ambitious journalist still at home in the conservative atmosphere of the *Scherl Verlag*. The following incident is reported by Axel Eggebrecht in his autobiography, *Der Halbe Weg* (*Halfway*), 1975:

> The summer of 1929 found me sharing an attic with Kurt von Molo. . . . I used to hang about at the *Toppkeller* on the Schweriner Strasse, a sort of low-class bar where everybody from the West Side of Berlin would congregate. . . . The chief attraction and challenge was a beam into which anyone was invited to drive a nail with a single blow. If you could do it, you got a free glass of brandy. . . . I tried it once just to show off before a sexy young girl. Afterwards, I sat down with her and her husband, who introduced himself as an editor on the staff of Hugenberg's magazine, *Sport im Bild*. . . . He liked being a snob, left the bar with a cane and great coat and had a Fiat. I was invited to come home with both of them. We had drinks and looked at his aquarium. . . . He wasn't at all disturbed that I was actually making a pass at his wife. . . . Thus, I began a month's liaison with Jeanne (sic), the wife of Erich Maria Remarque. . . . I soon found out he himself was having an affair with another woman. . . . I took trips with Jeanne into the Lusatian Alps. . . . He saw us off on the train. . . . She was sharp, but very indolent. . . . She told me that she had fallen in love with a friend of mine, Franz Schulz. . . . In the meanwhile, *All Quiet on the Western Front* had appeared in the *Vossische Zeitung*, then in book form. . . . Remarque became well off. . . . He was now driving an expensive sports car and I bought his little car. . . . The last time I ever met him was in the spring of 1929, when I interviewed him for the *Literarische Welt*. . . . He was terribly pessimistic. . . . But eventually, whether he liked it or not, Remarque became a populariser of democratic and humanistic ideas. . . . I suppose I should never have given him another thought if it had not been for one memory of him that coloured my feelings towards him. . . . After Remarque made a fortune, he became terribly conventional. He demanded faithfulness and obedience from Jeanne. He had her shadowed during her liaison with Franz Schulz. After that she submitted to his tyranny. At Davos, where she went for a lung cure, I had proof of

his conformism. I saw both of them, from a distance, in Ascona, during the Autumn of 1932. They were together, he and she; neither of them returned my greeting. (241-44)[4]

If it is true that Remarque, who was moving on in the world did not necessarily view Weimar bohemianism as the great leveler, he understood the virtue of dropping anyone who did not fit into his new scheme of personal and artistic advancement. He realized the futility of making his way in Berlin's Grub Street in 1928 by writing facile magazine articles. Neither *Dream Room* nor *Station* had received serious critical attention. He was suffering from bouts of mental depression and his efforts to survive them, Remarque called his therapy "intentional analysis", would indicate that the first drafts of *All Quiet* were born of spiritual and cathartic reasons. In June 1929 Remarque elaborated in all candor on this period of his life. Referring to his "general condition of emptiness, and scepticism," he went on to say:

> Formerly, I had never thought of writing about the war. At that time . . . that is, in the Spring of last year (1929) . . . I was busy with work of a different kind. I was employed as a 'picture editor' of a periodical. The evenings I devoted to a variety of things. Thus, for instance, I made a number of attempts to write a play, but I was never successful in that I suffered from rather violent attacks of despair (and) my mind reverted to my experiences during the war. I was able to observe quite similar phenomena in my acquaintances and friends. We all were, and still are to the present day, the victims of restlessness. We lack a final object to our striving. At times we are supersensitive, at times indifferent. . . . The shadows of the war oppressed us, and particularly so when we did not think of it at all. On that very day on which these ideas swept over me, I began to write, without lengthy reflection. This was continued for six weeks—every evening when I returned from the office—and by that time the book had been completed. . . . In the beginning, I had no confidence whatsoever in my work as a literary product, because it was the first time I had written in such a style. . . .[5]

These lines describe well the immediate reasons leading to Remarque's decision to write his great war novel. It begs the question, as one critic had suggested, that *All Quiet* bore all the trademarks of a German best-seller and that Remarque had planned to invade a writer's market (Bance 362). However, almost ten years had passed since the surrender and the collapse of the German Empire. The German people now had the time, if not the perspective, to reassess the harsh years of war in which the nation had suffered dire privation and humiliation. The idea of war novels was in the air, soon to be taken up by German film makers for a series of war movies. War fiction hit upon a central nerve of the time, expressly that continued presence of the military establishment in all phases of German life and culture. Dissolution of the Age of Security under the Emperor made the return home for the War's survivors—Remarque's generation—especially precarious. German Business, along with the Courts and the Universities, remained under the control of the Middle and Upper Classes. It was clear to Germany's more progressive elements that little had changed from the time of William the Second. When the Social Democrat, Police Chief Zörgiebel, shot at a group of striking workers in 1929 during a routine demonstration on the streets of Berlin, the German Right was ready to act and suggest its own measures for the restoration of order and discipline. In this sense, the Western Front had really changed its setting to one closer to home. There were now reasons to fear the collapse of the Weimar government and its immediate troubles were attributed by both the Right and Left to the deposed Imperialist Regime. That regime's policies, especially the War of 1914-1918, became a burning issue for all levels of German citizens. The debate on national accountability had begun.

On the one hand, Conservatives laid claim to their position that the late war was a prologemena for the renewal of national spirit and purpose. There had been no real defeat, except on the part of the Socialist Democrats. Conservatives said that the war was, in fact, the basis for future moral regeneration of the German nation. Nietzsche, the German philosopher of the Superman, had spoken eloquently on this issue. It was revived in the work of the novelist Ernst Jünger, whose book *In Stahlgewittern* (*Storm of Steel*, 1920) defined the ethos of German heroism. The book was hailed by the Right as a Bible for German youth because it propagated those values so dear to the conservative mind: Personal Duty, Family, and the Fatherland. War was a rite of passage beyond *Frontkamaradschaft* to a higher purpose, *Gemeinschaft*, now a sacred word in the German vocabulary. A new society, not the comradeship of war, was the new national priority!

Opposed to nationalist sloganeering, the German Left began to find its spokesmen among those foreign writers and novelists inclined to challenge the Rightist myth of war as purification. Among the first of these tests were two early French novels: Barbusse's *Le Feu* (*Under Fire*, 1918) and *Les Croix de bois* (*Wooden Crosses*, 1920) by Roland Dorgeles. Spain and the United States had also contributed notable pacifist texts in the campaign against the war. These were the novels of Blasco-Ibanez (*The Four Horsemen*, 1919), Willa Cather (*One of Ours*, 1923) and John Dos Passos (*Three Soldiers*, 1922).

At least a decade after the war's end, however, Germany began to correct the tide of foreign pacifist literature. Some of the more notable contributions were texts written by Johannes Becher (*Levisite*, 1926), Arnold Zweig's *Der Streit um den Sergeanten Grischa* (*Sergeant Grisha*, 1927) and Ludwig Renn's novel *Krieg* (*War*, 1928). Arnold Zweig's book, later part of his trilogy on the "white men's war," told the fate of a semi-legal military case, but the atmosphere of war was secondary. The plot concerned the struggle for the life of a poor Russian prisoner of war, Grischa, who escapes from his camp, steals the paper of a dead Russian deserter, is then captured and condemned by the Germans to death. Grischa's real identity is discovered but the German officer in charge decides he must die as an example and die he does. Grischa's competition for popularity among the German Left was Renn's book *War* and it, too, found an enduring place in German war fiction of the '20's. Renn purported to offer a straightforward, classic account of life and combat behind the German lines. *War*'s style and technique were very different from the sensitive, impressionistic manner of *All Quiet*. Renn claimed first-hand experience on the Front from start to finish. The author, a former Saxon nobleman turned pacifist, recorded the experiences of his hero 'Ludwig' with little effort and great simplicity. If the incidents and events making up the daily routine of Renn's German enlisted man were recognized here for their authenticity, this enthusiasm came from the German Officer Corps as well, who admired its objective and impartial report of the recent conflict. Some of the reasons for the book's critical and popular success are found in this commentary written by Carl von Ossietzky in 1929:

> (Renn) adopts a form of expression which has nothing visionary in its woodcut-like hardness, but which creates a rounded picture of extraordinary impressions—Every frightful wound is recorded with the faithfulness of an old Dutch painter of martyrs. . . . Renn's fanatical realism . . . misses no nuance. . . . He projects enormously much of what he saw and heard; but in the same measure he is sparing with what happened within him. He is, in succession, Soldier Renn, Lance-Corporal Renn, Corporal Renn, a single tiny wheel in the vast machine of war. . . . One understands why this bloody infamy could last for four years. There were innumerable Renns on all fronts and under all flags. They functioned so well because they loved people around them in all their misery and dirt. . . .[6]

Remarque, living in the center of German publishing and journalism, was undoubtedly aware of the commercial and artistic potential of writing a war novel and may have begun to form his own ideas of writing such a novel of the Western Front, surrounded as he was by the tide of personal recollections of the war and the flood of war fiction found in Germany from national and foreign sources. He had read Barbusse and Jünger and might have known George Duhamel's book *Civilisation* that was written in 1919. He spoke highly of Knut Hamsun and the American writers Theodore Dreiser and Upton Sinclair, both of them novelists concerned with socialist and economic issues. More to the point perhaps was his signed review in June 1928, in the pages of *Sport* where Remarque discussed the war fiction most Germans were then reading. There he touted the ideal components of a German war novel: simple style, the comradeship of men at war and at the Front and the device of viewing the war through a combat unit of enlisted men. In his concept of the ideal war novel, "the war itself would form only a backdrop to everything else" (*Soldat Suhren* 185).

By the Spring of 1928, Remarque had submitted the manuscript of *All Quiet* to his employer, the *Scherl Verlag*. Rejection was a foregone conclusion, considering the stance of publisher Hugenberg, who could hardly sponsor a work so contrary to German nationalist aspirations. One can only surmise the reasons behind Remarque's decision to submit his book to *Scherl*. Perhaps it was a matter of professional courtesy or even the memory of *Scherl's* favorable response to Remarque's early society novel, *Station*. Rejection, however, amounted to refusal; and at this point, Remarque was urged by the Chief Editor of *Sport*, Konrad Elert, to use the help of a fellow-employer, Paul Eipper. Eipper was responsible for bringing *All Quiet* to the attention of the *S. Fischer Verlag*, prestige publishers of German authors, poets and playwrights. In an extensive history of that publishing house, writer Peter de Mendelssohn traces the extensive passage of *All Quiet* from *Scherl* to *Fischer*. Mendelssohn's information itself comes from a letter sent by Remarque to the author and there Remarque notes:

> *All Quiet on the Western Front* was sent to *S. Fischer Verlag* in the Spring of 1928 by Konrad Elert, Chief Editor of *Sport im Bild*. Elert used Paul, one of our colleagues as an intermediary. . . . Samuel Fischer called me in later and told me he did not think the book would make him any money—nobody was interested in the war anymore. I was free, however, to go elsewhere. As far as I remember, he returned the manuscript to me. Several days later, I sent him a letter giving dates of books or the war and their many editions. I continued to be hopeful and therefore asked him to recon-

sider his decision. Perhaps my book would sell a thousand copies. He didn't answer back and a few months later the book was sent to Ullstein, who immediately bought it.[7]

Fischer's costly and short-sighted error is now part of German publishing history. Gottfried Bermann Fischer, successor to the firm, records that he tried to save the novel for his father-in-law, though it is not clear whether that gentleman ever got to read the manuscript.[8] In any event, Fischer seems never to have regretted his decision to say "no" to the young writer. Pressed for a more complete response, Fischer remarked that his firm's readers had made the point that Remarque would never write a second novel and that *All Quiet* was not a suitable book for a listing by Fischer in a stable of luminaries like Arthur Schnitzler, Thomas Mann and Hugo von Hofmannsthal. The jury was out, indeed, on the question of Remarque's permanent literary status. These decisions would be settled, in fact, far from any publisher's office and in the marketplace where books were bought and read by the German public itself. Remarque's immediate problem, however, was still that of finding a sympathetic publisher and at this point he was once again encouraged by Paul Eipper to send on the manuscript of *All Quiet* to *Ullstein's*, *Scherl's* competitor in Publisher's Row, where after some hesitation, Remarque was successful in placing the text of his novel into the hands of an equally prestigious and important German publishing house.

The true story of Remarque's contact with *Ullstein's* will probably never be known. The manuscript arrived shortly after Easter 1928 at the desk of Max Krell, a reader in the fiction section of *Ullstein's*. Every child in Berlin knew the name of this outstanding German publishing house, whose affiliates were scattered all over the city. Each branch of *Ullstein* was adorned with the firm's distinctive colophon, an owl. Behind the display windows of *Ullstein* were exhibited copies of the management's newspapers and magazines; the *Vossische Zeitung*, the *Berliner Morgenpost*, the *B. Z. am Mittag*. There was a total of twelve.

Its telegrams and photographs of recent world events were changed frequently for street traffic. All of these activities, some of them financial, others cultural and intellectual, defined *Ullstein's* position of communication leadership in the Berlin metropolis. In his autobiography *Das alles gab es einmal* (*It Was Once All There*, 1961), Max Krell relates the background of these key events at *Ullstein*. The cast of characters includes himself:

> The manuscript landed on my desk. It was shortly after Pentecost, at a time when there was little to read, so I had the leisure to do it. The tone of the manuscript impressed me. Situations and characters were rendered with journalistic accuracy. There was a strange world, since I had not fought in the recent war. I tried to tell my colleagues about my strong feelings for the book, but I was turned away. 'War'? And especially a war written by a soldier who never heard the sound of a bullet. (159-60)

Krell tells further that he was able to get the attention of Cyrill Soschka, chief of the newspaper division. Soschka read the manuscript and spoke up for it among his subordinates at the weekly executive conference. One of Remarque's defenders and perhaps the one whose voice cast the final vote for *Ullstein's* sponsorship was that of Monty Jacobs, the actor-critic of *Ullstein's* intellectually respectable newspaper, the *Vossische Zeitung* (Krell 161). The "Voss", as it was fondly called by both its writers and the buying public, was once under the guiding hand of Lessing, a stellar figure in the firmament of German eighteenth-century dramatic literature. It was thus no minor accomplishment for Remarque when in August 1928, he was able to sign a contract for publication in the "Voss" from the 10th of November to the 9th of December. The contract stipulated that the book's hardcover edition would hinge on its reception in the newspaper. It was the best offer that Remarque was able to garner and he accepted it.[9]

From the very moment of its birth as a serialized novel in the "Voss", *All Quiet* was to be a subject of controversy, censorship, banning and other difficulties. There were differences initially, both in style and content, between the novel printed in the newspaper and its later German hardcover edition.[10] Remarque's novel of the First World War was introduced to its readers, however, with little fanfare. Taking its modest turn in the literary and cultural sections of the newspaper, its appearance was a historical occasion, but hardly alluding to the *cause célèbre* that it would later become. There were signs that the public was responding to it; newspaper circulation figures for the "Voss" increased notably. Remarque left his job with *Scherl* on the 15th of November, about ten years to the day after the end of the Great War which his book was about to immortalize. He was surely fired by his conservative employer Hugenberg for reasons attributable to the novel's publication.[11] The "Remarque Case" and its subsequent turn into a media event had now begun.

Ullstein was thus compelled to keep its final contractual commitment to Remarque and *All Quiet* was published as a hardback novel on 31 January 1929. Its first printing was in *Ullstein's* quality publishing subsidiary, the *Propyläen Verlag*. The novel was now brought out complete and uncensored, unlike the newspaper serialization. There was an initial printing of approximately 30,000 copies.

Remarque's book began with its famous preface advising the reader that:

> This book is to be neither an accusation nor a confession, and least of all an adventure, for death is not an adventure to those who stand face to face with it. It will try simply to tell of a generation of men who, even though they may have escaped its shells, were destroyed by the war.[12]

We learn that a group of former classmates are now soldiers behind the front lines. They were advised by their teacher Kantorek to join in the fight for the glory of the Fatherland. Kantorek had urged them all to report as volunteers to the *Bezirkskommando*, the local training camp:

Kantorek had been our schoolmaster, a stern little man in a grey tail-coat, with a face like a schrew mouse. . . . It is very queer that the unhappiness of the world is so often brought on by small men. . . . During drill-time, Kantorek gave us long lectures until the whole of our class went, under his shepherding, to the District Commandant and volunteered. I can see now, as he used to glance at us through his spectacles and say in a moving voice: 'won't you join up, Comrades?' (15)

Basic Training takes ten weeks. Kropp, Müller, Kemmerich and Paul Bäumer (Remarque) are put together in a unit under Himmelstoss, a tyrant corporal. Some of the novel's most typical episodes treat Himmelstoss as a resented symbol of authority. Now in the front lines of the German Army, a strong sense of comradeship and common destiny are experienced by all. Bombardments and actual combat, however, gradually dispersed the academic rhetoric and nationalistic jingoism, with which they began their military service. It was their mistake, Paul Bäumer says to himself at a point of reflection, and under it the world as it was taught them had disappeared. Kemmerich has his leg shot off and then amputated. His subsequent death in a hospital ward is the first of many tragedies that Bäumer will witness in the war:

An hour passes. I sit tensely and watch every moment in case he may perhaps say something. . . . But he only weeps, his head turned aside. . . . He is entirely alone now with his little life of nineteen years and cries because it leaves him. This is the most disturbing and hardest parting that I have ever seen. . . . (33)

Kemmerich's boots are left not to Bäumer but to Müller who admires them. Bäumer, however, is sent out on wiring fatigue duty (again as a parallel with soldier Remarque) and there follows a strangely beautiful and moving description of exploding shells and shrapnel near the front lines. Bäumer says at this point:

An uncertain red glow spreads along the skyline from one end to the other. It is in perpetual movement, penetrated with the burst of flame from the nozzle of the batteries. Balls of light rise up high above it, silver and red spheres which explode and rain down in showers of red, white and green stars. 'Bombardment', says Kat. (55)

There next follow a few episodes of trench warfare, a gas attack and subsequent battle near a cemetery, all of these events deepening Paul's disillusionment with the war only further. When he is wounded, Bäumer is permitted a leave of absence after he comes out of his hospitalization. Going home for a visit to his home town (Remarque's Osnabrück), Paul is subject to distressful memories of his unhappy life at home. Neither his father nor his mother are exempt from this analysis where he says, "We were never very demonstrative in our family: poor folks who toil and are full of cares are not so. It is not their way to protest what they already know" (138).

His father, curious and proud of his soldier son in a way that Bäumer finds unusual, seems not to have changed, while his mother is sick and dying of cancer. Paul returns to the front once again to search for his comrades. One day, Paul Bäumer finds himself in a trench with the wounded and dying body of the "Enemy", the Frenchman Gérard Duval:

'Comrade, I did not want to kill you' (Bäumer soliloquizes). 'If you jumped in here again, I would not do it, if you would be sensible too. But you were only an idea to me before, an abstraction that lived in my mind and called forth its appropriate response. It was that abstraction I stabbed. But now, for the first time, I see you are a man like me. . . . Forgive me comrade. We always see it too late. Why do they never tell us, that your mothers are just as anxious as ours, and that we have the same fear of death, and the same dying and the same agony—forgive me, comrade, how could you be my enemy?' (191)

The controversial theme of this passage, namely the comradeship between German and French soldiers on grounds of a commonly shared destiny, was surely a primary reason why *All Quiet* was burned by the Nazis in May 1933.[13] Meanwhile, the summer of 1918 is the worst that Bäumer experiences, since no food or weapons are available for the dispirited German soldiers. There are rumors of armistice and reconciliation with the Allies. The Germans, however, are urged to continue fighting and Bäumer's best friend and helpmate, the older soldier Katczinsky (Kat), is killed by a piece of shrapnel. Paul is the last remaining survivor of seven recruits from his class. In October 1918, during a period of complete peace on the Western Front and when the army report declared as usual to the German people that "there is nothing new", Bäumer dies and his face has an expression of calm, as though he was glad of his death.

In *All Quiet*, Remarque had not only tried to speak out for his own non-political generation, for whom the Great War had lasted too long to be an adventure in heroism for nationalist or philosophical reason. The pessimism of this group was clearly put in Bäumer's reflection that "if we go back we will be weary, broken, burnt out, rootless, and without hope. We will not be able to find our way any more" (246).

There was, of course, a good bit of Remarque's life in the book, centering on (1) his life in Osnabrück, and (2) Paul Bäumer's experiences on the front lines. The most challenged chapters of the novel by German nationalists claimed to speak firsthand about direct combat on the battlefield[14] and to this day, *All Quiet* remains that kind of classic war novel in which the reality of the First World War experience blends with the wider dimensions of fiction itself. Goethe's autobiography was called *Dichtung und Wahrheit* (*Poetry and Truth*) and in the same sense, Remarque's limited but active participation as a combatant in that conflict showed how painful the distinction had become for those who refused to accept the novel as an authentic account of the war. We may ask, however, what was "fictional" in a book that described the common basis of an experience shared by most young Germans of Remarque's generation. The political underpinnings of the Imperialist regime had led naturally into the conflict. If *All Quiet* "is remarkably free from the obligation to documentary that is common to most war books" (Bance 361), then it is equally true that such documentation would have removed it (for many readers) from the realm of the fictional to that of the documentary and had made the book a factual record rather than the moving spiritual account that it still remains. In his redefinition of *Kameradschaft* especially, Remarque restated the personal bonds between men across personal and national boundaries. His pacifism was the logical and sensible end for a generation of young Germans and young Europeans and Englishmen—as Herbert Read said in 1929—who were unable to believe in Democracy, Socialism or the League of Nations (Read 116). To insist that the book be a rallying cry for political change, however, was in fact, too great a burden for the novel to carry. Its *raison d'être* was the common German soldier's *Fronterlebnis* (experience on the front line), rather than the suggestion that it could offer any specific formula for social or political change. Because it was a war novel, however, meaning many things to all its readers, it sets itself up for direct criticism.

There is little doubt, as recent scholarship has uncovered, that young soldier Remarque experienced the outbreak of the Battle of Flanders in the Summer of 1917 and that he was wounded by shrapnel from British artillery fire, behind the lines. As reported elsewhere in this text, Remarque was evacuated to a field hospital and from the middle of August he began recuperating at Saint Vincent's Hospital in Duisberg, Germany. His friend and biographer, Hanns Gerd Rabe, has spoken clearly on this unsettled portion of Remarque's life for most of his critics. Two events from Remarque's army career (1916-1918) were to make lasting impressions upon the later novelists, that of his wiring fatigue duty behind the front lines where he was constantly exposed to shells and bombing from the combat around him and finally his subsequent recuperation in the army hospital, during which time he could observe the direct effect of the war upon sick and mutilated soldiers. In Rabe's "Remarque and Osnabrück", we read the following:

Both of these experiences were taken over and fictionalized in his novel, *All Quiet on the Western Front*. However, the skilled eye of a soldier will soon realize that the book contains no incidents portraying an actual attack upon or even the repelling of an enemy unit. He must have realized that he had no direct experience with either of these kinds of incidents, despite the first hand accounts he received from wounded soldiers in the hospital. I myself told Remarque about my own experiences as a company commander on the Western Front. (214)

Paul Bäumer's fellow comrades on the Front, as Rabe further indicates, were based on Remarque's own contemporaries:

Officer Himmelstoss was derived from the Osnabrück family name Himmelreich, of whom there were still survivors in 1969. The teacher "Kantorek" was based only indirectly on Remarque's preparatory school instructor Konschorek. 'Kat' or Katczinsky, the provider and protector of young recruits, and for whom Bäumer suffers the pain of seeing wounded and dead, was based on Remarque's close friend Theo Christian Kemmerich, whom Remarque saved in 1917 during an incident on the Flanders line, has his own name in the novel. (232)

The novel bears witness to Remarque's memories of childhood and youth in Osnabrück, chiefly in those several passages describing Bäumer's leave with his parents. Through the eyes of *All Quiet*'s first person narrator, the reader sees that romantic city emerge as in a dream from the pages of literary text: (1) the *Pappelgraben* (young Remarque's playing grounds); (2) the *Altstadt* (streets and shops and homes in the old city); (3) The *Bahnhof* (train station) and the *Westberg* (the novel's "Klosterberg", where Bäumer and his friends go through Basic Training). All of these places help to identify the city of Osnabrück for the attentive reader and set the tone for what Rabe suggests is Remarque's love-hate affair with his birthplace.

Once his novel was published, however, Remarque found himself a *cause célèbre* among all segments of the German public. These included the general uncommitted populace as well as the more vocal elements of the Right and Left. "Der Kampf um Remarque" (*Battle around Remarque*) neatly summarizes the opposing sides in the contest for the book's acceptance or condemnation. This was, in fact, a brochure issued by *Ullstein* for publicity reasons.[15] There was in it a letter from a blinded combatant in the last war that promotes the book as the "only" truly representative text of that conflict. The brochure next includes signed statements from leading newspapers in the key German centers of Berlin, Cologne, Dresden and Dusseldorf. Here it can be seen how the German press itself contributed to the fire surrounding the controversy over the truth or the lie concerning the documentary and fictional aspects of the book. Some newspapers of conservative bent pointed out the dangers to German youth in Remarque's doubtful portrait of the German soldier. Elsewhere in the Press there were signed reviews and critiques by German writers as distinguished as Thomas Mann, Stefan Zweig and Fritz von Unruh.[16] In his appreciative review for *Ullstein's* journal, the *Berliner Illustrirte* (sic), the Austrian dramatist Carl Zuckmayer's comments, though laudatory, were indicative of Weimar Germany's progressive elements who believed naively that Remarque had written the war novel leading to incontrovertible end of War (*Aufruf* 93-94). They asked quite openly how the concept of war could now be defended in the national interest. The German Right, however, was not to be silent on the matter and had its turn in the ensuing controversy that was to develop. Rudolf G. Binding, P. Kolb and Otto Strasser were typical of the mixed group of establishment critics, former military officers and fascist hangers-on who attacked the validity of the pacifist ethos propounded in *All Quiet*. The *Völkischer Beobachter*, house organ of the Nazi party, published a violent critique of the book and its pacifist platform. Written in June 1929, the review openly called Remarque a Jew. Here was the source of the later rumor that Remarque's family name, Kramer (English translation: "little shop keeper"), was proof of his Jewish family name origins.

Remarque's opponents accused him of knowing singularly little of the details he described, that the situation and events he wrote of were fictitious and denigrating to himself and the German people. In a number of interviews, Remarque tried to ward off the attacks that began to circulate concerning his own person and the making of his novel. The earliest of these interviews and perhaps the most important was given to Axel Eggebrecht when Remarque said in his own defense:

> They asserted that my name was Kramer and this was considered a crime, just as if no other pseudonym had ever occurred in German literature. My name has never been Kramer. Others declared without further ado that I was a French Jew. . . . Above all, they designated me as a man whose service had been exclusively confined to Germany, who had never served at the Front, and therefore I naturally could not have known anything of the experience of active soldier's service at the age of twenty years. . . . These people declared that I had edited the diary of a comrade killed in the war. . . . None of these assertions had any basis. I have never changed a line in my manuscript, either for a progressive or for a conservative editor. I went into the war when I was eighteen. I was only a common soldier at the western Front, where I was wounded repeatedly, once in such a manner that I am still suffering from the consequences thereof. . . . (*Boston Evening Transcript*)

He entered into correspondence and exchanged letters with the British General, Ian Hamilton. They debated the politics and credibility of war fiction. Hamilton was a military man with strong literary capabilities. He reminded Remarque that "the pen is mightier than the sword," and that only a good novelist might write a book balancing the "counterpower of the romance and beauty of war." Remarque replied that he had wanted to present the war as seen through the small compass of the front-line soldier ("The End of War").[17]

All Quiet rendered a total experience of war as a profound event, pieced together out of many separate situations, out of minutes and hours, out of struggle, fear and death. Remarque's objectivity was genuine and uncommitted; it excluded with all deliberation any suggestion of political or sociological questions concerning the Great War. The German Left, however, saw this neutrality as a cardinal weakness for the cause of its own political platform. It felt justified in giving only limited approval to *All Quiet*. Leftists pointed out that the book did not go far enough, that it lacked any sense of revolutionary temperament. The novel, they said, failed to delineate more closely the Imperialist causes of the Great War, that according to the Left's own position, were attributed to the Wilhelmine Empire. The leftist novelist Arnold Zweig indicated that both Ludwig Renn's *War* and Remarque's *All Quiet* were dishonest in the sense that they continued to portray war as the Grand Adventure for the common man, a kind of temporary aberration in the course of human events. It was Zweig's position that German war fiction failed to ask the right questions; namely those centering on the economic and social causes of the war: "Who started this conflict?" "What are these men doing here at the front line?" Writers of fiction had a bound duty, Zweig said further, to show the common man that in war, the jingoistic tunes of patriotism originated on the drafting boards of landowners, industrial cartels and the banks ("Kriegsromane").[18] Other Leftist commentary on *All Quiet* appeared in the house journals of the German Communist Party, by then spreading its wings and flexing its young muscles in the pages of the *Linkskurve* and the *Rote Fahne*. Both the "Left Curve" and the "Red Banner" reminded the faithful that it was false to expect anything other than lukewarm revolutionary ideas from a writer of Remarque's dubious caliber. His value lay rather in the story he told of the Bourgeois apocalypse: the end of the dead society of a dying Empire (Br(and)).

However, Remarque and his book were not entirely beyond the pale of leftist redemption. *Das erste Volksbuch vom Grossen Krieg* (*The First Chapbook on the Great War*, 1929) was the first important attempt on the part of the German workers' movement to anthologize the contributions of those writers acceptable in the canon of war fiction. The book contained an eloquently written preface by Johannes Becher, later East Germany's Minister of Culture. Both Ludwig Renn and Remarque were included,[19] and here Becher noted the impossibility of taking a neutralist position on war by trying to write without a "tendency" (German: *tendenzlos*) or bias. Remarque's contribution to war fiction was that he portrayed war uniquely as a sensual experience: "scenes are worked out sensitively and exactly, involving the reader" (Kläber 9). Becher ends with the cryptic statement that Remarque failed when he began to intellectualize and probe at the causes behind the origins of the conflict itself.

Reviewing the Left's position on Remarque one feels that in 1929 the German revolutionary movement was still waiting for a war novel that would settle forever the rhetorical question of war as a viable experience for the human race. Specifically, this meant a war novel written from the standpoint of the proletariat, not one desiring and observing war, but burying and silencing it in such a way that the world would be changed from the bottom up. Both German socialists and Communists thought they had found their man in Remarque and his novel in *All Quiet*, but as was pointed out earlier, the Left was disappointed with Remarque's refusing to sponsor the cause of any political party or movement and this fateful decision would haunt him forever. He would continue to be "suspect" in certain leftist circles, despite the later evidence of his literary productivity. Because *All Quiet* was indeed an event of literary and political achievement, it was effective beyond the boundaries of conventional pacifist sensibilities. Everybody in Germany took up positions, but Remarque withdrew, as the writer Carl von Ossietzky said in 1932, into a kind of essay neutrality, leaving to his friends and enemies the argument as to what *All Quiet* really meant to say:

Such an attitude may be excused when it is adopted by an aesthete who craves peace and quiet; but it is more difficult to excuse on the part of a writer who had dealt actually with the most exciting theme of our time, a theme which divides Germany into camps: the theme of war. ("The Remarque Case")[20]

Ossietzky was correct. Remarque chose not to join his leftist comrades on the sandbags that lined the streets of Weimar Berlin as a matter of daily routine. For the moment at least, withdrawal meant assessment and evaluation, even if Remarque's purported objectivity was to be sorely tested in the months ahead.

From relative obscurity a year ago, Remarque blazed both in 1929 as an international celebrity and money maker. His rise to fame was not without certain disadvantages to himself. There were rumors about his "flight" to Davos, Switzerland, a center for medical care. Marlene Dietrich notes in the pages of *Stern* that Remarque was burdened by the quick success of his first book ("Mein Leben"). In June 1929, Remarque wrote a letter to the Austrian novelist Stefan Zweig, at which time he thanked him for early support and encouragement. Zweig had responded warmly to Remarque's poetic scribblings in 1919. In his second letter Remarque reminded Zweig how he had saved the disconsolate Osnabrück youth from suicide, that his kind words earlier had prevented him from turning to a more practical calling, as his father had hoped.[21] Remarque remembered that his father, a simple man, had been content to work as a mere book binder most of his life. An entry in the *Diaries* of the German diplomat and writer Count Harry Kessler (August 1929) tells how young Remarque showed up in Kessler's Berlin apartment to discuss "contracts." Kessler, whose satirical turn of mind could appreciate the notoriety with which Remarque's name had appeared before all Germans, said at first of his petitioner, "He has the head of a Saxon peasant boy, an incisively contoured face with furrows, fair-haired with blue eyes beneath fair eyebrows, firm expression that sometimes slips into lyricism" (366).

Kessler ends this passage with the observation that to Remarque, "it always seemed to him extraordinary, that he should exist at all. . . . The success of his novel has depressed rather than gladdened him. Previously he thought that success could bring contentment, but now he has realized that it cannot suffice a man" (367).

The contracts mentioned in Kessler's entry were probably those concerning film negotiations between Remarque and Carl Laemmle, Head of Universal Studios. Remarque disavowed any proposed film or stage adaptations of *All Quiet* yet Laemmle had pursued Remarque to Europe, where announcements of Laemmle's coup were carried by the London and New York press. Remarque and Laemmle, the complete Hollywood financier, posed for pictures for the photographers. "I want to hear how (Remarque) himself thinks the book should be filmed," Laemmle said to reporters in Prague ("Laemmle Will Film").[22] In any event, the head of Universal promised to make a serious film for a world audience.

Laemmle's attention had been drawn to Remarque by the high sales of the English-language edition of *All Quiet*. Unpublished correspondence in 1929 between Putnam's (London) and Little, Brown (Boston) reveals the competitive nature of publication rights to Remarque's book in the American market. Viking Press, Simon & Schuster and Alfred A. Knopf had all tried to sign on the German author, envisaging the profits to be made from sales of the novel. The winner was the old-line Boston firm, Little, Brown and Company, who were obliged to use Putnam's London as an intermediary in dealing with Remarque.[23] Putnam's in turn had its own arrangement with *Ullstein's* in Germany. The complexity of these arrangements is suggested from the side of Little, Brown in a letter to the English firm. Written a week before the American publication of *All Quiet*, the letter states they were hoping to deal with Putnam "in all matters" having to do with Remarque. Little, Brown hoped further to have an option on Remarque's work covering American rights (Little, Brown 25 May 1929). Little, Brown was alert to protect its future financial investment and it would remain responsible negotiators in its dealings with Remarque during his journeyman publishing days. Successful and best-selling writers must be courted and in its letters Little, Brown asked their English contacts for pictures of Remarque and a statement from him considering the extraordinary success of his book. Remarque was defended by Little, Brown against accusations of slander and an alleged "Jewish" background by the German Right. This was the time when Remarque's enemies asserted that his family name was Kramer.[24] Would there be a repeat novel, Little, Brown asked, and could Remarque write a book about Germany after the war? Here was, in fact, a reference to the topic of Remarque's second novel, *The Road Back*, to be published in 1931.

The huge sums to be made on the sale of *All Quiet* brought forth the indefatigable talents of Remarque's Berlin agent, Otto Klement, whose name appears like Ariadne's thread in future business negotiations between Remarque and foreign publishing interests.[25] It was Klement who instructed Remarque on moving through the maze of future book contracts. It is not clear when Otto Klement entered the scene; but once front and center only death could remove him. Later he would bring the largest possible sums of royalties from publishers at that time. Klement's role was a tangible sign that Remarque had left the workaday environment of the *Scherl Verlag*. He gave Klement a free hand to deal with publishers as he saw fit, since he himself could never have peddled his own copy. There was a fracas surrounding the American edition of *All Quiet*, an event that did not proceed without its special act of problems. Remarque's novel was involved in censorship charges by the *New York Times* and American periodicals.[26] The President of Little, Brown, Alfred R. McIntyre, was asked for an explanation and in a letter to the *New Republic*, he explained that a kind of censorship had indeed occurred:

> When we read the English translation we knew that the book as it stood would offend some people by its frankness, and that under the Massachusetts law, which judges a book not as a whole but by as little as a single

phrase, its sale would probably be stopped in Boston, a very serious matter for a Boston publisher. . . . We decided, however, to take this risk, and did not more than delete three words having to do with the bodily functions. We then offered the book to the Book-of-the-Month Club. . . ."[27]

Pursuing the recommendation of William Allen White, Kansas publisher and an editor of the Book-of-the-Month Club, Little, Brown had moved to print *All Quiet* in an expurgated edition (Jenkins). In addition to the changes mentioned above, two passages or episodes were expunged in America, one dealing with latrine matters of the German soldier on the open field and the other with sexual contact between a convalescing soldier and his visiting wife. Neither the German nor the British editions of the novel had undergone any form of censorship in its hardcover editions.[28]

It is certain that Little, Brown would not have made an advance sale to the Book Club had the company not agreed to censor, yet a letter from Putnam's publisher Huntington to Little, Brown (21 March 1929) conveys permission from Remarque "to do what, in your judgement, is in the best interests of the book." Years later, the deleted passages and words were indeed restored in all American editions.[29] In 1929, advance sales of *All Quiet* to the trade amounted to about 25,000 copies. The Book-of-the-Month Club USA ordered 60,000 copies for its membership.[30] These initial figures were excellent for an otherwise unknown writer in the American publishers' market.

From *Erich Maria Remarque: A Thematic Analysis of His Novels* (1988), pp. 29-64. Copyright © 1988 by Peter Lang. Reprinted with permission of Peter Lang.

Notes

1. The *Ullstein* firm was founded in 1877 by Leopold Ullstein, the son of a Jewish paper wholesaler. It followed an aggressive policy of acquiring Berlin newspapers, employed many foreign correspondents and had its own wire service. It was under the direction of five Ullstein brothers during the 1920's, when Remarque was

in Berlin. See Max Krell, who was the head of its book publication department, and Herman Ullstein, *The Rise and Fall of the House of Ullstein* (New York: Simon, 1943).

2. Remarque and Ilse were married on 14 October 1925 in the Charlottenburg district of Berlin. The "Heirats-Urkunde" (Marriage Announcement) can be found in "Mynona" 253-54. Articles by Remarque's wife are also indicated in the bibliography of "Mynona" 257-58.

3. "Station" was published as a supplement to Nos. 24-26 (1927) and was continued in Nos. 1-4 of 1928. As far as I can determine, it was never translated into English. An earlier version of "Station" is Remarque's sketch "Das Rennen Vanderveldes," *Sport* 12 (1924): 684. Both items are typical examples of the kind of facile journalism with which Remarque was preoccupied at the time.

4. For another personal account of Remarque as editor of *Sport* see: Felicitas von Reznicek, "So war Erich Maria Remarque."

5. The article is an English-language translation of an interview in the *Boston Evening Transcript* originally found in Eggebrecht's "Gespräch mit Remarque," *Literarische Welt*.

6. Carl von Ossietzky, "Ludwig Renn," *Die Weltbühne*, 5 March 1929. Quoted from *The Stolen Republic: Selected Writings of Carl von Ossietzky*, ed. Bruno Frie (East Berlin: Seven Seas, 1971) 211-12.

7. *S. Fischer und sein Verlag* (Frankfurt: S. Fischer, 1970) 1116. A reliable account of the publishing history of *All Quiet*, especially after all others have been considered. Cf. relevant pages in Barker and Last.

8. *Bedroht-Bewahrt: Weg eines Verlegers* (S. Fischer Verlag, 1967) 68-70.

9. Some of the stipulations are found in Richard Katz, *Gruss aus der Hängematte* (Zurich: Albert Müller Verlag, 1958) 169. The contract date is cited in Kerker, "Der unbekannte Remarque," 23.

10. Changes are in some instances extensive, including omission of entire paragraphs, sentence corrections and chapter divisions.

11. Remarque's dismissal from *Scherl's* is mentioned by Martin Stoss 934 and by A. W. Smith 16. *Die Tat*, one of Germany's prestigious cultural magazines, was founded in 1909 and was eventually turned into a conservative revolutionary journal under the editorship of Hans Zehrer.

12. Erich Maria Remarque, *All Quiet on the Western Front*, trans. A. W. Wheen (1929; Boston: Little, 1975). All English quotes from the rpt. 1975 edition. This convenient Little, Brown edition restores excised passages from earlier American editions published by Little, Brown and is in line with an English-language edition originally published by Putnam in England in 1929.

13. The Nazi position was expressed much earlier, however, in a review of *All Quiet* by Eduard A. Mayr for the Party newspaper.

14. Three examples of polemics notorious for their attacks on Remarque's personality and character and intended to challenge the veracity of *All Quiet*: (1) Klietmann; (2) Nickl; (3) "Emil Marius Requark."

15. Copy in my files. The brochure is approximately twelve pages with extensive quotations from authors and publishers of newspapers both in Germany and abroad.

Date of the brochure is late June or July 1929 since it contains a reprint of Axel Eggebrecht's interview with Remarque on 14 June 1929.

16. Fritz von Unruh, *Vossische Zeitung* 5 Feb. 1929. Zweig is quoted in the brochure, *Kampf um Remarque*.

17. The article reproduces two important letters between Remarque and General Ian Hamilton (2 Apr. and 1 June 1929).

18. Another liberal writer, Karl Hugo Sclutius, criticizes *All Quiet* as an example of "pacifistic war propaganda."

19. Remarque is excerpted on pg. 58.

20. Though his comment was made in 1932, Ossietzky's position is typical of the German Left's lingering disappointment with Remarque's silence on political and social issues, i.e., his failure to speak out in 1929 in the public arena.

21. Photocopy of letter in my possession. The original is in the Stefan Zweig Archives, State University College, Fredonia, New York.

22. On 10 Aug. 1929 Laemmle was in Berlin and conferred with Remarque on the making of the film (*New York Times*, Sec. 1: 8). The London *Times* had reported earlier on 6 July 1929, page 14, that "film rights to Erich Maria Remarque's book 'Im Westen Nichts Neues' . . . have been acquired by Deutsche Universal Production, a German-American concern" (*All Quiet*).

23. Letter to Alfred R. McIntyre of Little, Brown. (Little, Brown had accepted American publishing rights to *All Quiet* on 4 Mar. 1929.) The agent in this transaction was probably European Books Limited, 30 Henrietta Street, Covent Garden, London. This letter as well as others cited or referred to in the subsequent discussion of American publishing rights to *All Quiet* are in the files of Little, Brown (Boston) and were generously made available to me for inspection. Copies of these letters are in my files.

24. Putnam's gives an answer to McIntyre's questions on the "Kramer myth" in a letter dated 30 May 1929.

25. For further background of Klement, see: "Otto Klement," 526. Klement would remain in Germany until the Nazi takeover in the early 1930's and then moved to London and eventually the United States. In his many-faceted career, he was active as a publisher, play broker, stage producer and literary agent. Klement was very active in Remarque's negotiations with Hollywood film studios.

26. "Volume expurgated on Book Club Advice. German War Story, issued today by Little, Brown and Co. Toned Down for Americans," *New York Times* 31 May 1929: 23. See a related article: "Nice Nellie, the Censor," *New Republic*, 24 July 1929; 264.

27. McIntyre's answer relates to the *New Republic*'s article of 26 June 1929.

28. Canadians were very active in criticizing these "decisions" of Little, Brown and the Book-of-the-Month Club. See "Preferences" in *Canadian Forum*, and a follow-up letter (MacCallum).

29. For example, in the 1975 rpt. of Little, Brown that was based on the 1929 London edition. Interestingly, a popular Grosset and Dunlap rpt. (New York) published in 1930 was "complete" and appears to have been based on the London edition.

30. Discussed in a letter from Little, Brown to Putnam (London) dated 31 May 1929.

Works Cited

Bance, Carol. "The Reception of Exiled Writers in the Nazi and Conservative German-Language Press of California: 1933-1950." Diss. U. of SC, 1972.

Barker, Christine R. and R. W. Last. *Erich Maria Remarque*. London: Oswald Wolff, 1979.

De Mendelssohn, Peter S. *Fischer und sein Verlag*. Franfurt: S. Fischer, 1970.

Dietrich, Marlene. "Mein Leben." *Stern* 7 Oct. 1979: 118-30. Pt. 4 of a series.

Eggebrecht, Axel. "Erich Maria Remarque Meets an Interviewer." Trans. of "Gespräch mit Remarque." *Boston Evening Transcript* 21 Sept. 1929: 1.

_____. "Gespräch mit Remarque." *Literarische Welt* 14 June 1929: 1-2.

_____. *Der Halbe Weg: Zwischenbilanz einer Epoche*. Reinber: Rowohlt, 1975.

Fischer, Gottfried B. *Bedroht, Bewahrt: Weg eines Verlegers*. Frankfurt: S. Fischer, 1967.

Friedrich, Otto. *Before the Deluge*. New York: Harper, 1972.

Huntington, C. Letter to Alfred R. McIntyre. 21 Mar. 1929. Little, Brown, Boston.

_____. Letter to Alfred R. McIntyre. 14 Apr. 1931. Little, Brown, Boston.

_____. Letter to Alfred R. McIntyre. 20 July 1934. Little, Brown, Boston.

Der Kampf um Remarque. Brochure. Berlin: Propyläen Verlag, 1929.

"Kampf um Remarque." *Vossische Zeitung* 7 Dec. 1930.

Katz, Richard. "Ein Soldat der Wahrheit." *Forum* June 1958: 226-27.

_____. *Gruss aus der Hängematte*. Zürich: Albert Muller Verlag, 1958.

Kessler, Count Harry. *The Diaries of a Cosmopolitan*. Trans. and ed. Charles Kessler. London: Weidenfeld and Nicolson, 1971.

Klaber, Kurt, ed. *Der Krieg: Das erste Volksbuch vom Grossen Krieg*. Berlin: Internationaler Arbeiter-Verlag, 1929.

Klietmann, Franz Arthur. *Im Westen wohl was Neues*. Berlin: Verlag C. Nonnemann, 1931.

Krell, Max. *Das alles gab es einmal*. Frankfurt: Verlag Heinrich Scheffler, 1961.

"Laemmle will film Remarque war book." *New York Times* 6 Aug. 1929: 8.

Little, Brown. Letter to Putnam's London. 23 May 1929. Little, Brown, Boston.

_____. Letter to Putnam's London. 25 May 1929. Little, Brown, Boston.

_____. Letter to Putnam's London. 31 May 1929. Little, Brown, Boston.

_____. Letter to Remarque. 19 Sept. 1933. Little, Brown, Boston.

_____. "Talk with Klement." Memorandum of a letter. 10 Oct. 1934. Little, Brown, Boston.

_____. Letter to Remarque. 24 Feb. 1936. Little, Brown, Boston.

_____. Letter to Otto Klement. 25 Aug. 1937. Little, Brown, Boston.

_____. Letter to Remarque. 13 June 1939. Little, Brown, Boston.

Mayr, Eduard A. "Im Westen nichts Neues." Rev. of *All Quiet on the Western Front*. *Völkischer Beobachter* 16-17 June 1929: n. pag.

"Mynona: (Salomo Friedlander). *Hat Erich Maria Remarque wirklich Gelebt?* Berlin: Paul Steegemann Verlag, 1929.

"Nice Nellie, the Censor." *New Republic* 26 June 1929: 142.

Nickl, Gottfried. *Im Westen nichts Neues* und sein wahrer Sinn. Eine Betrachtung über den Pazifismus und Antwort auf Remarque." *Heimgarten*. Sonderheft. 1930: 20.

Ossietzky, Carl Von. "The Remarque Case." *Die Weltbühne* 12 April 1932: n. pag. Rpt., in *The Stolen Republic: Selected Writings of Carl von Ossietzsky*, ed., Bruno Frei. East Berlin: Seven Seas, 1971. 217.

_____. "Remarque Film." *Die Weltbühne* 16 Dec. 1930: 889-91.

"Preferences." *The Canadian Forum* Aug. 1929: 386-87.

Putnam's, G.P. Letter to Little, Brown. 30 May 1929. Little, Brown, Boston.

Rabe, Hanns-Gerd. 3 vols. *Erich Maria Remarque Collection*. State Archives, Osnabrück, Germany.

_____. "Erich Maria Remarque: Eine unbekannte Episode seines Lebens." *Heimat-Jahrbuch: Osnabrücker Land*. Osnabrück: 1976.

_____. "Junglehrer Erich Paul Remark: *Merian* (Emsland) 24.7: 47-48.

_____. "Remarque und Osnabrück: Ein Beitrag zu seiner Biographie." *Osnabrücker Mitteilungen* 77 (1970): 196-246.

"Remarque, Emil Marius: Vor Troja nichts Neues." Rev. of *All Quiet*. *Books Abroad* Jan. 1930: 86-87.

Remarque, Erich Maria. *All Quiet on the Western Front*. Trans. A. W. Wheen. Boston: Little, 1929.

_____. *Arc de Triomphe*. Zürich: Micha, 1946.

_____. *Arch of Triumph*. Trans. Walter Sorell and Denver Lindley. New York: Appleton, 1946.

_____. *The Black Obelisk*. Trans. Denver Lindley. New York: Harcourt, 1957.

_____. "Die Dame und der kleine kleine Wagen." *Der Montag* (*Berliner Lokalanzeiger*) 19 Apr. 1926: n. pag.

_____. *Flotsam*. Trans. Denver Lindley. Boston: Little, 1941.

_____. *Der Funke Leben*. Köln: Kiepenheuer u. Witsch, 1954.

_____. *Drei Kameraden*. Amsterdam: Querido Verlag N.V., 1937.

_____. *Heaven Has No Favorites*. Trans. Richard and Clara Winston. New York: Harcourt, 1961.

_____. *Der Himmel kennt keine Günstlinge*. Köln: Kiepenheuer u. Witsch, 1961.

_____. *Im Westen nichts Neues*. Berlin: Propyläen, 1929.

_____. *Liebe Deinen Nächsten*. Batavia: Bermann Fischer-Querido Verlag, 1941.

_____. "Melchior Sirrs Verwandlung." *Sport im Bild* 3 (1926): 98.

_____. *Die Nacht von Lissabon*. Köln: Kiepenheuer u. Witsch, 1963.

_____. *The Night in Lisbon*. Trans. Ralph Manheim. New York: Harcourt, 1964.

_____. "Das Rennen Vanderveldes." *Sport im Bild* 12 (1924): 684.

_____. *The Road Back*. Trans. A. W. Wheen. Boston: Little, 1931.

_____. *Schatten im Paradies*. München: Droemer Knaur, 1971.

_____. *Der schwarze Obelisk: Geschichte einer verspäteten jugend.* Köln: Kiepenheuer u. Witsch 1956.

_____. *Shadows in Paradise.* Trans. Ralph Manheim. New York: Harcourt, 1972.

_____. *Soldat Suhren. Ringen an der Somme. In Stahlgewittern. So war der Krieg. Sport im Bild* 12 (1928): 895.

_____. *Spark of Life.* Trans. James Stern. New York: Appleton, 1952.

_____. "Station am Horizont." Beginning of the serialized novel. *Sport im Bild* 24-26 (1927).

_____. "Station am Horizont." Conclusion of the serialized novel. *Sport im Bild* 1-4 (1928).

_____. *Three Comrades.* Trans. A. W. Wheen. Boston: Little, 1937.

_____. *A Time to Love and a Time to Die.* Trans. Denver Lindley. New York: Harcourt, 1957.

_____. *Die Traumbude: Ein Künstlerroman.* Dresden: Verlag der Schönheit, 1920.

_____. *Der Weg zürück.* Berlin: Propyläen, 1931.

_____. *Zeit zu leben und Zeit zu sterben.* Köln: Kiepenheuer u. Witsch, 1954.

Reznicek, Felicitas von. "So war Erich Maria Remarque." *Schweizer Rundschau* 69.6 (1970): 398-400.

Smith, A. W. Rev. of *The Road Back. Atlantic Monthly* June 1931: 16.

Stoss, Martin. "Die Front Marschiert: die Tragödie Remarque. *Die Tat* Mar. 1929: 934-37.

Ullstein, Herman. *The Rise and Fall of the House of Ullstein.* New York: Simon, 1.

Unruh, Fritz von. Rev. of *All Quiet. Vossische Zeitung* 5 Feb. 1929: 1.

Zuckmayer, Carl. *Aufruf zum Leben: Porträts und Zeugnisse aus bewegten Zeiten.* Frankfurt: S. Fischer, 1976.

_____. "Front der Unzerstörten." *Vossische Zeitung* 21 Dec. 1930: n. pag.

_____. *A Part of Myself.* trans. Richard and Clara Winston. New York: Harcourt, 1970.

Zweig, Friderike. *Stefan Zweig.* trans. Erna McArthur. New York: Crowell, 1946.

Remarque's Abyss of Time:
*Im Westen nichts Neues*_____

Richard Schumaker

Despite its great commercial success and continuing popularity, Erich Maria Remarque's *Im Westen nichts Neues* has seldom received the critical attention or respect that it deserves. All too often this novel is read as a mere war novel with dubious claims to objectivity, as a political novel with questionable ideological biases, or as a psychological novel that expresses the disenchantment of an entire generation. In fact, although Remarque's novel is indeed set during the Great War, and does, obviously, contain political and psychological themes, its full significance is grasped only when these considerations are related to the novel's central problematic—the effect of World War I on the sense of temporality of the novel's main characters. The structure of the three temporal dimensions and their relationship to each other form the backbone of this novel. Once the relationship between problematic and theme is brought into clear focus, the novel's place in twentieth century literature becomes quite clear.

Im Westen nichts Neues begins on a serene and almost jocular note. The soldiers at the foreground of the novel are behind their own battle-lines. They are relaxed and absorbed in menial, inoffensive routine. Yet there has already been a casualty: the future. The political and social culture of the young men has not inculcated them with values that will resist the vicissitudes of historical evolution. Thus, the young men move into the future bereft of emotional and moral anchors.

> For us lads of eighteen they [their mentors] ought to have been mediators and guides to the world of maturity, the world of work, of duty, of culture, of progress—to the future. (*All Quiet* 12)

The sham guidance and hypocritical morality of the mentors do not survive even the first shells and the first deaths of the war. Paul realizes that there is a relatively superficial and an extremely serious side to his shattered future. He has never really believed in the conventional phrases and the formulas; he has, however, believed in the "authority," "greater insight," and "manlier wisdom" (12) which the leaders of his culture represent. It is this latter authority, this unconscious surge toward the future, which is destroyed by the Great War. As Paul says, "the first bombardment showed us our mistake . . . the world as they taught it to us broke in pieces" (12).

This sense of being deprived of a future intensifies as the novel progresses. Remarque seldom explores the external aspect of this dilemma; he is interested for the most part in analysing what it is like to have crucial, dangerous combat responsibilities and, at the same time, be incapable of believing in any conventional sense of purpose, goal, or aim.

> The breath of desire . . . shall fill me again, melt the heavy, dead lump of lead that lies somewhere in me and wakens the impatience of the future, the quick joy in the world of thought. . . . (10)

The chagrin expressed in these lines deepens as the war drags on. The soldiers worry not only about having lost their aims and goals, but also about ever again restructuring a system of values.

> Here my thoughts stop and will not go any farther. All that meets me, all that floods over me are but feelings . . . but no aims. . . . Now if we go back we will be weary, broken, burnt out, rootless, without hope. We will not be able to find our way any more. (174)

Im Westen is not, however, a novel of dejection and despair. Despite their shattered sense of purpose, despite the inevitable negative psychological development that must accompany such a traumatic experience, the young soldiers in this novel are not mere passive victims of an intransigent fate. They are capable of personal growth and insight of the deepest possible sort: they are capable of generating new values.

Remarque's novel is punctuated with surges of insight into values that could sustain life after the war. The author uses these insights to evaluate the values of Wilhelmine Germany and to evoke fresh possibilities for the future. First, the future must be devoted to avoiding war. Paul had been brought up to believe in the necessity of war. This was only possible because war had been an abstraction. Killing the French printer, G. Duval, forces him to confront the stark, odious reality of being involved in killing people. Paul realizes that rejection of killing and personal integrity condition each other in a profound and intimate way. He pledges his future to avoiding repetitions of the Great War:

> But if I come out of it, comrade, I will fight against this, that has struck us both down; from you, taken life—and from me—Life also. I promise you . . . it shall never happen again. (138)

Second, during the war Paul comes to understand the importance of the class system in his life. Before the war he had an instinctive respect for the authority of his mentors and community leaders. He comes to realize that they are his real enemies, that class is based on arbitrary and pernicious values, and that such a system is what led the country to war. As he says,

> Any non-commissioned officer is more of an enemy to a recruit, any schoolmaster to a pupil than they [the Russians] are to us. (119)

Finally, Paul begins to think in internationalist terms. He observes the kindly simplicity of the Russian prisoners and realizes that he has much in common with them: he can feel no hatred of any kind.

> I know nothing of them except that they are prisoners, and that is exactly what troubles me. Their life is obscure and guiltless;—if I could know more of them. . . . (118)

Thus, Paul projects himself into a future based on values which are different from those that he has known as a child. Anti-militarism, a rejection of the class system, and internationalism seem to him, at least as he fights in the trenches, the values which would secure a better future. He also realizes that these values are dangerous: they cannot be articulated while he is fighting; they go against the entire grain of his culture.

> I am frightened: I dare think this way no more. This way leads to the abyss. It is not now the time; but I will not lose these thoughts. I will keep them, shut them away until the war is ended. . . . this is the aim, the great, sole aim, that I have thought of in the trenches. (119)

The future is not a closed dimension for the young soldiers in this novel. They begin to articulate new values in a lucid, intelligent way. They have considerable inner reserves, untapped by the pre-war culture.

The past seems to be the tragic dimension for Remarque. Paul and his childhood friends experience the past in a fashion that is almost wholly negative and destructive. The personalities of the soldiers are significantly weakened because of the impossibility of maintaining a living, healthy relationship with the past. Remarque's analyses are psychologically precise and of considerable originality.

Rootlessness vis-à-vis the past is one of the primary characteristics of the young men described in this novel. Remarque explores this rootlessness from several different perspectives. First, the young men in a certain sense never possess a past. "There are sights there he has not forgotten because he never possessed them—perplexing yet lost to him" (61). In the context of his novel, Remarque means at least two things by this: it would seem that the soldiers do not receive much from their original environment. A few shards of moral guidance, some vague, rather banal feelings of family intimacy, and a sense of place are about all they carry with them to the front.

We young men of twenty, however, have only our parents, and some, perhaps a girl. That is not much, for at our age the influence of parents is at its weakest and girls have not yet a hold over us. . . . And of this nothing remains. (12)

Moreover, because the soldiers are so young when they go away to war, they have had little time to assimilate personally the values of their culture. Had they stayed at home, had they had to test the conventional wisdom of their culture for themselves, they might have had time to deepen or reject their rather pathetic axiological heritage. But they don't get the chance; the war deprives them of this possibility.

We had as yet taken no root. The war swept us away. For the others, the older men, it is just an interruption. (16)

Thus, the young men of Paul's generation have their pasts undermined—retroactively.

Rootlessness in this novel is experienced as *Angst*, confusion, a kind of dread of life. The soldiers feel disoriented because the war isolates them from their already fragile past lives. They not only see the worthlessness of their past experiences; they are also "cut off" from whatever might have been of some value.

But a sense of strangeness will not leave me, I can find nothing of myself in all these things. There is my mother, there is my sister, there is my case of butterflies, and there is the mahogany piano—but I am not myself there. There is a distance, a veil between us. (16)

The fragile, suddenly distant past leaves the soldiers in a state of ontological insecurity. It is easy for them to feel bitter and cynical about the institutions that nurtured them as children and adolescents.

All I do know is that this business about professions and studies and so—it makes me sick, it is always disgusting. I don't see anything—I don't see anything at all. . . . (56)

It's a bit better. But it's rot all the same, everything they teach you. (55)

It is this rootlessness, this unnatural inner distance that causes the eerie, muffled tone of the novel. The brutal noises and the murderous flying metal of war encircle and engulf Remarque's soldiers, but the deepest damage is done to the souls of these young men. They are severed from their earliest, most tender experiences, and thus it is impossible for them to develop and mature normally.

A series of neurotic symptoms results from this existential rootlessness. The very tenor of conscious life seems to be diminished for these young soldiers. They realize that *something* of a very fundamental nature is happening to them, but they are incapable of reflecting on their experiences in a conscious, systematic manner.

My strength is exhausted as always after an attack, and so it is hard to be alone with my thoughts. They are not properly thoughts; they are memories. . . . (74)

And these memories are mere transient images which dissolve with the light of the next shell blast. Pinioned between a horrific present and a half-assimilated past, the soldiers find it difficult to pursue these memories. Instead they develop the habit of fleeing from them. They develop an inner resistance to self-examination and contemplation. They don't *want* their own lives. They have the inner stiffness of much older people.

He is right. We are not youth any longer. . . . We are fleeing. We fly from ourselves. From our life. We are eighteen and had begun to love life and the world; and we had to shoot it to pieces. . . . The first explosion burst in our hearts. (75)

Consequently, the affective tenor of the lives of these frontline soldiers becomes melancholy and oddly calm.

> It is strange that all the memories that come have these two qualities. They are always completely calm . . . and even if they are not completely calm, they become so. (75)

> Their stillness is the reason why these memories of former times do not awaken desire so much as sorrow—a strange incomprehensible melancholy. (76)

This is not the calm of self-possession and mastery; it is depression which results from their lucidity; the soldiers realize that they have been cheated out of life in any real sense of the term. Moreover, they intuit that the dimness and fragility of their memories are symptomatic of a profound injustice.

Just as Paul's hope for a valuable future diminishes as the war continues into its third and fourth years, his calm and melancholy about the past turn into cynicism and hopelessness.

> Once we had such desires but they return not such desires . . . they belong to another world that is gone from us. (76)

He realizes that a profound, definite dislocation has occurred in his life: some kind of fracture or annihilation of the very core of Paul's temporal being.

> Speak to me . . . Life of my youth . . . receive me. Images float through my mind, but they do not grip me, they are mere shadows and memories. Nothing—nothing—. A terrible feeling of foreignness suddenly rises up in me. I cannot find my way back, I am shut out. . . . (107)

The young soldiers of this novel experience not only danger in the trenches; the total experience of the war—its length, its horrors, its senselessness, its multi-faceted unfairness—victimizes the most intimate parts of their souls. Their relationship with and adhesion to the past is destroyed. Moreover, the novel contains very few passages where any affirmative sense of the past is maintained by the soldiers. Yet in these scarce passages, Remarque reveals two important qualities in his characters. First, they do try to rekindle the energy and spontaneity of the past:

> The pure fragrance of the water and the melody of the wind in the poplars held our fancies. We loved them dearly, and the image of those days still makes my heart pause in its beating. (75)

Second, the young soldiers are frighteningly lucid: they realize that they are themselves battlegrounds between a deeply destructive process and a vague, almost incomprehensible surge of life.

> . . . and it is the alarm of their silence that forces me to lay hold of my sleeve and my rifle lest I should abandon myself to the liberation and allurement in which my body would dilate and gently pass away into the still forces that lie behind these things. (75)

In this passage, the German soldier *lives* his past; this dimension of his being is not extinguished, only maimed and suppressed by the war. He senses the power of his past but dares not explore this intuition too deeply. As we have learned, such exploration is the way to the abyss.

Remarque goes beyond the triviality of most war novels by showing that the war affects the deepest levels of the personality. The men in *Im Westen* are worthy; they endure a horrible experience. They are also punished for their endurance; their memories, their half-formed emotions, their rudimentary intuitions about life are all but effaced by the war. Moreover, Remarque has the simple, dignified audacity to show us that this punishment, this temporal mutilation, is caused only partially by battle. Society itself—its culture, its religion, its greed—is just as guilty, maybe more so.

Remarque's characters live at the apex of a shattered future and an atrophied past. Thus, the present is deprived of fullness and resilience. But, paradoxically, the present is the most complex temporal dimension in *Im Westen nichts Neues*. The present is horrific: the soldiers submit to physical agony beyond description. The present is demeaning: the war causes psychological humiliation. The present is also the temporal dimension where the true stature and dignity of these soldiers are revealed.

In order to endure life at the front, the soldiers must renounce (*aufgeben*) many important facets of themselves (17). Remarque explores this reductive psychological process in different ways. He shows that the first and most obvious effect of battle is a loss of one's sensibility: "But the shelling is stronger than anything. It wipes out the sensibilities" (20). Thus, almost immediately the men are hardened: "we become hard, suspicious, pitiless, vicious . . ." (20). The experience at the front oscillates between habit and brutality (71, 86). Thus, in addition to being severed from its natural, healthy relationship to the past and future, the present is further diminished by the psychological adaptation that must occur to survive the daily horrors of battle and military routine.

Remarque is careful to show that this reductive process is not temporary; it is destructive and definitive. The soldiers are not merely dulled by habit: they are reduced to being automatons.

> . . . the earth is the background of the restless, gloomy world of automatons, our grasping is the scratching of a quill, our lips are dry, our heads are debauched with stupor—we stagger forward. . . . (72)

> . . . we are insensible, dead men who through some trick, some dreadful magic, are still able to run and kill. (73)

Remarque tends to explore the deeper psychological effects of the war in images and metaphor. His language is especially powerful and appropriate when he describes the inner maiming of his main characters. Early in the novel, Paul says, "Our faces are encrusted, our thoughts are devastated . . ." (83). Later in the novel, this kind of expression reappears in somewhat stronger form:

> Our thoughts are clay, they are moulded with the changes of the days;—when we are resting they are good; under fire, they are dead. Fields of craters within and without. (162)

Thus, the soldiers have less and less personal strength with which to resist the horrors of war. They become mere reflections of the shell-blasted landscapes of the Great War. The soldiers are so worn down that they no longer perceive the passage of time: "We count the weeks no more" (161).

The destructive process becomes more and more demonic as the war continues. The themes of rage/madness/breakdown emerge early in the novel: "We have become wild beasts" (71). But at this point in the novel it is only an occasional phenomenon, connected with the frenzy of battle and self-defense. Insanity and mental breakdown become dominant traits of the experience of the late stages of the war. After he has killed G. Duval, Paul realizes that his "brain is taxed beyond endurance" (138). Paul becomes obsessed by the theme of madness and meditates on it:

> Were we more subtly differentiated we must have long since have gone mad, have deserted, or have fallen. . . . I often sit over against myself as before a stranger, and wonder how the unnameable active principle that calls itself Life has adapted itself even to this form. (163)

The latter part of the novel would suggest that Paul has only the slightest hold on life; he meditates on the fragility of the human personality and the presence of darkness:

And at night, walking out of a dream, overwhelmed, and bewitched by the crowding faces, a man perceives with alarm how slight is the support, how thin the boundary that divides him from the darkness.

Every day and every hour, every shell and every death cuts into this thin support, and the years waste it rapidly. . . . (164)

Remarque multiplies anecdotes (the Berger incident, for example) and allusions to death, cadavers, and insanity as the novel closes. He also insists that this somber experience is punctuated by positive, affirmative perceptions and insights. New levels of understanding do emerge from the war: his characters, for all their rootlessness and trauma, do break new existential ground.

The experience of the war forces the soldiers to experience life for themselves. They feel, think, and see in a way that would have been impossible without the experience of the war. The soldiers are separated from their families, towns, and culture; thus, they are liberated from the trivialities of convention; they are also forced to discover spiritual depths in themselves. Remarque emphasizes the intensity of the front:

Our faces are neither pale nor more flushed than usual; they are not more tense nor more flabby—yet they are changed. We feel that in our blood a contact has shot home. . . . It is the front, the consciousness of the front, that makes this contact. (36)

The intensity of this experience individualizes and, almost despite the young men, produces a profound psychological metamorphosis.

Every time it is the same. We start out for the front plain soldiers . . . then come the first gun-emplacements and every word of our speech has a new ring. (36)

Paul likens this experience to a mysterious whirlpool, and, in the most telling phrase of all, he wonders if it is "our inner and most secret life that shivers and falls on guard" (36).

The inner transformation is accompanied by a renewed experience of the natural world. The war sunders and destroys nature; it also farces a renewed sense of the preciousness of the earth and all its manifestations. At times, Paul expresses feelings of mystical affirmation of the earth: "O Earth thou grantest us the great resisting surge of new-won life" (37). At times Paul uses his intense reverence for natural phenomena as a springboard to recapture his past.

> The parachute-lights shoot upwards—and I see a picture, a summer evening. I am in the cathedral cloister and look at the tall rose trees that bloom in the middle of the cloister garden. . . . (74)

> Between the meadows behind our town there stands a line of old poplars by a stream. The pure fragrance of the water and the melody of the wind in the poplars held our fancies. (75)

Paul's responsiveness to nature becomes at once obsession and metaphysical reflection:

> I often become so lost in the play of soft light and transparent shadow, that I almost fail to hear the commands. It is when one is alone that one begins to observe Nature and to love her. (116)

> Summer of 1918—Never has life in its niggardliness seemed to us so desirable as now:—the red poppies in the meadows round our billets, the smooth beetles on the blades of grass . . . the mysterious trees of the twilight. (170)

The war forces the soldiers to behave in an inhumane way; it also makes them able to transcend the conventional, superficial relationships of normal civilian life: "It awakened in us a strong, practical sense of *esprit de corps*, which in the field developed into the finest thing that arose out of the war-comradeship" (20). Throughout this novel, the author reserves some of his strongest, most poignant passages for this sense of frontline fraternity.

> They are more to me than life, these voices, they are more than motherliness and more than fear; they are the strongest, most comforting thing there is anywhere: they are the voices of my comrades. (130)

In passage after passage, we see how Paul realizes that allegiance to his friends not only keeps him sane but also allows him to retain his self-respect.

There is yet another positive trait which the war engenders in Remarque's characters. These characters do not simply *live* the enigmatic mixture of destruction and growth that has been described here; they also think hard about what is happening to them. They grapple with the meaning of the war and what it is doing to them. Paul is extremely lucid as he realizes that he is being emotionally destroyed by the war.

> —it has transformed us into unthinking animals in order to give us the weapon of instinct—it has reinforced us with dullness, so that we do not go to pieces. . . .
> Our inner forces are not exerted toward regeneration, but toward degeneration. (163)

Paul is equally lucid when he realizes that there is still life left in him—even if it is only spasmodic and wan:

> —the years will pass by and in the end we shall fall into ruin. . . . But perhaps all this that I think is more melancholy and dismay, which will fly away as dust, when I stand once again beneath the poplars and listen to the rustling of their leaves. (175)

Once again Paul attempts to understand his experience at its deeper level. This is not a mere expression of puerile nostalgia, but an attempt to understand how his future, past, and present have been transformed by the war. *Im Westen nichts Neues* is anything but a novel of disenchantment and despair: it is a phenomenological account of the way the Great War wears away at the personalities of a group of young men— without destroying their deepest engagement in life. One of the novel's final passages demonstrates perfectly this double-edged, typically Remarquian view:

> Let the months and years come, they bring me nothing more, they can bring me nothing more. I am so alone, and so without hope that I can confront them without fear. The life that has borne me through these years is still in my hands and my eyes. Whether I have subdued it, I know not. But so long as it is there it will seek its own way out, heedless of the will that is within me. (175)

> Mögen die Monate und Jahre kommen, sie nehmen mir nichts mehr, sie können mir nichts mehr nehmen. Ich bin so allein und so ohne Erwartung, daß ich ihnen entgegensehen kann ohne Furcht. Das Leben, das mich durch diese Jahre trug, ist immer noch in meinen Händen und Augen. Ob ich es überwunden habe, weiß ich nicht. Aber solange es da ist, wird es sich seinen Weg suchen, mag dieses, das in mir "ich" sagt, wollen oder nicht. (*Im Westen*, 203)

In order to determine the deepest effects of the war on Paul's life Remarque explores the three temporal dimensions. As for the future, Paul realizes that very little of a positive nature can come to pass ("Let the months and years come . . ."). The war has continued so long, it has been so physically gruelling, his pre-1914 values have so utterly shattered, that imagining any kind of positive outcome in the near future is impossible for the young soldier. Paul's attitude toward the present is one of tranquil endurance: "I am so alone and so without hope that I can confront them without fear." As for the past, it is, as we have seen, the ravished dimension. Paul refers to it without much comment, without much interest: "The life that has borne me throughout these years is still in my hands and my eyes." This somber, brooding sense of temporality is accompanied, as we have seen here, by a positive, affirmative one. Paul, as a product of a given culture, has been destroyed. Very few, if any, of the social, political, and cultural values of his childhood and adolescence endure the war. The war has, as the saying goes, caused them to become what they are. On the other hand, Paul realizes that there is more than these corrupt and corrupting values. The values of Western civilization are not identical with life itself:

> But so long as it is there it will seek its own way out, heedless of the will that is within me.

Thus, Remarque succeeds in expressing our basic condition: although we stand for little besides domination, militarism, and disrespect for the earth, we do at times produce individuals capable of expressing a deeper, more worthy sense of life.

Im Westen nichts Neues is an extremely coherent novel. The experience of World War I, a political and social reflection of life in Wilhelmine Germany, and carefully, subtly drawn psychological analyses are all integrated into a probing, intelligent, and dignified work of art by exploring the interplay of the three temporal dimensions. By doing this, Remarque enters into a dialogue with the Greeks, with St. Augustine, and with many of the finer writers our own age. Understanding the importance of temporality in this novel assists us in conceptualizing the deep poetic resonance that so many readers have responded to. The formula "Im Westen nichts Neues" is a *fait divers*: things are, as the English title tells us, quiet on the battlefield. In the context of the novel, the *fait divers* has considerable poignancy, for the novel's main character dies when the war is almost over. But *Im Westen* also signals the real scope of the novel. It is not just about Wilhelmine Germany, for the temporal shattering, rootlessness, and metaphysical disorientation which are at the heart of the novel characterize the entire West. The novel presents an image of life in the twentieth century which is rare in its rigor. For until we are capable of understanding the underlying corruption, danger, and violence residing in our finest social, moral, and religious values, there will be *nichts Neues* in the West.

From *Focus on Robert Graves and His Contemporaries* 1, no. 11 (Winter 1990-91): 24-36. Copyright © 1990 by the University of Maryland. Reprinted with permission of the University of Maryland.

Works Cited

Remarque, Erich Maria. *All Quiet on the Western Front*. New York: Crest, 1962.
_____. *Im Westen nichts Neues*. Köln: Ullstein, 1987.

"Der Krieg hat uns für alles verdorben":
The Real Theme of *Im Westen nichts Neues*_____

Richard Littlejohns

Indictment or Confession?

There are, admittedly, good reasons for a sceptical attitude towards the brief declaration which forms a kind of preface to *Im Westen nichts Neues*.[1] It runs, it will be remembered, as follows:

> Dieses Buch soll weder eine Anklage noch ein Bekenntnis sein. Es soll nur den Versuch machen, über eine Generation zu berichtep, die vom Kriege zerstört wurde—auch wenn sie seinen Granaten entkam. (p. 40)

> [This book is intended neither as an accusation nor as a confession, but simply as an attempt to give an account of a generation that was destroyed by the way—even those of it who survived the shelling.]

This statement, despite its seductively modest claims and the directness of its laconic formulations, is certainly less transparent and straightforward than it appears at first sight. The reader may for instance be inclined to question Remarque's assertion that the book is not intended to be either an indictment or a confession, for self-evidently it does include no small measure of criticism of the society which propelled his generation into a senseless war and more than a little reflection of Remarque's own experiences and feelings whilst serving in the German army. And indeed, ever since the publication of *Im Westen* in book form in 1929, its critics have chosen to maintain that indictment or confession do represent the main point of the novel, regardless of Remarque's explicit denial of such intentions. Again and again the book has been assessed as if it were documentary literature or reportage; and at the same time praised or vilified, according to the politics of the critic, as a pacifist polemic against militarism.[2]

Nevertheless, Remarque's statement of intent, however incomplete or disingenuous it may appear to be, is essentially validated by the text. *Im Westen* is not an historical or autobiographical work, on the contrary it marks a departure from the countless war diaries and officers' memoirs which had flooded the market after 1918, and which by the late 1920s seemed too devoted to factual reporting to afford any means of accommodating the emotional experiences involved in the war. Remarque himself told Axel Eggebrecht in an interview in 1929 that his novel was insufficiently representative to purport to be a documentary account of the war, since it showed only the subjectively observed experiences of one small group of young infantrymen on one short sector of the front during one phase of the war.[3] *Im Westen* is a work of fiction. Although it makes use of numerous details from the past of Erich Paul Remark (to give him his real name), from his youth in Osnabrück, from his period at a military training camp, and from his stay in a Catholic hospital in Duisburg, it transforms them and weaves them into an imaginative pattern quite distinct from historical fact.[4]

Remarque's other disclaimer, that the novel is not intended to level accusations, deserves even closer attention. It is tempting to suppose that the theme of *Im Westen* is the futility or obscenity of war, and both the critical portrayal of military values and the gruesome descriptions of broken bodies seem to support this reading. Thus Brian Rowley writes in an article on the novel that its fundamental theme is 'the monstrous unacceptability of modern trench warfare'.[5] The same view dominates Brian Murdoch's Introduction to the text: *Im Westen* 'remains an indictment of the modern mechanized war', he states, '. . . its message, though not overtly stated, is perfectly clear, that war is evil' (p. 26). Here, however, Murdoch falls into the trap of imposing on the novel the predictable theme which it might be expected to contain rather than elucidating the more original ideas actually expressed in the text. In fact the horrific aspects of war are not discussed as a theme anywhere in *Im Westen*, rather they are taken for granted, reported with matter-of-fact bluntness and accepted as inevitable. Remarque himself said as much to Eggebrecht:

Der Krieg ist als Tatsache vorausgesetzt. Die wenigen Reflexionen, die in dem Buch stehen, beschäftigen sich nur mit diesem rein menschlichen Erleben des Krieges.[6]

[The war is a given fact. The few reflections in the book are concerned only with the purely human experience of war.]

It might be objected that *Im Westen* contains rather more than occasional reflections, but Remarque's main point is correct: the book is not about the war itself, but about the way in which certain human individuals experience the war.

Such pacifist sentiments as the novel does contain are vague and scattered platitudes, which are never developed into an argued case;[7] and they are compromised by the perverse pleasure which Bäumer and his mates take in the earthy physicality of life at the front. A careful reading of the text suggests even that Remarque does not entirely disapprove of the war, or perhaps rather that he has failed to work out an unequivocal moral stance towards it. One recent German critic, Hans-Harald Müller, has argued plausibly that the theme enunciated in Remarque's opening declaration, the traumatic effect of the Great War on both those participants who fought it and those who survived it, represents only part of the import of the book; and that there is a subordinate theme which remains unstated in this prefatory remark, namely nostalgia for the undemanding comradeship of the trenches.[8] These two themes co-exist in uneasy duality in the text, the one emphasizing the negative consequences of the war, the other less obtrusively and less self-consciously dwelling on its dubiously positive aspects. Remarque is not then concerned with anything as morally simplistic as 'the evil of war', but rather with the psychological impact of the war on the troops and its implications for their future, for those who have one, in a post-war civilian world. As his opening statement correctly asserts, he seeks to portray a generation which is being 'vom Kriege zerstört', mentally even if not physically.

Brutalization

It is the realist Katczinsky who remarks that any human being is 'zunächst einmal ein Biest'; decency and altruism are merely social accretions, like dripping spread on a slice of bread (p. 71). The war has scraped this surface layer off its participants and exposed the brute in them. Bäumer himself reflects, with surprising ambivalence, on the reduction of their lives to a primitive state in which nothing matters to them but their animal existences (p. 227-28). This brutalized condition is also their means of survival, he maintains, for any vestige of sensitivity or fastidiousness would have long since driven them insane, caused them to desert or made them fatally careless under fire. The deaths of Detering and Berger shortly afterwards prove him right. In the trenches all normal human emotions in the soldiers have been suppressed, so Bäumer thankfully observes, and instead they are governed by 'Stumpfheit', a zombie mentality which causes them to act only on instinct. They have become 'denkende Tiere' [thinking animals], living a 'Dasein äußerster Oberfläche' [existence of complete superficiality] like some primitive tribe in the bush before civilization. On reflection he realises that they are morally inferior to the aboriginal natives: whilst savages live contentedly and know no other way, the soldiers have forced themselves into this state, it is a conscious 'Anspannung zur Ruhe' [stress in silence]. The aborigines may in time use their intelligence to become more civilized, but the soldiers at the front have abused theirs by reversing the course of civilization. In the trenches they have deliberately regressed to a prehistoric animality: 'unsere inneren Kräfte sind nicht auf Weiter-, sondern auf Zurückentwicklung gerichtet' [our inner forces are not geared to development, but to regression] (p. 228). When in isolated moments he compares their present state to their past lives in normal human society, he can only marvel that such a radical adaptation has occurred.

In the description of the hand-to-hand combat following the French offensive Bäumer reports that he and his comrades have become 'gefährliche Tiere' [dangerous animals] (p. 119). Seeing a prone

French soldier's eyes staring at him, he hesitates for a second, but then hurls a hand grenade at the man's face, overwhelmed again by the instinct to slaughter rather than be slaughtered. In the German counterattack an entrenching spade is used to cleave the features of an enemy soldier, and a bayonet is plunged into a Frenchman's back. The impetus of battle has turned immature schoolboys into inexorable killers, 'zu Wegelagerern, zu Mördern, zu Teufeln meinetwegen' [into highwaymen, into murderers, I suppose into devils]. How will such savage animals ever be able to resume a peaceful civilian routine? As Kropp points out (p. 101), ridding themselves of a state of mind in which killing has become a way of life will not be as simple a matter as taking off their socks. The extent to which normal human feelings have been overturned in the soldiers is revealed by Bäumer's remark (p. 119) that they would kill their own fathers if they happened to be in the ranks of the advancing enemy. Later, observing the Russian prisoners of war during his leave, he reflects that they look like amiable German farmers. He has no quarrel with them, less so than with the German NCO's, but some document signed at a distant table by obscure politicians has decreed that on the field of battle he should kill them remorselessly (p. 174). Murder, in peacetime the supreme crime, has become the supreme goal. Moral imperatives appear to have been reversed: Detering's love of nature and of his home lead to his court-martial for desertion, and Berger's sympathy for a suffering animal causes him to be mown down in a hail of enemy fire.

Earlier in the novel Bäumer remarks that the sadistic discipline of their military training had inured them to the horrors they were later to suffer: 'Wir wurden hart, mißtrauisch, mitleidlos, rachsilchtig, roh— und das war gut' [we became tough, suspicious, hard-hearted, vengeful and rough—and a good thing too] (p. 59). The gains from their brutalisation are however outweighed by the losses. As adolescents they may enjoy the liberation from genteel propriety, the unabashed vulgarity about sexual and lavatorial matters, and the impossibility of personal hygiene. Yet in moments of reflection they know that the dehumanisation which they have undergone, their transformation into 'Menschentiere' [human animals] (p. 79), has impoverished them, making them 'roh und traurig und oberflächlich' [rough, sad, superficial] (p. 126). After being wounded Bäumer is ashamed when on the hospital train a young nurse offers him a bed with clean sheets; he feels like a dirty pig, unable to cope with this modicum of civilised existence (p. 209). How then would he manage with a lifetime of human decency? The war has suspended social and educational differences and made it possible to take revenge on bullies like Himmelstoß and on pompous autocrats like the teacher Kantorek. This measure of equality has, however, only been achieved by destroying individual identities, as if they were coins of various realms melted down into a uniform common currency (p. 226). They have all been reduced to nothing but soldiers, trained like circus animals to perform their military functions, forced into an 'Aufgeben der Persönlichkeit' [surrendering our individual personalities], a loss of human dignity more degrading than that suffered by the most menial of servants (p. 56).

From the perspective of the life-and-death existence of the Flanders trenches they mock an authoritarian educational system obsessed with the encyclopaedic memorising of abstruse facts. What relevance to them has the structure of Schiller's plays compared to the reality of a bayonet in the guts? Did Leer's aptitude for mathematics save him from the shrapnel which tore away his hip? Yet such sarcasm derives from the bitterness of despair, and in their private moments soldiers like Bäumer realise that in jettisoning culture and intellect they have also lost a part of themselves as human personalities. During his leave he sits in his bedroom at home looking at the books, drawings, letters and pictures which had meant so much to him as a sixth-former, trying in vain to recover 'das Feuer der Wünsche . . . die Ungeduld der Zukunft, die beschwingte Freude an der Welt der Gedanken' [the wind of desire . . . the impatience of the future, the soaring delight in the world of the intellect] (p. 159). The brutalising effect of the war has destroyed his emotional sensitivity and deprived him of his youthful hopes, dreams and ideals. He has no heart within him, only a 'schweren, toten Bleiblock' [a heavy, lifeless lead weight]. Nothing matters but the facts (p. 55).

A Generation in Limbo

Bäumer's generation has been denied a whole phase of their lives. In mental and psychological terms they have missed out the best of their adult years and grown old before their time. Thinking of Kantorek's jingoistic description of them as the 'eiserne Jugend' [iron youth] of Germany, Bäumer comments bitterly 'Wir sind alle nicht mehr als zwanzig Jahre. Aber jung? Jugend? Das ist lange her. Wir sind alte Leute' [None of us is more than twenty. But young? Young men? That was a long time ago. We are old now] (p. 53). Whilst physically barely beyond puberty they have acquired the fatalism, the world-weariness and the readiness to compromise of the elderly. Like Prince Leonce in Büchner's *Leonce und Lena* they have 'Den Frühling auf den Wangen und den Winter im Herzen' [spring on their cheeks and winter in their hearts]. In fact Bäumer dreams of himself as 'der Soldat mit den großen Stiefeln und dem zugeschütteten Herzen' [a soldier with big boots and a heart that has been buried alive] (p. 107). Later he makes a similar point by using two parallel images: 'Wir kennen Unterschiede wie Handler, und Notwendigkeiten wie Schlächter' [we perceive differences only in the way tradesmen do and we see necessities like butchers] (p. 126); he and his mates have learned to base their actions on hard-bitten shrewdness and callousness. They have jumped straight to this premature cynicism from the early years of eagerness and good will, from the 'Bereitsein der Jugend' [ready-for-anything world of youth] (p. 159). As young men at school they had felt

> das Weiche, das unser Blut unruhig machte, das Ungewisse, Bestürzende, Kommende, die tausend Gesichter der Zukunft, die Melodie aus Büchern und Träumen, das Rauschen und die Ahnung der Frauen. (p. 241)

[the tenderness that troubles our blood, the uncertainty, the worry, all the things to come, the thousand faces of the future, the music of dreams and books, the rustling and the idea of women.]

This tender and hesitant anticipation of adulthood was never fulfilled, however, for the war intervened. Now they have no desire to change the world or take it by storm, only to escape from it and themselves. They are shut off 'vom Tätigen, vom Streben, vom Fortschritt' [from real action, from getting on, from progress] (p. 102), from that unquestioning energy and belief in progress, however naïve, which are the prerogative of the young.

In general these young men have a strong sense of being separated by a gulf from their own youth. During their training in 1916, as their boyish ideals were drilled out of them, their memories of the past had still been part of them and they had fought to retain them; now, at the end of the war, these 'Bilder des Früher' [earlier images] (p. 124) are only a faint glimmer on the horizon, lost and unattainable. When Bäumer refers in this passage to the 'Landschaft unserer Jugend' [landscape of our youth], he is thinking of a metaphorical landscape in which the topographical features are the experiences and sensations which he shared with his friends at school and which separated his generation from the world inhabited by their parents. Even if they could now be transported back into that youthful landscape, he concludes, they would be like tourists rather than natives, affectionately admiring the view but unable to relate to it. Sitting in his old bedroom Bäumer experiences a 'fürchterliches Gefühl der Fremde' [a terrible feeling of isolation] (p. 160). He feels shut out of his own past, it has turned away from him. The loss of continuity, of any sense of belonging or identity, will evidently make it difficult or even impossible to integrate into normality after the war. For not only are he and others of his generation cut off from the past, they have no role in the future.

The peculiar social limbo in which they find themselves is analysed several times in the novel (especially pp. 54-55 and 240-41). The older soldiers have wives and homes and jobs, in short adult lives, which bind them to the past and provide a framework to which they hope to return. The generation following Bäumer and his class, not having taken part in the war, or at least not having been in the trenches long enough to be shattered by the experience, has its youth intact and can build a future for itself. Only the young men of his generation are aimless and superfluous, uprooted from their past and too demoralised and alienated from normal human society to face the future. At the time of their recruitment none of their interests and plans had amounted to a 'Daseinsform', a purposeful way of life which might have survived the war. Now, after the enormity of what they have lived through, it seems to them absurd and repugnant to envisage settling into a civilian routine. They ought, says Bäumer, to do something extraordinary after the war; but he can think of nothing appropriate. What he seeks is a 'Daseinsmöglichkeit nach dieser Katastrophe aller Menschlichkeit' [a reason for going on living after this universal catastrophe is over] (p. 174-75), some inspiring and purposeful future to compensate for the horror of the trenches; but the pacifist and egalitarian ideas which he entertains at this point remain too speculative and indefinite to constitute a coherent plan. He can gladly offer the dying Gérard Duval twenty years of his own life: 'nimm mehr, denn ich weiß nicht, was ich damit noch beginnen soll' [take more, because I don't know what I'm going to do with all the years I've got] (p. 194). It is no wonder that Bäumer dies with a look of composure and even relief on his face, for his death has exempted him from a future which the war had rendered him incapable of handling.

Perspective and Structure

Much earlier in the novel, when the group of soldiers had concluded that they were part of a whole generation without a future, Albert Kropp had summed up by saying 'Der Krieg hat uns für alles verdorben' [the war has ruined us for everything] (p. 102). He and the others seem in the midst of the war to be endowed with a remarkable capacity to stand back from their situation and analyse its consequences. The reason is of course that Remarque is writing about 1918 in order to explain and come to terms with the problems of 1928. He has the advantage of a decade's hindsight and knows about the predicament of the 'Heimkehrer', the demobilised soldiers unable to settle down in the ensuing 1920s. As he claims in his prefatory statement, his aim is to describe the destruction of a generation by the war, 'auch wenn sie seinen Granaten entkam'. A novel apparently about the horror of the war turns out on closer analysis to be more about the difficulty of coping with the subsequent peace. As Alan Bance has demonstrated, *Im Westen* in many respects reflects attitudes prevalent in the Weimar Republic, such as the sense of powerlessness in the face of modern technology and the fear of social disintegration.[9] Bäumer even predicts the disorientation which Remarque and the other survivors were to experience:

> Wir werden wachsen, einige werden sich anpassen, andere sich fügen, und viele werden ratlos sein;—die Jahre werden zerrinnen, und schließlich werden wir zugrunde gehen. (p. 241)

> [We shall grow older, a few will adapt, others will make adjustments and many of us will not know what to do—the years will trickle away, and eventually we shall perish.]

Such arguably anachronistic statements have led Hans-Harald Müller to suggest that Remarque is trying in this novel to provide a justification for his own drifting in the 1920s and for the failure before 1928 of his pre-war ambitions as a writer.[10]

Be that as it may, it is clear that the war itself, paradoxically, is not the focus of interest in *Im Westen*; and this fact also determines the form of the novel. Critics have frequently noted the absence of any proper plot in *Im Westen*. Alfred Antkowiak describes Bäumer's narrative as a chain of loosely connected subjective experiences and, quoting a dissertation by Hans Joachim Bernhard, as a 'mosaic', in which individual sections could be transposed without disrupting the logical train of events.[11] Even the successive deaths of the group of soldiers do not represent turning points in this static narration, for they are seen as inevitable and registered mechanically. In fact there is hardly any sequence of cause and effect in *Im Westen* at all, only a shifting back and forwards from the front, during which there are repeated discussions and reflections on the significance and implications of the war. It is a structure, as Christine Barker and Rex Last put it in their biography of Remarque, of 'theme and variation'.[12] Bäumer proceeds episodically and associatively, using flashbacks and memories and dreams like clips from a film in order to turn the issues over in his head. The emphasis is not on the external events of the war but rather on the states of mind which they engender.

Remarque was not alone in his generation in discovering that the war was remarkable less for death and horror than for the degradation of the human personality. Forty years later Carl Zuckmayer was to write in his memoirs that it was not the fear of death that had made life at the front in the Great War into a hell:

> Hier galt es zu lernen, ein 'gemeiner Mann' zu sein, dem keiner etwas erließ oder erleichterte, und der seine graue, anonyme, schmutzige Arbeit machen mußte, statt 'Heldentaten' zu begehen. Man mußte das Härteste erfahren, das . . . so schwer erträglich war: die ungeheure Langeweile, die Nüchternheit, das Unheroische, Mechanische, Alltägliche des Kriegs, in das sich das Grauen, das Entsetzen, das Sterben nur einfügte wie das Anschlagen einer Kontrolluhr in einem endlosen Fabrikationsprozeß.[13]

> [What you had to do was learn to be a 'common man,' to whom nobody made any concessions or gave any relief, and who had to carry out his grey, anonymous and dirty tasks rather than engaging in heroic deeds. You had

to experience the toughest thing, the thing which was so hard to bear: the dreadfully boring, matter-of-fact, unheroic, mechanical, everyday nature of the war, into which horror, terror and death simply fitted like the ticking of the factory clock in some endless manufacturing process.]

What is special about Remarque's novel is that he shows with journalistic verve and immediacy the destructive effect of this dehumanisation and brutilisation on the personalities of those who were subjected to it. Writing in 1929 to General Sir Ian Hamilton, Remarque stated that his book was never intended to have any political message, either pacifist or militarist. 'I have not felt myself called upon,' he maintained, 'to argue about the war. . . . I merely wanted to awaken understanding for a generation that more than all others has found it difficult to make its way back from the four years of death, struggle and terror, to the peaceful fields of work and progress'.[14]

From *Modern Languages* 70, no. 1 (March 1989): 89-94. Copyright © 1989 by the Modern Language Association. Reprinted with permission of the author.

Notes

1. The following article was first delivered as a lecture at a German Sixth-Form Day at the University of Birmingham in 1988, and has been adapted and expanded for publication. The text of *Im Westen nichts Neues* is quoted from the edition by Brian Murdoch in the Methuen's Twentieth Century Texts series (London, 1984).

2. The early course of this debate is well charted in Alfred Antkowiak and Pawel Toper, *Ludwig Renn. Erich Maria Remarque. Leben und Werk*, Berlin (East), 1965, pp. 113-18.

3. Axel Eggebrecht, 'Gespräch mit Remarque', *Die literarische Welt*, 5, Issue 24 (14 June 1929), p. 1.

4. Cp. the remarks on the complex relationship between personal experience and fiction, in a quite different literary context, in my essay 'Autobiography and Poetry: the example of Goethe's *Römische Elegien*,' in *Modern Languages*, 67, 1986.

5. Brian A. Rowley, 'Journalism into Fiction: *Im Westen nichts Neues*,' in: *The First World War in Fiction*, ed. Holger Klein, London, 1976, p. 110.

6. As Note 3.

7. See A. F. Bance, '*Im Westen nichts Neues*: a Bestseller in Context', *Modern*

Language Review, 72, 1977, p. 365. Bance rightly describes the pacifism of the book as 'generalised' and 'diluted'.

8. Hans-Harald Müller, *Der Krieg und die Schriftsteller. Der Kriegsroman der Weimarer Republik*, Stuttgart, 1986, pp. 54-58.

9. As Note 7. See especially pp. 364-69.

10. As Note 8, p. 48.

11. As Note 2, pp. 128-33. Critics have been too eager to dismiss Antkowiak's analysis of *Im Westen* on account of its Marxist perspective. He makes a number of thoughtful observations about Remarque's characterisation technique and about the structure of the novel.

12. Christine R. Barker and R. W. Last, *Erich Maria Remarque*, London 1979, p. 58.

13. Carl Zuckmayer, *Als wär's ein Stück von mir*, paperback edition, Frankfurt am Main, 1969, p. 184.

14. *Life and Letters*, 3, 1929, p. 406.

From the Frog's Perspective:
Im Westen nichts Neues
and *Der Weg zurück*_____

Brian Murdoch

The title of this chapter, which considers Remarque's two novels of the First World War, is a literal translation of the German phrase *aus der Froschperspektive*, which is usually translated as "worm's eye view," although frogs, unlike worms, have harsh voices as well as eyes. Remarque treated the First World War in both novels from this perspective, and although the second of them is set for the most part after the cessation of hostilities, the war informs it so completely that *Der Weg zurück* (*The Road Back*), is not simply a sequel to *Im Westen nichts Neues* (*All Quiet on the Western Front*), but almost a second part of its famous predecessor.[1]

Im Westen nichts Neues made its first appearance in serial form in Germany in 1928, and then, with a great deal of sometimes not entirely truthful publicity (its composition and the revision process had taken longer than was claimed), in a slightly changed and expanded book version in January 1929. It sold a million copies by 1930,[2] was translated into an enormous number of languages,[3] and provoked personal attacks, parodies, and imitations. It remains a bestseller and has been filmed twice, both times in English, and the first version remains one of the classics of early sound cinema. When it was first shown in Berlin in 1930 it was famously disrupted, on the orders of Goebbels, by Nazi activists releasing mice.[4] Remarque was later condemned by the Nazis for "betraying the front-line soldier" and his novel was publicly burned in May 1933.[5]

The popularity of the novel seems sometimes to have baffled the critics. In 1985, for example, Jost Hermand wrote a piece with the revealing title "Versuch, den Erfolg von Erich Maria Remarques *Im Westen nichts Neues* zu verstehen" (An attempt to understand the success of Erich Maria Remarque's *Im Westen nichts Neues*), while a few years earlier, Alan Bance, having noted that "perhaps because of its phenomenal commercial success, it has received relatively little serious discussion," went on to state that "no one would want to claim for the novel a place in the ranks of first-class literature." But there precisely is a case for placing the work in the category of first-class literature. There is no critical law defining a great work as one that can be read or understood only by an intellectual elite, and the focus on the work as a commercial phenomenon has often distracted from proper considerations of style, structure, and content.[6]

Some basic misunderstandings were associated with *Im Westen nichts Neues* from the start. Some of the first critics assumed somewhat unreasonably (given the death of the narrator) that Remarque was completely identifiable with Paul Bäumer.[7] Of the literary responses—many of which appeared with covers imitating Remarque's novel—Klietmann's *Im Westen wohl was Neues* (Not Quiet on the Western Front) is the most extreme example of a parodistic attack (carrying the heading *Contra Remarque*), with Nickl's *"Im Westen nichts Neues" und sein wahrer Sinn* (The True Meaning of "All Quiet on the Western Front") the most nationalistic and anti-Semitic in its attack on the publisher, Ullstein. Otto's *Im Osten nichts Neues* (All Quiet on the Eastern Front) is a simple imitation, and *Vor Troja nichts Neues* (All Quiet on the Trojan Front) by "Emil Marius Requark" a not uninventive parody that manages one or two telling blows against the marketing strategy adopted for the work.[8] The influence of Remarque's novel was enormous, not only in German, as is clear even from the novel title *Not so Quiet . . .* by Evadne Price, for example, writing as Helen Zenna Smith in 1930.[9]

In 1931 Remarque published *Der Weg zurück*. The first war novel is set in 1917 and 1918, and its sequel begins with a prologue set immediately after, and referring to, the death of the narrator of *Im Westen nichts Neues* in October 1918. The main part takes place in 1919, immediately following the last month of the war, although an epilogue takes us briefly into 1920. The work is set, then, in the period of the establishment of the Weimar Republic.[10] The new first-person narrator is so similar to that of the first novel in name, background, and attitude that he could be Bäumer brought back to life, but this reinforces the point that the young soldiers of the First World War were both representative *and* individual. *Der Weg zurück* did not meet with the same enthusiasm as the first war novel, although it too was widely translated and also filmed.

Both novels are part of an international body of literature concerned with the war and produced in the late 1920s and early 1930s. The universality of the experience of the trenches was emphasized by the appearance in Germany during the Weimar period not only of many native novels, but of German translations of numbers of war novels from abroad. Most of the contemporary German war novels, even the more obscure ones, were also translated into English, French, and other languages. In Germany the novels included both pacifist anti-war works and novels that took the opposite stance and presented the war as heroic, and as a testing and strengthening of German virtues in the storm of steel.[11] The emergence of the pacifist *Im Westen nichts Neues* as the leading war novel in an international context is all the more impressive.

Im Westen nichts Neues

That a historical event of the magnitude of the First World War, which cost around ten million lives from most nations of the world, could be encapsulated to any extent in a novel the paperback edition of which has little more than two hundred pages is an achievement in itself.[12] The fact that the body of the novel is a convincingly presented first-person narrative means that it *does* still need to be spelled out that Bäumer is not Remarque, who drew without doubt upon his own experiences in the war and at home in Osnabrück. But *Im Westen nichts Neues* is a work of fiction, and most importantly it has only one character. With two small but significant exceptions, the young soldier Paul

Bäumer delivers the work directly to the reader, and therefore everything we see or hear is through him. It testifies to Remarque's skill that Bäumer remains consistent throughout the work, and it is Bäumer's character and background that dictates the style.[13] The choice of a narrator is significant; because Bäumer, drafted in 1916, was still a schoolboy in 1914, he bears no personal responsibility for the war itself, nor indeed does he understand much about it. Equally, Remarque does not permit him any prescience (although of course he speculates) about what happens *after* the war. This has an effect on the way in which other figures are presented to us, and criticism has been leveled at the book for the apparent one-sidedness of some of the characters encountered, or for the limited view of the fighting troops. But since they are all presented through Bäumer, his close friends would clearly be in far sharper focus than an anonymous and unpleasant major, or even an attractive French girl met on one occasion only. Bäumer would in reality have been unlikely to know the names of either of them. Nor would he have had much of a view of the war beyond company level, and his immediate experience with senior or even junior officers would be limited. The most senior officer glimpsed in the work is in fact Kaiser Wilhelm, when he comes to review the troops, but apart from one major and his own second lieutenant, Bäumer mentions no one else above the noncommissioned ranks. *Im Westen nichts Neues*, and to an extent the sequel, seem by this approach to claim the advantages of a diary—that is, its immediacy—with none of the drawbacks of a precise chronology, and Bäumer (and Birkholz in *Der Weg zurück*) present their thoughts, experiences, and reflections directly to the reader.[14]

The individual private soldier Paul Bäumer nevertheless sees himself for most of the novel as part of a group, so that it is the first person plural that predominates much of the work, and the move away from it at the end to Bäumer as an individual gains in significance thereby. Nor, of course, must we forget Remarque as the (concealed) structuring author behind the character, controlling the work as a whole in the variation in chapter lengths, or in the balance of action and periods of inaction, of reported discussion and private reflection. Remarque allows Bäumer to send signals to the reader to consider how single events need to be multiplied by thousands, for example, or indications that a particular train of thought will be able to be taken to a logical conclusion only after the war.

It is also sometimes overlooked that *Im Westen nichts Neues* is not a contemporary account of the First World War. Although both novels contain episodes based upon historical reality,[15] *Im Westen nichts Neues* was not written in 1918, but in 1928, recreating within the Weimar Republic events that had happened ten or more years before, even if those events were part of the experience of many of those living in the new postwar German state. *Im Westen nichts Neues* is historical fiction, and so is *Der Weg zurück*, although by the time of the latter, the sense that history was moving on was more apparent.[16] That Remarque chose to set the two novels during and just after the war itself means that they cannot be historically reflective in themselves, but both raise questions to which the narrator was never in a position to give answers. The burden of finding answers is thus placed upon the reader, whether in 1930 or in the present, and wherever he or she may be responding to the work.[17] In the first instance the target audience was the Weimar Republic itself, because both novels reflect the shared history of those reaching maturity in a postwar Germany that was already beginning to look insecure. But they were addressed, also, to the contemporary world, sending out a specifically pacifist message to Germany's former enemies. Beside these two time levels—that of the action and that of the contemporary reception—stands a third, the time of the present reader. They are addressed also to an international posterity and remain important in their general implications.

There are two places in *Im Westen nichts Neues* in which Bäumer is not in control of the narrative. There is a prefatory statement by the author that was omitted in some translations and appears in others with a significant variation from the text of the first German edition. It may be cited in German from a prepublication version; with the translation by

A. W. Wheen, who included it in full in his 1929 translation; the sentence in italics was left out of the first German book edition:[18]

Dieses Buch soll weder eine Anklage noch ein Bekenntnis, *vor allem aber kein Erlebnis* sein, *denn der Tod ist kein Erlebnis für den, der ihm gegenübersteht.* Es soll nur den Versuch machen, über eine Generation zu berichten, die vom Kriege zerstört wurde;—auch wenn sie seinen Granaten entkam.

[This book is to be neither an accusation nor a confession, and least of all an adventure, for death is not an adventure to those who stand face to face with it. It will try simply to tell of a generation of men who, even though they may have escaped its shells, were destroyed by the war.]

The statement in its original form was necessary because there were many examples of literature that did present the war in that light. More importantly though, it categorizes the work as a *Bericht*, a report, reminding us that although the fictive narrator would have been dead for ten years when the book appeared, other soldiers had survived. As a parallel with this opening statement, the final half-dozen lines of the novel are spoken by a new third-person narrator within the historical fictionality of the book, commenting on the death of Bäumer.

It was argued early in the criticism of the novel that the presentation of the war by a single individual could not portray a valid picture of the war.[19] There are various responses to this: one is that the first person in the novel is, as indicated, frequently the plural *wir*, so that Bäumer speaks for other soldiers and their experiences. Furthermore, even the notion of "other soldiers" can mean a variety of things, ranging from just Bäumer and Katczinsky (Kat), his mentor, to his immediate groups of school or platoon comrades, to his company, to the German army, or even the Germans as a whole. Refining it again, it might refer to the ordinary German soldier, or indeed to the ordinary soldier as such. Remarque permits Bäumer and his comrades to stress their representative status by pointing out that most of the soldiers of all countries are also ordinary people, and also by introducing overtly what might be seen as a multiplication factor at key points. Thus Bäumer says of the teacher, Kantorek, who had bullied them into signing up: "Es gab ja Tausende von Kantoreks" (18, there were thousands of Kantoreks), and more significantly towards the end of the novel, of the military hospital, which shows the true measure of war: "es gibt Hunderttausende in Deutschland, Hunderttausende in Frankreich, Hunderttausende in Russland . . ." (177, there are hundreds of thousands of them in Germany, hundreds of thousands of them in France, hundreds of thousands of them in Russia).

The *Froschperspektive* need not, then, be as restricted as it might appear.[20] But the narrator is also an individual; wars may be expressed in terms of the often unimaginably large numbers of those who fought or were killed, but such statistics are always made up of individuals. Remarque reduces the *wir* element gradually throughout the work in parallel to what was a war of attrition that ultimately reached the single individual, when at the end Paul Bäumer is not just left alone, but is thrown onto his own inner resources without support from any side. The ultimate expression of Bäumer's existentialist realization of the nature of life in the face of the extreme situation of war links this work with Remarque's oeuvre as a whole.

The fictional time of the novel begins in 1917, well after the outbreak of the war, and the reader is aware of time—more specifically of the seasons—passing until October 1918. Bäumer's own thoughts and conversations with others take the reader back to earlier periods, but in the fictional present the deadly monotony and constant attrition is completely established. The first chapter begins with *wir*, which refers on this occasion to a company of 150 men, just back from what was supposed to be a quiet sector after heavy losses, and with only eighty survivors. The battle has not been an important one, and the reason for the losses is casually put:

Nun aber gab es gerade am letzten Tage bei uns überraschend viel Langrohr und dicke Brocken, englische Artillerie, die ständig auf unsere Stellung trommelte, so daß wir starke Verluste hatten und nur mit achtzig Mann zurückkamen. (11)

[But then, on the very last day we were taken by surprise by long-range shelling from the heavy artillery. The English guns kept on pounding our position, so we lost a lot of men, and only eighty of us came back.]

The slang (*Langrohr und dicke Brocken* cannot really be imitated in translation) and the offhand manner of describing the death of nearly half the company is striking, and even more so is the stress on the pure mischance that there just happened to be unexpected heavy shellfire. The impression is one of passivity. The role of Bäumer and the other ordinary soldiers as victims rather than warriors is immediately established.

The first person plural now shifts to two smaller groups: Bäumer and three former classmates, Kropp, Müller, and Leer, who have joined the army straight from high school, then four more friends who were workers—Tjaden, a locksmith; Westhus, a peat-digger; Detering, a farmer; and finally Katczinsky, the father figure of the group, who is already forty and who is presented as someone with enormous capabilities for spotting and avoiding trouble and for finding things that are needed. We have, therefore, a cross section of those fighting at the lowest and largest level, although, for different reasons, none of them understands precisely why they are fighting.

Paul Bäumer is nineteen when the action of *Im Westen nichts Neues* begins, and we learn that he joined up directly from a *Gymnasium* (classical high school). He is educated along traditional lines, is thoughtful, but does not have enough experience to draw full conclusions, especially since he has been thrust into the extreme situation of war. The consistency of the character is made clear in numerous small ways: when wounded and on a hospital train, he is still too embarrassed to ask a nurse when he needs to relieve himself, although he has been under heavy shellfire. On another occasion he describes how Tjaden, his ex-locksmith friend, insults their drill corporal, Himmelstoss, who has been sent to the front: "Tjaden erwidert gelassen und abschliessend, ohne es zu wissen, mit dem bekanntesten Klassikerzitat. Gleichzeitig lüftet er seine Kehrseite" (64, Tjaden gives an unworried and conclusive reply, quoting, though he doesn't know he's doing so, one of Goethe's best-known lines, the one about kissing a specific part of his anatomy. At the same time he sticks his backside up in the air). The quotation is from Goethe's *Götz von Berlichingen*, and it is often truncated in print anyway, though the sense ("you can kiss my ass") is clear and is here even made graphic. The passage is difficult to translate, because the quotation is not known in English, but the real point of Bäumer's report of this small incident is that Tjaden has used the literal expression, but does not know about any literary allusions. Bäumer, on the other hand, uses the literary reference to avoid actually saying what Tjaden has said, and even in describing Tjaden's gesture he uses a euphemism. Bäumer notes several times that everything they learned at school has now become worthless, and this is true; but he cannot escape from his background.[21]

Im Westen nichts Neues presents the war as such being shown with the vivid and deliberately shocking realism associated with the term *neue Sachlichkeit* (new objectivity). The approach here and in many comparable war novels is a quasi-documentary one, but the style is not only one of objective authenticity.[22] The structure is episodic, something that would become a hallmark of Remarque's novels, holding the interest by moving rapidly from one scene to another and alternating the kinds of scenes presented, while picking up themes from one episode to another in twelve chapters that vary in content, emphasis, and length. This enables the work to present a wide range of experiences of the war: we see the soldiers recovering behind the lines, visiting and being treated in a military hospital, on wiring duty, on reconnaissance patrol, under fire in a dugout, going over the top and attacking another trench, going on leave. Further experiences, including a soldiers' brothel, are filled in by *Der Weg zurück*. Movement from the immediate present to the remembered past also enables Bäumer to give us scenes of basic training as well.

The first three chapters are set behind the lines, the work opening with an apparently trivial incident in which Bäumer and his associates receive a double ration of food; we soon discover, however, that it is because they have just sustained the loss of half of the company, and the attrition continues when the reinforcements sent to bring them back to strength are raw recruits, who fall in large numbers. Discussions between the soldiers take us back to the training period under the martinet Himmelstoss as drill corporal, and then in the third chapter the soldiers recollect the satisfactory revenge that they had taken, beating him up when he is drunk, and thus utilizing the pragmatism of violence that he has instilled in them, and in fact is vital for their survival. Revenge on the noncommissioned officer (NCO) is probably part of the fantasy of any soldier, and it certainly has literary antecedents in German.[23] The character of Himmelstoss, however, is developed in the work. Initially frightened when forced to go into battle, he is shamed into gathering his courage, and eventually becomes friendly towards the former recruits. The first two chapters each end, however, with a visit to one of Bäumer's school-friends, Fritz Kemmerich, who is badly wounded in a field hospital in the first, and dead by the end of the second.

Various key themes are voiced in these early chapters. Attention has been paid to a comment by Bäumer describing the feeling of solidarity engendered first by their training, which "im Felde dann zum Besten steigerte, was der Krieg hervorbrachte: zur Kameradschaft" (27-28, grew, on the battlefield, into the best thing that the war produced— comradeship in arms). It is possible to make too much of this comment, and most certainly the development of a close comradeship is not to be taken as a justification for the war; it is just that the war, as an extreme situation, permits it to develop more strongly. The comradeship in *Im Westen nichts Neues* is born of mutual help in battle, and in *Der Weg zurück* Remarque would make clear that while it is a necessity in war, it does not necessarily always survive in peacetime. Equally important is a motif first voiced at the end of the third chapter, in response to someone's reference to them as *eiserne Jugend* (22, iron youth), Bäumer comments that none of them is young, even if they are only nineteen or twenty. Their youth has been taken away from them, and they feel that they are—this is a common literary motif with other writers, too—a betrayed, a lost generation.[24]

The novel now shows the young soldiers in action, first on duty laying barbed wire, and then, after a further period behind the lines, in the field, although we rarely see the soldiers engaged in actual fighting. The episode when they are laying wire shows them being fired upon, rather than firing. Various striking incidents remain in the mind from this section of the work: the young recruit who loses control of his bowels under fire; the slow and grotesque death of a horse (in a scene that once again has literary parallels before and after Remarque), a gas attack, and the fact that the men come under fire in a cemetery and have to take cover against death among the graves and coffins of the fairly recently dead (a sleeve is apparently still intact on one of the bodies). The symbolism of the cemetery scene is clear enough, but it is not gratuitous, nor grotesque sensationalism, as has been suggested.[25] In this incident, too, the young recruit from the earlier scene who soiled himself under fire, is fatally wounded. Kat wants to shoot the horribly wounded soldier, but cannot do so because other soldiers are around. The irony in his being prevented from mercy killing, when they are forced to kill otherwise, is underlined again in the reaction of Detering, the farmer, who wants to shoot the wounded horse, but cannot, because this would draw fire upon them.

The fifth chapter, which contains the arrival of Himmelstoss at the front and Tjaden's insult, is set behind the lines, again a respite from the horrors of the previous chapter. A discussion between the young soldiers focuses upon the realization of the high school recruits that their knowledge has become worthless and they are now unable to

Critical Insights

think beyond the war. The atmosphere of a more or less flippant conversation gradually gives way to something close to despair in Bäumer's thoughts. He reports one of his friends as saying: "Der Krieg hat uns für alles verdorben" (67, the war has ruined us for everything), and sums up for the reader—in the Weimar Republic and afterwards—their collective state of mind, developing the idea of the loss of youth: "Wir sind keine Jugend mehr. Wir wollen die Welt nicht mehr stürmen. Wir sind Flüchtende. [. . .] . . . wir glauben an den Krieg" (67, We're no longer young men. We've lost any desire to conquer the world. We are refugees . . . we believe in the war). The chapter concludes, however, with a scene in which the ever-resourceful Kat, aided by Bäumer, requisitions—steals—a couple of geese and roasts them. The incident may have adventurous, or even comic elements, but the long process of cooking the geese permits Bäumer to think further, and to comment for the benefit of the reader upon what he has become. He and his older mentor are close, and although Kat, too, will fall before the end of the work, for the moment Bäumer is aware of them both simply as "zwei Menschen, zwei winzige Funken Leben, draußen ist die Nacht und der Kreis des Todes" (72, two human beings, two tiny sparks of life; outside there is just the night, and all around us, death). That spark of life—possibly the most important recurrent theme in Remarque's novels—will survive in Bäumer to the end.

The central sixth chapter is one of the longest in the work, two dozen pages in the standard paperback, as against the final chapter, which is barely two pages long, and although it does show the soldiers fighting, the concept of the soldier as victim as well as aggressor is maintained. The precise nature of the enemy is important, too. The realistically presented fighting makes a deliberate assault on all of the senses, in particular that of hearing. The massive and permanent noise of war is probably the feature that those who experienced it recollected most.

Plötzlich heult und blitzt es ungeheuer, der Unterstand kracht in allen Fugen unter einem Treffer, glücklicherweise einem leichten, dem die

Betonklötze standgehalten haben. Es klirrt metallisch und fürchterlich, die Wände wackeln, Gewehre, Helme, Erde, Dreck und Staub fliegen. Schwefeliger Qualm dringt ein. (81)

[Suddenly there is a terrible noise and flash of light, and every joint in the dugout creaks under the impact of a direct hit—luckily not a heavy one, and one that the concrete blocks could withstand. There is a fearsome metallic rattling, the walls shake, rifles, steel helmets, earth, mud, and dust fly around. Sulphurous fumes penetrate the walls.]

Cinema audiences in the early 1930s were horrified when films with a realistic soundtrack were first shown. The sound of war in particular, but also sight, feeling, and smell are all invoked in a chapter that makes clear the physical aspects of frontline warfare. The soldiers fight like automata when they go over the top, and they suffer from *Unterstandsangst* otherwise, driven crazy in the confinements of a dugout under heavy shelling. A severely wounded man calls out constantly for some days, but cannot be reached, large numbers of untrained recruits, referred to as *Kinder* (children), are killed, as are some of Bäumer's friends. Tjaden, however, has to be stopped from trying to knock the fuse off a dud shell; a natural survivor, he appears in *Der Weg zurück*, the only member of the group to do so. The novel began with the return of eighty out of 150 men, and this chapter, at the halfway point, ends with the return of only thirty-two. In terms of actual plot, the ironic major achievement in this part of the offensive is the welcome capture of five cans of corned beef.

The physical realism is balanced by Bäumer's thoughts. In an earlier chapter, the front was for Bäumer a whirlpool, sucking him in as a helpless victim, and now it is a cage, again an image of external entrapment, while later on it will be an inescapable fever. Dominating everything is *Zufall* (chance), another key theme throughout the work. An indifferent universe can inflict upon any human being what it will, and in the war a bullet may strike at any time, which leaves the soldier believing in chance and chance alone. The soldiers themselves become not men but dangerous animals, who fight to stay alive, something that also—significantly—distances their actions from those of hatred for any specific human enemy.

> Aus uns sind gefährliche Tiere geworden. Wir kämpfen nicht, wir verteidigen uns vor der Vernichtung. Wir schleudern die Granaten nicht gegen Menschen, was wissen wir im Augenblick davon, dort hetzt mit Händen und Helmen der Tod hinter uns her. . . . (83)

> [We have turned into dangerous animals. We are not fighting, we are defending ourselves from annihilation. We are not hurling our grenades against human beings—what do we know about all that in the heat of the moment?—the hands and the helmets that are after us belong to Death itself. . . .]

The breathless style of the passage is noteworthy, and the length of the chapter also underlines the comments by Bäumer that the horror seems to go and on with no sign of relief. Episodic variation permits us to see periods of waiting, which can be as bad as the fighting, killing rats, and preventing the dugout-crazy recruits from running out into the open. There are calmer moments—at one point two butterflies are seen near their trenches—but the return is always to the fighting, until the few remaining exhausted soldiers return behind the lines.

The next chapter matches this in length; after a brief incident when some of them visit some French girls, Bäumer returns home on leave, and is confronted with his now unimaginably distant earlier life. Here he has to cope with the uncomprehending worries of his dying mother, and with the differently uncomprehending attitudes first of the military—an unpleasant major is critical of Bäumer's *Frontsitten* (frontline manners)—and of civilians, as a group of well-meaning middle-aged men at an inn instruct him on what the army ought to do. Neither the major nor the civilians have any idea of the realities of life at the front, which have just been shown so graphically to the reader. Bäumer also has to report to Franz Kemmerich's mother how he died, swearing (ironically) on his own life that Kemmerich died instantly. Bäumer and the others may feel that they are no longer young, but Kemmerich's mother reminds us sharply of the real situation when she asks why "you children" are out there. The conclusion Bäumer draws is that he should never have gone on leave.

A brief interlude in which Bäumer is detailed to guard some Russian prisoners of war reminds us that this was a war on more than one front, and is followed by a return to his unit and the ceremonial visit by the Kaiser, which provides occasion for the soldiers to discuss the nature of the war once again. It is followed, however, by a reconnaissance patrol in which Bäumer kills in terror a French soldier—the only enemy soldier seen closely, and certainly the only one named, Gérard Duval—against whom he is quite literally thrown in a shell hole and whom he stabs. His experience, trapped in no man's land while Duval dies slowly, brings Bäumer close to madness as he realizes that this is a real person, with a name and a family. While trapped with the dying French soldier, Bäumer makes promises to him, declaring that "Es darf nie wieder geschehen" (154, It must never happen again). That last statement is directed at the outside world, of course, from a Weimar Republic concerned to remove the image of Germany as the aggressor. However, when he finds his way back to his own trench, Bäumer is made to watch a sniper at work, and to find a kind of comfort in the circular notion that *Krieg ist Krieg*, war is war. That might during the war itself be enough, but whether it would work afterwards is left open.

The original version of the prefatory statement warned against seeing war as an adventure, and that criticism has been leveled at the incident when Bäumer and his comrades are placed in charge of a food supply dump. They take advantage of this and organize a feast, but Bäumer points out the need for the soldiers to seize any opportunity of light relief, contextualizing this passage as a respite, rather than as an adventure. It is the same reflex action that makes the soldiers use jokey slang evasions for the idea of being killed. The meal, which gives the participants diarrhea, is conducted under heavy shellfire, and immediately afterwards Bäumer and others are wounded and hospitalized, giving him the opportunity to see and to comment upon for the reader another aspect of the war. He enumerates soberly and in detail the various types of wounds—a long list of all the places in which a man can be hit by a bullet—and notes that this is the real indicator of the reality of war: "Erst das Lazarett zeigt, was Krieg ist" (177, only a military hospital can really show you what war is).

Bäumer's mood seems to reach complete despair in the two final short chapters. The penultimate chapter is still characterized by the *wir* opening: "Wir zählen die Wochen nicht mehr" (183, we've stopped counting the weeks), but not many of Bäumer's friends are left, and the war seems never-ending. Again some incidents stand out: the farmer Detering's apparent desertion, although he is actually heading homewards towards his farm, rather than trying to escape to the Netherlands; the attempt, also caused by frontline madness, by another soldier to rescue a wounded dog. The horrors of war have been shown in telegrammatic enumeration at earlier points, and here again the style sounds almost like an expressionist poem by, say, August Stramm:[26]

Granaten, Gasschwaden und Tankflottillen—Zerstampfen, Zerfressen, Tod.
Ruhr, Gruppe, Typhus—Würgen, Verbrennen, Tod.
Graben, Lazarett, Massengrab—mehr Möglichkeiten gibt es nicht. (190)

[Shells, gas clouds and flotillas of tanks—crushing, devouring, death.
Dysentery, influenza, typhus—choking, scalding, death.
Trench, hospital, mass grave—there are no other possibilities.]

A further stylistic variation stressing the apparent endlessness of the war is seen in a sequence of four paragraphs beginning: *Sommer 1918* (Summer 1918), full of the desire not to be killed at this late stage, coupled with the desperate feeling that surely it has to end soon?

Bäumer is still able to voice comments on the nature of the war, castigating the profiteers, for example: "Die Fabrikbesitzer in Deutschland sind reiche Leute geworden—uns zerschrinnt die Ruhr die Därme" (188, the factory owners in Germany have grown rich, while dysentery racks our guts). He also comments on why the war is ending for the German army. It is simply because they are tired and hungry, yet are faced with a well-provisioned and stronger opposition force—America had finally joined the war in 1917, and the allied blockade had affected supplies to Germany itself. But the German army, says Bäumer—and the *wir* voice is highly significant here—has not been defeated in a purely military sense:

Wir sind nicht geschlagen, denn wir sind als Soldaten besser und erfahrener; wir sind einfach von der vielfachen Übermacht zerdrückt und zurückgeschoben. (192)

[We haven't been defeated, because as soldiers we are better and more experienced; we have simply been crushed and pushed back by forces many times superior to ours.]

Historically Germany had in any real terms been defeated; but Bäumer's wartime interpretation, while certainly not in line with the famous notion that she had been "stabbed in the back" by left-wing political forces (the *Dolchstosslegende*),[27] may still have struck a chord with the former soldiers in the Weimar Republic who were the first audience for the book. The Nazis, who accused the work of insulting the frontline soldier, presumably overlooked this passage. Remarque himself, however, was specific enough on Germany's actual defeat later, and in a piece written in 1944 he criticized the plethora of books published in the years after the First World War with titles like *Im Felde unbesiegt* (Undefeated in Battle). In *Der Weg zurück* the idea is neatly countered when the new narrator thinks of an essay he wrote at school on the subject of why Germany is bound to win, and considers that the low grade it received was probably about right in the circumstances.[28]

Juxtaposed with the comments and thoughts of Bäumer in the penultimate chapter is a quickening of the final attrition, as the last of his friends are killed. Müller leaves to Bäumer the boots he had inherited from Kemmerich, and which became probably the most commented-upon motif in the work—Tjaden will get them next, and he of course survives.[29] Then Kat is killed by a random piece of shrapnel while Bäumer is carrying him to a dressing station to have another minor wound treated. The loss of the man with whom he had shared the moment of isolation in the battlefield as the spark of life leaves him with an immense feeling of isolation, and means that Bäumer is alone in a final two-page chapter.

Had they returned in 1916, Bäumer thinks that they could have unleashed a revolution—the idea will be developed in other novels—but now he feels that there is weariness without hope. However, this state of mind gives way fairly suddenly to a new attitude: this might, he thinks, just be a transitory melancholy, the trees are green, there is much talk of peace, and he himself becomes very calm: "Ich bin sehr ruhig" (197). Whatever happens, there will be inside him an independent spark of life that will carry him onwards, whether his own individuality wants it or not. Bäumer has used the *wir* voice a great deal, but now he is forced into the first person singular as the last survivor of his group. Beyond this, his thoughts move still further away from the individual that he has become to focus on the independent life force, from the *ich* to the *es*. "Aber so lange es [das Leben] da ist, wird es sich seinen Weg suchen, mag dieses was in mir 'ich' sagt, wollen oder nicht" (197, but as long as life is there it will make its own way, whether my conscious self likes it or not).

But things go further. Bäumer is killed, and now he is completely objectivized as *er*, seen by a third party. His death is as random as Kat's in reality, although in literary terms we recall his promise to Kemmerich's mother that he may not return if he is not telling the truth, and there is also perhaps a sense of expiation for the death of the French soldier. He dies in October 1918, on a day when there is—hence the title—"nichts Neues zu melden" (197, nothing new to report). It is difficult to stress enough the importance of this final section of the novel, in which an objective observer not only reports the death, but speculates on Bäumer's mind at the end: he looked, he tells us, "als wäre er beinahe zufrieden damit, daß es so gekommen war" (197, as if he were almost happy that it had turned out that way). The subjunctive "as if he were" and the qualifier "almost" are both warnings that this is only speculation. The reader has been privy to Bäumer's actual thoughts and experiences, and may well think differently. Of course there will always be an ambiguity: no one can know whether another individual was content to have died at any point. Nor, of course, do we know what happens next: there is no indication of whether Bäumer even believed in an afterlife, let alone whether he now enters one, and the work, like most of Remarque's, is agnostic in that sense.

Im Westen nichts Neues provokes thought about the nature of war in various different ways. The most obvious is the direct presentation of the horrors: parts of bodies hanging in trees, the wounded soldier calling out from no man's land, the slow gurgling death of the French soldier. Sometimes the telegrammatic lists of forms of attack, or weapons, or types of wounds make their point. The reader is, however, also prompted to consider the nature of war by being privy to the inconclusive and often humorous discussions by the young or uneducated soldiers. Thus when the visit of the Kaiser leads to a discussion between the *Gymnasium* pupils and the working-class soldiers of how wars come about, one of the former declares that wars happen when one country insults another. The answer comes that it is impossible for a mountain to insult another mountain; when this is countered by the fact that a nation can be insulted, Tjaden—not one of the high school group—points out that he does not feel insulted and should therefore not be there. The only people to profit from war, the soldiers feel at this point, are those like the Kaiser, who need a famous victory. Of course there is no conclusion. Müller comments that it is better that the war should be fought in France than in Germany, and Tjaden responds that the best of all would be no war at all. Eventually a consensus is reached that the discussion is pointless because it will change nothing. This may be true in the immediate historical context; the message to the Weimar reader, though, is that perhaps things might be changed.

Sometimes Bäumer's comments are addressed directly to the reader. In the second chapter the soldiers visit Franz Kemmerich, who is dying in a field hospital, and Bäumer thinks:

Da liegt er nun, weshalb nur? Man sollte die ganze Welt an diesem Bette vorbeiführen und sagen: Das ist Franz Kemmerich, neunzehneinhalb Jahre alt, er will nicht sterben. Lasst ihn nicht sterben! (29)

[Now he is lying there—and for what reason? Everybody in the whole world ought to be made to walk past his bed and be told: "This is Franz Kemmerich, he's nineteen and a half, and he doesn't want to die! Don't let him die!"]

The novel has done precisely what Bäumer has asked: the world has been led past that bed. Later, when he is in a *Lazarett* (military hospital) himself, Bäumer makes a personal statement that gradually develops into a philosophical attitude to the war as a whole:

Ich bin jung, ich bin zwanzig Jahre alt; aber ich kenne vom Leben nichts anderes als die Verzweiflung, den Tod, die Angst und die Verkettung sinnlosester Oberflächlichkeit mit einem Abgrund des Leidens. Ich sehe, dass Völker gegeneinander getrieben werden und sich schweigend, unwissend, töricht, gehorsam, unschuldig töten. (177)

[I am young, I am twenty years of age; but I know nothing of life except despair, death, fear, and the combination of completely mindless superficiality with an abyss of suffering. I see people being driven against one another, and silently, uncomprehendingly, foolishly, and obediently and innocently killing one another.]

Most striking is the idea of the victim as killer, the paradoxical *unschuldig töten* (innocently killing). These almost exculpatory words are again clearly directed at the ex-soldiers who survived the war. Bäumer also wonders how the older generation would react if they called them to account. This, too, is what the novel is doing.

Often Bäumer himself is unable to think things through because, since he is actually in the war, those conclusions would lead to madness.[30] For the time being he is forced to cling to the circular statement that "war is war"; sometimes, however, Bäumer decides consciously to store up ideas for later, and thus Remarque permits him to present ideas directly to the later readership. When on guard-duty over the Russian prisoners, for example, he has time to speculate.

> Ein Befehl hat diese stille Gestalten zu unseren Feinden gemacht; ein Befehl könnte sie in unsere Freude verwandeln. An irgendeinem Tisch wird ein Schriftstück von einigen Leuten unterzeichnet, die keiner von uns kennt; und jahrelang ist unser höchstes Ziel das, worauf sonst die Verachtung der Welt und ihre höchste Strafe ruht. (134)

> [An order has turned these silent figures into our enemies; an order could turn them into friends again. On some table, a document is signed by some people that none of us knows, and for years our main aim in life is the one thing that usually draws the condemnation of the whole world and incurs its severest punishment in law.]

Bäumer stops: "Hier darf ich nicht weiterdenken" (I mustn't think along those lines any more), but the importance of this passage for the novel and for Weimar is clear. The distancing from responsibility is as marked as the inclusivity implied by the first person plural, and the questions of guilt and murder will be raised in *Der Weg zurück* and elsewhere. The question of responsibility for war on an individual basis, however, is not addressed until we reach the Second World War and *Zeit zu leben, und Zeit zu sterben*,[31] by which time conditions for Germany were very different.

A war implies an enemy. For Bäumer, however, the principal enemy faced by all soldiers is death itself, and after that the bullying noncommissioned officers of their own army. The declared enemy—the British or French soldiers—are usually invisible, although we are aware of their guns. Bäumer himself meets only the *poilu* Duval and the Russian prisoners of war whom he guards. The absence of a specific enemy was a programmatic policy message for the Weimar Republic. The consistent portrayal of Bäumer as a victim, who was too young to be involved even with the hysteria associated with the outbreak in 1914, and who understands little and can influence even less, is also appropriate to the novel's Weimar context and to the generation that survived the war. The Weimar Republic welcomed the realistic and graphic presentation of the horrors of the war in a way that showed the participants free of responsibility, if not of guilt. Other unresponsible and even guilt-free narrators and protagonists in Weimar anti-war novels of the period include stretcher bearers, women, children, or schoolboys too young to join up, and most extreme of all, but most clearly a participant who is an innocent victim of bestial humanity, Liesl the mare, used as the narrator in Ernst Johannsen's unjustly forgotten *Fronterinnerungen eines Pferdes* (Front Line Memoirs of a Horse).[32] What unites all these involved narrators is the complete lack of awareness of the reasons for war as such, or for this war.

Im Westen nichts Neues needs more than any of Remarque's later works to be located in various contexts, first of all in the genre of the war novel. This itself, however, requires some subdivision: *Im Westen nichts Neues* is a novel about the First World War, but not one written either during that war, like Henri Barbusse's *Le Feu* (*Under Fire*), or just afterwards, such as Ernst Jünger's *In Stahlgewittern* (*Storm of Steel*), nor, on the other hand, at a historical distance so far removed as to be completely divorced from the actual experience (as with recent novels by, for example, Pat Barker). It is a historical novel addressing as its first audience Germans who shared the experiences presented in the work and survived, and it can be contextualized therefore as Weimar literature and hence is a German novel for reasons other than the simply linguistic. As one of the many novels produced at around the same time that took a similarly pacifist and anti-war stance, however, it is both national and international. *Im Westen nichts Neues* is a German novel in that it shows us German soldiers worn down to what amounts to a defeat in 1918. The war in the novel has no beginning, nor do we see the end, because Bäumer dies before the armistice, so that questions of responsibility and indeed of whether or not Germany was ultimately defeated are not raised. It is also worth noting—though the Nazi critics again missed the point—that there is no lack of patriotism in general terms on the part of Remarque's soldiers. All these elements would have elicited a response from those in the Weimar Republic trying to come to terms with the war. At the same time, the intentional internationalism of the novel is clear in the presentation precisely from the viewpoint of the ordinary soldier and member of the lost generation. Equally clear is the expressly pacifist message. In fact, some English-language reviews criticized the novel for offering too mild a presentation of the German soldier. Nevertheless, the work is a clear indictment of all wars. Wars are still fought, even if not in the trenches, and they still give rise to political chaos. They are still fought largely by the young and uncomprehending, who are themselves forced by killing to incur a guilt that they do not necessarily deserve, while the major questions, such as why wars happen at all, often still go unanswered. One criticism of the work was that Remarque did not take a political stand, which means that he did not allow Bäumer to do so. This is partly justified by the consistent character of the narrator, but in fact the work does have a political dimension in various respects. Its pacifist stance and the emphasis on the soldiers as victims of the war are both contributions to the political agenda of Weimar Germany, and in general terms, the attacks on a prewar social system embodied in teachers like Kantorek, and the references to the capitalist profiteering are clear. As an antiwar novel, too, its message could hardly be clearer.

Within Remarque's novels as a whole, the fate of Bäumer may also be taken beyond the confines of the war itself. Remarque shows us a historical event, but also makes clear the way in which it faces an individual with an extreme situation. Bäumer is eventually stripped of all support and left alone, which forces him to the existential realization that the life force will carry him onwards regardless, because it is all that there is. That life force is represented by the spark of life that is with Kat on the battlefield at night in the surrounding sea of destruction. The force is there, too, in nature, which saves Bäumer physically—when he presses himself to the earth, praising it in what is almost an echo of an Homeric hymn[33]—and also spiritually at the end, when his near despair gives way after the promptings of the natural world. He is not content to die, his death is a final reminder of the force of chance, seemingly malignant but actually completely impartial, which is heightened in a war, but is always present in Remarque's novels. The same awareness will come to many of Remarque's later figures. The novel is not just a pacifist work. The human theme of the inextinguishable nature of the spark of life is just as significant.[34]

It is overly tempting to view all of Remarque's other novels in the light of *Im Westen nichts Neue*, but themes first found here do recur and are developed. *Zeit zu leben und Zeit zu sterben* has a number of actual echoes, such as the scenes in the hospital, but picks up and develops the idea of the responsibility of the soldier in a later war where this was far more a German issue. The concentration camp novel *Der Funke Leben* (*The Spark of Life*)—the title harks back to *Im Westen nichts Neues*—uses the narrative technique of shocking realism again, and rather than a soldier in a war, we have an even more extreme situation in which the spark of humanity must struggle even harder to survive. There were, however, aspects of the work that Remarque realized could be misunderstood, and there is indeed some danger in his chosen methodology of placing the burden of discourse upon a later reader. Remarque does indeed allow Bäumer to praise *Kameradschaft* in war, but it is offset by the need to cope with the attrition that takes away all of Bäumer's friends one by one. The closest friendship—with Kat—is fortuitous, and it is brought to an end by and in the war. The ties that bound the men together in war, too, are shown to break down in *Der Weg zurück*, and some of the other important ideas—such as what constitutes murder, or whether war is a justification in itself of the deeds done within it—are also brought back and re-examined in the new novel. Remarque called the second work a necessary one.[35]

Der Weg zurück

The First World War is nominally finished by the time the main part of *Der Weg zurück*[36] begins—there is an *Eingang*, an introductory section set in the last days of the war—but the shooting is not over. Three shots are fired in the course of the new novel, and these are of the greatest importance: the first is at another soldier (although he is a German soldier); the second is at a hated enemy (although he is a German civilian); and the third and final shot is a suicide. In a close parallel to the death of Bäumer, killed by an unseen enemy sniper not long before the armistice in November 1918, the First World War is effectively brought to an end for Remarque's soldiers with the closing scene of *Der Weg zurück* proper, with the death of one of the characters, a former soldier, by his own hand, back on the western front at the end of 1919. He is not the narrator, but he represents at least part of the narrator's attitudes. Following the stylistically distinctive death of Georg Rahe, an *Ausgang*, an epilogue, gives an indication that even if the First World War is over, a new war will come. A phrase like "the Great War of 1914-1918" is in any case open to question. When the war began is clear, but when did it really end? The Allied Victory medal issued to British soldiers after the war was engraved "The Great War for Civilisation 1914-1919," although qualification was based on service from the beginning of the war to the Armistice in 1918. There was no peace treaty until 1919, and given the aftereffects, there is a good argument for claiming that the conflict did not actually end until the death of the First World War corporal, Adolf Hitler, in 1945. *Der Weg zurück* is, like its predecessor, a work for, and of, the Weimar Republic as well as a historical novel of the First World War, although the possibility of another war was becoming increasingly clear when it was written.

The title of the work is as ambiguous as that of the earlier novel. The narrator, the ex-soldier Ernst Birkholz, discovers in the course of the work that although the troops have physically made their way back to Germany, the road back into life cannot lead them back to their premilitary existence. The only way possible on the road back is forward. Birkholz and Bäumer have similar name elements (*Baum, Birke, Holz*: tree, birch, wood), their backgrounds are identical, and they seem to live in pretty well the same house. Moreover, they have had the same experiences—we learn in the course of the novel that Birkholz had stabbed a French soldier (132), and later on he refers to what sounds like the scene in *Im Westen nichts Neues* in which the soldiers enjoy a feast in a supply dump while under fire.[37] That the recollection comes in a scene in which a presumed war profiteer is holding a formal dinner party indicates that Remarque is drawing a conscious connection between the two novels. At all events, the characters are so similar that one can see Birkholz as living the postwar experiences that Bäumer would have had. In the last analysis, Birkholz is not Bäumer: they are both representative members of the same generation. Bäumer was a fictitious character who did not survive the war, and this novel refers to him and the others, Kat, Haie, and so on, as having been killed.

Although the later novel is also, for the most part, at least, a first-person narrative, the style is not quite the same as in the earlier work. This time two other characters, Ludwig Breyer and Georg Rahe, close friends of the narrator, play a greater part than any of the figures in the earlier novel, and their ideas in particular are foregrounded in a way that does not happen in the earlier work. Remarque again uses discussions by the now former soldiers as a starting point for the reader to consider matters further, but the discussions reported by Birkholz, especially between Breyer and Rahe, are fuller and more serious, as they do have the experience of the war behind them. The work is in that sense more political, but it must be remembered that it remains within its historical context, and the narrator remains consistent. Just as Bäumer probably would have had no clearly formed political views, Birkholz is still learning in 1919, and acts as an intermediary for the Weimar audience, passing on the debates for further consideration. Once again, too, the novel is not entirely a first-person narrative, though the matter is not as clear as with *Im Westen nichts Neues*. The work also operates on several levels. The progress and learning process of the individual, in the person of the narrator, represents one level; but through him not only do we hear of political debates and see the events of 1919 as they happen—the revolutionary conflicts, the food shortages—but we see too the difficulties of coming to terms with the war and the breakdown of some aspects of society in social as well as political terms. Nor is this just a work of the generation robbed of its youth, since older comrades are considered as well. Finally, of course, the work continues the indictment of war, and this is especially clear with some of the motifs that are picked up directly from *Im Westen nichts Neues*.

After the *Eingang*, which is set during the war and in which people are still being killed, the survivors return to a Germany without firm government and with polarized left- and right-wing forces, and must begin to reconstruct their own lives against this chaos. Just as some survived in the war and others did not, some find it easier to adapt to civilian life than others; even en route back to Germany, one of the soldiers manages to strike a business deal with souvenir-hungry American soldiers, a motif that will recur in *Der Funke Leben*. But although the main part of the novel is set in 1919,[38] the war is kept close through the memories, words, and sometimes the actions of Birkholz and his friends. Birkholz has survived, but he is aware of his own unashamed exultation in still being alive, and comments that "Vielleicht ist nur deshalb immer wieder Krieg, weil der eine nie ganz empfinden kann, was der andere leidet" (33: Maybe that is why there is always a war, because one person can never really feel another person's suffering). This, too, is a key theme in Remarque's work.

The debate in Germany about the war was polarized into those who saw it as a disaster to be avoided in the future, and those who stressed the heroic aspects, and this is already apparent among the soldiers as they return. The *Oberleutnant*, Heel, stresses the heroic side, and the Jewish soldier Max Weil, voices the view that the price was simply too high. Soldiers' and sailors' councils are already established in Germany, and when Birkholz's group returns, Ludwig Breyer, the lieutenant, is attacked by members of such a council, young soldiers and sailors, because he is an officer. One of the others, Willy Homeyer, a large, strong man who plays this somewhat stylized role throughout the work, defends him in a violent confrontation. The attitude of the returning frontline soldiers is scornful towards the sailors, whose role in the war was not great, and to the raw recruits turned revolutionaries, but an older soldier defuses the situation, going so far as to salute them. Birkholz comments that the salute is neither for the uniform, nor for the war, but for the comradeship of the war, which is fast vanishing.

The lack of comprehension by their families of what the soldiers have been through leads to conflicts and sometimes to farce, as when Homeyer "requisitions" a cockerel that belongs to a neighbor. Willy uses soldiers' words—*requiriert, besorgt, gefunden* (requisitioned, acquired, found)—but the return to a civilian moral code now demands the word *gestohlen* (stolen). The soldiers themselves, however, need to achieve a kind of closure, just as Weimar Germany needed to come to terms with the war as such. In one incident, an intensified parallel to the revenge taken upon Himmelstoss, the group of soldiers encounters a former sergeant, Seelig, who had effectively caused the death of the friend of one of the group, Kosole, by refusing him leave. The friend had been killed (the story is one of the extended flashbacks to the war itself), and Kosole seeks revenge. But now Seelig is an innkeeper, and even Kosole feels that this is not the same man. Only when he spots that this innkeeper, who does not even remember the incident, is still wearing his uniform trousers does the military Seelig come back to him, and he is jolted into taking the revenge he needed.[39]

This incident, observed by Birkholz, shows how one character does achieve a personal closure. In parallel to the attrition in the earlier novel, here some of the former soldiers make good, among them Tjaden, who marries a butcher's daughter, while others, who had been good soldiers, fall on hard times. The comradeship of the front vanishes, since it was in any case determined by conditions at the front, and an uncomfortable reunion draws attention to the fact. In a case that merits special attention, we follow the tale of a married soldier, Adolf Bethke, who has returned to his home in the countryside to find that his wife has been unfaithful to him. When Birkholz visits Bethke, who was one of their group, he is at first silent, but then Birkholz tells the reader: "Schließlich höre ich dann alles" (125, then at last I get the whole story), which may then be given as a third person narrative. Despite his wife's genuine contrition, Bethke's initial reaction had been to take revenge on the other man, but this method of closure proves impossible. Later, after a kind of reconciliation, he and his wife are forced by gossip to sell up in the village, and move into the town and to an uncertain and unhappy future. Bethke comments to Birkholz when he sees him at this later stage that he wishes they were still at the front, where things were simpler. The war has destroyed, or at least damaged, a relationship, and this time there are further-reaching social ramifications as well.

More physical results of the war are still visible. Bäumer wished for the world to be paraded past the bed of Kemmerich; Birkholz observes a parade of the war-wounded as a part of a demonstration against rising prices as they move past a newly built dance hall. He also visits one of his comrades in an asylum, to show that minds were broken as well as bodies. For these men the war has not ended at all—they ask for news of it—and Giesecke, whom the others are visiting, is obsessed with a desire to return to Fleury, where he had been buried alive.[40] The idea of returning to gain closure in that way makes an impression upon them.

Ernst Birkholz himself has to make his own way back into the more normal aspects of life. His experiences at home recall strongly Bäumer's home leave and the isolation that he had felt. The situation again becomes farcical when Birkholz dines with a rich uncle, and in the course of a formal meal forgetfully picks up a chop in his hands, to the consternation of the other guests. The devaluation of formal niceties when set against what he has been through is of some interest. Only when he goes off secretly to catch sticklebacks in a river as he had done as a child and there encounters Georg Rahe on a similar mission is there any real recapturing of the past, but that past is too far away. The ex-soldiers had gone into the war as schoolboys, and they try at first, in vain, to pick up their lives from that point. At a dance, Birkholz encounters a girl he had known in those days, but is told that he has become too serious. When the girl leaves him because she has arranged to meet someone else, he says: "Ich nehme die. Mütze ab und grüsse sie tief, als nähme ich einen grossen Abscheid—nicht von ihr—von allem Früheren" (178, I take off my cap and give her a sweeping bow, as if I were making a grand farewell—not from her, but from everything that came before).

Birkholz and the others return to the school itself, determined to take emergency examinations. Those that have returned—the roll call shows us how many have not done so—are sometimes wounded, and all of them have been hardened by their experiences, so that there is a significant confrontation when the head teacher refers to those who "sleep as fallen heroes beneath the greensward." The ebullient Willy Homeyer will have none of this cant, and demythologizes it vigorously. Homeyer is speaking from the immediacy of 1919, of course, but by the time the novel was written the tendency to romanticize and sanitize the heroic dead was that much more common, and proportionately more dangerous. The war dead are not sleeping, shouts Homeyer:

Im Trichterdreck liegen sie, kaputtgeschossen, zerissen, im Sumpf ver-
sackt. Grüner Rasen! Wir sind nicht doch nicht in der Gesangstunde! [. . .]
Heldentod! Wie ihr euch das vorstellt! Wollen Sie wissen, wie der kleine
Hoyer gestorben ist? Den ganzen Tag hat er im Drahtverhau gelegen und
geschrien, und die Därme hingen ihm wie Makkaroni aus dem Bauch.
Dann hat ihm ein Sprengstück die Finger weggerissen. [. . .] Als wir dann
herankonnten, nachts, war er durchlöchert wie ein Reibeisen. Erzählen Sie
doch seiner Mutter, wie er gestorben ist, wenn Sie Courage haben!" (114-15)

[They're lying in filthy shell holes, shot to pieces, ripped apart, sunk in the
swamp. Greensward! This isn't choir practice! [. . .] A hero's death!
You've no idea! Would you like to know how little Hoyer died? He was lying on the wire all day and screaming, his guts hanging out like macaroni.
Then some H. E. took his fingers off. [. . .] By nightfall, when we could get
to him he was as full of holes as a sieve. Go and tell his mother how he died,
if you're up to it.]

Presented with the realities of the war in the language of *Im Westen
nichts Neues*, and with the pseudo-heroic images debunked, the school
authorities give way and the ex-soldiers are allowed to qualify on their
own terms. Willy Homeyer and Ernst Birkholz becomes teachers in a
neighboring village, and although they are able to surprise the local
worthies by drinking them under the table, Ernst himself, who lacks the
toughness of his friend, is unable to cope for long with the task of
teaching children because he cannot escape from the war, either in his
dreams or in the classroom. He has nothing to offer these children,
when all that he himself has ever really learned is how to make war.

The difference between the necessarily inconclusive debates in the
earlier novel and those between Ludwig Breyer and Georg Rahe (in the
reporting presence of Birkholz) is marked in the fourth chapter, near
the center of the work.[41] Rahe observes the political chaos. "Sieh dir
an, wie sie sich bereits gegenseitig in den Haaren liegen, Sozial-
demokraten, Unabhängige, Spartakisten, Kommunisten" (195, Look

at the way they are already at each other's throats, Social Democrats, Independents, Spartacists, Communists), but Breyer sees the blame in themselves. Echoing Paul Bäumer's comments at the end of the earlier novel, Breyer feels that by 1918 they were simply too beaten down:

> Wir haben mit zu wenig Haß Revolution gemacht, und wir wollten gleich von Anfang an gerecht sein, dadurch ist alles lahm geworden. Eine Revolution muss losrasen wie ein Waldbrand, dann kann man später zu säen beginnen; aber wir wollten nichts zerstören und doch erneuern. Wir hatten nicht einmal mehr die Kraft zum Hass, so müde und ausgebrannt waren wir vom Krieg. (195)

> [Our revolution didn't have enough hate in it, and we wanted to be just from the beginnings, and so it all flopped. A revolution should roar away like a forest fire, and then after that you can start to sow seeds again. Only we didn't want to destroy anything, just renew. We didn't even have the strength to hate, because we were so tired, so burnt out by the war.]

Though evident from an early stage, this was becoming clear by the time the book was written; only an organized and unified revolution could have established a stable and liberal republic after the war, and that never happened. The two men agree that they still have the war in their bones, but while Breyer feels that they have to—and can—struggle to make sure that it was not all in vain, Rahe thinks they are no longer fit for the task, and in desperation sets out to try to rediscover the old comradeship. He sets his road backward and resolves to rejoin the army. Ludwig is equally aware of the damage done to his generation, and although he feels—for the moment—that he has to go on trying, it soon becomes apparent that he, too, is unable to shake off the war.

The underlying political conflict between the right and the left develops to a climax in the later part of the novel, to the point in which the first of the important three shots are fired. Oberleutnant Heel is now part of the new *Reichswehr*, whose steel helmets are noted (the *Stahl-*

helm was the right-wing veteran's group), and they fire on a workers' group during a demonstration over food prices, in spite of being addressed by the unarmed demonstrators as *Kameraden*. As Birkholz and some of his friends, including Breyer, watch, Max Weil, on the demonstrators' side, is shot and killed at the command of Heel. The comradeship of the front has broken down to the extent that the soldiers are shooting now not at an enemy, but at each other. As they take cover, Birkholz realizes:

> Wir sind wieder Soldaten, es hat uns wieder, krachend und tobend rauscht der Krieg über uns, zwischen uns, in uns—aus ist alles, die Kameradschaft durchlöchert mit Maschinengewehren, Soldaten schiessen auf Soldaten, Kameraden auf Kameraden, zu Ende, zu Ende! (252)

> [We are soldiers again, it's got us again, the war roars over us, loud and raging, between us, in us—it's all over, comradeship has been drilled full of holes by machine-gun fire, soldiers are shooting at soldiers, comrades at comrades, it's over, it's over.]

Breyer offers Heel ironic congratulations, and Birkholz reiterates a little later that the war has started again, but the comradeship has gone.

If that shot is political, however, the next shot fired is personal. Albert Trosske shoots a man he has found with his girl, and despite the efforts of the others to persuade him to escape, he gives himself up, and at the end of the work is tried for murder. The point that comes out in the trial is that the soldiers have been trained to kill people they do not hate, but now one of them has killed in hatred. He is given a fairly lenient sentence, because it is made clear that less than a year before he was in the trenches, but the reader is left, as in the earlier novel, to draw conclusions about war and what constitutes murder. Shortly before the trial, Birkholz visits another old comrade, Bruno Mückenhaupt, who had been a sniper. Bäumer had been made to watch a sniper just after his return after killing Duval, and he had seized upon the notion of

"Krieg ist Krieg" as a temporary consolation. Birkholz now finds that Mückenhaupt, a solid family man with a child, is still proud of his "hits," and is unquestioning about these acts of killing, seeing no need for justification beyond the fact that it was war, and he had been obeying orders. Indeed, anyone who thinks otherwise is, says Mückenhaupt, some kind of Bolshevik. Various ways of coping with the past are shown in the work, but this complete rejection of the idea that there might even be cause for guilt, is hardly likely to have been uncommon in reality.

In the event, neither Georg Rahe, who tries to go back to the army, nor Ludwig Breyer, who tries to carry on, is able to survive. Ludwig, we discover, has contracted syphilis in one of the official brothels during the war, a fairly clear image (which he himself points out) of the war still in his blood. Although he can be cured, his despair reaches a point where he can only rid himself of the war by cutting his veins. The passage describing his death is not strictly part of a first-person narrative, and on this occasion we do not even have the distancing devices used for the retelling of Bethke's story. However, Birkholz is summoned, finds Ludwig, and after this falls into a state of shock, so that the paragraph describing Breyer's last moments might be ascribed to the fevered imagination of the narrator.

Breyer's suicide is a removal of the war from his system by a knife rather than a bullet, but one final shot remains. Georg Rahe has attempted to rejoin the army and try to reclaim the lost comradeship, but returns and tells Birkholz that the attempt failed. The army, he found, is now a disparate collection of idealists, those afraid to go back into civilian life, adventurers and mercenaries, all presenting a caricature of the comradeship, and making clear that that comradeship was just a product of the war. As soon as he was faced with a fight against supposed communists, actually workers, some of whom had been at the front, he was (unlike Heel) unable to fire. For him there had been a kind of honesty about the war, but now things are different, and he realizes that war as its own justification functions only when there actually is a war: "Krieg war Krieg. Aber diese toten kameraden in Deutschland—erschossen von früheren Kameraden—aus, Ernst" (283, the war was the war. But these dead comrades in Germany—shot by former comrades—that's enough, Ernst). Georg Rahe feels that he has only survived by mistake, and now picks up the idea voiced in the asylum: the return to Fleury.

The resolution of his story is the last section of the final chapter of the novel proper, and it is stylistically different, told by a third person omniscient narrator who is neither Birkholz nor a speculative reporter as in the final lines of *Im Westen nichts Neues*. Rahe returns to the rusting barbed wire of the battlefields until he finds a cemetery, a row—a regiment—of black crosses. Greeting the dead with the words "Kameraden! Wir sind verraten worden! Wir müssen noch einmal marschieren! Dagegen!—Dagegen—Kameraden" (301, Comrades-in-arms, we were betrayed! We must march again. Against it all—against it—comrades!), he fires the last shot of the novel—and of the First World War?—killing himself, and is able to march with the dark army of the dead.[42] Bäumer did not want to die, but Rahe does. Driven by despair and survivor's guilt, he finds that a return to the battlefields is not enough.

Where Bäumer's death marked the end of the novel, *Der Weg zurück* has a coda, an *Ausgang*, separate from the work proper, but nevertheless still part of it, and it reminds us that the third member of the trio, the narrator Ernst Birkholz, whose difficulties we have also seen, does survive. At the end of the book he, like Bäumer, is alone: his friends have either died or moved away, and he has commented on the difficulty of relationships with women, underlined in the tales of Bethke and Trosske. In this epilogue the few remaining friends—we are told that they now rarely meet—gradually leave.[43] But he, too, is *ruhig und gefasst*, calm and composed, and he now, like Bäumer, sees a way forward—not back—a way that will be difficult and in which for most of it he will be alone, but he will be given strength by nature:

Ich will weitergehen und nicht umkehren. Vielleicht werde ich nie mehr ganz glücklich sein können, vielleicht hat der Krieg das zerschlagen, und ich werde immer etwas abwesend sein und nirgendwo ganz zu Hause— aber ich werde auch wohl nie ganz unglücklich sein, denn etwas wird immer da sein, um mich zu halten, und wären es auch nur meine Hände oder die atmende Erde. (311)

[I shall go onwards and not turn back. Perhaps I shall never be able to be completely happy again, perhaps the war has finished that off and I shall always be a little absent, and shall not feel completely at home anywhere— but I shall probably also never be completely unhappy, because there will always be something there to sustain me, even if it is only my own hands or the living earth.]

There is no more external support, and the central figure faces again the existential crisis. But the *ich* voice of Ernst Birkholz, who in this passage sounds virtually identical to Bäumer just before he was shot, is alive. Nature, the life force that is in everything, would have sustained Bäumer, and it is there for Birkholz.

Der Weg zurück is as much about the war as its predecessor. Equally, it is just as much a Weimar novel, although one that is more inward looking, showing to contemporary German society the dangers of political polarization while presenting a variety of ways of overcoming the past, and indeed the failure in some cases to get the war out of the system. Bäumer's final thoughts had been right: some would simply come to terms and get on with things, and some could compartmentalize the war and feel nothing for the killing; others could not cope at all. But the answer is one for the individual to discover alone. The First World War may be over, but the ambiguity of Birkholz's position and the difficulties he will have to face are already indicated in the *Ausgang*. In spring 1920, the small group of ex-soldiers comes across some young *Wandervögel*, members of the prewar youth movement, which was partly taken over by the right-wing *Freikorps*, being drilled as soldiers. When Birkholz and his friends—who are not many years older—object, they are called cowards and traitors. The roots of a new war were becoming much clearer, of course, by the end of the Weimar Republic, but they were there in 1920. "Ja" says one of the ex-soldiers, "so geht es wieder los" (307, Yes, that's the way it starts again).[44] The further development of the right-wing groups in the Weimar years would be portrayed after the end of the Second World War, in Remarque's "delayed" novel, *Der schwarze Obelisk*; by 1923 these semi-politicized *Wandervögel* had become teenage Nazis.

Notes

1. Texts cited are the 1998 KiWi editions of *Im Westen nichts Neues* and *Der Weg zurück*, both with afterwords by Tilman Westphalen (Cologne: Kiepenheuer and Witsch, 1998). The earlier KiWi edition of the former (1987) has a slightly different afterword (referring to the first Gulf War) and a useful selection of materials on the work from 1929 to 1980. The first edition of *Im Westen nichts Neues* was published in Berlin under Ullstein's Propyläen imprint in January 1929 after a *Vorabdruck* in Ullstein's *Vossische Zeitung* starting just before Armistice Day in 1928, ten years after the end of the war. *Der Weg zurück* appeared under the same imprint in 1931, also after a preprint in the *Vossische Zeitung* at the end of 1930. For a full bibliography of editions, including picture books, and translations into all languages of *Im Westen nichts Neues*, see Thomas F. Schneider, *Erich Maria Remarque: Im Westen nichts neues: Bibliographie der Drucke* (Bramsche: Rasch, 1992).

2. See Thomas F. Schneider, *Erich Maria Remarque: Im Westen nichts Neues: Text, Edition, Entstehung, Distribution und Rezeption, 1928-1930* (Habilitationsschrift: University of Osnabrück, 2000; now published in Tübingen: Niemeyer, 2004 as a book plus CD), and his booklet *Erich Maria Remarque: Im Westen nichts Neues: Das Manuskript* (Bramsche: Rasch, 1996). Schneider notes on page 12 that Remarque's contract with Ullstein demanded that if the book were not to be a success, Remarque would have to work off the advance paid by working for them as a journalist. Remarque claimed in a 1966 piece for the newspaper *Die Welt* that he worked on the novel for only five weeks: "Grössere und kleinere Ironien meines Lebens," *Ein militanter Pazifist*, 141; *Das unbekannte Werk*, vol. 4, 439; *Herbstfahrt*, 257.

3. The translation by A. W. Wheen as *All Quiet on the Western Front* (London:

G. P. Putnam's Sons 1929; Boston: Little, Brown, and Company, 1929) was made, as were other translations, from a typescript and is slightly different from the German book version. It was bowdlerized when first published in the United States, and the full version was only readily available in a Fawcett paperback after 1979. The quality of Wheen's translation was attacked on publication, although Remarque seems to have liked it, calling it "eine englische Originalarbeit" (an original English work): see the letter by Herbert Read in *Time and Tide* on 26 April 1929. The reviewer for *Time and Tide*, Cicely Hamilton, pointed out gently that Remarque was perhaps not an authority on English. Richard Church praised the translation in the *Spectator* for 20 April 1929. For more detail, see Claude R. Owen, "*All Quiet on the Western Front*: Sixty Years Later," *Krieg und Literatur/War and Literature* 1 (1989): 41-48, and my papers "Translating the Western Front: A. W. Wheen and E. M. Remarque," *Antiquarian Book Monthly Review* 18 (1991): 452-60 and 102, and "We Germans . . . ? Remarques englischer Roman *All Quiet on the Western Front*," *Jahrbuch* 6 (1996): 11-34. On Wheen, see Ian Campbell, "Remarking Remarque: The Arthur Wheen Papers," *National Library of Australia News* 8, no. 7 (April, 1998): 3-7, with illustrations of the drafts, showing the shift from "No News in the West" to "All Quiet in the West," with the familiar title only emerging at galley stage. My own translation (London: Cape, 1993) retains Wheen's by now established title. In spite of its flaws (mostly of register), Wheen's translation played an important part in the establishing of the novel as a masterwork of world literature: see the comments by General Sir Ian Hamilton in 1929 in: "The End of War?" *Life and Letters* 3 (1929): 399-411, see 403.

4. Lewis Milestone directed *All Quiet on the Western Front* for Universal in 1930. The script, by George Abbott, Maxwell Anderson, and Dell Andrews, is available in German translation by Jürgen Schebera together with full documentation of its first performance, in *Der Fall Remarque, "Im Westen nichts Neues"—eine Dokumentation*, ed. Bärbel Schräder (Leipzig: Reclam, 1992), 104-73 and 289-409; see 409 on the change from the intended final scene to its famous replacement in which Bäumer is killed reaching out for a butterfly. Much secondary literature has been devoted to the film, including most of issue 3 of the 1993 *Jahrbuch*. See Wagener, *Understanding*, 122, on the United States reissue in 1939 and its showing in Germany in 1952. Examples of secondary studies are: Kevin Brownlow, *The War, the West, and the Wilderness* (London: Secker and Warburg, 1979), 214-19; George J. Mitchell, "Making *All Quiet on the Western Front*," *American Cinematographer* 66 (1985): 34-43; Andrew Kelly, "*All Quiet on the Western Front*: 'Brutal Cutting, Stupid Censors, and Bigoted Politicos'," *Historical Journal of Film, Radio, and Television* 9 (1989): 135-50—see also his book *Filming All Quiet on the Western Front* (London and New York: I. B. Tauris, 1998); John Whiteclay Chambers, "*All Quiet on the Western Front* (1930): the Anti-war Film and the Image of the First World War," *Historical Journal of Film, Radio, and Television* 14 (1994): 377-411. Milestone's film compares well with the exactly contemporary German Nerofilm *Westfront 1918*, based on a novel by Ernst Johannsen and directed by Georg W. Pabst; see Kathleen Norrie and Malcolm Read, "Pacifism, Politics, and Art: Milestone's *All Quiet on the Western Front* and Pabst's *Westfront 1918*" in *Remarque Against War*, ed. Brian Murdoch, Mark Ward, and Maggie Sargeant (Glasgow: Scottish Papers in Germanic Studies, 1998), 62-84. *All Quiet on*

the Western Front was remade for television for Norman Rosemont productions, directed by Delbert Mann.

5. There is an anecdotal but interesting historical report on the reading in 1944 of this proscribed book by Klaus Gruhn, "'Wehrkraftzersetzend': Schüler des Gymnasium Laurentianum Warendorflernen 1944 *Im Westen nichts Neues* kennen," *Jahrbuch* 15 (2005): 93-100, and see for the response to exile books in schools after 1945 Hermann Glaser, "Das Exil fand nicht statt," in *10 Mai 1933*, ed. Walberer, 260-84. In a brief résumé of his life and works in 1956, Remarque noted that the book was banned in Italy from 1929-45, in Germany from 1933-45, but that it had subsequently been banned in the Soviet Union in 1947 and at that stage still was: *Das unbekannte Werk*, vol. 5, 167.

6. Jost Hermand, "Versuch, den Erfolg von Erich Maria Remarques *Im Westen nichts Neues* zu verstehen," in *Weimar am Pazifik: Festschrift für Werner Vordtriede*, ed. Dieter Borchmeyer and Till Heimeran (Tübingen: Niemeyer, 1985), 71-78; A. F. Bance, "*Im Westen nichts Neues*: a Bestseller in Context," *Modern Language Review* 72 (1977): 359-73, cited 359, and see the comments by Firda, *All Quiet*, 12, whose book attempts a full-scale "Literary Analysis and Cultural Context." On the work as a bestseller, see Hubert Rüter, *Erich Maria Remarque: "Im Westen nichts Neues": Ein Bestseller der Kriegsliteratur im Kontext* (Paderborn: Schöningh, 1980). On the style see Brian Rowley, "Journalism into Fiction: *Im Westen nichts Neue*," in *The First World War in Fiction*, ed. Holger Klein (London: Macmillan, 1976), 101-11; Brian Murdoch, "Narrative Strategies in Remarque's *Im Westen nichts Neues*," *New German Studies* 17 (1992-93): 175-202; Howard M. De Leeuw, "Remarque's Use of Simile in *Im Westen nichts Neues*," and Harald Kloiber, "Struktur, Stil, und Motivik in Remarques *Im Westen nichts Neues*," *Jahrbuch* 4 (1994): 45-64 and 5-78 respectively; and Thomas Schneider, "Es ist ein Buch ohne Tendenz—*Im Westen nichts Neues*: Auto- und Textsystem im Rahmen eines Konstitutions- und Wirkungsmodells für Literatur," *Krieg und Literatur/War and Literature* 1 (1989): 23-40.

7. Most famously by Peter Kropp, *Endlich Klarheit über Remarque und sein Buch Im Westen nichts Neues* (Hamm: Kropp, 1930), which sold well, as did Wilhelm Müller-Scheld, *Im Westen nichts Neues eine Täuschung* (Idstein/Taunus: Grandpierre, 1929). See the survey by Barker and Last, *Remarque*, 38-44 as well as Owen, *Bio-Bibliography*, and Schräder, *Der Fall Remarque*. See also Thomas F. Schneider on the critical response, "'Die Meute hinter Remarque': Zur Diskussion um *Im Westen nichts Neues* 1928-1930," *Jahrbuch zur Literatur der Weimarer Republik* 1 (1995): 143-70, and Robert Neumann's original "Die Meute hinter Remarque," *Die Literatur* 32 (1929-30): 199-200. I have examined the imitative works in detail in my edition: Erich Maria Remarque, *Im Westen nichts Neues* (London: Methuen, 1984; rev. ed. Routledge, 1988), 4-6 and in my monograph *Remarque: Im Westen nichts Neues*, 2d rev. ed. (Glasgow: Glasgow University French and German Publications, 1995), 1-13. See on the work *Hat Erich Maria Remarque wirklich gelebt* by Mynona [Salomo Friedlaender] (Berlin: Steegemann, 1929): Manfred Kuxdorf, "Mynona versus Remarque, Tucholsky, Mann, and Others: Not So Quiet on the Literary Front," in *The First World War in German Narrative Prose: Essays in Honour of George Wallis Field*, ed. Charles N. Genno and Heinz Wetzel (Toronto, Buffalo, and London: U of Toronto P, 1980), 71-91. The

dust jacket of Friedlaender's book calls it "eine Denkmalsenthüllung" (uncovering/ unmasking a monument).

8. Franz Arthur Klietmann, *Im Westen wohl was Neues* (Berlin: Nonnemann, 1931); Carl A. G. Otto, *Im Osten nichts Neues* (Zirndorf-Nürnberg: Sanitas, 1929); Emil Marius Requark (M. J. Wolff), *Vor Troja nichts Neues* (Berlin: Brunnen/ Winckler, 1930); Gottfried Nickl, *"Im Westen nichts Neues" und sein wahrer Sinn*, published by the journal *Heimgarten* as a *Sonderheft* (Graz and Leipzig: Stocker, 1929), referring to the novel as a *Schandmal* (monument of shame), and subtitled *Antwort auf Remarque* (answer to Remarque). E. Erbelding, *Im Westen doch Neues* (Something New on the Western Front) (Munich: Ebering, 1930), is a pro-war piece that merely uses Remarque's title. Most of these works do not bear reading, but their existence makes its own point. I have examined Wolff's parody in detail in "All Quiet on the Trojan Front: Remarque's Soldiers and Homer's Heroes in a Parody of *Im Westen nichts Neue*," *German Life and Letters* 43 (1989): 49-62. These imitations must be distinguished from literary texts that did, nevertheless, take a positive approach to the military aspects, such as those by Ernst Jünger; see Thomas Nevin, *Ernst Jünger and Germany: Into the Abyss, 1914-1945* (London: Constable, 1997), 143, also on diaries. There is an important comparison by Heinz Ludwig Arnold, "Erich Maria Remarque und Ernst Jünger," in *Jahrbuch* 10 (1999): 5-17. As an aside on modern reception, Günther Grass allows Jünger and Remarque to discuss the First World War in his *Mein Jahrhundert* (Göttingen: Steidl, 1999), and trans. M. H. Heim, *My Century* (New York: Harcourt, 1999).

9. Brian Murdoch, "'Hinter die Kulissen des Krieges sehen': Evadne Price, Adrienne Thomas—and E. M. Remarque," *Forum for Modern Language Studies* 28 (1992): 56-74.

10. For a historical overview see such works as Werner Conze, *Die Zeit Wilhelms II und die Weimarer Republik* (Stuttgart: Metzler, 1964); *Die Weimarer Republik*, ed. Friedrich Krummacher and Albert Wucher (Munich: Desch, 1965, illustrated); Hans Herzfeld, *Die Weimarer Republik* (Frankfurt am Main: Ullstein, 1966). In English, see John McKenzie, *Weimar Germany 1918-1933* (London: Blandford, 1971) and J. W. Hiden, *The Weimar Republic* (London: Longman, 1974).

11. The best survey remains that by Hans-Harald Müller, *Der Krieg und die Schriftsteller: Der Kriegsroman der Weimarer Republik* (Stuttgart: Metzler, 1986). See also, however, the following selective chronological list: J. K. Bostock, *Some Well-known German War Novels 1914-30* (Oxford: Blackwell, 1931); William K. Pfeiler, *War and the German Mind* (1941; reprint, New York: AMS, 1966); Wilhelm J. Schwarz, *War and the Mind of Germany I* (Bern and Frankfurt am Main: Peter Lang, 1975); Michael Gollbach, *Die Wiederkehr des Weltkrieges in der Literatur: Zu den Frontromanen der späten zwanziger Jahre* (Kronberg im Taunus: Athenaeum, 1978); M. P. A. Travers, *German Novels of the First World War* (Stuttgart: Heinz, 1982); Margrit Stickelberger-Eder, *Aufbruch 1914: Kriegsromane der späten Weimarer Republik* (Zurich and Munich: Artemis, 1983); Herbert Bornebusch, *Gegen-Erinnerung: Eine formsemantische Analyse des demokratischen Kriegsromans der Weimarer Republik* (Frankfurt am Main: Peter Lang, 1985); Ulrich Baron and Hans-Harald Müller, "Weltkriege und Kriegsromane," *LiLi: Zeitschrift für Literaturwissenschaft und*

Linguistik 19 (1989): 14-38; Ann P. Linder, *Princes of the Trenches: Narrating the German Experience of the First World War* (Columbia, SC: Camden House, 1996); *Von Richthofen bis Remarque: Deutschsprachige Prosa zum 1. Weltkrieg*, ed. Thomas F. Schneider and Hans Wagener (Amsterdam and New York: Rodopi, 2003).

12. There is a large body of secondary literature on the novel (some cited elsewhere in this chapter), and it is usually discussed in studies of war novels as such: George Parfitt's *Fiction of the First World War* (London: Faber, 1988) is a study of English-language novels with reference otherwise only to Remarque, Ernst Jünger, Jules Romains, and Henri Barbusse, and this is true too (minus Romains) of Bernard Bergonzi, *Heroes' Twilight: A Study of the Literature of the Great War* 2d ed. (London: Macmillan, 1980). There are monograph-length studies of *Im Westen nichts Neues* by the present writer, *Remarque: Im Westen nichts Neues*, as well as by Firda, *All Quiet*, and Rüter, *Bestseller*. There are various papers in the *Jahrbuch* 10 (2000), and many studies compare the work with other novels of the war: Helmut Liedloff; "Two War Novels," *Revue de Littérature Comparée* 42 (1968): 390-406 (with Hemingway); Holger M. Klein, "Dazwischen Niemandsland: *Im Westen nichts Neues* und *Her Private We*," in *Grossbritannien und Deutschland: Festschrift für John W. P. Bourke*, ed. Ortwin Kuhn (Munich: Goldmann, 1974), 488-512 (with Manning); Holger M. Klein, "Grundhaltung und Feindbilder bei Remarque, Céline und Hemingway," *Krieg und Literatur/War and Literature* 1 (1989): 7-22. Some studies are less useful than others: David J. Ulbrich, "A Male-Conscious Critique of Erich Maria Remarque's *All Quiet on the Western Front*," *Journal of Men's Studies* 3 (1995): 229-40 is not enlightening. Given the clarity of the novel it is intriguing to note the continued production of "study guides" in English, which do little more than provide a detailed plot summary (Cliffs Notes, 1965; Monarch Notes, 1966; Coles Notes, 1984; Sparknotes, 2002). See in German however the rather different introductions by Peter Bekes, *Erich Maria Remarque, Im Westen nichts Neues* (Munich: Oldenbourg, 1998), and Reiner Poppe, *Erich Maria Remarque: Im Westen nichts Neues* (Hollfeld: Beyer, 1998). An adapted and abridged version of the English text was published for foreign students of the English language (such has it become part of the English canon): *Remarque: All Quiet on the Western Front*, adapted by Colin Swatridge (London: Macmillan, 1987).

13. As noted by Rowley, "Journalism into Fiction," 108. Rowley also indicates the importance of the chapter division and their varying lengths on 109. Rowley's reference, however, to a "curiously unrealistic cross-section of the fighting-troops" (109) is surely explained by the fact that this, too, is dictated by Bäumer's "frog's eye view," a term Rowley cites, 108.

14. An early subtitle was "Aus den Tagebüchern des Freiwilligen Georg Bäumers" (From the Diaries of the Volunteer Soldier Georg Bäumer—the name was changed later, too). See Schneider, *Text, Edition, Entstehung*, 463. See my paper "Paul Bäumer's Diary" in Murdoch, Ward, and Sargeant, *Remarque Against War*, 1-23.

15. The debate about the actual reality of the presentation of the war in the novel has continued in various forms since the first objections by those critics who wanted it to be autobiographical. See Günter Hartung, "Zum Wahrheitsgehalt des Romans *Im Westen nichts Neue*," *Jahrbuch* 1 (1991): 5-17. See also my "Paul Bäumer's Diary."

Paul Fussell, *The Great War and Modern Memory* (London: Oxford UP, 1977), 183, counters the notion that the work is as "real and intimate" as letters from the front.

16. Hans-Harald Müller makes the point clearly in "Politics and the War Novel," in *German Writers and Politics 1918-39*, ed. Richard Dove and Stephen Lamb (London: Macmillan, 1992), 103-20, esp. 112.

17. On Remarque's discourse technique, already apparent in these early novels, see Heinrich Placke on the works of the 1950s: *Die Chiffren des Utopischen: Zum literarischen Gehalt der politischen 50er Jahre-Romane Remarques* (Göttingen: Vandenhoek and Ruprecht, 2004).

18. The much-reprinted French translation and at least one of the recently reprinted Yiddish versions (by Isaac Bashevis Singer) omit the statement, known as "the Motto," entirely. In other translations it is tucked away on the verso of the title page. The English is from Erich Maria Remarque, *All Quiet on the Western Front*, trans. A. W. Wheen (London: G. P. Putnam's Sons, 1929; also in the American edition, Boston: Little, Brown, and Company, 1929). In these and the German first edition it is prominently displayed on a separate preliminary page. Wheen translated from a typescript; my own translation follows the printed German text (thus omits the italicized parts). For variant versions of the Motto, see Schneider, *Text, Edition, Entstehung*, 465-67 (and I am indebted to Thomas Schneider for guiding me through the complexity of this situation). The translation of *Erlebnis* as "adventure" is not exact, but there were many books that did see the war as an adventure. Gunther Plüschow's *Die Abenteuer des Fliegers von Tsingtau*, another bestseller from Ullstein, originally 1916, but printed in 610,000 copies by 1927, and translated as *My Escape from Donington Hall* (London: Bodley Head, 1929), is adventurous, although a single airman who escapes from a POW camp (hence the English title) is not representative; the publishers added a preface in 1927 claiming that it was being presented *nicht als Kriegsbuch* (not as a war book).

19. As by Rudolf Huch, for example, in a review discussed by Roger Woods in "The Conservative Revolution and the First World War: Literature as Evidence in Historical Explanation," *Modern Language Review* 85 (1990): 77-91, see 86-87. The conservative literature of the war, which justified and to an extent glorified it, objected that the individual could form no overview of the inner sense of the conflict.

20. See Woods, "The Conservative Revolution," 87-88, discussing Rudolf Huch's criticism of Remarque and the *Froschperspektive*. See also Travers, *German Novels*, 134.

21. Various German novels blame teachers: see Caroline Martin, "The Conflict of Education: Soldiers, Civilians, a Child, and a Teacher," in Murdoch, Ward, Sargeant, *Remarque Against War*, 39-61. There is an interesting contrast with the situation in English, where the opposite was (or seemed often to be) the case, soldiers drawing strength from what they had learned at British public (that is, private) schools: see on this Peter Parker, *The Old Lie: The Great War and the Public School Ethos* (London: Constable, 1987), 283-84, with reference to Remarque.

22. See on the style (with comments on "pseudo-authenticity") especially David Midgley, *Writing Weimar. Critical Realism in Weimar Literature 1918-1933* (Oxford: Oxford UP, 2000), especially 14-56. I have discussed the question with regard to Re-

marque in "Paul Bäumer's Diary," and see Thomas Schneider, "'Krieg ist Krieg schließlich': Erich Maria Remarque: *Im Westen nichts Neues* (1928)," in Schneider and Wagener, *Von Richthofen bis Remarque*, 217-32. On *Neue Sachlichkeit*, see Helmut Gruber, "'Neue Sachlichkeit' and the World War," *German Life and Letters* 20 (1966-67): 138-49.

23. See my "Narrative Strategies," 180, referring to [Fritz Oswald] Bilse's *Aus einer kleinen Garnison: Ein militärisches Zeitbild* (Braunschweig: Sattler, 1903) (*Life in a Garrison Town*, London: Bodley Head, 1904), which contains also a discussion of comradeship and a scene where a soldier fails to salute a superior.

24. See Robert Wohl, *The Generation of 1914* (London: Weidenfeld and Nicolson, 1980) for an international overview of the lost generation. Richard Littlejohns, "'Der Krieg hat uns für alles verdorben': the Real Theme of *Im Westen nichts Neues*," *Modern Languages* 70 (1989): 89-94 takes this as the principal theme of the novel, rather than the war as such.

25. Fussell, *The Great War*, 196 misrepresents the scene, both misunderstanding the text—it is not a civilian cemetery—and by mischievously using phrases, unlike Remarque, such as "graves torn asunder," "stinking cerements" or "the narrator and his chums." There is no doubt of the potential reality of what is clearly also a symbolic scene and it is certainly not a "Gothic fantasia"; the dead were often not left in peace.

26. Stramm (1874-1915) was himself killed in the war: see his brief poems in *Lyrik des Expressionistischen Jahrzehnts* (Munich: dtv, 1962), 133-34. There are translations of two in *The Penguin Book of First World War Poetry*, ed. Jon Silkin (Harmondsworth: Penguin, 1979), 227.

27. Hindenburg, in his memoirs, commented that "unsere ermattete Front" (our exhausted front line) fell Eke Siegfried, with Hagen's spear in the back: Generalfeldmarschall [Paul] von Hindenburg, *Aus meinem Leben* (Leipzig: Hirzel, 1920), 403. Hitler himself claimed that "Germany was not defeated by the sanctions but exclusively by the internal process of revolutionizing"—thus the English translation of a letter from Hitler to the press baron Lord Rothermere, dated 20 December 1935, in *Fleet Street, Press Barons, and Politics: The Journals of Collin Brooks*, edited by N. J. Crowson (London: Royal Historical Society, 1998), 286. Both recognize a defeat of some sort.

28. As late as 1940 a pamphlet appeared in a World Affairs series by Cyril Falls called *Was Germany Defeated in 1918?* (Oxford: Clarendon, 1940). See also the larger historical studies of 1918 by John Terraine, *To Win a War* (London: Sidgwick and Jackson, 1978); John Toland, *No Man's Land* (London: Eyre Methuen, 1980); Gordon Brook-Shepherd, *November 1918* (London: Collins, 1981). Terraine's book carries a quotation on the title page from David Lloyd-George's war memoirs: "the conclusion is inescapable that Germany and her allies were in fact defeated in the field." H. Essame, *The Battle for Europe 1918* (London: Batsford, 1972) has a final chapter titled "The Politicians Take Over," and Niall Ferguson's *The Pity of War* (Harmondsworth: Penguin, 1998) ends with two chapters titled "The Captor's Dilemma" and "How (Not) to Pay for the War." See on the (sometimes avoided) question of the opening of the war the papers in: *Forging the Collective Memory*, ed. Keith Wilson (Providence, RI and Oxford: Berghahn, 1996). On the literary response to the concept of defeat in

the Weimar republic, see Linder, *Princes of the Trenches*, 151-78. Remarque's 1944 comments were in an unpublished piece surviving in English, titled "Practical Education Work in Germany after the War," now in German translation by Thomas Schneider in *Ein militanter Pazifist*, 66-83 (see 72) as "Praktische Erziehungsarbeit in Deutschland nach dem Krieg" (also in *Das unbekannte Werk*, vol. 5, 387-403 and *Herbstfahrt*, 226-42).

29. Even Remarque commented ironically on the boots ("Kemmerichs Stiefel in *All Quiet*") in a diary entry on 1 August 1950: *Das unbekannte Werk*, vol. 5, 427. Of course they are a symbol of death, but the real point, alluded to by Remarque in his diary, is their utilitarian value; only because they are of no use to Kemmerich does Müller take them.

30. This happens in Edlef Koeppen's *Heeresbericht* (Berlin: Horen, 1930 and Reinbek bei Hamburg: Rowohlt, 1986). For example, see my "Documentation and Narrative: Edlef Koeppen's *Heeresbericht* and the Anti-War Novels of the Weimar Republic," *New German Studies* 15 (1988-89): 23-47.

31. See Hans Wagener, "Erich Maria Remarque, *Im Westen nichts neues—Zeit zu leben und Zeit zu sterben*: Ein Autor, zwei Weltkriege," *Jahrbuch* 10 (2000): 31-52, See 39.

32. See Brian Murdoch, "Tierische Menschen und menschliche Tiere: Ernst Johannsen: *Vier von der Infanterie* und *Fronterinnerungen eines Pferdes* (1929)" in Schneider and Wagener, *Von Richthofen bis Remarque*, 249-60. The same collection contains articles on many comparable works and also a useful indication of sales figures, 12-11. The other texts referred to here are Ernst Glaeser, *Jahrgang 1902* (1928; reprint, Frankfurt am Main and Berlin: Ullstein, 1986), translated as *Class of 1902* by Willa and Edwin Muir (London: Secker, 1929); Alexander Moritz Frey, *Die Pflasterkästen* (1929; reprinted in the *Verboten und verbrannt/Exil* series, Frankfurt am Main: Fischer, 1986), translated as *The Crossbearers*, no translator given (London: G. P. Putnam's Sons, 1931); Adrienne Thomas's *Die Katrin wird Soldat* (1930) is in the same series (Frankfurt am Main: Fischer: 1987), trans. Margaret Goldsmith, *Katrin Becomes a Soldier* (Boston: Little, Brown, and Company, 1931).

33. Bäumer draws life and strength from the earth in the fourth chapter. The motif is a classical one, which Bäumer, as a product of a classical *Gymnasium* (see his dismissive references to Plato and to classical history) might have absorbed: the Homeric hymn to the earth as a mother is in Karl Preisendanz, *Griechische Lyrik* (Leipzig: Insel [1936]), 5, for example, a collection the first edition of which had appeared in 1914.

34. Remarque made the point in his "Grössere und kleinere Ironien," *Ein Militanter Pazifist*, 141; *Das unbekannte Werk*, vol. 4, 438; *Herbstfahrt*, 256. See Richard Schumaker, "Remarque's Abyss of Time: *Im Westen nichts Neues*," *Focus on Robert Graves and his Contemporaries* vol. 1, No. 11 (Winter 1990): 124-35.

35. Friedrich Luft, "Das Profil: Gespräch mit Erich Maria Remarque" in *Ein militanter Pazifist*, 118-33, cited 120. The point is made in the perceptive analysis (principally of *Im Westen nichts Neues*) by Modris Eksteins, *Rites of Spring: The Great War and the Birth of the Modern Age* (London: Transworld, 1990), 368-97. See more on the two works in Kathleen Devine, "The Way Back: Alun Lewis and Remarque," *Anglia* 103 (1985): 320-35. The new work was not well received: see Antkowiak, *Remarque*,

53; Jost Hermand, "Oedipus Lost," in *Die sogenannten zwanziger Jahre*, ed. Reinhold Grimm and Jost Hermand (Bad Homburg: 1970), 218, and Wagener, *Understanding*, 41. American criticism thought more highly of the work: see Barker and Last, *Remarque*, 69.

36. Again the English translation of the novel was by A. W. Wheen, *The Road Back* (London: G. P. Putnam's Sons, 1931). The film *The Road Back* was made in 1937, also by Universal but directed by James Whale, with a screenplay by Charles Kenyon and R. C. Sherriff, the writer of what is possibly the best-known drama of the First World War, *Journey's End*. It was not critically acclaimed, possibly because of the inevitable comparisons with Milestone's *All Quiet on the Western Front*, and it came under considerable pressure from the German consul as Hitler's representative in Los Angeles: see Jay Hyams, *War Movies* (New York: Gallery, 1984), 46. The summary there indicates that the film emphasised some of the shots fired in the novel. Apparently no 35 mm negative now exists.

37. See Antkowiak, *Remarque*, 52, and (referring to Remarque's own comments), Taylor, *Remarque*, 88, and Firda, *Thematic Analysis*, 65. Ludwig Bodmer, the first-person narrator of *Der schwarze Obelisk* might also be taken as a further development of the same character at some years' distance of writing, as indeed might Robby Lohkamp in *Drei Kameraden*.

38. The timing is sometimes confused in criticism, but the indicators are clear in the novel itself. See my paper: "Vorwärts auf dem Weg zurück," *Text+Kritik* 149 (2001): 19-29, esp. 20.

39. See my "Vorwärts auf dem Weg zurück" for a discussion of the passage in the context of closure, with reference also to Arnold Zweig's 1935 novel *Erziehung vor Verdun* (*Education before Verdun*), which uses the notion of precisely such a revenge as the major plot.

40. See the two stories originally published in English in *Collier's Magazine* and included in Erich Maria Remarque, *Der Feind*, re-translated by Barbara von Bechtolsheim (Cologne: Kiepenheuer and Witsch, 1993): "Karl Broeger in Fleury" (Where Karl had Fought, 1930), 26-33, and "Josefs Frau" (Josef's Wife, 1931), 34-44. There is a Karl Bröger in *Der Weg zurück* (and one is shot in a putsch in 1920 in *Drei Kameraden*). The title story, "Der Feind" (The Enemy, 1930), 9-17, is reported by a friend as coming from Ludwig Breyer, who is described as having fought at Verdun, the Somme, and in Flanders. All the stories are also in *Das unbekannte Werk*, vol. 4, 324-69.

41. The centrality is underlined by Mark Ward in his analysis "The Structure of *Der Weg zurück*," ed. Murdoch, Sargeant and Ward, *Remarque Against War*, 85-97, esp. 94f. See John Fotheringham, "Looking Back at the Revolution" in the same collection, 98-118; and Anthony Grenville, *Cockpit of Ideologies* (Bern: Peter Lang, 1995), 80-97. On the revolutions and the effect on the Weimar Republic, see Benjamin Ziemann, "Die Erinnerung an den Ersten Weltkrieg in den Milieukulturen der Weimarer Republik," in *Kriegserlebnis und Legendenbildung*, ed. Thomas F. Schneider (Osnabrück: Rasch, 1998), 1, 249-70. For a general history, see Richard M. Watt, *The Kings Depart: The Tragedy of Germany: Versailles and the German Revolution* (London: Weidenfeld and Nicolson, 1969).

42. Marching with the dead is a traditional motif, used in the context of the first world war in films like Abel Gance's *J'accuse* and plays like Chlumberg's *Wunder um Verdun* of 1931: see my paper "Memory and Prophecy Amongst the War-Graves: Hans Chlumberg's Drama *Miracle at Verdun*," in *The Commemorative Century*, ed. William Kidd and Brian Murdoch (Aldershot: Ashgate 2004), 92-104; Malcolm Humble: "The Unknown Soldier and the Return of the Fallen," *Modern Language Review* 93 (1998): 1034-45; and Linder (with reference to Rahe's suicide) *Princes of the Trenches*, 102. In *Der Weg zurück* and several other works, the dead from *Im Westen nichts Neues* are invoked as a means of linking the novels.

43. Barker and Last, *Remarque*, 77, stress this, and Antkowiak, *Remarque*, 55, sees the work as a novel of the collapse of comradeship; neither study links this with existential isolation.

44. Prewar youth groups were taken over from 1919 onwards by parties from the different right- and left-wing political extremes. By 1926 the Hitler Youth was already in being, but became prominent in 1933. See Peter D. Stachura, *The German Youth Movement 1900-1945* (London: Macmillan, 1981), 40-45. For interesting comments on the Wandervögel before the war, see Wohl, *Generation of 1914*, 203-9. On the political situation after the First World War and the links—or lack of them—between Versailles and the Second World War, see Zara Steiner, *The Lights that Failed: European International History 1919-1933* (Oxford: Oxford UP, 2005).

"There must be a reason . . .":
The Uses of Experience_____

Ann P. Linder

My discussion has thus far concentrated on the experience of the First World War—its physical realities and the reactions, individual and collective, to those realities. But an analysis of the experience itself fails to answer the question that haunted the combatants and has bedeviled students of the war ever since: Why? What did the war mean, and how did the combatants arrive at that meaning? Did the men who fought learn anything from their experience, and if so, what? Or was it a meaningless slaughter of the innocents? I am not here referring to the belated analyses of historians, generals and politicians, who, for the most part, spent the war far from the trenches. The critical question is what the combatants made of their own experiences.

The British literary reaction to the war is, for the most part, a bitterly ironic denunciation of its massive human cost. One need only recall Sassoon's vitriolic condemnation of incompetent generals and uncomprehending bishops, or the bitterness of Owen's "old lie" to grasp the sense of irremediable and meaningless loss that characterizes the British and French war literatures.[1] Although the proponents of similar views are in the minority and the tone is entirely different, the literature of disillusionment also existed in Germany. The leading spokesman of the German "lost generation" was Erich Maria Remarque. The now-famous epigraph of *All Quiet on the Western Front*, which triggered an immediate sympathetic response in the English-speaking world, earned him as much opprobrium as praise in his native country. His book, he said, ". . . is to be neither an accusation nor a confession, and least of all an adventure, for death is not an adventure to those who stand face to face with it. It will try simply to tell of a generation of men who, even though they may have escaped its shells, were destroyed by the war."[2]

Despite the disclaimer, the book is both a confession and an accusation. As one of the earliest of the major war novels in Germany, Remarque's claim to speak for a generation physically or psychologically destroyed by the fighting placed him at the center of the expanding re-examination of the war. His contention that his generation was wasted in a war created by their elders was welcomed by many veterans. But it was indignantly rejected by even greater numbers of front soldiers, with accusations that Remarque had depicted a "latrine war" from a "worm's-eye" or "frog's-eye" view, and had completely ignored the spiritual aspect of the experience in order to describe the war in the crudest material way. The opening pages of the book, which center on a frank description of communal field latrines, were frequently cited as an example of Remarque's "latrine" vision.[3] The similarity of Re-marque's experience of the war to that of many British writers largely accounts for the adulation with which the book was received in Britain, and for its continuing popularity in the English-speaking world as "the" novel of the First World War.

Although Remarque occupies the chair of minority spokesman, he was by no means the only German writer nor, indeed, the first to focus on the loss, horror, and insanity of the war. The heavily pacifistic expressionists had opposed the war from the beginning. The last and most extreme of a series of literary revolts beginning with *Sturm und Drang*, and equally dependent upon the subjectivism and radicalism of the earlier movements, the expressionist movement peaked between 1910 and 1918, and declined rapidly after the conclusion of the war. Most of the early war books in Germany—books written during or just after the war, as distinguished from the much greater number that appeared between 1928 and 1935—are either expressionistic or influenced by the expressionists. These books share a number of typical characteristics: revolt against the war and established authority, extreme contrasts, a utopian vision of human brotherhood, and a messianic belief in the ability of spirit to transform social and political realities.[4] The political wing of the expressionist movement was in the vanguard of anti-war sentiment throughout the war, particularly during the early years when opposition was almost unheard of. Even the Democratic Socialists and other leftist parties had joined in signing the disavowal of political strife—the *Burgfrieden*—in the first patriotic flush of 1914. They also voted the necessary war credits in the parliament, thereby proving their patriotism, but incidentally damaging their future credibility in the Weimar Republic.

On the literary side Fritz Pfembert's leftist journal *Die Aktion*, primarily a vehicle for expressionist work, published anti-war and avant-garde material until its dissolution in 1917, most notably the war poems of Stramm, Stadler and other "advanced" poets. The war verse of these poets is only now becoming known, largely because it was submerged by the tidal wave of patriotic occasional verse at the beginning of the war (one critic estimated over one million poems in the last five months of 1914), and in the twenties by the general disparagement of experimental verse in the rising tide of conservatism.[5]

The most important expressionist war narrative is Fritz von Unruh's *Opfergang* (Way of Sacrifice) written in the field in 1916, but not published until 1919. Its publication was forbidden during the war because of its pacifistic and humanitarian views. The title itself is ironic. The German word *Opfer* was much used by writers during the war in its positive patriotic sense of "sacrifice." In letters and diaries soldiers often speak of being "opferbereit," ready to sacrifice their lives for the good of the fatherland. These youthful writers of 1914-1918 were following a well-established, patriotic tradition in their use of the word. Prussian writers, especially, had enshrined the idea of sacrifice to king and country in the mythos of the Prussian, and later, German, state. Frederick the Great for example was glorified as the symbol of heroic sacrifice to duty.[6] But *Opfer* can also carry the far less heroic meaning of "victim," and there is little doubt that Unruh saw the war less as a way of sacrifice than as a parade of victims. For Clemens, one of the characters, the skulls of the regiments of men marching into Verdun (the locus of the book) were part of a charnel-house ("ein Beinhaus").[7]

Indeed, the controlling symbols in Unruh's book are the charnel-house, the madhouse, and the theater. The image of the charnel-house is, in various guises, a commonplace of the German war literature.[8] That of the madhouse is less common, although it appears in a number of the anti-war novels, most effectively in Edlef Köpper's *Heeresbericht* (1930, translated as *Higher Command*, 1931). Theatrical analogies, on the other hand, are rather rare (unlike the British literature, where they are quite common). After his vision of the marching charnel-house, Clemens in despair finally calls Verdun a comedy ("Lustspiel"), no doubt a blackly ironic one. Unruh's involvement with the theater is apparent not only in that image, but also in the construction of the book. It consists of a series of vivid scenes, loosely tied together by theme and image. The scenes equally provide an opportunity for the exclamatory speeches so typical of expressionist writing.

The same episodic construction and declamatory style also characterizes the other major expressionist work about the war, Leonhard Frank's *Der Mensch ist Gut* (Man Is Good, 1918). In Frank's work the utopian aspect of expressionism is at its most apparent. If ironic despair typifies Unruh, a vision of an ideal future infuses *Der Mensch ist Gut*. The epigraph combines a warning from Matthew III with a dedication to the coming generation. Like *Opfergang*, it is organized in a series of loosely-connected episodes, each focused on a nameless representative generic figure. The action takes place in a German city rather than at the front, and shows first those who stayed at home: the father, the mother, and the war widow. Frank then moves to the couple, and finally to the war cripples.

The father of the opening section is a waiter. He has sacrificed everything for the son he adores and wants to make into a good German bourgeois. When the son is killed in 1915 "on the field of honor" as the official language has it, "a whole world was slain."[9] In his despair and distraction, he sells food for too little money and loses his job. In the simple, declamatory style typical of the book, he addresses a crowd that turns into a protest march. For him a lack of love is the enemy and the root cause of all wars. "All Europe weeps because all Europe can no longer love. All Europe is mad because it can no longer love."[10]

The second section, "The War Widow," opens with her despair:

"How many women is it then? Two million perhaps who sit in their rooms and, like me, think of their dead husbands? Who look out the window and think of their dead husbands, who dust, wait for children, knit stockings, cook, go to work and think of their dead husbands, think of their dead husbands, think of their dead husbands. Who go to bed at night and think of their dead husbands."[11]

The reiteration of the single phrase interwoven with the catalogue of daily activities gives this passage surprising power and is a fine example of Frank's style at its best. The widow cannot imagine the "Altar of the Fatherland" on which her husband has been sacrificed. For her he has been sacrificed in the barbed wire of the Fatherland (22). The irony of the word "sacrifice" is worth noting here, and for the same reason as in Unruh. Like the father, the war widow joins the growing crowd of war protesters.

The third section, "The Mother," is essentially a continuation of the protest march in progress, but the mother provides a symbolic level of meaning. She has a vision of the trenches as an enormous wreath of graves ("ein Riesen-Kreis-Grab")—a funeral wreath—spanning a silent Europe (62). The scene shifts to the front where her son is obsessed by a man he saw die in the barbed wire (the war widow's husband, naturally). After his terrible experiences, he concludes that all the best people have to die because there are only two ways to tolerate the slaughter of the war: to grow accustomed to it, or to go mad (82-83). The section doses with the cry (Schrei) of the mother—the symbol of European humanity. A vision of Christ lowers itself into her arms, and two streams of people form a human cross with the mother and Christ at the center. Despite the expressionist's rebellion against traditional society, the Christian symbolism fits into the framework of Frank's utopian and humanitarian vision.

The fourth section, "The Couple," is largely given over to a rambling and confused philosophical discourse on the war, turning primarily on the idea that everything in Germany has been created by the war, and everyone who does not oppose it is also a part of it (101). This echoes the earlier theme of war-guilt introduced by the father and the war widow—a theme common to leftist writers throughout the Weimar period.

The final section, "The War Cripples," centers on wounded and crippled veterans. Frank dwells on the horrors of a forward surgical unit, which he calls a butcher's kitchen (120), before shifting to the hospital train returning the wounded to Germany. They realize that all cripples are comrades (152). The book ends in the city with a festival of cripples who join the protesters. The cries of suffering are transformed into songs of love in an ecstasy of brotherhood and peace. At the end, militarism is banished from the world: "The uniform disappears. Disappears out of the world" (171).

I have examined the work of Unruh and Frank at some length because, along with Latzko's 1918 book, *Menschen im Krieg* (translated as *Men in Battle*) they represent the earliest fictional responses to the war. Leaving aside for the moment predictable pacifist propaganda and the attempts of eminent writers (such as Thomas Mann) to come to terms with the war, these works share a number of characteristics. First, they were all written during the war, and they possess, for better or worse, an emotional immediacy that later works rarely demonstrate. Secondly, they all expound pacifistic views. There are a number of reasons for the pacifism of wartime works. In some cases, such as that of Latzko, the writers were, before the war, already pacifists by conviction. Latzko was at the center of an important pacifist group in Switzerland throughout the war. Others, like Unruh and Frank, became pacifists through their experience of the war. Fritz von Unruh presents a particularly interesting case. Descended from a Prussian noble family of strong military traditions, he had spent his youth in cadet schools and as the companion of two of the Kaiser's younger sons. He rejected the army in favor of the bohemian theatrical life of Berlin, but when the war broke out he returned immediately and voluntarily to the army, where he spent the remainder of the hostilities as an officer in the trenches, including service at Verdun, which led him to write *Opfergang*.

The decline of expressionism after the war is linked to its espousal of pacifism during the war. Even late in 1917 and 1918, pacifism represented a radical revolt against established authority and the general tenor of public opinion. That was particularly true when the pacifism was of the international humanitarian variety found in Frank and Unruh. Utopian visions of universal brotherhood and peace which characterized the leftist-internationalist-pacifist world view ran entirely contrary to the nationalism and conservatism common to German thought. In the wake of the defeat, pacifist writers were not perceived as seers who had predicted the *suffering* of war, but as betrayers who had undermined the German will to fight.[12] The innate conservatism of German readers also militated against experimental form as well as against pacifist and internationalist content. The brief flash of expressionist sound and fury was followed, with a couple of exceptions, by a long literary silence about the war that was scarcely broken until 1928.

The silence was broken by the unprecedented success of the classic liberal (to borrow Leed's term) war novel, Remarque's *All Quiet on the Western Front*. Remarque's pacifism, unlike that of the expressionists, emerges from a realistic depiction of the horrors of trench warfare.[13] *All Quiet* and its 1931 sequel *Der Weg zurück* (translated as *The Road Back*, 1931) provide the best-known examination of the liberal experience of the war. The other major liberal texts are Ludwig Renn's *War* and *Afterwar* (*Krieg*, 1928; *Nachkrieg*, 1930), and Arnold Zweig's tetralogy *The Great War of the White Men* (Der Grosse Krieg der weissen Manner).[14] Leaving aside Zweig's attempt at a panoramic historical account of the war, Remarque and Renn are particularly pertinent to an analysis of the uses of the war experience, as both authors follow their characters into postwar Germany. In both cases, despite feelings of hopelessness and loss, there is a driving need to make some sense of the war, and to find some use for all of the horror. It is precisely on the last point that the German liberal experience seems to differ from the British experience of the war. The German writers, however pacifistic, seem unable to accept the war as meaningless loss, or their experience of it as useless. The German belief in experience as formative and creative prevents even terrible experiences from being viewed as purely destructive.

The final chapter of *All Quiet*, set in the autumn of 1918, mirrors the hopelessness of the troops. Paul Bäumer has lost all of his friends, and is the last of the seven volunteers from his class. Had the soldiers returned home in 1916, he thinks, "out of the suffering and the strength of our experiences we might have unleashed a storm. Now if we go back we will be weary, broken, burnt out, rootless and without hope. We will not be able to find our way anymore."[15] The utter exhaustion and despair of men trapped in a seemingly endless war appear consistently in writing about the last months of the war. Even Schauwecker, who stands at the opposite philosophical pole, speaks of the soldiers as "victims of fate" and of the "vanity of human plans, of human thought."[16] Remarque's use of the word *wurzellos* (rootless) is especially appropriate here, as it reinforces the alienation and superfluity that Remarque treats at length in *The Road Back*. Bäumer's meditation ends with the quiet conviction that he has lost everything that it is possible to lose, his ideals, his friends, the chance for a happy, productive life, so "let the months and years come, they can take nothing from me, they can take nothing more. I am so alone, and so without hope that I can confront them without fear."[17] In the famous conclusion, Bäumer dies on a day in October 1918 so quiet that the army report is the single sentence which serves as the book's title. When found, his face is calm "as though almost glad the end has come."[18] The irony here, and Remarque is one of the rare German writers to employ irony in the English manner, is twofold: Bäumer's death just before the armistice, and the implication that even had he survived to the end, the war would not be over for him. The only escape from war is death. The irony is more pointed in the culminating image of Lewis Milestone's 1930 film of *All Quiet*. Although it does not appear in the book, the image of Paul Bäumer's hand reaching out of the trench for a butterfly and thereby exposing himself to a sniper remains one of the most evocative images of the First World War, embodying, as it does, the ironic contrast between the beauty and fragility of life and the universality of death in war.

The sense of profound loss that shapes *All Quiet* continues through *The Road Back*, published two years later in 1931. Again the title is ironic. The soldiers may have come back from the front, but the return is purely physical. Any attempt to return to a pre-war life or to realize a dream of "home" is doomed to futility. The abiding effect of the war on the combatants appears in several guises, often elaborations on earlier themes and scenes. Most evident is the unbridgeable gap between soldiers and civilians, and by extension between the life of the soldier and that of the civilian to which they are attempting to adjust. To take one example among many, Ernst, the protagonist, having just been demobilized, is invited to a party by his wealthy uncle and aunt.[19] He's somewhat reluctant to go, but is persuaded by his mother, who feels indebted to Uncle Karl for gifts of food during the war. Remarque slyly implies that Uncle Karl, who passed a safe war as a senior paymaster, had not been overly generous. In any event, Ernst goes to the party, is greeted first by a pompous butler, then by his uncle, resplendent in full uniform, including spurs. Ernst, noting the spurs, makes a bad joke about having roast horse for dinner, which only annoys his uncle. At one point before dinner he uneasily scratches his back and his aunt stops in the middle of a conversation to ask him what he's doing. He calmly responds that it's probably a louse, as it takes a while to get rid of them all. As she steps back in horror, he reassures her that lice don't jump like fleas, so she is quite safe. She exclaims and signals him to be quiet, as if he had said something stupid. That, Ernst concludes, is the way these people are. "We are supposed to be heroes, so they don't want to know anything about lice."[20] He completes his disgrace by eating his food (real pork chops fried in real fat) with his hands. His embarrassment quickly turns to rage against all those people who "go on living their trivial lives as a matter of course, as if the monstrous years had never been, when only one thing existed: death or life and nothing else."[21] I have detailed this incident at some length because it represents a classic postwar confrontation. Essentially, it is an exacerbated version of the earlier confrontations on home leave. But in this case, the veteran, who ought to be seen as a heroic figure, is instead treated as a social outcast by the very society that he has suffered to protect. What is worse, he has been permanently altered by the war; the smug, self-satisfied civilians seem entirely untouched by it. Renn, for example, is astonished by showily dressed women in a café—he didn't know that such elegance *still* existed (my emphasis).[22] Disenchantment with the race of civilians is by no means the exclusive province of the liberal novelists. The gap between front and rear cuts across the entire literary corpus. At the opposite end of the philosophical spectrum, Bucher gives a different twist to the common feeling of betrayal and suspicion. Toward the end of *In the Line* he presents the most overtly political formulation of the theme. After the failure of the 1918 offensive, "the arguments of the pacifist conspiracy had begun insidiously to destroy our will to fight on,"[23] and then lashes out at the homeland's betrayal of their sacrifice with references to the desperation of the last battles, the enormity of the human losses, and the insinuations that the soldiers were prolonging the war (quoted earlier).

Bucher's formulation, however extreme, cannot be discounted. Even if one ignores the usual conservative clichés—the pacifist agitators from a weak homeland, the glorification of German will, the melodramatic invocation of fallen comrades—the passage still reeks of genuine bitterness, betrayal and suffering, and there is little doubt that Bucher and others (Wehner, Hoffmann) spoke for the thousands who joined conservative veterans' organizations such as the Stahlhelm after the war. The majority of those who mouthed conservative platitudes were probably more bewildered than truly spiteful. They had, they felt, done their duty, and more than their duty. If the war was lost, the blame must lie elsewhere.

For the returning soldier, the loss of his comrades and his belief in his countrymen was augmented by yet another loss: loss of his ideals. Unlike the theme of civilian betrayal, or at the very least willful civilian ignorance, the theme of loss of ideals is mostly limited to the liberal novel. Where it exists in the conservative novel, loss of belief is of a special limited type, to which I shall return. Disillusionment, particularly about war, is, on the other hand, a broadly-based and inevitable phenomenon. Given the standard German patriotic education and the nature of the First World War, disillusionment with "Hurrah-patriotism," "the spirit of 1914," and similar notions of traditional combat was entirely predictable.

Fussell's remark that pre-war Britain was a world in which "the certainties were still intact"[24] is, in a different philosophical context, just as accurate for Germany. The whole framework of German idealism and nationalism must, in the heady days of August 1914, have appeared unshakable. That was particularly true for the German bourgeoisie with its devotion to spiritual values and traditional culture. The loss was, therefore, particularly striking among the bourgeois student-soldiers who exchanged the classroom for the trenches. As noted above, the growing meaninglessness of traditional culture for Paul Bäumer appears clearly during his home leave in *All Quiet*.

The loss of that link to the past is even starker in *The Road Back*, particularly when the young men return to school. They had volunteered before taking their final exams, and after the war must finish their studies. Returning to the old school building, Ernst remarks that before they were soldiers "these buildings enclosed our world. Then it was the trenches. Now we are here again. But this is no longer our world. The trenches were stronger."[25] The situation deteriorates when the school director greets the soldiers with a patriotic speech, which they shout down with demands for separate, practical courses; their demands reduce the methodical director to bewildered silence. Later, as the men try to plan a curriculum to present to the education authorities, they can scarcely believe that any of it had been of value to them (141-142).

Not only are *Bildung* and traditional learning no longer of value, the spiritual values have been replaced by material ones. The war-profiteer is the most obvious example of that change, but it appears among the soldiers as well. Karl Bröger, who before the war had been a voracious book collector, sells all his books with the words "a centimeter of business knowledge is worth more than a kilometer of Bildung."[26] Schauwecker's diatribe against percentages is only a more radical version of this use of units of measure to suggest the relative importance of spiritual and material values. The triumph of materialism is a constant theme in the liberal novels, as its opposite is in the conservative ones (for example, those of Schauwecker, Wehner, Zöberlein). Throughout his tetralogy on the war Arnold Zweig paints scathing portraits of self-centered, materialistic officers and men, most notably of the scheming and cowardly Sgt. Niggl of *Education before Verdun* and of General Schieffenzahn (the name means "crooked tooth") in the last two volumes, the incarnation of the modern, middle-class, technologically-adept general officer, said to be a portrait of Ludendorff. In Zweig's books, it is the Schieffenzahns of the world who triumph.

But for Remarque, the most terrible loss is the loss of his comrades and of comradeship itself, which he regarded as the only positive thing to come out of the war. He becomes aware of the change at the first regimental reunion after the end of the war (194-203). Most of the men have continued to wear their old uniforms as daily attire, but in honor of the reunion they all appear in civilian clothes for the first time. The pre-war social distinctions instantly reappear in their suits, causing some embarrassment. Tjaden accuses Kosole of having bought his suit from the rag man, making Kosole suddenly aware that some of the others are wearing much better suits. Men who were excellent soldiers and were in positions of responsibility at the front wear pre-war clothes and are patronized by worse soldiers who have returned to good jobs or made quick money on the black market. The world of comradeship that Ernst had known is suddenly topsy-turvy. These men are, he concludes, "still our comrades, and yet not any more; that's what makes it so sad. Everything else was destroyed in the war, but we had believed in comradeship. And now we see: What death has not brought to an end, life has. It separates us."[27] The resurgence of civilian society shatters the fragile community of the trenches, which depended upon the uniqueness of the situation. When the war ends, the community collapses. Renn likewise complains of the loss of comradeship in terms of loss of love.[28]

But it goes further than that. After the riot in the city, in which one group of soldiers fires upon another, Ernst concludes that, "We are at war again, but comradeship no longer exists."[29] The one thing that had sustained them through the war would not sustain them through the civil insurrections of post-war Germany. So, in the end, everything of value has been lost, except life itself. And for Ernst, what hope there is lies only in the fact that he is still alive and must make a way for himself in life. Interestingly enough, the language in which he couches his resolution recalls the language of *Bildung*. Life, he says,

> . . . is almost a task and a way. I will work on myself and be ready, I will use my hands and my thoughts, I will not make myself important and I will go forward, even when I sometimes want to stay still. There is a lot to be rebuilt, and almost everything to make good, things that were buried alive in the years of grenades and machine guns must be dug up. . . . Then the dead will be quiet, then the past will no longer pursue me, but help me.[30]

What Ernst is attempting is nothing less than the creation of a new personality that will integrate his war experience into productive life. Remarque emphasizes the transformation of character by referring to the war in terms of its mechanical destruction ("grenades and machine guns"), and by using the German verb *ausgraben*, to dig up, the antithesis of *eingraben*, to dig in, that is, to entrench—an emblematic verb of the war.

The essential characteristic of German First World War narratives, even novels as nihilistic as those of Remarque and Renn, is an attempt to endow the war with some meaning, be it personal, moral or historical; or, failing that, to derive from it some lesson or means by which a survivor can continue with his life. Remarque, clearly, is on the latter path. For him the war's only significance was its destruction, physical or mental, of a generation of German men. The men who survived appear to him to have gained nothing from the experience except survival itself. But even Remarque hints that there must be a use for the past, if only he can find his way to it.

From *Princes of the Trenches: Narrating the German Experience of the First World War* (1996), pp. 85-96. Copyright © 1996 by Camden House-Boydell & Brewer, Inc. Reprinted with permission of Camden House-Boydell & Brewer, Inc.

Notes

1. In Britain and France there were minority voices who attempted to bestow on the war a meaning other than meaningless loss. But, as in Germany, the prevailing myth was too strong. Although the respective national myths were virtual opposites, the loss of minority views beneath the monolithic unity of those myths is similar. See Hynes, *A War Imagined*, 449-455 for the British minority writers.

2. Remarque, *All Quiet*, 5. "Dieses Buch soll weder eine Anklage noch ein Bekenntnis sein. Es soll nur den Versuch machen, über eine Generation zu berichten, die vom Kriege zerstört wurde—auch wenn sie seinen Granaten entkam" (Dedication).

3. On the reception of *All Quiet* see Gollbach, *Die Wiederkehr des Weltkrieges*, 275-309.

4. Walter Sokel, *The Writer in Extremis: Expressionism in Twentieth-Century German Literature* (Stanford: Stanford UP, 1959), 2.

5. For an appreciation of the German war verse see Marsland, *The Nation's Cause* and especially Bridgewater, *German Poets of the First World War*.

6. See Stirk, *The Prussian Spirit*, for an analysis of Frederick the Great as the embodiment of Prussian virtues. A famous National Socialist poster depicts Hitler as the heir of Frederick and Bismarck.

7. Unruh, *Opfergang*, 44.

8. The image of the charnel-house reaches back to the Thirty Years' War and the poetry of Andreas Gryphius. In visual form, it is an important component of Otto Dix's war paintings, especially *Der Schatzengraben* and the central panel of *Der Krieg*. See Otto Conzelmann, *Der andere Dix: Sein Bild vom Menschen und vom Krieg* (Stuttgart: Klett-Cotta, 1983) for a thorough analysis of Dix's war imagery.

9. Leonhard Frank, *Der Mensch ist Gut* (1918, reprint Munich: Nymphenburger, 1953), 8. "Eine Welt war erschlagen."

10. Frank, 14-15. "Das Nichtvorhandensein der Liebe ist der Feind und die Ursache aller Kriege. Ganz Europa weint, weil ganz Europa nicht mehr lieben kann. Ganz Europa ist wahnsinnig, weil es nicht lieben kann."

11. Frank, 21. "Ja wieviel Frauen sind's dann? Zwei Millionen vielleicht, die in ihrem Zimmer sitzen und, wie ich, an ihren toten Mann denken? Zum Fenster hinaus sehen und an ihren toten Mann denken, Staub wischen, Kinder warten, Strümpfe stricken, kochen, auf die Arbeit gehen und an ihren toten Mann denken, an ihren toten Mann denken, toten Mann denken. Sich abends ins Bett legen und an ihren toten Mann denken."

12. For sources on the history of German pacifism, see chapter 6, notes 80 and 81. The influence of pacifism in France, on the other hand, was especially pervasive among veterans, although it was not usually of the internationalist sort. See Antoine Prost, *Les Anciens combattants et la société française, 1914-1939*, 3 vols. (Paris: Presses de la Fondation nationale des sciences politiques, 1977), 3:35-119.

13. Sontheimer, *Antidemokratisches Denken*, 119. Remarque's view of the war is not unlike that of a number of French memoirists, especially Roland Dorgelès in *Les croix de bois*, which may help to account for the enthusiastic reception for the French translation of Remarque's novel.

14. The tetralogy includes *Junge Frau von 1914* (1931, *Young Woman of 1914*), *Erziehung vor Verdun* (1935, *Education before Verdun*), *Der Streit um den Sergeanten Grischa* (1927, *The Case of Sergeant Grischa*), and *Die Versetzung eines Konigs* (1938, *The Crowning of a King*). All of the published translations are by Eric Sutton.

15. Remarque, *All Quiet*, 371-318. ". . . wir hätten aus dem Schmerz und der Stärke unserer Erlebnisse einen Sturm entfesselt. Wenn wir jetzt zurückkehren, sind wir müde, zerfallen, ausgebrannt, wurzellos und ohne Hoffnung. Wir werden uns nicht mehr zurechtfinden können" (261-262).

16. Schauwecker, *The Furnace*, 270. "Sie waren dem Schicksal verfallen . . . Die Vergeblichkeit menschlichen Planens und Deutens war ihnen hart und undurchdringlich beschlossen" (307).

17. Remarque, *All Quiet*, 319. "Mögen die Monate und Jahre kommen, sie nehmen mir nichts mehr, sie können mir nichts mehr nehmen. Ich bin so allein und so ohne Erwartung, daß ich ihnen entgegensehen kann ohne Furcht" (262-263).

18. Remarque, *All Quiet*, 320. ". . . als wäre er beinahe zufrieden damit, daß es so gekommen war" (263).

19. Remarque, *Road Back*, 111-117.

20. Remarque, *Road Back*, 113. "Helden sollen wir sein, doch von Läusen wollen sie nichts wissen" (126).

21. Remarque, *Road Back*, 116-117. ". . . die so selbstverständlich mit ihrem

Kleinkram dahinlebt, als waren die ungeheuren Jahre niemals gewesen, in denen es doch nur eins gab: Tod oder Leben und nichts sonst" (129).

22. Renn, *After War*, 30.

23. Bucher, *In the Line*, 270. "An unserem Willen beginnen die Hetzreden unsichtbarer Verschwörer zu wüten" (314).

24. Fussell, *Great War*, 21.

25. Remarque, *Road Back*, 118. "Ehe wir Soldaten wurden, umfaßten diese Gebäude unsere Welt. Dann wurden es die Schützengräben. Jetzt sind wir wieder hier. Aber dies ist nicht mehr unsere Welt. Die Gräben waren stärker" (131).

26. Remarque, *Road Back*, 167. "Ein Zentimeter Handel ist besser als ein Kilometer Bildung . . ." (182).

27. Remarque, *Road Back*, 200. "Es sind noch unsere Kameraden, und sie sind es doch nicht mehr, das macht gerade so traurig. Alles andere ist kaputtgegangen im Kriege, aber an die Kameradschaft hatten wir geglaubt. Und jetzt sehen wir: Was der Tod nicht fertiggebracht hat, das gelingt dem Leben: es trennt uns" (217).

28. Renn, *After War*, 211.

29. Remarque, *Road Back*, 277-278. "Es ist wieder Krieg, aber die Kameradschaft ist nicht mehr" (303).

30. Remarque, *Road Back*, 342. "Das ist beinahe eine Aufgabe und ein Weg. Ich will an mir arbeiten und bereit sein, ich will meine Hände rühren und meine Gedanken, ich will mich nicht wichtig nehmen und weitergehen, auch wenn ich manchmal bleiben möchte. Es gibt vieles aufzubauen und fast alles wieder gutzumachen, es gibt zu arbeiten und ausgraben, was verschüttet worden ist in den Jahren der Granaten und der Maschinengewehre. . . . Dann werden die Toten schweigen, und die Vergangenheit wird mich nicht mehr verfolgen, sondern mir helfen" (366-367).

Works Cited

Bridgewater, Patrick. *The German Poets of the First World War.* London: Croom Helm, 1985.

Bröger, Karl. *Bunker 17.* Jena: n.p., 1929. Translated by Oakley Williams as *Pillbox 17.* London: Butterworth, 1930.

Bucher, Georg. *Westfront 1914-1918. Das Buch vom Frontkameraden.* Vienna-Leipzig: Konegen, 1930. Translated by Norman Gullick as *In the Line: 1914-1918.* London: Cape, 1932.

Conzelmann, Otto. *Der andere Dix: Sein Bild vom Menschen und vom Krieg.* Stuttgart: Klett, 1983.

Frank, Leonhard. *Der Mensch ist Gut.* 1918. Reprint, Munich: Nymphenburg, 1953.

Gollbach, Michael. *Die Wiederkehr des Weltkrieges in der Literatur.* Kronberg/Taunus: Scriptor, 1978.

Hoffmann, Helmut. *Mensch und Volk im Kriegserlebnis.* Germanische Studien 189, 1-81. Berlin: Ebering, 1937.

Hoffmann, Richard. *Frontsoldaten*. Hamburg: Fackelreiter, 1928.

Hynes, Samuel. *A War Imagined: The First World War and English Culture*. New York: Atheneum, 1991.

Köppen, Edlef *Heeresbericht*. Berlin-Grunewald: Horen, 1930. Tr. as *Higher Command*, no translator listed. London: Faber, 1931.

Latzko, Andreas. *Menschen im Krieg*. Zurich: Rascher, 1918. Tr. by Adele N. Seltzer as *Men in Battle*. London: Cassell, 1918.

Mann, Thomas. *Betrachtungen eines Unpolitischen*. Berlin: Fischer, 1918.

_____. *Briefe I*. Frankfurt am Main: Fischer, 1961.

_____. "Gedanken im Kriege." *Friedrich und die große Koalition*. Berlin: Fischer, 1916. Tr. H. T. Lowe-Porter, *Three Essays*. New York: Knopf, 1929.

_____. *Von Deutscher Republik*. Berlin: Fischer, 1923.

Marsland, Elizabeth A. *The Nation's Cause: French, English and German Poetry of the First World War*. London: Routledge, 1991.

Prost, Antoine. *Les Anciens combattants et la société française 1914-1939*. 3 vols. Paris: Presses de la Fondation nationale des sciences politiques, 1977.

Remarque, Erich Maria. *Im Westen nichts Neues*. Berlin: Propyläen, 1929. Tr. by A.W. Wheen as *All Quiet on the Western Front*. London: Putnam, 1929.

_____. *Der Weg Zurück*. Berlin: Propyläen, 1931. Tr. by A.W. Wheen as *The Road Back*. Boston: Little, 1931.

Renn, Ludwig. *Krieg*. Frankfurt: Frankfurter Societäts-Druckerei, 1929. Tr. by Edwin and Willa Muir as *War*. London: Secker, 1929.

_____. *Nachkrieg*. Berlin: Agie, 1930. Tr. by Edwin and Willa Muir as *After War*. London: Secker, 1931.

_____. *Krieg und Nachkrieg*. Berlin: Aufbau, 1985. (Ed. cited).

Sassoon, Siegfried. *Complete Memoirs of George Sherston*. London: Faber, 1937.

Schauwecker, Franz. *Aufbruch der Nation*. Berlin: Frundsberg, 1930. Tr. by R. T. Clark as *The Furnace*. London: Methuen, 1930.

_____. *Der feurige Weg*. 1926. Reprint, Berlin: Frundsberg, 1929. Tr. by Thonald Holland as *The Fiery Way*. London: Dent, 1929.

Sokel, Walter H. *The Writer in Extremis: Expressionism in Twentieth-Century German Literature*. Stanford: Stanford UP, 1959.

Sontheimer, Kurt. *Antidemokratisches Denken in der Weimarer Republik*. Munich: Nymphenburg, 1962.

_____. "Der Tatkreis." *Vierteljahrshefte für Zeitgeschichte* 7:3 (1959): 229-260.

Stirk, S. D. *The Prussian Spirit, 1914-1940*. Port Washington, N.Y.: Kennikat, 1969.

Unruh, Fritz von. *Opfergang*. Berlin: Eriss, 1919.

Wehner, Josef Magnus. *Sieben vor Verdun*. Munich: Langen/Muller, 1930. Reprint, Hamburg: Deutsche Hausbücherei, 1932.

Zöberlein, Hans. *Der Glaube an Deutschland*. Munich: Nachfolger, 1931.

Zweig, Arnold. *Einsetzung eines Königs*. Amsterdam: Querido, 1937. Tr. by Eric Sutton as *The Crowning of a King*. New York: Viking, 1938.

_____. *Erziehung vor Verdun*. Amsterdam: Querido, 1935. Tr. by Eric Sutton as *Education before Verdun*. New York: Viking, 1936.

_____. *Junge Frau von 1914*. Berlin: Kiepenheuer, 1931. Tr. by Eric Sutton as *Young Woman of 1914*. New York: Viking, 1932.

_____. *Der Streit um den Sergeanten Grischa*. Potsdam: Kiepenheuer, 1928. Tr. by Eric Sutton as *The Case of Sergeant Grischa*. New York: Viking, 1928.

Iron Men and Paper Warriors:
Remarque, Binding, and Weimar Literature_____

Kim Allen Scott

> More and more we are to be counted among the dead, among the es-
> tranged—because the greatness of the occurrence estranges us, rather than
> among the banished, whose return is possible.[1]

This poignant expression of the destructive alienation experienced
by war veterans could have been written at any time in human history.
Contemporary Americans can find an identifiable pathos in the statement when considering the plight of Viet Nam veterans, but it is likely
that soldiers returning to civilian life from any of the wars recorded in
the annals of western civilization could sympathize with its meaning.
What is significant about this passage is that it represents the viewpoint
of a German veteran of the First World War and that the seemingly pacifistic work from which it was taken is not Remarque's *All Quiet on the
Western Front*. The estranged veteran who penned these lines in 1925
was Rudolf Georg Binding, an ex-cavalry officer whose work, *A Fatalist at War*, anticipated Remarque's later classic by four years.

In the decades following the First World War, Germany was the
scene of both confused political turmoil and experimental artistic cre-
ativity. While economic and political conditions followed a roller-
coaster course of heights and depths, social and artistic changes reflected the despair of a defeated nation. One of the voices of despair
could be heard in the war literature springing from the typewriters of
ex-soldiers attempting to find some meaning in their experiences. Two
such writers, Rudolf Georg Binding and Erich Maria Remarque, produced books which were at once alike, yet poles apart. By examining
the similarities and differences of their stories this paper will illustrate
some of the cultural forces which helped shape the war literature of the
Weimar period.

One question presents itself at the outset of this inquiry. Both Binding and Remarque wrote on the futility of war and the insanity of using force to settle modern international disputes, but only Remarque came to be identified with a solidly pacifistic viewpoint and suffered persecution under the Nazi regime. The bonfires which consumed *All Quiet on the Western Front* and other works considered "degenerate" by the National Socialists did not include Binding's indictment. While Remarque was forced to flee Germany in 1933 and officially stripped of his citizenship in 1938, Binding continued to write and publish in Hitler Germany, enjoying moderate success as a popular author. Why Binding's book escaped the auto-da-fé reserved for Remarque's can be more clearly understood after a brief review of how historians have interpreted the Weimar Republic's cultural roots.[2]

The Nazi seizure of power was not a sudden takeover by a demonic minority, but rather a gradual process of centralization that exploited the public's acceptance of the basic tenets laid down by the cultural critics. Hitler's ideal state, towards which the Nazi political machine relentlessly rolled, was one where individuals and institutions were nationalized. As George Mosse defines it, Nazi "nationalization" meant the subordination of the self to the "Volk" or folk culture.[3] The arts, commerce, industry, in short, all phases of life were to be integrated into this larger sense of community and belonging, burying forever the forces of division and alienation wrought by political liberalism.

The first casualties of this cultural revolution were obviously the artists, those creative people for whom self-expression took precedent over maintaining any sort of cultural unity. Experimental works in painting, writing, and the cinema had always been subject to some distrust in Germany; under the Nazis' control they became stifled and all but ceased to exist. A key element in Hitler's will to power included control of the publishing industry, and if a printing plant could not be directly supervised by the Nazi party its output could be restricted by carefully monitoring paper allocations. Among approved literature was a genre of novels identified as "Fronterlebnis" (Life at the Front). Richard Grunberger identifies these stories as tales concerning "the alchemy whereby life at the front transmuted a motley of self-centered atoms into an oath-bound band of brothers."[4]

One of the Weimar war novels that the Nazis found unacceptable was Erich Maria Remarque's *All Quiet on the Western Front*. Partly because in its depiction of the 'Fronterlebnis' and the soldiers as a 'band of brothers' it resembled more right-wing novels, *All Quiet on the Western Front* had been a phenomenal success when it was first published in 1928/29. It sold over one million copies in a year[5] and translations in English and French reached the reading public across Europe and the Atlantic. Some German reviewers seemed openly amazed that a war book could achieve such popular success,[6] but a brief examination of the novel helps us understand at least part of the reason for Remarque's literary triumph.

All Quiet on the Western Front is the story of a common soldier named Paul (modeled on the author himself) who enlists with his school mates at the opening of hostilities. Written in the present tense, the first person narrative follows Paul and his comrades during the course of the slaughter with a terse, almost detached prose style. Two major themes dominate Paul's description of life at the front: the senselessness of war in general and the betrayal of the youth who bear the weapons by the older generation in charge of the state.

The generational betrayal is illustrated in a number of vignettes throughout the novel. Schoolteachers, army officers, capitalists who run the factories, are all in turn targets of Paul's indictment:

> For us lads of 18 they ought to have been mediators and guides to the world of maturity, the world of work, of culture, of progress—to the future. We often made fun of them and played jokes on them, but in our hearts we trusted them. The idea of authority, which they represented, was associated in our minds with a greater insight and manlier wisdom. But the first death shattered this belief. We had to recognize that our generation was more to be trusted than theirs. They surpassed us only in phrases and cleverness.[7]

In this expression of generational betrayal, *All Quiet on the Western Front* is a good example of the "revolt of the son" among Weimar artists and intellectuals. Just like the Weimar expressionist painters and artists, Remarque's characters are in constant opposition to authority in the guise of the older generation.[8] When the protagonist Paul returns home on leave he is amused to find his former teacher, Kantorek, is now a soldier in a home guard unit under the command of a former schoolmate named Mittelstaedt. Paul watches one day as his chum drills the former teacher mercilessly:

> Mittelstaedt encourages Kantorek the Territorial with quotations from Kantorek the Schoolmaster. "Territorial Kantorek, we have the good fortune to live in a great age, we must all humble ourselves and for once put aside all bitterness."[9]

In this sarcastic episode Remarque is not only expressing generational condemnation of the old order, but is also mocking one of the basic pillars of the Nazi credo: the concept of the "Volk," or folk community.

The novel's condemnation of war is consistent throughout. "We had fancied our task would be different," reflects Paul on the differences between combat and basic training, "only to find we were to be trained for heroism as if we were circus ponies."[10] Paul and his comrades long to be survivors rather than heroes, even if any were naive enough to believe in heroics anymore. When Paul becomes unsettled after spending a hellish evening in a no-man's-land shellhole with a dying enemy soldier he has knifed, he speaks to the corpse: "Comrade, I did not want to kill you. If you jumped in here again I would not do it, if you would be sensible too."[11] Later on he vows to his victim, "Comrade . . . today you, tomorrow me. But if I come out of this, comrade, I will fight against this, that has struck us both down."[12]

In 1930 the Universal Film Company of Hollywood, California, filmed a movie based on *All Quiet on the Western Front*. Although asked by the producers to write the screenplay and star in the picture,

Remarque declined in order to continue writing.[13] The film was completed with American actors and screenwriters, but it was dubbed in German and premiered in Berlin on December 5, 1930. Apparently right wing extremists feared the medium of film even more than the book because they exercised every imaginable tactic of disruption during the premiere showing and maintained sufficient subsequent agitation to result in the movie being banned in Germany. Remarque became all too aware that he was a marked man by the Nazis, and although he continued writing in Germany for the next few years, he fled the country for Switzerland just a few days before Hitler assumed the Chancellorship in 1933. On May 12 of the same year, *All Quiet on the Western Front* was publicly burned. The offensive novel, which had suggested among other heresies that Germany's defeat had been due to factors other than the "stab in the back" at home by corrupt politicians, was purged from Hitler's new order.

But another book, similar in style and tone to Remarque's, was both spared burning and actually reprinted in 1941 when paper for publishing was strictly controlled by the Nazis' initial efforts during World War II: Rudolf Binding's *Aus dem Krieg—A Fatalist at War.*[14]

Rudolf Georg Binding was born to a wealthy family August 13, 1867, in Basel, Switzerland. He attended university at Leipzig and Berlin and began to write poetry and stories before the end of the nineteenth century. World War I found the affluent patrician 47 years old, yet still captured by the enthusiastic thralldom of his younger countrymen for the coming holocaust. Unlike Remarque, Binding enlisted in the army even though he could have easily avoided military service. Commissioned as a captain in a cavalry regiment, he saw action on both fronts. Binding received minor wounds on several occasions, but escaped serious injury until the final months of the war when chronic dysentery ended his military career. Following the war, he continued writing, publishing a romantic narrative entitled *Reitvorschrift für eine Geliebte* (*Riding Instruction for a Lover*) in 1924. The next year he wrote an account of his military adventures called *Aus dem Krieg*. An

English translation by Ian Morrow entitled *A Fatalist at War* appeared in 1929.[15]

Like Remarque's novel, *A Fatalist at War* is written in the present tense, conveying a sense of the immediacy of a soldier's existence. The style takes the form of a series of journal entries and letters home, written in the same stark economy of language as Paul's story. Where it differs from *All Quiet on the Western Front* is not in the constant questioning of the institution of warfare, but in the absence of any generational conflict between the narrator and those from whom he receives his orders. Binding had lived the bulk of his early adult years in the relative tranquillity of late nineteenth century Germany. While Remarque's Paul is ordered into the fray by his elders, Binding takes his orders from his peers. As a result the cavalry officer is ready to criticize stupidity when he sees it in the military command structure, but he does not ascribe it to a corrupt older order. In the course of one entry Binding complains about an order issued by his superiors that instructs the troops to alter the structure of French three-wheeled carts whose original design is best suited for the narrow roads. "This natural wisdom, sprung from the soil centuries ago, could not penetrate the imagination of the German officers of high rank."[16] The officers are wrong in Binding's view, not because they represent mindless authority in the form of stern, paternal overlords, but because they do not have the flexibility to use the wisdom of their own elders.

The theme of alienation is present throughout the book, but when Binding discusses the estrangement wrought by the war his protests almost seem like endorsements: "If one really lives in the War, I mean if one puts Peace resolutely behind one—one gains a pleasant feeling of detachment from all that one has known."[17] While the author admits his battle experiences have altered him, we gain no sense that the alteration will permanently affect his ability to adjust to civilian life. Unlike Remarque's youthful footsoldier, Binding has half a lifetime of experiences and memories to cushion the disorientation of combat.

As a cavalry officer Binding views the mechanized war from horseback, but this anachronistic perspective never seems to dawn on him when discussing the futility of war in general. At one point he describes the moonscape remaining on a battlefield near Beaucourt, France:

> The area ought to remain as it is. No road, no well, no settlement ought to be made there, and every ruler, leading statesman or president of a republic ought to be brought to see it instead of swearing an oath on the Constitution, henceforth and forever. Then there will be no more wars.[18]

This passage, which reflects none of the human suffering endured by the infantrymen in the trenches, reads more like a gratuitous nod towards pacifism rather than a scathing indictment of warfare.

To counter whatever anti-war sentiments he may express, Binding constantly looks for some sort of meaning in the carnage. As might be expected, the German writer finds solace in the Nietzschean model:

> And again comes the quite extraordinary counter-sensation that one should not wish to lose any of these years out of one's life . . . that one would hope to win something by the very length of one's endurance, that one is prepared to suffer even worse, even more revolting things, out of a lust for things that leads one to extremes. It seems in all this there lay something positive, some worth, some change for the better.[19]

At one point during Binding's recurrent attempts to place Nietzsche in a steel helmet he reflects on the philosopher's differences with the writings of Plato. Binding concludes that perhaps a "thoroughbred," resistant to genetic degeneracy, is as vital to mankind as Nietzsche's "superman" who will lead.[20]

But the human suffering caused by the war is unavoidable, and when Binding climbs down from Valhalla into the trenches he is almost uncomfortable with the necessary description of the mangled corpses strewn across no-man's land. Again and again the cavalry officer tries to wrap his horror in the cloak of the "superman." One entry tells of his experience informing a military chaplain that the minister's son has been killed by a sniper:

> As he spoke to me about his boy his face lit up under his tears. To have experienced this grief seemed to him a marvelous achievement. He was proud to have been so rich that so much could be taken from him.[21]

Exact sales figures of Binding's book when it appeared in the 1925 German edition would be difficult to establish, but it is a safe assertion that it was not a runaway best seller. The work waited four years before being published in an English translation, whereas *All Quiet on the Western Front* was rendered into English in a matter of weeks. It is significant that *A Fatalist at War* was ready for English readers shortly after Remarque's book, leading one to assume its translation was undertaken because of the impressive success of *All Quiet on the Western Front*. The timing of the two books' release and the surface similarities helped color the reviews in the English press. A reviewer with the *Boston Transcript* hailed *A Fatalist at War* as "a powerful pacifist argument from the military point of view and impresses strongly with its sincerity."[22] A possibility exists that the critics who read Binding's account in 1929 had done so after digesting Remarque and over-emphasized the weaker pacifistic argument presented in *A Fatalist at War.* When the Nazis gained control of Germany four years later they saw no such similarity between the two books.

Binding's viewpoint as an aristocrat, an officer, and an adult citizen of Hohenzollern Germany allowed his work to bridge the gap between Nazi Germany and the fabled years of Teutonic greatness in the late nineteenth century. *A Fatalist at War* was thus able to transcend the "junkyard" of the Weimar years while *All Quiet on the Western Front* was tainted with the innovative experimentalism of the era. Remarque's novel makes a prime example of Weimar's rebellious son, irreconcilable with the stern father represented first by the Hindenburg government and later by the Nazi regime. Binding was able to reconcile with the father because he never truly rebelled in the first place.

Among the passages that men in Hitler's government would read with approval in Binding's book are those dealing with the German spirit, anti-Semitism, and the failure of democracy. "I tell you now," Binding preaches after musing over Germany's prospects in March 1917, "if only Germany could attain real inspiration she would still win the war."[23] Here the author is willing to overlook the logistical impossibility of victory by a belief in a triumph of the will. When he tries to illustrate the inflexibility of his superiors for refusing to promote a worthy Jewish soldier, Binding readily admits "a number of incidents have shown that Jews are unsuitable as officers and for positions of command."[24] The captain expresses little confidence in the government on the home front when he blurts, "All the same, a man is doing his job here defending his country; the same cannot be said of his elected representatives in the Reichstag."[25] By championing the spirit of the "Volk," condemning the conduct of the Jews, and casting doubt on the worth of democratic institutions, Binding proved to be a worthy spokesman for the National Socialist world view.

As the 1930s waned and Hitler's government advanced along the road to another world war, Rudolf Binding and Erich Remarque followed very different pathways. Remarque lived for a time in Paris, writing other novels that were eventually made into American movies. He moved to the United States in 1939 and afterwards became an American citizen. The Nazis never forgave his heresies, though. The German consul in Los Angeles, California, protested vigorously against *The Road Back*, a film based on one of his subsequent novels, and Remarque's sister, Elfriede Scholz, was executed in December, 1943, by Germany for her "defeatist" views.

Binding continued to write and publish during the Nazi years. His *Antwort eines Deutschen an die Welt* (*A German Answers the World*), was published in 1933 and was a defense of National Socialism. He died in 1938, but a collection of his works, *Dies War das Maß* (*These were the Most*), which included *A Fatalist at War*, was published post-humously in 1941.[26]

Weimar Germany was an intermission between two cataclysmic world wars in which veterans of the first wrote their memoirs in antici-pation and dread of the next. Some pulled out all the stops in exposing the military life as a lunatic's institution, such as Jaroslav Hašek's *The Good Soldier Schweik*. Not as sarcastic but just as accusatory was Re-marque's novel which, like Hašek's, received the ultimate honor by the Nazis, who banished them due to unacceptable pacifistic content. Binding's essays belong to another class, whose qualified pacifism re-stricted itself to the actual execution of World War I rather than an in-dictment of warfare as a means of settling international disputes. Finally, it was the "Fronterlebnis" stories, the novels that glorified the experience while ascribing defeat to political circumstances, that found ready acceptance in Hitler's Germany.

Another plunge into the abyss of total war has left the Weimar war narratives in a new perspective of causation and reaction to human conflict. "Why" is the question they all asked in varying degrees, and the answer is one which still eludes the present-day questioner. If Re-marque finds pointlessness in the sacrifice of young men in the meat grinder called the front, and even the aristocratic Binding can find fault in those who order the slaughter, one understandably ponders why warfare still found such a ready acceptance among the Germans of mil-itary age in 1939. The answer can only partially be uncovered by look-ing beneath the surface of these books.

Notes

1. Rudolf G. Binding. *A Fatalist At War*. Trans. Ian F. D. Morrow. New York: Houghton Mifflin, 1929,1.

2. See Fritz Stern. *The Politics of Cultural Despair.* Berkeley: University of California Press, 1963; Eric Bentley. *A Century of Hero Worship.* New York: J. B. Lippincott, 1944; Gordon A. Craig. *Germany 1866-1945.* New York, Oxford: Oxford UP, 1978; Peter Gay. *Weimar Culture: The outsider as insider.* New York: Harper & Row, 1968.

3. George L. Moss. *Nazi Culture: Intellectual, cultural, and social life in the Third Reich.* New York: Grosset and Dunlap, 1966, xx-xxi.

4. Richard Grunberger. *The Twelve Year Reich: A social history of Nazi Germany.* New York: Holt, Rinehart and Winston, 1971, 349.

5. Modris Eksteins. "War, Memory and Politics: The fate of the film *All Quiet on the Western Front*". *Central European History* 13 (1980), 60.

6. Modris Eksteins. "*All Quiet on the Western Front* and the Fate of War". *Journal of Contemporary History* 15 (1980), 353.

7. Erich Maria Remarque. *All Quiet on the Western Front.* Trans. A.W. Wheen. Boston: Little, Brown, 1929, 11.

8. Gay, 102-118.

9. Remarque, 180.

10. Ibid., 21.

11. Ibid., 226.

12. Ibid., 229.

13. Eksteins. "War, Memory and Politics", 61.

14. Rudolf G. Binding. *Dies war das Maß.* Potsdam: Rütten & Loening, 1941.

15. See Robert Wistrich. *Who's Who in Nazi Germany.* New York: McMillan, 1982, 18.

16. Binding, 1929, 29.

17. Ibid., 50.

18. Ibid., 217.

19. Ibid., 198.

20. Ibid., 80-81.

21. Ibid., 196.

22. M.M. *Boston Transcript*, 16.03.1929, 3.

23. Binding, 1929, 150.

24. Ibid., 55.

25. Ibid., 189.

26. Wistrich, 18.

All Quiet on the Western Front (U.S., 1930):
The Antiwar Film and
the Image of Modern War _____

John Whiteclay Chambers II

More than any other American feature film in the interwar years, *All Quiet on the Western Front* (U.S., 1930) came to represent the image of World War I. In a poignant saga of the life and death of a sensitive young German recruit, the film vividly portrays the senseless horror of trench warfare on the western front. Explosive sound effects accompany powerful visual images—it was one of the first "talking" pictures—to produce an emotionally wrenching viewing experience. It directly contributed to the widespread revulsion against such slaughter and against industrialized mass warfare in general.

All Quiet on the Western Front became the classic antiwar movie, hailed as a brilliant and powerful work of film art and widely imitated.[1] It achieved that classic status for historical and political reasons as much as for the cinematographic excellence with which it brought to the screen the war novel of an embittered young German veteran and writer, Erich Maria Remarque.[2] For the film speaks to ideology and history as well as to art.

Half a century later, the very title remains highly evocative. It has emotional significance even for those whose understanding of World War I comes primarily from sepia pictures in history books. Now blended in public memory, the novel and film have come, like the young protagonist, the schoolboy-soldier Paul Bäumer, to symbolize the transformative horror of the western front. It is a horror that remains embedded in Western consciousness as a consequence of World War I.

The film was based on the tremendously popular novel *All Quiet on the Western Front* (in the original German, *Im Westen nichts Neues* [literally, Nothing New on the Western Front]). The book was a semiautobiographical work, based on Remarque's brief experience in the German army in the last years of the war. It was also clearly a product of the disillusionment that he and many other veterans felt about the war and about the dislocations of the postwar era.

Remarque wrote the manuscript in the winter of 1927/1928 when he was twenty-nine years old. Originally published in Germany in January 1929 and in Britain and United States six months later, the book sold more than 2 million copies within a year. (In the United States, the Book-of-the-Month Club made the work its June 1929 selection, and Little, Brown sold 300,000 copies the first year.) By the end of 1930, it had been translated into twelve languages and had sold 3.5 million hardbound copies worldwide. Fawcett Crest acquired the paperback rights in 1958, and the first 175,000 copies sold out in a few months. By the time Remarque died in 1970, this classic had been translated into forty-five languages and had sold nearly 8 million copies, a figure that by now has probably exceeded 12 million. The book sells well to the present day.[3]

After the publication of Remarque's semiautobiographical novel, there was considerable interest in his military record. He began his compulsory military service in November 1916, entering at eighteen with his school classmates. He underwent basic and advanced recruit training at the Caprivi Barracks in Osnabrück, his hometown in Westphalia. In June 1917, he was sent with the Second Guards Reserve Division to a position behind the Arras lines on the western front. Assigned to a sapper (engineer) unit, which had responsibility for laying barbed wire and building dugouts and gun emplacements, Private Remarque and his unit were subsequently transported to Flanders to help block the major offensive being prepared by the British and French.

On July 31, 1917, after two weeks of artillery bombardment, the Allies began their assault (called Third Ypres or Passchendaele by the British). On the first day, Remarque, who had been working in the sapper unit, was wounded in the neck, leg, and forearm by fragments from a British artillery shell. His wounds were serious enough for him to be taken to a hospital in Duisburg, Germany, where he underwent surgery and then spent more than a year in convalescence, working part-time as a clerk in the office helping to process the new casualties from the front. Released from the hospital on October 13, 1918, as fit for garrison duty, Remarque was transferred to a reserve unit in Osnabrück. He was declared fit for active duty on November 7, 1918, four days before the end of the war.[4] Although Remarque had spent only about six weeks at the front, his experience was reinforced by his time with wounded and dying soldiers at the hospital and by correspondence with his schoolboy comrades in his old unit, several of whom were later killed or severely wounded.

* * *

The 1930 Hollywood version of Remarque's book was the result of the successful judgment of Carl Laemmle, an independent entrepreneur who had entered the industry by purchasing theaters and then expanding into distribution and finally into production, heading the Universal Pictures Corporation. *All Quiet on the Western Front*, directed by Lewis Milestone, starred both a young, relatively unknown actor, Lew Ayres, and a seasoned veteran, Louis Wolheim.[5] Ayres became personally identified with the film, for he perfectly captured the role of the protagonist, the sensitive, educated, young man, Paul Bäumer—the everyman trapped, corrupted, and destroyed by the horror of trench warfare. Like the book, the 1930 film continues to be available, now on videocassette. In 1979, an entirely new version, in color, was produced for television, starring Richard Thomas and Ernest Borgnine.

In August 1929, Laemmle rushed from Hollywood to his native Germany and acquired the film rights from the author.[6] He put his twenty-one-year-old son, Carl Laemmle, Jr., the studio's new general manager, in charge of production of *All Quiet on the Western Front*.[7] The younger Laemmle ("Junior," as he was called) hired Lewis Milestone as the director.

Born in Russia, Milestone had abandoned an education in mechanical engineering in Germany in 1913 at the age of eighteen and gone to New York City to pursue a career in the theater. He soon became an assistant to a theatrical photographer. When the United States entered World War I in 1917, Milestone enlisted as a private in the photography section of the U.S. Army Signal Corps. In the army, he first worked on training films in New York, then learned about editing at the film laboratory of the War College in Washington, D.C., where he worked with Victor Fleming, Josef von Sternberg, and a number of future luminaries in the motion-picture industry. Discharged from the army in 1919, Milestone became a U.S. citizen and soon moved to Hollywood. He worked as an assistant film cutter, a screenwriter, and, beginning in 1925, a director.[8] In 1927, *Two Arabian Knights*, a tale of two fun-loving American doughboys, earned Milestone the Motion Picture Academy Award for Best Comedy Direction.

Despite the objections of the younger Laemmle, Milestone hired Ayres, who was only twenty years old and largely unknown, for the starring role of Paul Bäumer.[9] Although inexperienced, Ayres had many of the qualities Milestone sought: he was handsome, earnest, intelligent, and somewhat broodingly introspective. Without a well-known actor in this leading role, the audience effectively saw the young soldier protagonist as a kind of everyman. Ayres's relative lack of experience was balanced by the veteran actor Wolheim, who personified Katczinsky (Kat), the knowledgeable, cynical, but compassionate oldtimer. It is Katczinsky who instructs the young recruits about how to try to survive in the deadly chaos of the front.

For the task of converting Remarque's novel into a screenplay for what the industry then referred to as a "talker," Milestone drew on a group of capable writers. Contrary to many accounts, playwright Maxwell Anderson was not responsible for the dramatic treatment; he simply wrote the first version of the dialogue.[10] Creating a chronological screenplay to replace the episodic form of the novel, Milestone and his associates helped give structure to a war-film genre: one that follows a group of young recruits from their entry into the military, through basic training, to the battlefront. In this case, the film begins with the young men together in the schoolroom just before they rush off to enlist, encouraged by their chauvinistic teacher, Kantorek, who shames them into enlisting and calls on them to become "Iron Men" of Germany.

The film, like the novel, emphasizes the war's senseless human waste, especially the waste of youth. The camera graphically illustrates the breakdown of romantic ideas of war, heroism, and defense of the nation in the squalor of the trenches and the brutality of combat. One by one, the young men are lost; finally death takes the veteran Katczinsky and shortly thereafter Paul himself. (Remarque ends his novel by stating that when Paul's body is turned over, "his face had an expression of calm, as though almost glad the end had come.")[11]

Milestone and his crew paid particular attention to the brutality and senselessness of war on the western front and to the sharp divergence between civilian and military society, between home front and battlefront. Civilian society is characterized by the strident chauvinism of influential males such as Paul's father and schoolteacher, or by the intense anguish of helpless women such as his mother and sister. In the training camp and at the front, civilian youths are transformed into soldiers. They form cohesive male fighting groups, bands of brothers. But the male bonding is not simply as a band of warriors but also, under the shock and pain of the war, as a family—caring, nurturing, even doing domestic chores—but a family without women.

The few women in this film have smaller roles. They, too, are victims. On home leave, Paul finds food in short supply, his mother ailing and out of touch with reality. At the military hospital, nurses and other medical personnel are overworked and unsympathetic. The book has little romantic interest, but Hollywood felt the need for some women and sex in the film. Indeed, one of the promotional posters used in the United States featured a pretty young French woman clearly alluring to the German schoolboy-soldiers as well as to potential ticket buyers. In a French village behind the German lines, three young women are so famished that they are willing to exchange sex for the soldiers' food rations. Although the book mentions this episode only briefly, Milestone expanded it into an important and moving sequence.

New motion-picture technology—sound equipment and more mobile cameras—gave "talkers" a distinct new feeling. Like many of the posters, paintings, and other art of the postwar period, film took on a new harder, sharper, more brutal aura. Milestone brought the brutal reality of the war to this picture. Together with his cinematographer, Arthur Edeson, the director used a combination of fast-moving sight and sound to heighten the impact of the violence of industrialized warfare. The two men built a number of powerful images: the pockmarked landscape of no man's land; flashes of artillery fire on the horizon; wisps of smoke and gas; soldiers climbing out of trenches and rushing into machine-gun fire and exploding artillery shells; bodies lying crumpled on the ground, hanging on barbed wire, or being hurled into the air by artillery blasts.

One of Milestone's most acclaimed—and imitated—photographic devices was a long, fast, parallel-tracking shot (moving sideways like a crab) along a German trench while maintaining its focus on the attacking French infantrymen. The shot was possible because Milestone mounted Edeson's camera on a giant wheeled crane so it could be rolled along behind the trench. In the film, for nearly a minute of uninterrupted camera movement, the picture travels rapidly along at eye level as machine-gun bullets mow down charging French *poilus*. When sound was added, the metallic staccato of the machine guns helped audiences believe they were *hearing* the authentic sounds of battle.

Milestone and Edeson drew on their experience in silent films to create appropriate visual imagery and movement. They shot the battle scenes with more maneuverable silent cameras, adding sound effects later. Outdoor dialogue scenes, however, were made with cameras and microphones. Edeson had been hired partly because he had developed a quieter camera whose whir would not be picked up by the microphone.

As cinematographer-historian George Mitchell has observed, Edeson used lighting and camera angles to particular effect.[12] He employed a low-key light level to emphasize the drama of the recruits' first nighttime barbed-wire duty and later to provide a claustrophobic effect of sustained artillery bombardment on the shell-shocked boys in their dugout. In one of the most important scenes—the shell-crater sequence—Edeson used a subtle but realistic lighting style to mark the passage from day to night to day again. At night, flashes of artillery fire light up the shell hole and its two occupants. With the morning light, a close-up reveals the dead French soldier's face, his eyes open and staring, as a wisp of smoke, a remnant from the battle, drifts into the frame. The camera cuts to Paul's anguished, pleading face. Thus the horror and remorse of individual killing is brought directly to the audience.

Universal worked to give an authentic World War I appearance to this historical drama, particularly since it was filmed in southern California, not northern France. Studio purchasing agents obtained actual French and German army uniforms as well as scores of tools, packs, helmets, rifles, machine guns, and even six complete artillery pieces. The focus on authenticity was in the visual details. As such, for example, the film illustrates the change in German army equipment during the war, from the initial spiked leather headgear (*Pickelhaube*) to the more practical steel helmets (*Stahlhelm*).

In the battle scenes, Milestone and Edeson produced some of the most effective pictures in the film. During the major attack sequence following the artillery bombardment, Edeson's main camera, mounted on a large crane, travels over the trenches as the German troops pour out of their dugouts and into position. It is joined by five other cameras shooting from different angles as French infantrymen charge toward the trenches and the mobile camera. Stern-faced German machine gunners open fire. The French are mowed down. Later in the editing room, Milestone repeatedly cut these shots with increasing brevity and speed. A hand grenade explodes in front of a charging *poilu*. When the smoke clears, all that remains is a pair of hands clutching the barbed wire. In the trench, Paul turns his face away in sickened revulsion. As the remaining French soldiers reach the trench, they lunge at the Germans with bayonets in hand-to-hand fighting. The Germans counterattack, but are temporarily halted by French machine guns. After taking the first line of French trenches, the German soldiers are ordered back to their own lines before the French can counterattack. The battle ends in a stalemate, each side exhausted and back in its original position.

Sound made action films such as *All Quiet on the Western Front* so powerful—the impact of music, the realism produced by the sound of rifle fire, the staccato rhythm of machine guns, and the deafening roar of exploding artillery shells. Milestone jolted his audience right onto the battlefield by simultaneously bombarding their senses and their emotions.

Milestone created powerful images of war for the public, but how did he, after having spent the war years in the United States, know the reality of combat? Milestone believed it had come from the year he spent in Washington, D.C., in the U.S. Army Signal Corps during World War I. There he had become quite familiar with photographic images of the war. As Milestone recalled in an interview published in 1969, "having examined thousands of feet of actual war footage while stationed at the Washington, D.C., War College during the war, I knew precisely what it was supposed to look like."[13] A decade later, he drew on that background in re-creating the battle scenes near Los Angeles. This is wonderfully suggestive phrasing by Milestone: what war was *supposed* to look like. He had never personally seen a battle or a battlefield. What he did was to draw on his experience with documentary photographic representation of the battlefront to create the "reality" for his dramatic representation of battle and the battlefront. He seems not to have questioned whether he was drawing on the illusions created by Signal Corps photographers, who were able to photograph battlefields only *after* the actual fighting.

The theme of disillusionment is heightened in *All Quiet on the Western Front*. The meaninglessness of the war is accentuated by having the frontline German soldiers discuss the fatuous nature of the official justifications from Berlin. However, it is most dramatically personalized in one of the key scenes of the film, the shell-crater scene. In the midst of battle, Paul, panic-stricken and hiding in a shell crater in the middle of no man's land, mortally stabs a French soldier who had leaped into the crater. While the Frenchman slowly dies, Paul begs his forgiveness, concluding that they are after all comrades forced to kill each other by the brutal mechanics of war. This certainly represents another powerful theme: all men are brothers.

The most unforgettable scene is the final one. On a quiet day shortly before the Armistice, Paul is killed by a French sniper's bullet as he reaches out to touch a butterfly just beyond the trench. Milestone juxtaposes the fragility and beauty of life against imminent death by means of ironic sound effects (a soldier's harmonica plays softly in the background) and by visual cross-cutting among shots of the French rifleman, Paul, and the butterfly. The camera focuses on a close-up of Paul's hand reaching out across the parched, lifeless earth to embrace life—the butterfly, which is also a symbol of Paul's lost innocence and youth, a reminder of his adolescent, butterfly-collecting days. But instead of life—death: the sharp crack of a rifle, the spasmodic jerk of Paul's hand, which slowly relaxes in death. The harmonica suddenly stops. The sensitive, young, schoolboy-soldier has become just another corpse in the trenches. It is, according to one observer, "one of the screen's most powerful, well-remembered moments."[14]

* * *

All Quiet on the Western Front was immediately hailed for its aesthetic excellence and trenchant realism. It officially premiered at New York City's Central Theater on April 29, 1930, a few days after opening at the Carthay Circle Theater in Los Angeles. Hearst's New York *American* reported that the film had played "before an audience stunned with the terrific power of stark, awful drama." The *New York Times* agreed that the spectators had been "silenced by its realistic scenes." "It is far and away the best motion picture that has been made . . . talking or silent," asserted the New York *Telegraph*.[15]

The film was a phenomenal financial success. "A money picture," reported *Variety*, the entertainment industry's weekly newspaper.[16] It actually cost $1.5 million to produce, a major sum for a motion picture at that time, and nearly double the $900,000 projected cost estimates. Universal was so embarrassed by the overrun that it publicized only $1.2 million.[17] Within two weeks after the premiere, however, it was evident that the studio would more than recoup its investment, even in the worst economic slump of the Great Depression. *All Quiet on the Western Front* broke box-office records and showed to sell-out crowds in city after city throughout the spring of 1930.[18]

Erich Maria Remarque first saw the film in August 1930. Universal's representative in London, James V. Bryson, flew to Germany with a print and provided a private showing for the author and his wife. Back in London the next day, Bryson told reporters that Remarque had said not a word during the showing but had "walked out of the theatre with tears in his eyes." According to Bryson, before parting Remarque had told him, "It is beautiful indeed. I can say no more."[19]

The success of *All Quiet on the Western Front*, the book and the film, convinced other studios to produce antiwar motion pictures. Two made in 1930 were particularly noteworthy both for their intrinsic merit and for their demonstration of the international nature of the phenomenon: *Journey's End* (Britain, 1930) and G. W. Pabst's *Westfront 1918* (Germany, 1930). Although James Whale's sound-film rendition of English veteran Robert C. Sherriff's play proved highly popular with British audiences and American critics, its lack of battle scenes limited its mass appeal in America. More comparable to Milestone was Pabst, whose artistry and "near documentary realism" were widely recognized and whose antiwar film based on the novel *Vier von der Infanterie* (*Four Infantrymen*) drew large audiences on the European Continent.[20]

From its first showing, *All Quiet on the Western Front* was recognized as a powerful emotional force for opposition to war, particularly modern industrialized mass warfare. Its message received support from many pacifists, liberals, and moderate socialists throughout Europe and, to some extent, in the United States as well.[21] But there was also considerable hostility to the film in many countries. Some cultural critics decried its horrifying images and its "vulgarities." Military and political opponents argued that it distorted and demeaned the patriotism and heroism of soldiers of all nations and that it undermined nationalism, military defense, and the ability to wage war. They considered it subversive pacifist propaganda.

German sensibilities had been evident in reactions to Remarque's book, which had been vehemently denounced by conservative nationalist opponents of the fledgling Weimar Republic. Consequently, the initial German-dubbed version prepared by Universal, finally released in December 1930, had included, with Remarque's consent, a number of cuts to obtain the approval of the Berlin Censorship Board. These cuts were not concerned with aspects controversial in other countries—others had objected to the use of earthy language and latrine scenes, the oblique bedroom scene of Paul and a young French woman, or the scene of Paul stabbing a French *poilu* to death—but with the image of Germany and the German army. Thus Universal, in the initial German version, deleted scenes showing the recruits beating up their tyrannical corporal, Himmelstoss, a symbol of Prussian militarism; soldiers starving for food and eating ravenously; soldiers blaming the kaiser and the generals for the war; the grim use of the boots of a dead comrade to show the loss of one soldier after another; and Paul's return to his former school and his antiwar remarks there.

Although *All Quiet on the Western Front* played to packed theaters in the United States, Britain, and a number of other countries, it was banned in Germany, first, for a time, by the Weimar Republic and then permanently in 1933 by the Nazi regime.[22] The German-dubbed film, which had opened to the general public in Berlin on December 5, 1930, almost immediately led to Nazi street demonstrations and theater disruptions.

Representatives of the German military and the War Ministry had already issued protests against the film for portraying German soldiers as ridiculous, brutal, and cowardly.[23] Now Nazi propaganda leader Joseph Goebbels took his brown-shirted toughs to the streets, directing a number of violent protests and demonstrations against what he characterized as "a Jewish film" filled with anti-German propaganda.[24] Inside the theaters, Nazis released snakes and mice and set off stink bombs.[25] Although both the Board of Censors and the government of Chancellor Heinrich Bruening denied that they were influenced by the Nazi demonstrations, the decision to ban the film was correctly seen as a capitulation to the right, including the Nazis. Pabst's antiwar film, *Westfront 1918*, produced in Germany, was being shown in many theaters without any disturbances or demonstrations. The Nazis had used the American film to force the issue, and they had won. Hailed in Germany by the nationalist press—Goebbels's newspaper called it "Our Victory"—the censorship decision was, nevertheless, denounced by most liberals and socialists there and throughout the West.[26]

The Bruening government's decision was vigorously attacked by the left-wing Social Democrats in Germany, but they were unable to lift the ban until late the following year. By June 1931, Universal Pictures was willing to make concessions to gain access to Germany, with 5,000 theaters the second-largest market in Europe. The Board of Censors lifted the general ban in September 1931 after Universal had agreed to eliminate the scene of Corporal Himmelstoss's cowardice at the front as well as Paul's panic in the graveyard attack, and Paul's contrition for having stabbed the French soldier to death. The shortened film (cut by nearly 900 meters, or approximately 33 minutes) played with great success in Germany through early 1932. Indeed, in 1931 and 1932, *All Quiet on the Western Front* was the sixth most popular film in Germany.[27]

Nazi-inspired censorship of the film had a lasting impact long after the debate in Germany in the 1930s. Indeed, it apparently had a long-term effect on the film and its showings in many countries. In its eagerness to enter the German market, Universal Pictures had agreed to delete offensive scenes not only from the film shown in Germany but from all versions released throughout the world.[28] Thus the versions of Milestone's *All Quiet on the Western Front* seen by millions of viewers in many countries for years thereafter were versions "sanitized" to please the German censors in 1931.

The history of the various versions and releases of *All Quiet on the Western Front* from 1930 to the present, as reconstructed in part by film scholar Andrew Kelly, demonstrates that Universal Pictures was as responsive to national sensibilities and political constraints as it was to economic opportunities in the international marketplace.[29] The film was banned entirely in Italy, Hungary, Bulgaria, and Yugoslavia. Austria, also under pressure from the Nazis, followed Germany's lead. The version shown in France (beginning in October 1930) did not contain the scenes of French women entertaining German soldiers and had a drastically cut shell-crater scene in which Paul kills the French soldier. Paris banned this and other antiwar films in 1938—the eve of World War II.[30]

In 1979, an entirely new, Technicolor version of *All Quiet on the Western Front* was shown on the CBS television network in the United States with subsequent release abroad in theaters and a decade later in videocassette.[31] The new version starred twenty-eight-year-old Richard Thomas as Paul and sixty-two-year-old Ernest Borgnine as "Kat" Katczinsky. It was financed by British film magnate Sir Lew Grade, who bought the rights from Remarque's widow, actress Paulette Goddard. Produced by Norman Rosemont, the remake was filmed somewhat paradoxically on the eastern front—in Czechoslovakia.

The nearly three-hour-long television format allowed the inclusion of a number of scenes from the book that had been omitted in the two-hour 1930 motion picture, such as a gas attack and a hospital sequence in which a blinded soldier tries to commit suicide by stabbing his chest with a fork. The 1979 film also captures and maintains the episodic intensity of the novel, keeping almost all the scenes brief and using a narrator, Paul Bäumer himself, to recount experiences and feelings, a role that Richard Thomas expresses with fine poetic shadings. Writer Paul Monash stuck much more closely than Milestone and his team to Remarque's original novel, employing flashbacks rather than straight chronology and, for example, softening a bit the character of Himmelstoss, who redeems himself in battle instead of remaining a sadistic and cowardly martinet.

Director Delbert Mann, whose career had led him to make television dramas from classic books, sought a harder edge and even more gruesome detail than the 1930 classic, drawing on standard techniques of late-twentieth-century American action movies: rapid cutting, extreme closeups, as well as assault on the senses by intensified battle noise and excruciating specificity of blood and gore, including impacting bullets, retching gas victims, gaping wounds and flowing blood, rat-besieged corpses, and incinerating flame throwers—all in vivid color. In place of the "butterfly ending," the 1979 version created a new image directly dramatizing Remarque's cryptic conclusion where Paul had simply been hit and fallen face down. While most American reviewers heralded the 1979 remake as powerful and poignant, some in the United States and many in Europe, where it was shown in theaters in 1980, criticized the new film as uninspired. As one British reviewer put it, "This ploddingly expensive film is as redundant a remake as one could conceive."[32]

Milestone's version of *All Quiet on the Western Front* had enormous impact. Its ideological message contributed to political debate about war and isolationism in the 1930s and later. And in its most lasting impact, it helped to shape public images and attitudes about trench warfare, about World War I, and, to some extent, about modern war in general. It also had an undeniable impact on the motion-picture industry. It encouraged directors to shift away from static, stage-like "talking pictures" and instead to combine sound with open, fluid, visual movement. Milestone's long tracking shots were widely and specifically imitated. Of broader and deeper influence was his effective combination of sight and sound to produce a new realism that became one of the most influential concepts of Hollywood in the 1930s.[33]

No wonder, then, that pacifists, antiwar activists, and isolationists—in the 1930s and in subsequent decades—have regarded the film as a powerful antiwar and antimilitary device. Its many subsequent re-releases (in 1934, 1939, and 1950)[34] and the creation of an entirely new version in 1979 both reflected and contributed to such tides of sentiment in the United States and perhaps elsewhere. Indeed, Lew Ayres was so affected by his role and by the antiwar sentiment of the 1930s that he became a conscientious objector in World War II, at first refusing to be a soldier, and only after much public censure, agreeing to serve as an unarmed medic in the Army Medical Corps.

Most important, *All Quiet on the Western Front* helped shape subsequent public perceptions of the nature of trench warfare and of World War I. In part, this was because the book and the film, the latter with its visual images matching—even exceeding—the inner power of Remarque's writing, were part of the outpouring of antiwar memoirs and novels of the period that recast and bitterly articulated the failure of the Great War in the story not of battles won but of individual lives lost—and lost for naught.

Photography, especially motion-picture photography, is part of the explanation of why World War I has been so powerfully implanted on the public consciousness. It was the first war to be extensively recorded by motion-picture cameras, particularly by official military and newsreel photographers of all the major belligerents.[35]

Because of inherent dangers in no man's land, the weight and immobility of the early cameras, and official restrictions of access to the front, actual infantry combat was seldom recorded on film. However, some enterprising cameramen staged simulated battle scenes using soldiers and trenches near the front. Audiences were unaware of this deception, and as with *The Battle of the Somme*, a full-length British documentary shown in London theaters in the autumn of 1916 within weeks of the onset of the battle, viewers thought they were seeing actual combat footage.[36] Such motion-picture images, together with the many black-and-white still photographs, created an entire audience who thought they had a real view of the war, despite the fact that they had not seen combat firsthand.

Widespread accessibility of photographic images gave World War I a mass audience, but it was an audience whose understanding of the "reality" of war was in fact mediated through images, just as much as it was interpreted by the printed word. Our visual image of World War I has for generations been informed by the grainy, black-and-white pictures of the western front. The original photographs were dictated in part by the bulky nature of the cameras and the limitations of their lenses, and in part by the restrictions placed on the photographers by the military authorities who rigorously controlled access to the front.

The dramatic films of World War I, whether the silents of the war years and the 1920s or the sound films of the 1930s, beginning with *All Quiet on the Western Front*, drew directly on those original images to build a sense of realism. Consequently, our image of the war is still dominated by the "reality" authenticated by such film footage. Indeed, one of the most jarring aspects of watching the 1979 television version of *All Quiet on the Western Front* was precisely its vivid color and smooth, modern film style, a format that so clearly separates it from the now distant war it portrays.

The popularity of *All Quiet on the Western Front* and some other antiwar films may also be due in part to more oblique reasons. Despite their so-called realism and their brutal images, the antiwar films of the 1930s about World War I may, as historian Jay M. Winter has suggested, actually have helped masses of people take the chaos and horror of the war and mentally organize them in a more understandable and manageable way. Most of these motion pictures, after all, focus on the surface of events, on action, on melodrama, usually even including some romance, or at least on a bit of comedy. In mythologizing the war (re-creating the conflict in a form more understandable and acceptable than the complex and chaotic event itself), such films offer a way to organize and contextualize events that are themselves fragmented and traumatic. They serve to "help people to bury the past and help people recreate it in a form they can accept," according to Winter.[37] In more generic terms and in a longer time frame, antiwar action pictures, from *All Quiet on the Western Front* to the anti-Vietnam War film *Apocalypse Now*, offer many viewers both the moral solace of a strong, antiwar message and the emotional appeal of an exciting, action-filled adventure.[38]

Regardless of how World War I is understood, it is clear that in cinematographic terms, the enduring public perceptions of the image of trench warfare were established in the 1930s. No single motion picture was more influential in fixing that visual representation than this one. After *All Quiet on the Western Front*, the "reality" of trench warfare in the public mind was a "reality" constructed in Hollywood.

Notes

1. See, for example, Martin Gilbert, *The First World War: A Complete History* (New York: Holt, 1994), p. 535; and Michael T. Isenberg, *War on Film: The American Cinema and World War I, 1914-1941* (London: Associated University Presses, 1981), pp. 30, 132, 138. Historical studies of the film's place in the larger political and cultural history of the period have been few and largely fragmentary—for example, Andrew Kelly, "*All Quiet on the Western Front*: Brutal Cutting, Stupid Censors and Bigoted Politicos, 1930-1984," *Historical Journal of Film, Radio and Television* 9, no. 2 (1989): 135-50; Jerold Simmons, "Film and International Politics: The Banning of *All Quiet on the Western Front* in Germany and Austria, 1930-1931," *Historian* 52, no. 1 (November 1989): 40-60; and Richard A. Firda, "*All Quiet on the Western Front*": *Literary Analysis and Cultural Context* (New York: Twayne, 1993), pp. 92-106. In a class by itself is Modris Eksteins, *Rites of Spring: The Great War and the Birth of the Modern Age* (London: Black Swan, 1990), pp. 368-97. A useful anthology is Bärbel

Schrader, ed., *Der Fall Remarque: Im Westen nichts Neues: Eine Dokumentation* (Leipzig: Reclam-Verlag, 1992). An earlier, if longer, version of this chapter appeared as John Whiteclay Chambers II, "'All Quiet on the Western Front' (1930): The Antiwar Film and the Image of the First World War," *Historical Journal of Film, Radio and Television* 14, no. 4 (October 1994): 377-411.

2. On his early life, see Christine R. Baker and R. W. Last, *Erich Maria Remarque* (London: Oswald Wolff, 1979), pp. 5-17.

3. Erich Maria Remarque, *Im Westen nichts Neues* (Berlin: Ullstein Verlag, 1929); Remarque, *All Quiet on the Western Front*, trans. A. W. Wheen (Boston: Little, Brown, 1929). A recent translation is Remarque, *All Quiet on the Western Front*, trans. Brian Murdoch (London: Jonathan Cape, 1994). In this chapter, all citations are to Wheen's translation, which is more widely read. Remarque died in 1970, and two major collections of materials related to him and his work have now become available: the Erich Maria Remarque Papers at the Fales Library, New York University, New York (cited hereafter as Remarque Papers), and the Erich Maria Remarque Archive/Research Center on War and Literature at the University of Osnabrück in Germany. I am indebted to Tilman Westphalen, Thomas F. Schneider, Claudia Glunz, Dieter Voigt, Michael Fisher, Annegret Tietzeck, and Nicole Figur for their assistance in my research in Osnabrück.

4. See the detailed investigation by Remarque's friend and biographer Hanns-Gerd Rabe, "Remarque und Osnabrück," *Osnabrücker Mitteilungen* 77 (1970): 211-13. The fullest account in English is Harley U. Taylor, Jr., *Erich Maria Remarque: A Literary and Film Biography* (New York: Lang, 1989), pp. 15-21.

5. *All Quiet on the Western Front* (Universal Pictures, 1930). Original sound version is 138 or 140 minutes, black-and-white (a silent version with synchronized music and sound effects ran longer). Carl Laemmle, Jr., producer; Lewis Milestone, director; George Abbott, Maxwell Anderson, and Del Andrews, screenplay; C. Gardner Sullivan, story editor; Arthur Edeson, director of photography; George Cukor, dialogue director; and David Broekman, music. The cast included Lewis Ayres (Paul Bäumer), Louis Wolheim (Katczinsky), George "Slim" Summerville (Tjaden), John Wray (Himmelstoss), Raymond Griffith (Gérard Duval), Russell Gleason (Müller), Ben Alexander (Kemmerich), Arnold Lacy (Kantorek), and Beryl Mercer (Mrs. Bäumer); in the silent version, ZaSu Pitts (Mrs. Bäumer); Marion Clayton (Miss Bäumer); and Yola D'Avril (Suzanne).

6. "Confers on New War Film," *New York Times*, August 11, 1929, p. A8.

7. "Mr. Laemmle Returns [from Germany]. Universal's President Discusses Film *All Quiet on the Western Front*," *New York Times*, October 6, 1929, sec. 9, p. 8.

8. Lewis Milestone and Donald Chase, *Milestones* (typescript of unfinished autobiography in the Lewis Milestone Collection, Margaret Herrick Library, Academy of Motion Picture Arts and Sciences, Los Angeles [cited hereafter as Milestone Papers]; Joseph R. Millichap, *Lewis Milestone* (Boston: Twayne, 1981).

9. See the somewhat differing accounts of Ayres's selection in the interview with Lewis Milestone, in Charles Higham and Joel Greenberg, *The Celluloid Muse: Hollywood Directors Speak* (Chicago: Regnery, 1969), pp. 152-54; and William Bakewell, *Hollywood Be Thy Name* (Metuchen, N.J.: Scarecrow Press, 1991), pp. 71-72.

10. See, for example, Millichap, *Milestone*, p. 39. Maxwell Anderson acknowledged a less important role (Anderson, interview, May 10, 1956, Columbia University Oral History Collection, New York).

11. Remarque, *All Quiet on the Western Front*, p. 291.

12. George J. Mitchell, "Making *All Quiet on the Western Front*," *American Cinematographer* 66 (September 1985): 34-43.

13. Milestone, interview in Higham and Greenberg, *Celluloid Muse*, p. 151. He told this story many times.

14. Mitchell, "Making *All Quiet on the Western Front*," p. 42. Milestone tried several different endings during production. See mimeographed copies of the shooting script, November 20, 1929, Remarque Papers, Series 1, Folder 4; and the continuity script, undated, Film Studies Center, Museum of Modern Art, New York City.

15. Excerpts in an advertisement by Universal Pictures, *Variety*, May 7, 1930, pp. 36-37.

16. [No first name given] Sime, Review of *All Quiet on the Western Front*, *Variety*, May 7, 1930, p. 21.

17. For the $1.2 million publicized figure, see ibid. The projected estimate was $891,000, according to "Estimated Cost Sheets," December 9, 12, 1929; the actual cost was $1,448,863.44, "Final Cost Sheet," May 7, 1930 (*All Quiet on the Western Front* file, Universal Pictures Collection, Doheny Library, University of Southern California, Los Angeles).

18. "Disappointments on [West] Coast Last Wk [*sic*]—'Western Front' Made Big Showing, $22,000 at $1.50 Top," *Variety*, April 30, 1930, p.9; "Only 'Western Front' at Over Capacity, $21,957, in $2 Central," *Variety*, May 14, 1930, p. 8.

19. "Bryson Meets Remarque. 'All Quiet' Author Moved to Tears," *Bioscope*, August 6, 1930; James V. Bryson, "I Meet Erich Remarque," *Cinema*, August 6, 1930 (clippings in Scrapbook, vol. 3, Milestone Papers). I am indebted to Sam Gill, archivist, Margaret Herrick Library, Academy of Motion Picture Arts and Sciences, for calling my attention to these articles.

20. On Whale's film based on the R. C. Sherriff play, see D. J. Wenden, "Images of War 1930 and 1988: *All Quiet on the Western Front* and *Journey's End*: Preliminary Notes for a Comparative Study," *Film Historia* 3, nos. 1-2 (1993): 33-37. On Pabst's film, see Michael Geisler, "The Battleground for Modernity: *Westfront 1918* (1930)," in *The Films of G. W. Pabst*, ed. Erich Rentschler (New Brunswick, N.J.: Rutgers University Press, 1990), pp. 91-102.

21. Modris Eksteins, "*All Quiet on the Western Front* and the Fate of a War," *Journal of Contemporary History* 15, no. 2 (April 1980): 355.

22. Simmons, "Film and International Politics"; Heiko Hartlief, "Filmzensur in der Weimarer Republik. Zum Verbot des Remarque-Films *Im Westen nichts Neues*: Eine Fallstudie im Geschichtsunterricht der gymnasialen Oberstrufe," *Erich Maria Remarque Jahrbuch* 3 (1993): 73-82.

23. U.S. Ambassador, Germany, to Secretary of State, December 17, 1930, received January 3, 1931, in *Foreign Relations of the United States, 1931* (Washington, D.C.: Department of State, 1931) vol. 2, pp. 309-10 [hereafter cited as *FRUS*].

24. Diary entries, December 5-12, 1930, Joseph Goebbels, *Die Tagebücher von Jo-*

seph Goebbels: Samtliche Fragemente, ed. Elke Frählich (Munich: Saur, 1987), vol. 1, pp. 641-45.

25. "Fascist Youth Riot as *All Quiet* Runs," *New York Times*, December 9, 1930, p. 17.

26. "Unser der Sieg! [Our Victory!]," *Der Angriff*, December 15, 1930, p. 1; Guido Enderis, "'All Quiet' Banned by Reich Censors," *New York Times*, December 12, 1930, p. 12; *New York Times*, [editorial], "Commercialism and Censorship," December 13, 1930, p. 20.

27. Simmons, "Film and International Politics," pp. 58-59; U.S. Ambassador, Germany, to Secretary of State, September 12, 1931, in *FRUS*, pp. 316-17; see also "Top 10 Films in Germany, 1925-1932" [table], in Joseph Garncarz, "Hollywood in Germany: The Role of American Films in Germany," in *Hollywood in Europe: Experiences of a Cultural Hegemony*, ed. David W. Ellwood and Rob Kroes (Amsterdam: VU University Press, 1994), pp. 123-24.

28. U.S. Ambassador, Germany, to Secretary of State, September 12, 1931, *FRUS*, p. 316.

29. Andrew Kelly, "*All Quiet on the Western Front*: Brutal Cutting, Stupid Censors, and Bigoted Politicos, 1930-1984," *Historical Journal of Film, Radio and Television* 9, no. 2 (1989): 135-50.

30. Although some studies claim that the film was not shown in France until 1963, a silent version with French intertitles (and perhaps some simulated sound effects) opened there in October 1930. In December 1930, the German-dubbed sound version with French subtitles brought the full impact of the battle scenes as well as the dialogue to enthusiastic French audiences. Apparently it was not until 1950 that a French-dubbed dialogue sound version was released. See "*A l'Ouest, rien de nouveau* vient d'être présenté à Marseille," *La Cinématographie française*, no. 624, October 17, 1930, p. 197; Fernard Morel, "Le Cinéma doit préparer la paix; on doit détaxer les films de ce genre," *La Cinématographie française*, no. 625, October 25, 1930, p. 49; "La Foire aux films," *L'Humanité*, November 23, 1930, p. 4; Emile Vuillermoz, "Le Cinéma: '*A l'Ouest, rien de nouveau*,'" *Le Temps*, December 27, 1930, p. 5; and, for the rerelease, Henry Magnan, "Le Cinéma: '*A l'Ouest, rien de nouveau*' Durable chef-d'oeuvre," *Le Monde*, December 30, 1950, p. 8.

31. *All Quiet on the Western Front* (Sir Lew Grade's Marble Arch Productions, England, 1979), three hours, premiered on CBS, November 14, 1979. Delbert Mann, director. The cast included Richard Thomas, already known for playing John Boy in the TV series *The Waltons* (Paul Bäumer); Ernest Borgnine (Katczinsky); Ian Holm (Himmelstoss); Donald Pleasence (Kantorek); and Patricia Neal (Mrs. Bäumer). A videocassette, running 131 minutes, was released by ITC, Avid Home Entertainment, in 1992.

32. John Pym, review in the *British Monthly Film Bulletin*, quoted in James Robert Parish, *The Great Combat Pictures: Twentieth Century Warfare on the Screen* (Metuchen, N.J.: Scarecrow Press, 1990), p. 16.

33. Millichap, *Milestone*, pp. 24-25; see also Michael I. Isenberg, "An Ambiguous Pacifism: A Retrospective on World War I Films, 1930-1938," *Journal of Popular Film and Television* 4, no. 2 (1975): 98-115.

---

34. Copies of the scripts for the 1930, 1934, and 1939 releases are in the New York Film Censor Records, New York State Archives, Albany, New York. I am indebted to Richard Andress, archivist, for providing these.

35. On photographing the western front, see Paddy Griffith, *Forward into Battle* (Chichester: Bird, 1981), pp. 43-74; Geoffrey Malins, *How I Filmed the War* (London: Jenkins, 1920); and S. D. Badsey, "Battle of the Somme: British War Propaganda," *Historical Journal of Film, Radio and Television* 3, no. 2 (1983): 99-115.

36. Roger Smither, "'A Wonderful Idea of the Fighting': The Question of Fakes in *The Battle of the Somme*," *Historical Journal of Film, Radio and Television* 13, no. 2 (1993): 149-68.

37. Jay M. Winter, *The Experience of World War I* (New York: Oxford University Press, 1989), p. 328.

38. Milestone himself went on to direct a number of war and antiwar films, among them *The General Died at Dawn* (1936), *The Purple Heart* (1944), *A Walk in the Sun* (1946), *Halls of Montezuma* (1951), and *Pork Chop Hill* (1959).

Pacifism, Politics, and Art:
Milestone's *All Quiet on the Western Front* and Pabst's *Westfront 1918*_____

Kathleen Norrie and Malcolm Read

1930 saw the première in Berlin of two of the most celebrated anti-war films ever made: G. W. Pabst's *Westfront 1918*, adapted from Ernst Johannsen's novel *Vier von der Infanterie*, was first screened on 23 May and, on 4 December, Lewis Milestone's adaptation of Remarque's *Im Westen nichts Neues* was first shown.[1]

Although both films were subsequently banned by the Nazis in April 1933 after the *Machtergreifung*, the initial reception of the films, and the political response to them in Germany, despite the films' similar content and avowedly pacifist tone, mark an interesting contrast.

Right-wing political resistance in Germany to the film adaptation of Remarque's novel had first become obvious in the refusal by Hugenberg's Ufa to permit use of its dubbing studios to prepare the German version,[2] or to show the film in its cinemas.[3] This hostility intensified in the weeks before its Berlin première. The film was eagerly anticipated by the public, because of reports of its enthusiastic reception in America and because of the popularity of the novel, but became the object of Nazi propaganda 'wegen seiner angeblich antideutschen Tendenz' [on account of its alleged anti-German attitude].[4] That the film was significantly more sympathetic in its portrayal of the Germans than previous films that Carl Laemmle had produced went unnoticed by such critics.[5]

When the film was to receive its first public showing, the Nazis responded with a sequence of well-rehearsed spontaneous demonstrations outside the cinema and created disruptive panic inside by throwing stink bombs and releasing white mice. The *Völkischer Beobachter* labelled it a 'Film der jüdisch-bolschewistischen Unterwelt' [a film from the Jewish-Bolshevik underworld],[6] and Goebbels, in a public address at a demonstration on 8 December, referred to the public release of the film as a government sanctioned 'Kulturschande' [cultural insult].[7]

Although the right-wing press attempted disingenuously to portray the disruption as a unanimous public rejection of the film, it is clear that the film was to become the focal point of a final, and fateful conflict between democratic freedom and fascist manipulation:

> Es ist natürlich sehr leicht, wie es die demokratische Presse tut, zu behaupten, diese Kundgebungen gegen den Film seien organisiert und von nationalsozialistsicher Seite in die Wege geleitet worden [. . .] aber wir sind überzeugt, daß der Anstoß zu den allgemeinen Kundgebungen des Mißfallens nur ein ganz geringer zu sein brauchte, denn jeder gesund empfindende Mensch wird die an mancher Stelle dieses Films geradezu widerliche Darstellung menschlicher Feigheit und Erbärmlichkeit von sich weisen.[8]

[It is of course very easy to assert, as the democratic press has done, that these objections to the film were organised and set in motion by the National Socialists . . . but we remain convinced that the impetus for this general expression of dislike needed only to be quite small, because every sound person would reject the positively repulsive representations of human cowardice and wretchedness seen in many places in the film.]

Such organised disruption, which continued for almost a week, was intended to demonstrate that the film posed a threat to public order and safety and thus to force the Berlin Censorship Board to ban the film.[9] The pressure was sufficient to persuade the censors to reconsider the film, though, even in their reporting of this decision, the right-wing press sought to stress that this was an independent decision and that 'die Entscheidung der Oberfilmprüfstelle nicht unter dem Druck der Straße gefallen [sei]' [that the decision of the Censorship Board had not given way to pressure from the street].[10]

The reasons given by the official censors for the public ban are illuminating, particularly when one considers that they had initially not raised objections to the film and had praised it for showing the daring bravery and steadfastness of the German army in the war.[11] In the official hearings, the legal representative of Universal Pictures argued that the film, though undeniably a product of a 'pazifistische Weltanschauung' [pacifist standpoint], presented the fate of nine individual volunteers in the war. The censors, however, upheld the claim that the film, in its depiction of serving soldiers, constituted a 'Gefährdung des deutschen Ansehens' [threat to German esteem], as the chairman explained:

Da der Film Weltanschauungsfragen darstelle, seien die spielenden Personen Typen und nicht Einzelschicksale. Und diese Typen seien geeignet, das Ansehen der Kriegsteilnehmer auf das empfindlichste zu schädigen. Es sei unstreitbar, daß es nur deutsche Soldaten seien, die jammerten und schrien, während die Franzosen, die gegen die Stacheldraht anrennen, schweigend stürben. Im ganzen werde der Film der Gemütsverfassung der Teilnehmer am Kriege nicht gerecht. Die Oberfilmprüfstelle habe sich im übrigen dem Standpunkt des Reichsinnenministeriums angeschlossen, daß der Film *die deutsche Niederlage* und *nicht den Krieg* zeige. Er möchte, so betonte der Vorsitzende, das Volk sehen, das sich die Darstellung der eigenen Niederlage gefallen lasse.[12]

[Since the film represents philosophical questions, the persons in it are types rather than individuals. And these types are likely to damage considerably the image of those who took part in the war. It is undeniable that only the German soldiers moan and scream, while the French run against the barbed wire and die in silence. Overall, the film does no justice to the mind of those who took part in the war. The Senior Film Unit agrees with the point of view of the Reichsministerium, that the film shows a German defeat, rather than the war. The chairman expressed the view strongly that he would be interested to see any nation that would be happy with a film of their own defeat.]

The representative of the *Auswärtiges Amt*, who had previously raised no objections to the film in his statements to the *Filmprüfungsgericht*, the body responsible for originally approving the general release of the film, refused to give specific reasons for the official change of heart. Others were less reticent in their objections. Two of the most vociferous, and influential opponents of the film who appeared before the Censorship Board were the representative of the *Reichsinnenministerium*, Ministerialrat Hoche, and the official spokesman for the *Reichswehrministerium*, Kapitänleutnant von Baumbach.[13] Hoche's criticism of the film centred on its general tone:

Der Film zeigt das Kriegserlebnis empfindsamer junger Menschen, deren anfängliche vaterländische Begeisterung im Ausbildungsdrill des Kasernenhofs ernüchtert ist und die nun ihrem Schicksal an der Westfront nicht mehr mit sieghaftem Idealismus, sondern nur noch mit ihrer leiblichen Natur, mit ihrem animalischen Lebensdrang gegenüberstehen. Es ist ein Kampf des Lebenstriebes gegen die Todesdrohung geworden, bei dem die reinigende und erlösende Sinngebung in einem höheren Zweck unbewußt geworden ist.

Der Film wird damit zu einer einseitigen Darstellung des allen gemeinsamen Kriegerlebnisses, zumal er auf die schwersten Notjahre des deutschen Volkes abgestellt ist.

In der Hauptsache zeigt er das deutsche Volk ausgehungert, erschöpft und das Heer ergänzt durch die allerjüngsten Jahrgänge. In dem letzten Aufgebot knabenhafter Gestalten wird die Niederlage nicht nur vor Augen geführt, sondern auch als schicksalsnotwendig dargestellt.

Der Film ist nicht eine Darstellung des deutschen Krieges, sondem eine Darstellung der deutschen Niederlage und wirkt daher auf den deutschen Beschauer qualvoll und niederdrückend.

[The film shows the war experiences of sensitive young men, whose initially patriotic enthusiasm is dampened by the drill sessions on the parade ground and who now face their fate on the Western Front not with victorious idealism, but only with a physical response, with their animal instinct for survival. It has become a battle of the life force against the threat of death, in which the purifying and redemptive sense of a higher goal is quite unknown.

Thus the film turns into a one-sided representative of the shared experience of the war, the more so as it is restricted to the years of the greatest suffering for the German people.

Principally it portrays the German people as starving and exhausted, while the armed forces are replenished by the youngest possible recruits. In the final presentation of boyish figures, the defeat is not only portrayed, but presented as necessitated by fate.

The film is not a portrayal of the German war, but of the German defeat, and thus its effect on the German audience is painful and depressing.]

That the speaker might have applied a similar, if not harsher, criticism to *Westfront 1918*, as is shown in the discussion below, serves to demonstrate how *All Quiet on the Western Front* was used by the Nazi propaganda machine to manipulate official opinion. The main thrust of von Baumbach's objections was that 'die Leistungen des deutschen Soldaten im Weltkrieg in den Augen der Welt geschmäht werden' [the efforts of the German soldier in the world war are insulted in the eyes of the world]. In particular, he found the following scenes unacceptable:

Das jämmerliche Heulen und Schreien der Freiwilligen beim Trommelfeuer und ihre ständig angstverzerrten Gesichter.

Ihr wildes, gieriges, unappetitliches Fressen.

Das Hineinwerfen der Rekruten in eine Schlammpfütze auf dem Exerzierplatz.

Die Szene, in der ein sterbender Kamarad besucht wird, dem die Beine abgeschossen sind, und in der die Freiwilligen darüber zu verhandeln beginnen, wer seine schönen neuen Stiefel bekommen soll.—Gerade diese Szene wird bei denjenigen Nationen, die den Krieg nicht mitgemacht haben, und bei denjenigen, die keine Stiefelnot im Krieg kannten, abstoßend wirken.

[The pitiful howling and screams of the volunteers when under fire, and their permanently twisted and tortured faces.

The fact that the recruits are hurled into a muddy puddle on the exercise ground.

The scene in which a dying fellow-soldier whose legs have been shot off is visited, and the volunteers start to haggle about who will get his fine new boots.—This scene above all will be found repulsive in countries which did not participate in the war, and in those in which there was no shortage of boots.]

Leaving aside the question of how a ban in Germany would in any way influence the reception of the film internationally, and how a domestic ban of a film that had been made in America, not Germany, would diminish 'die Gefährdung des deutschen Ansehens' [endangering the image of Germany], it is more interesting to consider the particular objections listed since they reveal either intentional confusion on the speaker's part or official manipulation of the speaker aimed at securing a ban of the film. When Universal Pictures prepared the German version, approved by Remarque, for public release and presented this to the Berlin Censorship Board, they had made the following cuts of what they considered particularly controversial sections from the original American version:

Scene showing recruits diving in mud a second time.
Scene where Himmelstoß is thrashed by troops.
Scenes where some soldiers eat ravenously.
The part of the conversation amongst troops following the meal where they talk about the causes of the war and where the Kaiser is blamed.
Sections relating to Kemmerich's boots.
Scenes where Himmelstoß goes to the front and is seen to be a coward.
The end of Paul Bäumer's speech to the classroom.[14]

Though this point has never been identified by historical commentators, it seems clear that the ban imposed on the film in Germany was not based upon an assessment of the film that had been released in Germany. The Berlin Censorship Board, in responding to objections to the general release of the film, viewed it 'in der für Deutschland bestimmten Form' [in the version destined to be shown in Germany],[15] though it is known that an original version of the film was made available to government officials to counter the claim of its 'deutschfeindliche Wirkung' [anti-German effect]:

> Hierüber hinaus hat die Deutsche Universale ihre Bereitschaft erklärt, vor einem Kreise von Behörden-Vertretern, an der Spitze den Preußischen Innenminister, den Film '*Im Westen nichts Neues*' in seiner *Originalfassung* vorzuführen, wie er im Auslande läuft.[16]

> [The German Ufa had furthermore declared itself prepared to show the film *All Quiet on the Western Front* in the original version as shown abroad, to a circle of representatives of the authorities, most notably the Prussian minister for internal affairs.]

Clearly, the Berlin Censorship Board sought to appease that section of public opinion that the Nazis had mobilised in order to suppress a particular film, with an obviously broad popular appeal, that projected a pacifist, anti-militarist message so detested by the Nazi ideologues. In order to justify their decision, the authorities even succumbed to objections raised about features of a version of the film that had not appeared in Germany. That the same Berlin authorities, who found the film one-sided because it did not show the 'heroic side of war', feared it might weaken the resolve of the younger generation to defend their country and criticised it for being profoundly defeatist,[17] had not banned *Westfront 1918*, which continued to be widely shown without disturbances or demonstrations,[18] further illustrates their obvious willingness to accommodate Nazi attitudes when the latter flexed their muscles and sought political confrontation on the matter of *All Quiet on the Western Front*.

That Pabst's film continued to be shown whilst *All Quiet on the Western Front* was banned, demonstrates how the authorities capitulated to the Nazi mob. As a less compliant journalist argued at the time, the Nazis, 'die bisher Kriegsfilme, welche alle Greuel und allen Jammer der Wirklichkeit zu zeigen sich bemühten, ruhig ertrugen' [which up to that point had accepted without complaint war films which made every effort to show all the horror and misery], singled out this film as part of their continued hate campaign against the 'Landesverräter' [traitor] Remarque.[19] This successful bid to coerce the official authorities was more than just a question of artistic freedom, it was a demonstration of the 'torpor and cowardice' of republicans[20] and a clear indication that the Nazis were, in effect, already in power.

That Pabst's film was more uncompromising in its denunciation of militarism is generally accepted today:

Westfront 1918 ist der einzige den Krieg denunzierende Film, der der Armee jede Gefälligkeit verweigert—in dieser Hinsicht ist es ein reineres Werk als das von Milestone.[21]

[*Westfront 1918* is the only antiwar film that makes no concessions whatsoever to the army—in this respect it is a purer film than that by Milestone.]

The film, for example, features a longer sequence with German soldiers coming under bombardment from their own artillery. The fact that the film did not become the object of political action does not mean that it went unnoticed by the Nazis. Though it was greeted coolly by Nazi sympathisers, they later, absurdly, referred to it as a 'Heldenepos' [Heroic epic] and used it to help denigrate the American film.[22] Furthermore, in 1934 after Hitler's seizure of power, Hans Zöberlin adapted his novel *Der Glaube an Deutschland* to produce *Stoßtrupp*

1917, a film that is a quite obvious response to *Westfront 1918*.[23] The films are, as Kracauer points out,[24] remarkably similar in their realistic and objective depiction of the horrors of the trenches. Zöberlin's film lacks any displays of heroism or exceptional bravery, and the front-line troops are shown in their despondency. Such features are common to both films. However, an intentional contrast emerges by presenting the last stages of the war not as senseless suffering but as having a higher purpose, namely the struggle for Germany's very survival. What could have been a pacifist statement is thus mutated into a Nazi statement of nationalist pride, imbuing war with the 'erlösende Sinngebung in einem höheren Zwecke' [the purifying and redemptive sense of a higher goal] that the 'democratic' Weimar bureaucrat Hoche prescribed for war films.[25]

The fact remains, however, that the Nazis' public response to the release of Pabst's film attracted none of the venom that was directed at *All Quiet on the Western Front*. This is, initially, hard to explain since the two films are, quite obviously, pacifist and have similar internationalist themes, for example in the relationship between a German soldier and a French girl, or in scenes that show solidarity between soldiers of the opposing sides. *All Quiet on the Western Front* has the scene in which Paul, lying in a crater beside the French soldier that he has stabbed, expresses his feeling of guilt, whilst in *Westfront 1918*, in the final scene set in the field hospital, the wounded Frenchman, not realising that Karl is dead, stretches out to take his hand and whispers: 'Moi comrade. Pas ennemi. Pas ennemi' [My comrade. Not enemy. Not enemy].

Both films concentrate on the suffering and the defeat of the German troops, this being perhaps more evident in *Westfront 1918* with its repeated shots of bodies and abandoned weapons in the German trenches, and neither seeks to heroise the central characters. In *Westfront 1918*, a request for a volunteer to carry a message from the front is followed by a panning shot across reluctant faces with a cut to a shot of ongoing bombardment. The *Student*'s offer to carry the message is met with incredulity by his comrades, who are unaware that his ulterior motive is to seize the opportunity to visit his girlfriend behind the lines. Similarly, Karl's hysterical response to the later discovery of the *Student*'s body provokes the exchange:

—Reiß dich zusammen, wir sind doch Helden.
—Wenn wir Helden wären, dann wären wir schon längst daheim.

[—Pull yourself together, we're heroes, you know.
—If we were heroes we'd have gone home long since.]

Westfront 1918 might also be said to more defeatist in tone than *All Quiet on the Western Front* and it is the former rather than the latter which depicts what Ministerialrat Hoche, in his objections to the American film, had referred to as 'die schwersten Notjahre des deutschen Volkes' [the years of the greatest suffering for the German people]. In its portrayal of life in Germany, *All Quiet on the Western Front*, unlike the novel, makes no mention of hardship on the home front (Paul is fed potato pancakes with blueberries), whereas, in *Westfront 1918*, the plight of civilians is explicitly referred to in an exchange between officers:

—Ich schicke nicht mehr gern die Leute auf Urlaub. Nachher versauen sie hier draußen bloß die Stimmung.
—Naja. Die sagen auch, sie hungern mächtig zu Hause.

[—I don't like to send people off on leave any more, when they come back they ruin the atmosphere here at the front.
—O.K. But they say there's a huge amount of food shortages at home.]

Furthermore, echoing Pabst's classic socio-critical film of 1925, *Die freudlose Gasse*, which portrayed the ravages of inflation in Vienna, *Westfront 1918* shows the war bringing not only privation but also moral decline. Karl returns to find his mother standing in a food queue and his wife sleeping with the butcher's boy in return for an extra ration of meat. The mother, 'Du bist zu large von zu Hause weggewesen' [You've been away too long], displays a reasoned acceptance of the collapse of the moral order, whilst the wife, 'Warum macht ihr denn da draußen nicht endlich Frieden?' [Why don't they make peace out there?], evinces as little comprehension of Karl's position as his failure to acknowledge the reasons for her infidelity does of hers. In its lack of idealism the film achieves, in form and content, the unemotional, detached quality of resignation so typical of *Neue Sachlichkeit*.[26]

Despite their common anti-war, pacifist stance, the two films can be seen to have strikingly contrasting features, as an analysis reveals. In general terms, *All Quiet on the Western Front*, with its emphasis on autonomous individuals, is thematically and stylistically more humanist than *Westfront 1918*.

In the American film, the main characters are introduced as a group of schoolboys through a long shot in the classroom, and are then divided into individuals by tracking shots ending on a close-up of each in turn, followed by a short subjective sequence revealing their individual background and their reasons for volunteering for the army.

In *Westfront 1918*, only Karl and Yvette, the *Student*'s lover, are given names, otherwise the characters are identified solely by rank, status, geographical provenance or, in the case of female characters, their relationship to a male character: *Der Leutnant*, *Der Student*, *Der Bayer*, *Karls Frau*, *Karls Mutter* [the lieutenant, the student, the Bavarian, Karl's wife, Karl's mother]. Also, there is no individual introduction or expository sequence as in classical narrative. The action begins *in medias res*, with the main characters found in a French tavern enjoying a lull in hostilities. The spectator has to piece together any character's individual features.

Such general contrasts apply, similarly, to technical aspects of the films. Whilst both combine static and mobile shots in similar proportions, there being a predominance of static camera combined with noteworthy travelling shots, these techniques are employed to different ends. As Mike Cormack in his study of ideology and cinematography points out, despite the many travelling shots, the dominant set-up of *All Quiet on the Western Front* is still completely immobile. The sub-code of camera movement is based on a static camera but with movement used in fairly limited, unambiguous ways, mainly to follow human characters. Such techniques suggest a particular view of personality, combined with belief in the ultimate value of the individual. This is all set in the stable context provided by the dominating static camera:

> It may seem odd to talk of a strong and stable context in a film which por-
> trays the destruction of society and which concentrates on the changes
> which occur in a group of boys but the point is that the value system does
> not change. Whether it is the boys' eagerness to save their country at the
> beginning, the relationship between the old soldiers and the young recruits
> in the middle of the film or Paul reaching out towards the beauty of the but-
> terfly at the end, the values of individualistic, patriarchal humanism are im-
> plicit. [. . .] The boys are always shown as exercising freedom of choice, a
> fundamental value of this system.[27]

In *All Quiet on the Western Front* camera movements can, therefore, be said to reinforce the emphasis on individuals.

Westfront 1918 also features travelling shots following human char-acters, notably in sequence where the *Student*, having volunteered to carry a message from the front in order to rejoin his girlfriend behind the lines, is shown running across no man's land. Here, however, it is not the human figure, but the eerie, deathly, nocturnal landscape, which predominates. The *Student* runs past barbed wire twisted like ghostly, distorted crosses in a graveyard, before falling in the mud near a shell hole containing the body of a messenger dog seen in a previous sequence. The scene prefigures his own end, when his body is left lying in the mud in no man's land after being killed in hand-to-hand combat. This motif of death is then picked up in the next scene featuring the *Student*, who is shown the following morning in a travelling shot walking past soldiers making white crosses for graves. These motifs of martyred humanity, with men dying like dogs, are then combined in the final sequence where the shell-shocked *Leutnant*, mad and howling like a dog, is transported to a military hospital in a bombed-out church. A travelling shot follows the *Leutnant*, carried by an orderly and a nurse in a lolling pose, suggestive of a *pietà*, past a fallen statue of the crucified Christ. As a sightless soldier still blindly screaming 'Disziplin' [discipline] passes through the shot, the *Leutnant* then disappears into the interior of the church, out of shot, leaving the camera to linger on general bedlam in a scene of wounded, broken bodies.

In *Westfront 1918*, then, primacy is given not to autonomous individuals, but to the landscape of the war which destroys them. Although the travelling camera may follow an individual, it is elements of the *décor*, frequently given symbolic significance, as in the secularised Christ figure, to suggest suffering humanity or the ruined church to represent a shattered 'Christian' culture, which stand out. This landscape of war also predominates in static shots, for example the final battle sequence, with a series of shots coinciding with the *Leutnant*'s descent into madness. A medium shot of carnage in the German trenches features a large hand of a corpse in the foreground and a rifle butt jutting up at odd angle, both of which dominate the frame and, together with dead bodies, form part of a strange still life. There is a cut to a long shot of the combat zone as seen from the trenches, and then a cut back to the same medium shot of the deathly still life, from which emerges the shell-shocked *Leutnant* as the sole survivor. The camera tilts up, following him as he stands and salutes, shouting: 'Zu Befehl, Majestät' [As you command, your majesty].

There follows a long shot of the trenches, with German troops going over the top. Although the camera pans to the left to show movement out of trenches, it then remains static. It does not track into combat with the soldiers, nor are there cuts to shots from a different perspective, to engage the spectator in the combat. The combatants are relegated to the background of the image, framed by barbed wire dominating the foreground. The effect is to deny the spectator any participation in the excitement of combat, or any identification with individual soldiers or any particular nationality. It emphasises the static, futile nature of trench warfare. The overall effect of this, together with the preceding shots, is to reduce the significance of living individuals, who are consigned to the background, and to emphasise the fundamental, objective realities of war and death.

Thus, the most important stylistic feature of Pabst's film, and the main bearer of meaning, is not camera movement but *mise-en-scène*. The most striking example of this occurs in the love scene between the *Student* and Yvette. The scene is filmed in German Expressionist style, and the signifying elements of *décor* and lighting underpin one of the fundamental themes of the film: the conflict of love (life) versus war (death).

The scene is part of the first sequence in the film, which is set in a tavern where German soldiers are fraternising with Yvette and her grandfather during a lull in the conflict. As the bombardment starts, Yvette and the *Student* take refuge beneath the stairs. The first shot isolates them as a pair, suggesting the inauspicious nature of the relationship through the low-key lighting and *décor*: they are surrounded by darkness, and the stairs cast shadows over their white, ghost-like faces.

The subsequent high-angle shot, with an overall lighter tone, has more white areas in the frame but still with significant shadow areas, shows them about to make love among the jumble under the stairs. As they embrace, the sound of boots is heard and:

> Voice off: Hallo! Jemand da? [Hallo! Is anyone there?]
>
> [*Student* looks up, moving eyes into band of shadow]
>
> Voice off: Ja, was ist denn los? [Yes, what's up?]
>
> Voice off: Kompanie angetreten ist befohlen [Company commanded to fall in].
>
> Voice off: Geht denn die Sauerei schon wieder los. [All the crap's starting again, then.]

There is a cut to a medium shot of soldiers abandoning their card game, and rushing up the stairs, with reluctant urgency, complaining, 'Mensch, zum Heldentod kommst du noch immer früh genug' [OK, you'll get to your heroic death quickly enough]. This is followed by a cut to the top of the stairs as a soldier returns, calling to the *Student*, and then a cut to an eye-level medium shot showing the white faces of the lovers framed between shadows cast by the handrail of the stairs, surrounded by darkness. The *Student*, with a haunted look, says, 'Ich muß weg' [I must away], and pulls Yvette, who is hanging round his neck, into the shadows as he rises to go. Yvette responds, 'Non. Ne partez pas. Restez près de moi. Restez' [No. Don't go. Stay close to me. Stay.] and pulls him back into the light. As they kiss, a shadow bar covers their necks, as if decapitating them. As a voice off calls, 'Korporalschaftsführer melden' [platoon leader report], the *Student* assures Yvette, 'Ich komme schon wieder' [I'll be back]. He then pulls away, drawing her into the darkness. She drops back. There is then a cut to a low-angle shot of the *Student* running up the heavily shadowed staircase. As he looks down, there is a cut to high-angle shot showing Yvette's inert, corpse-like body lying under the stairs, like a shell victim, then a cut back to a low-angle shot, with the *Student* running off up the stairs.

The constant movement from light into darkness, omnipresent shadows, Yvette's inert body, together with the scathing reference to 'Heldentod', prefigure the death of the *Student* and thus of the relationship, destroyed by war. This marks the beginning of the series of death motifs, for example the *Student*'s walk through no man's land past crosses, referred to above. The separation of the *Student* and his sweetheart, temporarily through the demands of combat and then finally through death, is mirrored in the progressive estrangement of Karl and his wife, first geographically, then emotionally, as Karl cannot forgive her infidelity, which, as indicated above, is explicitly attributed to the length of the conflict and the consequences for the civilian population, a view Karl belatedly accepts on his deathbed. Through these failed love affairs war is shown to be at odds with humankind's more life-affirming instincts.

If, in *Westfront 1918*, the fate of individual characters thus serves to illustrate the main theme of the film, the inherently destructive and futile nature of modern warfare, the primacy of the war environment itself being evoked in the elaborate *mise-en-scène*, in *All Quiet on the Western Front* the emphasis, as suggested above, is placed upon the individual, as the film, by focussing first on group of boys and ultimately on their leader, Paul Bäumer, demonstrates how a specific generation is affected by the war.

The main theme of Milestone's faithful adaptation of the original novel is announced in the prologue:

> This story is neither an accusation nor a confession and least of all an adventure, for death is not an adventure for those who stand face to face with it. It will simply try to tell of a generation who, even though they may have escaped its shells, were destroyed by the war. . . .

It is this theme of the alienating effect of war on a generation of young men which dominates the film, as, from the first sequence, Milestone gives cinematographic expression to Remarque's text, by indicating, through a subtle combination of camera movement and framing, the fate which will befall the boys.

The first two scenes show an initial situation of harmony, in which the boys are at one with the ideals of their society. The sense of social cohesion is conveyed in the linking of exterior and interior by means of travelling shots. In the brief opening scene the camera tracks forward from a hallway, where a caretaker is discussing German gains with a cleaning woman, into the street, where soldiers are marching, surrounded by waving crowds. In the second and more important scene, in which the central characters are introduced, the camera cranes back from the parade and cheering crowds outside the window and pans left to show Kantorek the schoolmaster standing at his desk, before moving back through the classroom.

This travelling shot reinforces the notion of unity, as the jingoistic enthusiasm (whipped up by Kantorek) of the boys within the classroom is linked with the patriotic fervour of the crowds outside. The link is also made by sound, as, initially, Kantorek's speech is drowned out by the brass band outside, which fades as the camera moves towards the back of the class. The camera movement is repeated at the end of the scene, when the boys, persuaded by Kantorek to leave their studies and enlist *en masse*, rush to the front of the classroom then into the street. The camera rises and cranes back, showing the group cavorting around, singing patriotic songs, and then joining the crowds outside windows, leaving the classroom deserted.

The subsequent loss of this initial harmony is already hinted at in the third scene of the film, which takes place in a military training camp. The beginning of the boys' separation from society is denoted by the lack of travelling shots joining the interior and exterior. The scene opens with a static long shot of the barrack gates, which open to reveal the soldiers within. The only movement between military and civilian world occurs in the form of a cavalryman who begins to ride out of the barrack gates towards the front of the frame, but only gets as far as the shadow cast by the gates when there is a cut to the next shot, an extreme high-angle long shot of the parade ground inside the barrack gates, which, by dwarfing the figures of soldiers, emphasises the oppressive power of military institution over individuals.

The suggestion that entering the army cuts the boys off from civilian life is reiterated in the dialogue, in the following speech by Himmelstoß, a character who is himself an indication of changed roles as in the first scene he appeared in civilian guise as a postman, showing respect to the boys, addressing one as 'Master Peter', but now assumes the role of sergeant, rejecting the previous familiarity and demanding respect and obedience:

Himmelstoß: I see you've come here with a slight misunderstanding. We'll correct that too. The first thing to do is to forget everything you ever knew, everything you ever learned. Forget, see. Forget what you've been, and what you think you're going to be. You're going to be soldiers, and that's all.

The notion of segregation is reiterated visually in the fourth scene, which shows the boys arriving at the front. The establishing shot, a high-angle long shot of the troop train arriving, is filmed through large station windows. The same set-up is used for the closing shot, the departure of the train. In both shots the windows establish a barrier, and thus a sense of being cut-off.

The process of gradual alienation suggested visually in these opening scenes is made explicit later in the film, in dialogue which exposes the dislocation between classical ideals of war preached by Kantorek and the realities of life at the front, and the boys' own realisation that their wartime experiences have left them unable to be reintegrated into society. One scene, in which the boys, now hardened veterans themselves, discuss life after the war with older men, includes the following exchange:

—You've got something to go back to, wives, children, job. What about us? What do we have to go back to? School?

—A man can't take all that rubbish they teach you seriously, after three years of shells and bombs.

—They never taught us anything really useful, like how to light a cigarette in the wind, or make a fire out of wet wood, or bayonet a man in the stomach instead of the ribs where it gets jammed.

The alienation of this 'lost generation' is made clearest in the home leave sequence, where Paul cannot adjust simply by removing his uniform:

Paul's mother: Paul, you're a soldier now, aren't you? Somehow I don't seem to know you.

Paul: I'll take these things off.

and in the second classroom scene, in which Kantorek is shown indoctrinating the next batch of boys, which reveals both verbally and visually the distance separating Paul and his classmates from their schooldays.

Initially welcomed by Kantorek as a shining example of Germany's *eiserne Jugend*, Paul refuses to endorse his idealised view of war, emphasising instead the alienating effect of life in the trenches:

Paul: I shouldn't have come on leave. Up at the front you're alive or dead and that's all, and you can't fool anybody about that very long. Up there, we know we're lost and done for, whether we're dead or alive. Three years we've had of it, almost four, and every day a year and every night a century and our bodies are earth and our thoughts are clay and we sleep and eat with death. And we're done for, because you can't live that way and keep anything inside you. I shouldn't have come on leave. I'll go back tomorrow.

On a stylistic level, the scene begins with a medium shot of a window, framing Paul walking forwards in the street outside, then panning left to Kantorek at his desk. This recalls the crane shot in the first classroom scene, but only to emphasise the difference. The street outside is empty apart from a woman pushing a cart with firewood, a contrast from the earlier jingoist crowds, and there is no craning backwards through the classroom.

In its use of camera movements linking interiors and exteriors, and its emphasis on boundaries dividing space (classroom and station windows, barrack gates) *All Quiet on the Western Front* can be likened to another classic pacifist film, Renoir's *La Grande Illusion* of 1937, where similar devices are used, albeit in a more sustained manner, as a stylistic expression of one of the film's main themes, namely the artificial nature of the barriers of nationality and class separating mankind.[28]

The theme that these devices are expressing in *All Quiet on the Western Front*, the alienation of a generation irrevocably damaged by war, is echoed in the treatment of Paul's brief love affair and his death, which is indicative of his inability to find a sustainable reality outside the trenches.

Whereas the relationship between the *Student* and Yvette in *Westfront 1918* is portrayed in an earthy, realistic manner (within the conventions of the period), Paul's sexual desire is idealised, in the sense that it is repeatedly presented as something which cannot be integrated into everyday reality. This is first indicated in the scene where Paul's company is drinking in a bar behind the lines. Paul and Albert see the picture of a young actress on a poster. She immediately becomes a figure of fantasy for them, a fact underlined in the unusual manner in which the scene is shot, the boys being shown in a minor, side by side with the poster. Thus, they too become mere images, divorced from the immediate reality of direct representation as they articulate their desire.

A similar phenomenon occurs in the sequence in which Paul and his comrades swim over to fraternise with three young French women. Initially, the tone is predominantly one of comedy: the boys arrive naked, and while Paul, significantly, retains his dignity in a military coat, the others are forced to drape themselves in sheets. Yet the comedy is linked with realism: the charms of the young men reside mainly in their ability to provide sausages and bread, upon which the women fall ravenously. Abruptly, however, the tone changes. The camera tracks back from the table containing the remains of the meal and a gramophone grinding silently on, signifying a movement away from the earthy pleasures of the flesh. It then moves slightly forward, and the shot dissolves to the bedchamber occupied by Suzanne and Paul. This is, however, represented only in the shadow cast by the bedstead on the wall, over which Paul's voice off explains, in ethereal tones, the significance of the encounter for him:

I'll never see you again, Suzanne, I wouldn't even know you if I did, and yet I'll remember you always, toujours. If you could only know how different this is from the women we soldiers meet. [. . .] It seems as though all the war, the tavern, the grossness, have fallen away from me like a miracle, like something I never believed.

The love relationship is defined as being inherently incompatible with, and completely apart from, the daily reality of war, an opposition already established in relation to the girl in the poster in the comment that her thin shoes would be no good for marching. This divorce from daily reality is underlined in its non-representation, its relegation to a shadow world, which, like the poster and mirror images of the earlier scene, suggests it exists on a different plane. In both instances, love is placed on a different temporal as well as spiritual and practical level. The poster girl is situated in the past, a pleasure that has been missed. Albert points out that the poster is months old, whilst Paul's moment of pleasure with Suzanne is defined as transitory.

In Lacanian theory, the mirror stage in the development of the infant is synonymous with illusion, the infant wrongly identifying with images which are not itself, but which give an illusion of wholeness and control.[29] The mirror scene is indicative of a regressive urge for the impossible return to this now closed world. War is the only reality, the rest is all illusion. This also represents their failure to go through normal teenage developmental processes, leaving them stranded in a psychological no man's land, neither boys nor men. This is a reiteration of the theme suggested in the exchange with the older men referred to above:

—You've got something to go back to, wives, children, job. What about us? What do we have to go back to? School?

Paul's death is the only logical outcome, and the only exit from a situation with no future. His manner of dying further suggests a futile attempt at regression, grasping for a lost childhood, the lost ideals of beauty which are now inaccessible, as his disillusioned speeches, and premature return from leave make clear. He falls victim to a sniper's bullet while reaching out for a butterfly. This change from the original ending of the novel, suggested to Milestone by cameraman Karl Freund,[30] is linked to his childhood through a reference to butterflies in the home-leave sequence, where Paul is shown looking at a display case of dead butterflies in his bedroom and reminiscing with his sister on how they caught them.

It could thus be argued that *All Quiet on the Western Front* is as much a melodrama[31] as a pacifist film, in that it concentrates on the fate of one group of boys, focussing finally on the Oedipal drama of one of them, although Paul's psychological trajectory can be seen as representative of the socio-political fate of a generation. Camera movements reinforce the emphasis on individual and group fate, both by following human figures and by expressing the theme of progressive alienation. By contrast, *Westfront 1918*, as other commentators have observed, foregrounds the horrors of trench warfare rather than the fate of individuals and does not encourage identification with main protagonists to the same extent as *All Quiet on the Western Front*:

Die Oberfläche der sichtbaren Realität transzendiert zum Bild der geschändeten Menschlichkeit. Dabei steht aber [. . .] niemals einzelnes symbolisch für das Ganze. In kunstlosen, langsamen und ungleichmäßigen Fahrten tastet die Kamera das Schlachtfeld ab und enthüllt im epischen Nebeneinander das Grauen.[32]

[The surface of visible reality is transformed to an image of ravaged humanity. But individual elements never stand as symbols for the whole. In artless, slow and uneven sweeps the camera gropes its away around the battlefield and reveals the horror by means of epic juxtaposition.]

Further, *Westfront 1918* is a more visual film than *All Quiet on the Western Front*, in that the *mise-en-scène* is of greater significance in the creation of meaning and there is less reliance on dialogue to communicate the film's theme. One can contrast, for example, the scene in which the *Student* walks past soldiers making crosses, in which the spectator is left to identify the death motif, or not, with a comparable sequence in *All Quiet on the Western Front*, when soldiers march past newly made coffins on their way to the front. Milestone feels obliged to offer a verbal reinforcement of the scene's significance:

—Have a look, nice new coffins. For us.
—I must say, that's a very cheerful preparation for this offensive.

The main weakness of Milestone's film lies in the often excruciating dialogue, for example Paul at Kemmerich's deathbed, looking to the sky with puppy-dog eyes and intoning, 'Oh God, this is Franz Kemmerich, only 19 years old. He doesn't want to die', or, similarly, in the shell-hole with the Frenchman, 'Oh God, why did they do this to us? We only wanted to live, you and I. Why did they send us out to fight each other?' Pabst, by contrast, indulges in visual excesses, for example shredded hands on barbed wire, which have an overstatedly 'gothic' quality. On balance, *Westfront 1918* strikes one now as probably less dated than the more sentimental *All Quiet on the Western Front*.

The debate as to the relative superiority and effectiveness of *All Quiet on the Western Front* or *Westfront 1918* continues today. Both are distinguished works, and both were praised by critics of the time, hostile or otherwise, for their innovative use of sound to convey the impact of the everyday reality of war, but Pabst's film is today generally regarded, in artistic terms, as the better. It has more sustained realism, less sentimentality, and, except in the 'contrived ending of the hospital sequences and the forced climax',[33] none of the 'obviously pacifist propaganda, which mars *All Quiet on the Western Front*'.[34]

Kracauer, in a review of December 1930, found *Westfront 1918* the more damning indictment of war.[35] Other contemporary critics, while admiring Pabst's pacifism, found it less effective than Milestone's *All*

Quiet on the Western Front, in its lack of any emotional appeal that might move and 'convert' apathetic spectators. Critics today, however, find the Milestone film more a Hollywood product than a personally felt work. Although it too deals with a German youth's realisation of the horrors of war, its theatrically arch dialogue compares poorly with Pabst's less ostentatious but more genuine work.[36] Whilst one cannot perhaps deny that it may be marred by sentimentality, one must also recognise that *All Quiet on the Western Front* still has tremendous impact, visually and intellectually.

The intellectual versus emotional appeal might certainly explain why the Nazis found *Westfront 1918* less of a threat to their militarist ideology than *All Quiet on the Western Front*. One recognises today the aesthetic qualities of 'die Authentizität und Sachlichkeit, von der sich Pabst die entscheidende Wirkung des Films versprach' [the authenticity and objectivity from which Pabst got the ultimate effect of the film],[37] but a contemporary commentator criticised Pabst's 'cold and generalised abstraction',[38] and spoke of his 'political and anthropological ignorance' because he employed 'intellectual terms which could not possibly exert any emotional spell over that audience,' which the critic regarded as a fatal weakness in film-makers whose purpose is to change minds.[39]

As documents of pacifism they, together with Victor Trivas' *Niemandsland* of 1931, which, like *Westfront 1918*, was not the victim of Nazi opposition, stood out against the rabid militarism and nationalism of Germany reflected in the 'militaristischen Filme und Kasernenhofklamotten' [militaristic films and parade-ground rubbish] which were made in the early 1930s and which were very popular, both as escapism and as a reinforcement of 'die Erneuerung der hierarchischen simplen Ordnungen, in denen die Welt aus Befehlen und Gehorchen besteht—ein auch visuell einfaches Modell der Krisenbewältigung' [the renewal of the order of a simple hierarchy, in which the world is made up of commanding and obeying—a visually simple model, too, for the management of crisis situations].[40]

The message of pacifist films ultimately failed, since they were either ignored or suppressed. The attempt to show *All Quiet on the Western Front* represented a final voice of reason in a Germany that stood before the abyss, as the celebrated Weimar political journalist Carl von Ossietzky, noted: 'The sole question is whether a deliberately moderate pacific way of thinking [. . .] should continue to be permitted or not'.[41]

In Weimar Germany, pro-Nazi opinion, so desperate to stifle all pacifist sentiment, would even attempt to distort *Westfront 1918* in order to counter what it saw as the pernicious influence of *All Quiet on the Western Front*:

> Wir haben diesen Film [*Westfront 1918*] damals abgelehnt, weil wir der Auffassung waren, daß in ihm Tendenzen zum Ausdruck kamen, die wir nicht verantworten zu können glaubten. Heute müssen wir unser Urteil revidieren. Dieser Film war an dem Machwerk, das man uns im Mozartsaal vorsetzt, gemessen, ein Heldenepos. [. . .] Die Ufa, von der wir wissen, daß sie sich gern in den Dienst der vaterländischen Idee stellt, könnte sich ein bleibends Verdienst erwerben, wenn sie in ihrem dem Mozartsaal benachbarten Ufa-Pavillon in den nächsten Wochen diesen deutschen Frontfilm noch einmal zur Aufführung bringen würde; denn dann hätten die Kinobesucher die Möglichkeit, selbst Vergleiche zu ziehen. Es ist uns nicht zweifelhaft, daß dieser Vergleich für 'Im Westen nichts Neues' katatstrophal ausfallen würde.[42]

> [We rejected this film [*Westfront 1918*] at the time because we were of the opinion that it contained tendencies for which we were not prepared to assume responsibility. Now we must revise that view. Compared with the cobbled-together piece shown to us in the Mozartsaal, this film is an heroic epic. [. . .] Ufa, which is, we know, happy to place itself at the service of the patriotic ideal, could do lasting good if it would show again this German film of the Western Front in the Ufa-pavilion, which is next to the Mozartsaal, in the coming weeks; that way cinema-goers would have the opportunity to make their own comparison. We have no doubt that this comparison would be a catastrophe for *All Quiet on the Western Front*.]

The successful pressure to get *All Quiet on the Western Front* banned was a turning point in the official response to the Nazis: 'Die nationalsozialistischen Eingriffe fanden nach der "erfolgreichen" mit Verbot gekrönter Störung des Remarque-Films [. . .] immer unverhüllter offizielle Duldung, ja Billigung' [After the "successful" disturbance of the Remarque film, which had culminated in its being banned, the Nazi attacks were received with an increasingly unconcealed official tolerance, indeed approval].[43] The full political significance of the banning of *All Quiet on the Western Front* was, however, obvious to only the few in 1930:

Und darin liegt die Lehre des Remarqueverbots für uns. Und sie ist allgemeiner Art. Wie in diesem Falle, so kann man auch im allgemeinen sagen, daß es nicht die eigene Kraft der Nazis ist, die ihnen zu ihren Erfolgen verhilft. Ihre moralische Position ist so schlecht, [. . .] daß ihr Krisen—und Verzweiflungserfolg dieses aufgeblähte Parteigebilde nicht auf die Dauer erhalten könnte, wenn nicht die direkte und indirekte Hilfe käme aus der Haltung der bürgerlichen Parteien, der Presse, der Polizei, der Gerichte, und schließlich auch [. . .] der Regierung.[44]

[And in that lies the message of the ban on Remarque. It is a general one. As in this particular case, one can also say in general terms that it is not the Nazis' own powers that have got them their results. Their moral position is so poor [. . .] that their successes of crisis and despair would not be able to maintain the overblown image of the party in the long term if they didn't get direct and indirect support from the attitudes of the bourgeois parties, the press, the police, the courts and finally even the government.]

From *Remarque Against War: Essays for the Centenary of Erich Maria Remarque, 1898-1970*, edited by Brian Murdoch, Mark Ward, and Maggie Sargeant (1998), pp. 62-84. Copyright © 1998 by Scottish Papers in Germanic Studies. Reprinted with permission of the authors.

Notes

1. For a general discussion of *Westfront 1918*, see L. Atwell, *G. W. Pabst* (Boston: Twayne, 1977), pp. 75-82. For details on the making of the film *All Quiet on the Western Front*, see G. J. Mitchell, 'Making *All Quiet on the Western Front*', *American Cinematographer*, 66 (1985), 34-43; H. U. Taylor, *Erich Maria Remarque: A Literary and Film Biography* (New York, Bern, Frankfurt am Main, Paris: Lang, 1989), pp. 77-80. For full bibliographical information on the film *All Quiet on the Western Front*, see C. R. Owen, *Erich Maria Remarque: A Critical Bio-Bibliography* (Amsterdam: Rodopi, 1984), pp. 162-95.

2. K. Kreimeier, *Die Ufa-Story* (Munich and Vienna: Carl Hanser Verlag, 1992), p. 218.

3. W. Faulstich and H. Korte, eds, *Fischer Filmgeschichte. Band 2: 1915-1944* (Frankfurt am Main: Fischer Verlag, 1991), p. 112.

4. H. Pol, 'Im Westen nichts Neues', *Vossische Zeitung* (Berlin), 5 December 1930. Quoted from *Der Fall Remarque*: '*Im Westen nichts Neues*'—Eine Dokumentation, ed. by B. Schrader (Leipzig: Reclam, 1992), p. 105.

5. H. Beller, 'Die Deutschen als Hunnen' in *Unser Jahrhundert in Film und Fernsehen*, ed. by K. F. Reimers, C. Hackl, and B. Scherer (Munich: Verlag Öhlschläger, 1995), pp. 11-33 (p. 29).

6. '"Im Westen nichts Neues": Proteststurm gegen die gemeine Beschimpfung des deutschen Soldaten und unserer Gefallenen', *Völkischer Beobachter* (Munich), 7/8 December 1930. Quoted from *Der Fall Remarque*, p. 134.

7. 'Goebbels' Protestrede gegen den Remarque-Film', *Völkischer Beobachter* (Munich), 10 December 1930. Quoted from *Der Fall Remarque*, pp. 142-43.

8. 'Weiße Mäuse bei Remarque', *Neue Preußische Kreuz-Zeitung* (Berlin), 7 December 1930. Quoted from *Der Fall Remarque*, pp. 135-36 (p. 136).

9. For further details on the historical background to the ban, see J. Simmons, 'Film and International Politics: The Banning of *All Quite on the Western Front* in Germany and Austria, 1930-31', *The Historian*, 52 (1989), 40-60; M. Eksteins, 'War, Memory, and Politics: The Fate of the Film *All Quiet on the Western Front*', *Central European History*, 13 March 1980, 60-82.

10. 'Der Hetzfilm verboten', *Neue Preußische Kreuz-Zeitung* (Berlin), 13 December 1930. Quoted from *Der Fall Remarque*, pp. 154-55 (p. 155).

11. Owen, *Erich Maria Remarque*, p. 163.

12. *Der Fall Remarque*, p. 155.

13. 'Warum der Remarque-Film verschwinden mußte. Die Gutachten des Reichswehrministeriums und des Reichsinnenministerums vor der Filmoberprüfstelle', *Neue Preußische Kreuz-Zeitung* (Berlin), 13 December 1930, 1. Beiblatt. Quoted from *Der Fall Remarque*, pp. 156-60. A full transcript of the German Censor's report can be found in the records of the German Ministry of the Interior, located in the Deutsches Zentralarchiv, Potsdam, File 15.01, folder 26080: NSDAP und Kulturpolitik, Remarque Film *Im Westen nichts Neues*.

14. A. Kelly, '*All Quiet on the Western Front*: "brutal cutting, stupid censors and bigoted politicos" (1930-1984)', *Historical Journal of Film, Radio and Television*, 9 (1989), 135-50 (p. 138). Kelly deals with the issue of censorship not only in Germany

---

but internationally. See also J. W. Chambers II, '*All Quiet on the Western Front* (1930): the antiwar film and the image of the First World War', *Historical Journal of Film, Radio and Television*, 14 (1994), 377-411 (p. 394).

15. 'Filmoberprüfstelle prüft', *Berliner Lokal-Anzeiger*, 11 December 1930. Quoted from *Der Fall Remarque*, p. 152.

16. 'Widerruf gegen *Im Westen nichts Neues*', *Licht Bild Bühne. Illustrierte Tageszeitung des Films* (Berlin), 8 December 1930. Quoted from *Der Fall Remarque*, pp. 143-44.

17. W. Laqueur, *Weimar. A Cultural History 1918-1933* (New York: Perigree Books, 1980), p. 247.

18. Chambers II, '*All Quiet on the Western Front* (1930)', p. 396.

19. Anna Siemsen, 'Politischer Anschauungsunterricht', *Der Klassenkampf* (Halle), Heft 1. 1931. Quoted from *Der Fall Remarque, pp.* 192-98 (p. 196).

20. P. Gay, *Weimar Culture* (Harmondsworth: Penguin, 1988), p. 144.

21. J. Hembus and C. Bandmann, *Klassiker des deutschen Tonfilms 1830-1960* (Munich: Goldmann Verlag, 1980), quoting R. Boussinet, *L'Encyclopédie du Cinéma* (1967).

22. K.-U. Henning, 'Film der Erbärmlichkeit', *Neue Preußische Kreuz-Zeitung* (Berlin), 6 December 1930, 2. Beiblatt. Quoted from *Der Fall Remarque*, pp. 121-24.

23. P. Cadars and F. Courtade, *Histoire du Cinéma nazi* (Paris: Eric Losefeld, 1972), pp. 117-19.

24. Siegfried Kracauer, *From Caligari to Hitler* (Princeton: Princeton University Press, 1947), p. 235.

25. See above, p. 65.

26. Kracauer, *From Caligari to Hitler*, p. 233. See also, Atwell, *G. W. Pabst*, p. 77.

27. M. Cormack, *Ideology and Cinematography in Hollywood, 1930-39* (New York: St. Martin's Press, 1994), p. 38.

28. For a discussion of the film, see A. Bazin, *Jean Renoir*, trans. by U. Feldbusch (Munich and Vienna: Carl Hanser Verlag, 1977), pp. 37-46.

29. For a discussion of Lacan, see R. Lapsley and M. Westlake, *Film Theory: An Introduction* (Manchester: Manchester University Press, 1989), pp. 67-104.

30. Kingsley Canham, 'Milestone: The Unpredictable Fundamentalist' in C. Denton, K. Canham, and S. Wood, *The Hollywood Professionals. Volume 2* (London: The Tantivy Press; New York: A. S. Barnes & Co., 1974), pp. 69-119 (p. 79).

31. For a discussion of the male melodrama in European and American cinema, see S. Hayward, *Key Concepts in Cinema Studies* (London and New York: Routledge, 1996), pp. 205-208.

32. U. Gregor and E. Patalas, *Geschichte des Films* (Munich: Bertelsmann, 1973), p. 147.

33. Chambers II, '*All Quiet on the Western Front (1930)*', p. 393. See also M. Azzopardi, *Guide des Films*, ed. by J. Tulard, 2 vols. (Paris: Laffont, 1990), II, 547.

34. Spears, 'World War I on the Screen: Part 2', *Films in Review*, 17 (1966), pp. 347-65 (p. 361).

35. S. Kracauer, 'Im Westen nichts Neues', *Frankfurter Zeitung und Handelsblatt*, 6 December 1930. See *Der Fall Remarque*, pp. 109-112.

---

36. Atwell, *G. W. Pabst*, p. 81, refers to Jean Paul Dreyfus and Jean-Georges Auriol in *La revue du cinéma* of 1930.

37. Hermand and Trommler, *Die Kultur der Weimarer Republik*, p. 292.

38. P. Rotha, *The Film Till Now* (London: Vision Press, 1949), p. 467.

39. Rotha, p. 582.

40. Hermand and Trommler, *Die Kultur der Weimarer Republik*, p. 292.

41. P. Gay, *Weimar Culture*, p. 144.

42. K.-U. Henning, 'Film der Erbärmlichkeit'. Quoted from *Der Fall Remarque*, pp. 121-24 (pp. 123-24).

43. J. Hermand and F. Trommler, *Die Kultur der Weimarer Republik*, p. 186.

44. Anna Siemsen, 'Politischer Anschauungsunterricht', *Der Klassenkampf* (Halle), Heft 1. 1931. Quoted from *Der Fall Remarque*, pp. 192-98 (p. 196).

RESOURCES

Chronology of Erich Maria Remarque's Life

1898	Erich Paul Remark is born on June 22 in Osnabrück, Germany, to Peter Franz Remark and Anna Maria Remark.
1900	A sister, Erna, is born.
1901	Remark's older brother Theodor dies.
1903	A sister, Elfriede, is born.
1916	While in his third year at a teacher's college in Osnabrück, Remark is conscripted into the German army at the height of World War I.
1917	Remark is posted on the western front in June. He is injured by shrapnel in July and spends the remainder of the war in a German army hospital. Anna Maria Remark dies.
1918	With the end of World War I, Remark returns to the teacher's college to complete his degree.
1919	Remark begins working as a teacher.
1920	*Die Traumbude* is published. Remark leaves teaching to begin working a variety of odd jobs.
1921	Wishing to distance himself from his poorly received first novel, the novelist changes his name to Erich Maria Remarque.
1925	Remarque begins working as the associate editor of *Sport im Bild*, a sports magazine. He marries Jutta Ilse Zambona, an actress.
1927-1928	*Station am Horizont* is published as a serial in *Sport im Bild*. Remarque writes *Im Westen nichts Neues* (*All Quiet on the Western Front*).
1928	*All Quiet on the Western Front* appears in serialized form in *Vossische Zeitung* in November.
1929	*All Quiet on the Western Front* is published as a book in January.

1930	Remarque and his wife divorce.
1931	*Der Weg zurück* (*The Road Back*) is published.
1933	Remarque leaves Germany permanently and settles in Porto Ronco, Switzerland, as the Nazi Party carries out a government takeover.
1937	*Three Comrades* (*Drei Kameraden*) is published in English. Remarque meets Marlene Dietrich in Venice and they begin a three-year romantic involvement and lifelong friendship.
1938	Remarque remarries Zambona to ensure that she will be able to remain in Switzerland rather than return to Germany. Remarque loses his German citizenship.
1939	Remarque immigrates to the United States and settles in Los Angeles.
1941	*Liebe deinen Nächsten* (*Flotsam*) is published. Remarque has a brief affair with Greta Garbo and then begins a seven-year relationship with Natasha Paley Wilson.
1942	Remarque moves to New York City.
1943	Remarque's sister Elfriede, who has remained in Germany, is arrested by the Nazis for "undermining morale." She is convicted and executed in December.
1945	*Arch of Triumph* (*Arc de Triomphe*) is published.
1947	Remarque becomes a U.S. citizen.
1948	Remarque returns to Switzerland, where he will live for the remainder of his life.
1951	Remarque begins a romantic relationship with the actress Paulette Goddard.
1952	*Der Funke Leben* (*The Spark of Life*) is published.

1954	*Zeit zu leben und Zeit zu sterben* (*A Time to Love and a Time to Die*) is published. Peter Franz Remark dies.
1956	*Der schwarze Obelisk* (*The Black Obelisk*) is published. The play *Die letzte Station* is produced in Berlin.
1957	Remarque is divorced from Zambona again.
1958	Remarque marries Goddard.
1961	*Der Himmel kennt keine Günstlinge* (*Heaven Has No Favorites*) is published.
1962	*Die Nacht von Lissabon* (*The Night in Lisbon*) is published.
1967	Remarque is awarded the Grosses Verdienstkreuz (Grand Cross of Merit) by the Federal Republic of Germany.
1970	Remarque dies in Locarno, Switzerland, on September 25.
1971	*Schatten im Paradies* (*Shadows in Paradise*) is published.

Works by Erich Maria Remarque

Long Fiction

Die Traumbude, 1920

Station am Horizont, 1927-1928 (serial), 1998 (book)

Im Westen nichts Neues, 1928 (serial), 1929 (book; *All Quiet on the Western Front*, 1929)

Der Weg zurück, 1931 (*The Road Back*, 1931)

Drei Kameraden, 1938 (*Three Comrades*, 1937)

Liebe deinen Nächsten, 1941 (*Flotsam*, 1941)

Arc de Triomphe, 1946 (*Arch of Triumph*, 1945)

Der Funke Leben, 1952 (*The Spark of Life*, 1952)

Zeit zu leben und Zeit zu sterben, 1954 (*A Time to Love and a Time to Die*, 1954)

Der schwarze Obelisk, 1956 (*The Black Obelisk*, 1957)

Der Himmel kennt keine Günstlinge, 1961 (*Heaven Has No Favorites*, 1961; also known as *Bobby Deerfield*)

Die Nacht von Lissabon, 1962 (*The Night in Lisbon*, 1964)

Schatten im Paradies, 1971 (*Shadows in Paradise*, 1972)

Drama

Die letzte Station, pr. 1956 (adapted by Peter Stone as *Full Circle*, 1974)

Screenplay

Der letzte Akt, 1955

Bibliography

Barker, Christine R., and R. W. Last. *Erich Maria Remarque*. New York: Barnes & Noble, 1979.

Bloom, Harold, ed. *Erich Maria Remarque's "All Quiet on the Western Front."* New York: Chelsea House, 2009.

Firda, Richard Arthur. *"All Quiet on the Western Front": Literary Analysis and Cultural Context*. New York: Twayne, 1993.

_____. *Erich Maria Remarque: A Thematic Analysis of His Novels*. New York: Peter Lang, 1988.

Gilbert, Julie. *Opposite Attraction: The Lives of Erich Maria Remarque and Paulette Goddard*. New York: Pantheon, 1995.

Gordon, Haim. *Heroism and Friendship in the Novels of Erich Maria Remarque*. New York: Peter Lang, 2003.

Kam, Rose. *Erich Maria Remarque's "All Quiet on the Western Front."* Woodbury, NY: Barron's, 1984.

Kelly, Andrew. *"All Quiet on the Western Front": The Story of a Film*. New York: Tauris, 1998.

Murdoch, Brian. *The Novels of Erich Maria Remarque: Sparks of Life*. Rochester, NY: Camden House, 2006.

Murdoch, Brian, Mark Ward, and Maggie Sargeant, eds. *Remarque Against War: Essays for the Centenary of Erich Maria Remarque, 1898-1970*. Glasgow: Scottish Papers in Germanic Studies, 1998.

Norris, Margot. "The Novel of Depopulation: Remarque's *All Quiet on the Western Front*." *Writing War in the Twentieth Century*. Charlottesville: University Press of Virginia, 2000.

O'Neill, Terry, ed. *Readings on "All Quiet on the Western Front."* San Diego, CA: Greenhaven Press, 1999.

Owen, C. R. *Erich Maria Remarque: A Critical Bio-Bibliography*. Amsterdam: Rodopi, 1984.

Taylor, Harley U., Jr. *Erich Maria Remarque: A Literary and Film Biography*. New York: Peter Lang, 1989.

Tims, Hilton. *Erich Maria Remarque: The Last Romantic*. London: Constable & Robinson, 2003.

Wagener, Hans. *Understanding Erich Maria Remarque*. Columbia: University of South Carolina Press, 1991.

CRITICAL INSIGHTS

About the Editor

Brian Murdoch is Emeritus Professor of German at the University of Stirling in Scotland. His doctorates (Ph.D. and Litt.D.) are from the University of Cambridge, and he taught earlier at the Universities of Glasgow and Illinois (Chicago). He has held visiting lectureships and fellowships at the University of Oxford and at Cambridge and is a Fellow of the Royal Historical Society. He is a medievalist, and many of his books and articles are concerned with literature and theology in German, Latin, English, and the Celtic languages and also with heroic poetry. In the modern field he has written widely on the literature of the world wars, especially on poetry, on comparative topics, and on the antiwar novels of the Weimar Republic, particularly Remarque's. In addition to a number of articles on the novel, he has published a student edition of the German text of *All Quiet on the Western Front* and a monograph introduction to the work. He delivered the Remarque memorial lecture in Osnabrück in 1996, and in 2006 he published a full study of all of Remarque's novels. He has translated a number of medieval and modern works into English, including, in 1994, *All Quiet on the Western Front*.

About *The Paris Review*

The Paris Review is America's preeminent literary quarterly, dedicated to discovering and publishing the best new voices in fiction, nonfiction, and poetry. The magazine was founded in Paris in 1953 by the young American writers Peter Matthiessen and Doc Humes, and edited there and in New York for its first fifty years by George Plimpton. Over the decades, the *Review* has introduced readers to the earliest writings of Jack Kerouac, Philip Roth, T. C. Boyle, V. S. Naipaul, Ha Jin, Ann Patchett, Jay McInerney, Mona Simpson, and Edward P. Jones, and published numerous now classic works, including Roth's *Goodbye, Columbus*, Donald Barthelme's *Alice*, Jim Carroll's *Basketball Diaries*, and selections from Samuel Beckett's *Molloy* (his first publication in English). The first chapter of Jeffrey Eugenides's *The Virgin Suicides* appeared in the *Review*'s pages, as well as stories by Rick Moody, David Foster Wallace, Denis Johnson, Jim Crace, Lorrie Moore, and Jeanette Winterson.

The Paris Review's renowned Writers at Work series of interviews, whose early installments include legendary conversations with E. M. Forster, William Faulkner, and Ernest Hemingway, is one of the landmarks of world literature. The interviews received a George Polk Award and were nominated for a Pulitzer Prize. Among the more than three hundred interviewees are Robert Frost, Marianne Moore, W. H. Auden, Elizabeth Bishop, Susan Sontag, and Toni Morrison. Recent issues feature conversations with Salman Rushdie, Joan Didion, Norman Mailer, Kazuo Ishiguro, Marilynne Robinson, Umberto Eco, Annie Proulx, and Gay Talese. In November 2009, Picador published the final volume of a four-volume series of anthologies of *Paris Review* interviews. *The New York Times* called the Writers at Work series "the most remarkable and extensive interviewing project we possess."

The Paris Review is edited by Philip Gourevitch, who was named to the post in 2005, following the death of George Plimpton two years earlier. A new editorial team has published fiction by André Aciman, Colum McCann, Damon Galgut, Mohsin Hamid, Uzodinma Iweala, Gish Jen, Stephen King, James Lasdun, Padgett Powell, Richard Price, and Sam Shepard. Poetry editors Charles Simic, Meghan O'Rourke, and Dan Chiasson have selected works by John Ashbery, Kay Ryan, Billy Collins, Tomasž Šalamun, Mary Jo Bang, Sharon Olds, Charles Wright, and Mary Karr. Writing published in the magazine has been anthologized in *Best American Short Stories* (2006, 2007, and 2008), *Best American Poetry*, *Best Creative Non-Fiction*, the Pushcart Prize anthology, and *O. Henry Prize Stories*.

The magazine presents two annual awards. The Hadada Award for lifelong contribution to literature has recently been given to Joan Didion, Norman Mailer, Peter Matthiessen, and, in 2009, John Ashbery. The Plimpton Prize for Fiction, awarded to a debut or emerging writer brought to national attention in the pages of *The Paris Review*, was presented in 2007 to Benjamin Percy, to Jesse Ball in 2008, and to Alistair Morgan in 2009.

The Paris Review was a finalist for the 2008 and 2009 National Magazine Awards in fiction, and it won the 2007 National Magazine Award in photojournalism. The *Los Angeles Times* recently called *The Paris Review* "an American treasure with true international reach."

Since 1999 *The Paris Review* has been published by The Paris Review Foundation, Inc., a not-for-profit 501(c)(3) organization.

The Paris Review is available in digital form to libraries worldwide in selected academic databases exclusively from EBSCO Publishing. Libraries can contact EBSCO at 1-800-653-2726 for details. For more information on *The Paris Review* or to subscribe, please visit: www.theparisreview.org.

Contributors

Brian Murdoch is Emeritus Professor of German at the University of Stirling in Scotland. He specializes in medieval studies as well as the literature of the world wars. He has written articles on and a student edition of the German text of *All Quiet on the Western Front*, as well as a monograph introduction to the work. He delivered the Remarque memorial lecture in Osnabrück in 1996, and in 2006 he published a full study of Remarque's novels. In 1994 he published a new translation of *All Quiet on the Western Front*.

Diane Andrews Henningfeld has held the positions of Professor of English and Director of Corporate and Foundation Relations at Adrian College in Michigan.

Ruth Franklin is a senior editor at *The New Republic* and the author of *A Thousand Darknesses: Lies and Truth in Holocaust Fiction* (2010). She has written also for *The New Yorker*, the *New York Times Book Review*, the *London Review of Books*, the *Washington Post Book World*, and *Slate*, among other publications.

Thomas F. Schneider is Director of the Erich Maria Remarque Peace Center, which is run by the town and university of Osnabrück, and a lecturer in literature at Osnabrück University. He has published several books and articles on the life and writings of Erich Maria Remarque. His special interests lie in the areas of German literature concerning World Wars I and II; twentieth-century war and antiwar literature in Germany, Britain, the United States, and France; German exile literature; and questions of the representations of modern war in the media.

Mark Ward is Professor of German Language and Literature at the University of Glasgow, Scotland, and is currently Head of the School of Modern Languages and Cultures. His previous positions at the University of Glasgow include Dean of the Faculty of Arts and Director of Studies and Recruitment for a satellite campus in Dumfries, Scotland. His publications are concerned mainly with nineteenth-century German literature, in particular Grillparzer and German realism, but he has also published on the eighteenth and twentieth centuries.

Peter Hutchinson is Reader in German at the University of Cambridge, England, and Director of Studies in Modern Languages at Trinity Hall. He has published widely on aspects of German literature from the eighteenth century to the present day (especially on fiction since 1945) and has edited a number of German texts and studies of German literature.

Matthew J. Bolton is Professor of English at Loyola School in New York City, where he also serves as the Dean of Students. He received his doctor of philosophy degree in English from the Graduate Center of the City University of New York in 2005. His dissertation at the university was titled "Transcending the Self in Robert Browning and T. S. Eliot." Prior to attaining his Ph.D., he also earned a master of philosophy degree in English (2004) and a master of science degree in English education (2001). His undergraduate work was done at the State University of New York at Binghamton, where he studied English literature.

Ian Hamilton was a British editor, literary critic, biographer, and poet. After he formed *The Review*, a poetry magazine, in 1962, he authored three full-length poetry books: *Sixty Poems* (1998), *Fifty Poems* (1988), and *The Visit* (1970). His other publications include *Keepers of the Flame: Literary Estates and the Rise of Biography* (1992), *Writers in Hollywood, 1915-51* (1990), and *In Search of J. D. Salinger* (1988).

Hilton Tims is an English film, theater, and music critic. He has contributed many reviews to the *Bristol Evening World*, the *Daily Mail*, the British Broadcasting Corporation, and the *London Evening News*. He is the author of *Erich Maria Remarque: The Last Romantic* (2004), *John Ruskin* (2002), and *Emotion Pictures: The "Women's Picture"* (1987).

Alan F. Bance is Professor Emeritus of German at the University of Southampton and a former President of the Conference of University Teachers of German in Great Britain and Ireland. He has published widely on German literature, military themes, and the intellectual's role in society.

Modris Eksteins is Professor of History at the University of Toronto Scarborough. His publications have focused primarily on modern European cultural history. He is the author of *Diaghilev Was Here* (2005) and *Walking Since Daybreak: A Story of Eastern Europe, World War II, and the Heart of Our Century* (1999). His 1989 publication *Rites of Spring: The Great War and the Birth of the Modern Age* received the Wallace K. Ferguson Prize of the Canadian Historical Association and the Trillium Award of the Province of Ontario.

Harley U. Taylor, Jr., was Professor Emeritus of German Literature at West Virginia University, where he taught for thirty-seven years. He is the author of numerous scholarly articles and reviews as well as *Erich Maria Remarque: A Literary and Film Biography* (1989), the first biography of the German author. He served as the state president of the West Virginia Modern Language Teachers Association and the American Association of Teachers of German.

Richard Arthur Firda is the author of *"All Quiet on the Western Front": Literary Analysis and Cultural Context* (1993), *Peter Handke* (1993), *Erich Maria Remarque: A Thematic Analysis of His Novels* (1988), and *The North-American Review, 1815-1860* (1967).

Richard Schumaker currently teaches courses in English and philosophy at the University of Maryland University College, where he also manages the college's WebTycho training program. He is the former editor of the journal *Focus on Robert Graves and His Contemporaries*.

Richard Littlejohns is Professor Emeritus at the University of Leicester, where he taught eighteenth- and nineteenth-century German literature. He is coeditor of *Myths of Europe* (2007).

Ann P. Linder is the author of *Princes of the Trenches: Narrating the German Experience of the First World War* (1996).

Kim Allen Scott is Professor and Special Collections Librarian and University Archivist at Montana State University in Bozeman. He is the author of *Yellowstone Denied: The Life of Gustavas Cheney Doane* (2007) and editor of *Loyalty on the Frontier, or, Sketches of Union Men of the South-West* (2003).

John Whiteclay Chambers II is Professor of History at Rutgers University. He is the author of *To Raise an Army: The Draft Comes to Modern America* (1987) and *The Tyranny of Change: America in the Progressive Era* (2000) and editor of *The Oxford Companion to American Military History* (1999) and *Major Problems in American Military History* (1998). His book reviews have appeared in *Journal of American History*, *American Historical Review*, and the *Washington Post Book World*.

Kathleen Norrie graduated from the University of Aberdeen with a degree in French and German and took her doctorate at Stirling University on French film of the 1930s, teaching at Stirling later in the Department of Film and Media.

Malcolm Read is head of the Department of German at the University of Stirling in Scotland. He writes primarily on modern literature and the novels of the Weimar Republic. His publications include *Ideologies of the Spanish Transition Revisited: Juan Huarte de San Juan, Juan Rodriguez, and Noam Chomsky* (2004) and *Educating the Educators: Hispanism and Its Institutions* (2003). He is coeditor, with Brian Murdoch, of *Early Germanic Literature and Culture* (2004).

Acknowledgments

"Erich Maria Remarque" by Diane Andrews Henningfeld. From *Dictionary of World Biography: The 20th Century.* Copyright © 1999 by Salem Press, Inc. Reprinted with permission of Salem Press.

"The *Paris Review* Perspective" by Ruth Franklin. Copyright © 2011 by Ruth Franklin. Special appreciation goes to Christopher Cox, Nathaniel Rich, and David Wallace-Wells, editors at *The Paris Review.*

"The End of War?" by Erich Maria Remarque and Ian Hamilton. From *Life and Letters* 3, no. 18 (November 1929): 399-411. Copyright © 1929 by New York University Press. Reprinted with permission of the Estate of the Late Paulette Goddard Remarque.

"*All Quiet on the Western Front*" by Hilton Tims. From *Erich Maria Remarque: The Last Romantic* (2003), pp. 51-61. Copyright © 2003 by Constable & Robinson. Reprinted with permission of Constable & Robinson.

"*Im Westen nichts Neues*: A Bestseller in Context" by Alan F. Bance. From *Modern Language Review* 72, no. 2 (April 1977): 359-373. Copyright © 1977 by the Modern Humanities Research Association. Reprinted with permission of the author.

"Memory" by Modris Eksteins. From *Rites of Spring: The Great War and the Birth of the Modern Age* (1989), pp. 368-398. Copyright © 1989 by Transworld. Reprinted with permission of Beverly Slopen Literary Agency.

"The Spokesman of a Generation" by Harley U. Taylor, Jr. From *Erich Maria Remarque: A Literary and Film Biography* (2003), pp. 61-69. Copyright © 2003 by Peter Lang. Reprinted with permission of Peter Lang.

"Post Mortem: *All Quiet on the Western Front*" by Richard Arthur Firda. From *Erich Maria Remarque: A Thematic Analysis of His Novels* (1988), pp. 29-64. Copyright © 1988 by Peter Lang. Reprinted with permission of Peter Lang.

"Remarque's Abyss of Time: *Im Westen nichts Neues*" by Richard Schumaker. From *Focus on Robert Graves and His Contemporaries* 1, no. 11 (Winter 1990-91): 24-36. Copyright © 1990 by the University of Maryland. Reprinted with permission of the University of Maryland.

"'Der Krieg hat uns für alles verdorben': The Real Theme of *Im Westen nichts Neues*" by Richard Littlejohns. From *Modern Languages* 70, no. 1 (March 1989): 89-94. Copyright © 1989 by the Modern Language Association. Reprinted with permission of the author.

"From the Frog's Perspective: *Im Westen nichts Neues* and *Der Weg zurück*" by Brian Murdoch. From *The Novels of Erich Maria Remarque: Sparks of Life* (2006), pp. 31-65. Copyright © 2006 by Camden House-Boydell & Brewer, Inc. Reprinted with permission of Camden House-Boydell & Brewer, Inc.

"'There must be a reason . . .': The Uses of Experience" by Ann P. Linder. From

Princes of the Trenches: Narrating the German Experience of the First World War (1996), pp. 85-96.Copyright © 1996 by Camden House-Boydell & Brewer, Inc. Reprinted with permission of Camden House-Boydell & Brewer, Inc.

"Iron Men and Paper Warriors: Remarque, Binding, and Weimar Literature" by Kim Allen Scott. From *Erich Maria Remarque Jahrbuch* 6 (1996): 39-47. Copyright © 1996 by Erich Maria Remarque Friedenszentrum. Reprinted with permission of the author.

"*All Quiet on the Western Front* (U.S., 1930): The Antiwar Film and the Image of Modern War" by John Whiteclay Chambers II. From *World War II, Film, and History*, edited by John Whiteclay Chambers II and David Culbert (1996), pp. 13-30. Copyright © 1996 by Oxford University Press, Inc. Reprinted by permission of Oxford University Press, Inc.

"Pacifism, Politics, and Art: Milestone's *All Quiet on the Western Front* and *Pabst's Westfront 1918*" by Kathleen Norrie and Malcolm Read. From *Remarque Against War: Essays for the Centenary of Erich Maria Remarque, 1898-1970*, edited by Brian Murdoch, Mark Ward, and Maggie Sargeant (1998), pp. 62-84. Copyright © 1998 by Scottish Papers in Germanic Studies. Reprinted with permission of the authors.

Feu, Le. See *Under Fire*
Fischer, Bermann, 96
Fischer, Samuel, 96, 145
Fisher, H. A. L., 152
For Whom the Bell Tolls (Hemingway), 78
France, Anatole, 148
Frank, Leonhard, 28, 118, 281
Frederic Henry. *See* Henry, Frederic
Freund, Karl, 349
Frick, Wilhelm, 150
Friedell, Egon, 155
Friedländer, Salomo, 42, 169
Funke Leben, Der. See *Spark of Life, The*

Georg Rahe. *See* Rahe, Georg
Gérard Duval. *See* Duval, Gérard
Germain, José, 134, 154
Goebbels, Joseph, 15, 35, 46, 109, 160, 232, 318, 328
Goldring, Douglas, 157
Good Soldier Schweik, The (Hašek), 305
Goodbye to All That (Graves), 111, 131, 133, 149, 157
Graeber, Ernst (*The Road Back*), 286
Grande Illusion, La (film), 346
Graves, Robert, 111, 130-131, 133, 136, 149, 154, 157
Grunberger, Richard, 297

Hall, Mordaunt, 45
Hamilton, Cicely, 269
Hamilton, Ian, 85, 142, 191, 230
Hašek, Jaroslav, 305
Hemingway, Ernest, 68, 99, 136
Henry, Frederic (*A Farewell to Arms*), 68
Hermand, Jost, 117, 232
Hertzberg, Hendrik, 16
Himmelstoss, Corporal (*All Quiet on the*

Western Front), 30, 121, 185, 240, 318, 344
Hirth, Friedrich, 167
Hitler, Adolf, 34, 44, 101, 111, 123, 156, 160, 173, 257, 274, 300, 335
Hoberg, Maria, 98
Hoche, Ministerialrat, 331, 337
Homeyer, Willy (*The Road Back*), 261
Horses, wounded, 19, 62, 113, 170, 242, 253
Hummel, Hermann, 40

Im Westen nichts Neues. See *All Quiet on the Western Front*
Imagery, 16, 19, 140; amputation, 17, 56; animals, 62, 113, 170, 242; boots, 17, 56, 63, 185; butterflies, 141, 207, 245, 269, 286, 315, 320, 339, 349; darkness, 212, 342; nature, 214; tears, 59
In Stahlgewittern (Jünger), 66, 115, 130, 179, 253
Irony, 53, 56, 242, 285
Isolation, 207, 226, 249, 261, 277

Jacobs, Monty, 97, 145
"Jahrgang 1899" (Kästner), 117
Jake Barnes. *See* Barnes, Jake
Jordan, Robert (*For Whom the Bell Tolls*), 76
Journey's End (Sherriff), 103, 136, 149, 276
Jünger, Ernst, 27, 66, 110, 115, 130, 139, 179, 253

Kantorek (*All Quiet on the Western Front*), 69, 121, 184, 189, 224, 238, 255, 299, 311, 344
Kästner, Erich, 117
Katczinsky (*All Quiet on the Western*